HEALTH SECURITY
AND GOVERNANCE

HEALTH SECURITY AND GOVERNANCE

Critical Concepts in Military, Strategic, and Security Studies

Edited by
Nicholas Thomas

Volume IV
Rights, Liberties and Laws

Routledge
Taylor & Francis Group

LONDON AND NEW YORK

First published 2013
by Routledge
2 Park Square, Milton Park, Abingdon, Oxon OX14 4RN

Simultaneously published in the USA and Canada
by Routledge
711 Third Avenue, New York, NY 10017

Routledge is an imprint of the Taylor & Francis Group, an informa business

British Library Cataloguing in Publication Data
A catalogue record for this book is available from the British Library

Library of Congress Cataloging in Publication Data
Health security and governance : critical concepts in military, strategic, and security studies / edited by Nicholas Thomas.
    p. ; cm. – (Critical concepts in military, strategic, and security studies)
    Includes bibliographical references and index.
    ISBN 978-0-415-67104-0 (set : alk. paper) – ISBN 978-0-415-67105-7 (v. 1 : alk. paper) – ISBN 978-0-415-67107-1 (v. 2 : alk. paper) – ISBN 978-0-415-67108-8 (v. 3 : alk. paper) – ISBN 978-0-415-67109-5 (v. 4 : alk. paper)
    I. Thomas, Nicholas, 1970– II. Series: Critical concepts in military, strategic, and security studies.
    [DNLM: 1. Health Policy. 2. Communicable Diseases, Emerging. 3. Human Rights. 4. Security Measures. 5. World Health. WA 530.1]
    LC classification not assigned
    362.1–dc23

                                                                            2011051203

ISBN: 978-0-415-67104-0 (Set)
ISBN: 978-0-415-67109-5 (Volume IV)

Typeset in 10/12pt Times NR MT
by Graphicraft Limited, Hong Kong

Publisher's Note
References within each chapter are as they appear in the original complete work

Printed and bound in Great Britain by the MPG Books Group

CONTENTS

CONTENTS

ACKNOWLEDGEMENTS

The publishers would like to thank the following for permission to reprint their material:

Public Library of Science for permission to reprint Nicole A. Szlezák, Barry B. Bloom, Dean T. Jamison, Gerald T. Keusch, Catherine M. Michaud, Suerie Moon and William C. Clark, 'The Global Health System: Actors, Norms, and Expectations in Transition', *PLoS Medicine*, (Vol. 7, Issue 1, January 2010), e1000183 doi:10.1371/journal.pmed.1000183.

Elsevier for permission to reprint Sabina Alkire and Lincoln Chen, 'Global Health and Moral Values', *The Lancet*, (Vol. 364, Issue 9439, September 2004), pp. 1069–74.

Taylor & Francis for permission to reprint A. Nunn, E. Da Fonseca, S. Gruskin, 'Changing Global Essential Medicines Norms to Improve Access to AIDS Treatment: Lessons from Brazil', *Global Public Health*, (Vol. 4, No. 2, 2009), pp. 131–49.

Taylor & Francis for permission to reprint Andrew Harmer, 'Understanding Change in Global Health Policy: Ideas, Discourse and Networks', *Global Public Health*, (Vol. 6, No. 7, 2011), pp. 703–18.

Taylor & Francis for permission to reprint Tony Evans, 'A Human Right to Health?' *Third World Quarterly*, (Vol. 23, No. 2, 2002), pp. 197–215.

L. Gostin for permission to reprint J. M. Mann, L. Gostin, S. Gruskin, T. Brennan, Z. Lazzarini, H. V. Fineberg, 'Health and Human Rights', *Health and Human Rights*, (Vol. 1, No. 1, 1994), pp. 6–23.

Johns Hopkins University Press for permission to reprint Brigit Toebes, 'Towards an Improved Understanding of the International Human Right to Health', *Human Rights Quarterly*, (Vol. 21, No. 3, 1999), pp. 661–79.

Wiley for permission to reprint Lance Gable, 'The Proliferation of Human Rights in Global Health Governance', *Journal of Law, Medicine & Ethics*, (Winter, 2007), pp. 534–44.

Hastings Center for permission to reprint Lawrence O. Gostin, 'Swine Flu Vaccine: What Is Fair?', *The Hastings Center Report*, (Vol. 39, No. 5, Sept/Oct 2009), pp. 9–10.

François-Xavier Bagnoud Center for Health and Human Rights for permission to reprint Sam Foster Halabi, 'Participation and the Right to Health: Lessons from Indonesia', *Health and Human Rights*, (Vol. 11, No. 1, 2009), pp. 49–59.

The Sheridon Press for permission to reprint Jeffrey Kullgren, 'Restrictions on Undocumented Immigrants' Access to Health Services: The Public Health Implications of Welfare Reform', *American Journal of Public Health*, (Vol. 93, No. 10, October 2003), pp. 1630–3.

Hastings Center for permission to reprint Anna Mastroianni, 'Slipping through the Net: Social Vulnerability in Pandemic Planning', *Hastings Center Report*, (Vol. 39, No. 5, September–October 2009), pp. 11–12.

Wiley for permission to reprint Richard Coker, Marianna Thomas, Karen Lock and Robyn Martin. 'Detention and the Evolving Threat of Tuberculosis: Evidence, Ethics, and Law', *Journal of Law, Medicine & Ethics*, (Vol. 35, No. 4, 2007), pp. 609–15.

The Sheridon Press for permission to reprint Cécile Bensimon, and Ross E. G. Upshur. 'Evidence and Effectiveness in Decisionmaking for Quarantine', *American Journal of Public Health*, (Supplement 1) (Vol. 97, April 2007), pp. S44–S8.

American Medical Association for permission to reprint Joseph Barbera, Anthony Macintyre, Larry Gostin, Tom Inglesby, Tara O'Toole, Craig DeAtley, Kevin Tonat and Marci Layton. 'Large-Scale Quarantine Following Biological Terrorism in the United States: Scientific Examination, Logistic and Legal Limits, and Possible Consequences,' *Journal of the American Medical Association*, (Vol. 286, No. 21, December 2001), pp. 2711–7.

Oxford University Press for permission to reprint Amy L. Fairchild, Ronald Bayer and James Colgrove. 'Privacy, Democracy and the Politics of Disease Surveillance', *Public Health Ethics*, (Vol. 1, No. 1, 2008), pp. 30–8.

Wiley for permission to reprint David P. Fidler, Lawrence O. Gostin, and Howard Markel, 'Through the Quarantine Looking Glass: Drug-Resistant Tuberculosis and Public Health Governance, Law, and Ethics', *Journal of Law, Medicine & Ethics*, (Winter 2007), pp. 616–28.

Andreas Schloenhardt for permission to reprint Andreas Schloenhardt, 'Keeping the Ill Out: Immigration Issues in Asia Concerning the Exclusion of Infectious Diseases', *Hong Kong Law Journal*, (Vol. 35, No. 2, 2005), pp. 445–80.

Oxford University Press for permission to reprint Robert Barde, 'Prelude to the Plague: Public Health and Politics at America's Pacific Gateway, 1899', *Journal of the History of Medicine*, (Vol. 58, April 2003), pp. 153–86.

Disclaimer

The publishers have made every effort to contact authors/copyright holders of works reprinted in *Health Security and Governance (Critical Concepts in Military, Strategic and Security Studies)*. This has not been possible in every case, however, and we would welcome correspondence from those individuals/companies whom we have been unable to trace.

INTRODUCTION

Debating health security: norms, rights and liberties

Nicholas Thomas

An outbreak of an infectious disease – and the resulting securitized shift to an emergency mode – does not simply draw in the necessary array of actors and institutions to combat the threat but does so in special circumstances. During the emergency, it is not simply the budgets, policies and/or practices of the state that are altered, it is also the normative and regulatory frameworks under which those resources are deployed. The priorities of the emergency implicitly alter the operation of the prevailing norms: not just for the state but also for those affected by the outbreak.

This raises a fundamental question as to what happens to the social contract – between the state and the individual – during an infectious disease outbreak. What are the rights of both parties and how far can those rights be altered (or even suspended)? These are not purely philosophical questions but ones that can have a profound impact on the management of the securitization response. They are also not questions that stem from a single political tradition. Regardless of the regime type, all states are fundamentally designed to safeguard their citizens. Different political systems yield different pathways to achieve this goal. So, at its heart, a shift into emergency mode can be said to challenge the rules by which the social contract normally operates.

The chapters in this volume have been selected to consider some of the issues and debates that are framed by or respond to this challenge. The first section reviews the types of norms and values that underpin the provision of health services. From this review, we then move on to consider the human rights issues that arise in planning for and reacting to health threats. Finally, the analysis is narrowed to consider the socio-political challenge of quarantine enforcement and the role of civil liberties in times of health crises. As infectious diseases continue to emerge or re-emerge and present existential threats to humanity, these issues will continue to re-occur as states try to react to health threats without jeopardizing their own legitimacy or the well-being of their citizens.

1

Public goods and social norms

Health is one of the few truly transarchical goods in the global system. Possibly only the economic order and the climate have a similar capacity to affect the global security and well-being of states and societies in far removed parts of the world. As such, the way health threats are perceived or 'owned' is critical to the response strategies followed by states, regions or the international community. As Chen *et al.* identified, ownership of health used to reside in the state but, as linkages and networks proliferate across borders and as pressure builds on the global commons, health threats are increasingly being perceived as issues that all states have a stake in resolving.[1]

Since 2005, the norms that underpin the international system – at least with respect to health threats – have been changing. These changes have occurred as new infectious disease outbreaks exposed the shortcomings of the international health system. As Szlezák *et al.* discussed in their series of papers on the global health system, the system is being rethought as more actors appear and as new challenges surface.[2] Harmer identified ideational changes in the way health is constructed at the global level as a key driver in this evolutionary process.[3] But despite this ideational evolution, traditional sovereign health actors are still present and have valid roles to play. As Nunn *et al.* show in their analysis of Brazil's HIV/AIDS strategy, the actions of the state to internationally protect its capacity to meet the needs of its infected citizens through the provision of affordable generic medicines not only provided greater health security in the country but also provided greater options for other developing states.[4] Here Alkire and Chen's conclusion that what is ultimately needed is an efficient and equitable architecture framed by greater clarity as to access rights, systemic capabilities and utility maximization provides a useful way of analysing the multiple drivers of change against possible outcomes.[5]

Human rights

The 1994 UNDP Report *New Dimensions of Human Security* listed health security as one of the seven essential categories that needed to be protected from fear and want if individuals, societies and states could be considered as secure. The changes to global public norms discussed in the previous section suggest that a better understanding – at the global level – of health as a fundamental right is necessary if health security is to be achieved. As Evans concluded, given that health risks have now been globalised, it is also necessary to globalise the right to health. A failure to do so effectively only exposes humanity to more chronic and infectious diseases.[6] But, as Gable showed, the multitude of understandings of health as a human right that exist at the global level, combined with the expansion of actors, requires a multilevel governance of health rights if good outcomes as well as better coordination of policies and resources is to be achieved.[7]

At the domestic level, it is essential that public health systems are responsive to social needs in the event of a health threat. Whether in developing or developed states, Mastroianni made the point that public authorities that understand the social context in which the policy responses are enacted are necessary if the threat from pandemics is to be mitigated.[8] However, there are not always easy options available to policy-makers responding to health threats. Using the provision of scarce anti-retroviral (ARV) therapies as a case in point, Ford *et al.* have shown that approaches that draw in all actors and institutions in transparent dialogues can help overcome resource allocation debates;[9] although in the event of an infectious disease outbreak with high mortality and rapid transmission, it remains debatable whether such an inclusive process would be possible. Indeed, in the case of the 2009 swine flu pandemic, what was actually seen was a hoarding of vaccine resources by the wealthier states to the detriment of the developing states, whose public health infrastructure placed their peoples most at risk.[10] This suggests that in times of threat and scarcity, the focus of health security providers return to sovereign concerns, even as the genesis and/or ultimate resolution of the threat remains abroad. In turn, it could be concluded that despite the growing acceptance of health as a global public good – where all states have a role in securing the global commons – supporting an appreciation of health security as a human right, sovereign concerns can still truncate that norm in favour of domestic priorities.

Quarantines and civil liberties

This tension between evolving global norms of health security as a human right, on the one hand, and traditional norms of sovereignty and priority, on the other, is a signature debate at the global level. When faced with threats from infectious disease outbreaks, there are similar ethical and normative debates within states as well. A good example of one such debate is the right of the state to isolate individuals infected (or believed to be infected), curtailing their rights and liberties, even though they themselves have not committed an offence and, indeed, may not even be sick.

The starting point for this debate is the simple fact that there is (as yet) no cure for the common cold or any other influenza virus. There is no cure for Ebola or hantaviruses or the Nipah virus. While medical advances can alleviate the symptoms, a cure remains elusive for many infectious diseases. Thus, in the face of a major infectious disease outbreak (of known or unknown aetiology), states and societies are reduced to the only response proven to prevent the spread of diseases: quarantine. Isolation for 40 days – a technique first developed during the time of the Black Plague – remains the only effective tool against infectious diseases. However, implementing this technique raises fundamental questions of civil liberties, and challenges the balance between individual security and the protection of society.

Quarantines were designed to stop infections at the borders. But as infected persons cannot be automatically stopped at the state's boundaries and as transportation networks now reach directly into a state's territory, how should such procedures be implemented? Since SARS, states around the world have increasingly relied on enforced quarantines – in the infected person's home, in camps, in hotels. It is a utilitarian position that presumes that the rights of a society to protect itself are greater than the rights of the individual. Given that contagious individuals will not necessarily be symptomatic and that people who do express symptoms may not have that particular disease, how should quarantines be implemented?

As Coker *et al.* discussed with respect to detention of individuals possibly affected by extremely drug-resistant tuberculosis (XDR-TB), European case law requires that quarantines or detentions be balanced against the severity of the health threat and in consideration of other alternative responses.[11] Jacobs, however, observed that, in the case of SARS, the utilization of quarantine measures varied across the Asia-Pacific states,[12] making a coherent transnational response strategy at the regional or global levels difficult to implement. These quarantine procedures also operate at the borders between states but, as Schloenhardt concluded, 'keeping the ill out' is a problematic strategy with limited utility in the face of an infectious disease outbreak.[13] Instead, what are needed to prevent infectious disease outbreaks – as has been shown in all the preceding volumes – are better preventative health systems backed up by socio-behavioural changes and deeper international cooperation.

Conclusions

From the preceding brief discussion – which will be explored in more detail in the following chapters – these fundamental issues are intrinsic to the securitization of infectious diseases and the governance structure that supports such responses. Without a comprehensive understanding of the ways by which such emergency actions affect the normal operations of state–society relations it is difficult to fully assess just how complete the securitization response has been. In turn, as the response to a disease transitions out of the emergency mode towards a normal mode of operation, a review as to how – and in what ways – the health emergency changed state–society norms can also reveal the impact of the threat. Thus, an understanding of any shifts in ethical frameworks or legislative systems that take place in response to an infectious disease response also provides another way to measure the securitization process and to evaluate the behaviour of those involved in its resolution.

Notes

1 Lincoln Chen, Tim Evans and Richard Cash, 'Global health as a public good,' in Inge Kaul, Isabelle Grunberg and Marc Stern (eds) *Global Public Goods: International Cooperation in the 21st Century*, New York: Oxford University Press, 1999, pp. 284–305.

2 Nicole A. Szlezák, Barry R. Bloom, Dean T. Jamison, Gerald T. Keusch, Catherine M. Michaud, Suerie Moon and William C. Clark, 'The global health system: actors, norms, and expectations in transition', *PLoS Medicine*, 7(1) (2010), 4 pp. (Chapter 95 in this volume).

3 Andrew Harmer, 'Understanding change in global health policy: ideas, discourse and networks', *Global Public Health* 6(7) (2011), 703–18 (Chapter 98 in this volume).

4 A. Nunn, E. Da Fonseca and S. Gruskin, 'Changing global essential medicine norms to improve access to AIDS treatment: lessons from Brazil', *Global Public Health* 4(2) (2009): 131–49 (Chapter 97 in this volume).

5 Sabina Alkire and Lincoln Chen, 'Global health and moral values', *Lancet* 364(9439) (2004): 1069–74 (Chapter 96 in this volume).

6 Tony Evans, 'A human right to health?' *Third World Quarterly* 23(2) (2002): 197–215 (Chapter 99 in this volume).

7 Lance Gable, 'The proliferation of human rights in global health governance', *Journal of Law, Medicine & Ethics* (Winter, 2007): 534–44 (Chapter 102 in this volume).

8 Anna C. Mastroianni, 'Slipping through the net: social vulnerability in pandemic planning', *Hastings Center Report* 39(5) (2009): 11–12 (Chapter 108 in this volume).

9 Nathan Ford, Alexandra Calmy and Samia Hurst, 'When to start antiretroviral therapy in resource-limited settings: a human rights analysis', *BMC International Health and Human Rights* 10(6) (2010), 9 pp. (Chapter 104 in this volume).

10 Lawrence O. Gostin, 'Swine flu vaccine: what is fair?', *Hastings Center Report* 39(5) (2009): 9–10 (Chapter 103 in this volume).

11 Richard Coker, Marianna Thomas, Karen Lock and Robyn Martin, 'Detention and the evolving threat of tuberculosis: evidence, ethics, and law', *Journal of Law, Medicine & Ethics* 35(4) (2007): 609–15 (Chapter 109 in this volume).

12 Lesley Jacobs, 'Rights and quarantine during the SARS global health crisis: differentiated legal consciousness in Hong Kong, Shanghai, and Toronto', *Law & Society Review* 41(3) (2007): 511–51.

13 Andreas Schloenhardt, 'Keeping the ill out: immigration issues in Asia concerning the exclusion of infectious diseases', *Hong Kong Law Journal* 35(2) (2005): 445–80 (Chapter 115 in this volume).

Part 15

PUBLIC GOODS AND SOCIAL NORMS

THE GLOBAL HEALTH SYSTEM

Actors, norms, and expectations in transition

*Nicole A. Szlezák, Barry R. Bloom, Dean T. Jamison,
Gerald T. Keusch, Catherine M. Michaud,
Suerie Moon and William C. Clark*

Source: *PLoS Medicine*, 7:1 (2010), e1000183.

The global health system: a time of transition

The global health system that evolved through the latter half of the 20th century achieved extraordinary success in controlling infectious diseases and reducing child mortality. Life expectancy in low- and middle-income countries increased at a rate of about 5 years every decade for the past 40 years [1]. Today, however, that system is in a state of profound transition. The need has rarely been greater to rethink how we endeavor to meet global health needs.

We present here a series of four papers on one dimension of the global health transition: its changing institutional arrangements. We define institutional arrangements broadly to include both the actors (individuals and/or organizations) that exert influence in global health and the norms and expectations that govern the relationships among them (see Box 1 for definitions of the terms used in this article).

The traditional actors on the global health stage—most notably national health ministries and the World Health Organization (WHO)—are now being joined (and sometimes challenged) by an ever-greater variety of civil society and nongovernmental organizations, private firms, and private philanthropists. In addition, there is an ever-growing presence in the global health policy arena of low- and middle-income countries, such as Kenya, Mexico, Brazil, China, India, Thailand, and South Africa.

Also changing are the relationships among those old and new actors—the norms, expectations, and formal and informal rules that order their interactions. New "partnerships" such as WHO's Roll Back Malaria Partnership (RBM), Stop TB, the Global Alliance for Vaccines and Immunization

---

Box 1. Defining the Global Health System

We understand global health needs to include disease prevention, quality care, equitable access, and the provision of health security for all people [16-18]. We define the global health *system* as the constellation of actors (individuals and/or organizations) "whose primary purpose is to promote, restore or maintain health" [19], and "the persistent and connected sets of rules (formal or informal), that prescribe behavioral roles, constrain activity, and shape expectations" [20] among them. Such actors may operate at the community, national, or global levels, and may include governmental, intergovernmental, private for-profit, and/or not-for-profit entities.

(GAVI), the Global Fund to Fight AIDS, Tuberculosis and Malaria (GFATM), and many others have come to exist alongside and somewhat independently of traditional intergovernmental arrangements between sovereign states and UN bodies (see Figures 1 and 2 for an illustration of the underlying governance principles). These partnerships have been emphasized– not least by WHO itself—as the most promising form of collective action in a globalizing world [2]. Large increases in international support for the newer institutions has led to relative and, in some cases, absolute declines in the financial importance of traditional actors [3].

The rise of multiple new actors in the system creates challenges for coordination but, more fundamentally, raises tightly linked questions about the roles various organizations should play, the rules by which they play, and who sets those rules. Actors may exercise power within the constraints of international institutions in hopes of achieving benefits and shared objectives [4]. Such a calculus helps to explain why actors are willing to fund multilateral initiatives such as WHO, GFATM, RBM, and Stop TB, despite the fact that doing so entails relinquishing considerable control over what is done with their resources. On the other hand, powerful and financially independent actors, such as national governments, may elect to use their resources to influence the outcomes from multilateral initiatives or create bilateral ones. The lack of a clear set of rules that constrain distortion of priorities by powerful actors can threaten less powerful ones. As a case in point, despite widespread support for its overarching goals, there is considerable discussion, in some cases even unease and some tension, around the prominent role played by the Bill & Melinda Gates Foundation, whose spending on global health was almost equal to the annual budget of WHO in 2007 [5–8].

Finally, this period of transition in actors and relationships comes at a time when the very nature of the challenges faced by health systems is itself

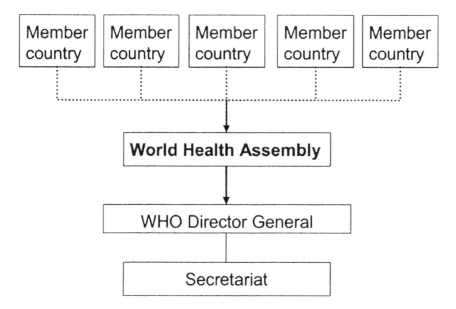

Figure 1 UN-type international health governance.
Based on the principles of the UN system, member countries are represented in the World Health Assembly (WHA), which functions as the central governing body. The WHA appoints the director general, oversees all major organizational decision making and approves the program budget.
doi:10.1371/joumal.pmed,1000183.g001

being transformed. The success of child survival efforts has meant that noncommunicable diseases, including cardiovascular disease, cancer, diabetes, and neuropsychiatric disease, are growing in prevalence alongside the continuing threats of communicable diseases [9–11]. The globalizing economy poses a new set of health challenges as the rules that govern trade in goods, services, and investment reach more deeply into national regulatory and health systems than have previous trade arrangements [12,13]. Finally, changes in climate and other environmental variables are likely to create unexpected and unpredictable health threats, both as a direct result of changing environments for disease vectors and as an indirect result of impacts on water and food security, extreme events, and increased migration [14,15].

The melee resulting from these interacting transitions has produced some extraordinary success stories, such as the drive that dramatically increased access to lifesaving antiretroviral therapy for people living with HIV/AIDS, unprecedented access to insecticide-treated bednets for malaria, and enhanced access to anti-TB drugs in the developing world within a span of a few short years. But there is also mounting concern that the increasingly complex nature of the evolving global health system leaves unexploited significant opportunities for improving global health, results in duplication and waste of scarce health resources, and carries high transaction costs. The ongoing

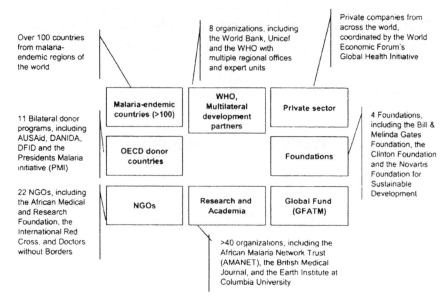

Figure 2 Global Health as partnership.
Today's Roll Back Malaria Partnership consists of more than 500 partners, including the major players WHO, the Global Fund, and the Bill & Melinda Gates Foundation. RBM was initiated in 1998 by WHO, UNICEF, UNDP, and the World Bank. WHO currently hosts RBM's secretariat and contributes in multiple ways. However, it is not presented as the central node of the partnership (*source*: http://www.rollbackmalaria.org/).
doi:10.1371/journal.pmed.l 000183.g002

global financial crisis makes the efficient and effective performance of the global health system all the more pressing.

Many have expressed doubts that today's global health system is remotely adequate for meeting the emerging challenges of the 21st century [21–24], A groundswell of opinion [25–35] suggests that new thinking is needed on whether or how practical reform of the present complex global health system can improve its ability to deal with such key issues as:

- Setting global health agendas in ways that not only build upon the enthusiasm of particular actors, but also improve the coordination necessary to avoid waste, inefficiency, and turf wars.
- Ensuring a stable and adequate flow of resources for global health, while safeguarding the political mobilization that generates issue-specific funding. How can the global burden of financing be equitably shared, and who decides? How should resources be allocated to meet the greatest health risks, particularly those that lack vocal advocates?
- Ensuring sufficient long-term investment in health research and development (R&D). Who should contribute, and who should pay? How can

the dynamism and capacity of both public and private sectors from North and South be harnessed, without compromising the public sector's regulatory responsibilities?

- Creating mechanisms for monitoring and evaluation and judging best practices—how can policy agreement be achieved when actors bring contested views of the facts to the table?
- learning lessons from the enormous variance in effectiveness and costs of various national and international health systems, from R&D to the delivery and monitoring and evaluation (M&E) of interventions in the field, to create improvements everywhere.

Roadmap of the series

In this series we undertook a study of the role of institutions in the global health system. The aims of the study were threefold: first, to advance current understanding of the interplay of actors in the system; second, to evaluate its performance; and third, to identify opportunities for improvement. The project was part of a larger program led by Harvard University's John F. Kennedy School of Government to advance thinking on the challenges of linking research knowledge with timely and effective action in an increasingly globalized and diverse world [36,37]. It drew together theoretical literature on global governance that has emerged from the field of international relations over the last half-century [20,38,39]; on empirical analysis of institutional design and performance in other sectors that, similar to public health, seek to mobilize scientific knowledge as a global public good (e.g., agriculture and environmental protection [40–42]); and on the engagement of several of the authors of this paper in contemporary policy debates on ways to improve the institutions that promote global health [43,44].

We focused on three central questions regarding the global health system: (1) What functions must an effective global health system accomplish? (2) What kind of arrangements can better govern the growing and diverse set of actors in the system to ensure that those functions are performed? (3) What lessons can be extracted from analysis of historical experience with malaria to inform future efforts to address them and the coming wave of new health challenges? To illuminate these questions, we built a series of case studies, workshops, and synthesis efforts, the results of which are reported in more detail elsewhere (http://www.cid.harvard.edu/sustsci/events/workshops/08institurtions/index.html).

In the papers presented in this series we summarize representative results from our work for one key actor in, and one key function of, the global health system. Thus, the second article in the series, by Frenk [45], reflects on the essential characteristics of functioning national health systems, which are the anchoring institutions of the global health system. The continued crucial importance of national health systems as connectors of research and development with populations, and as guarantors of the successful and sustained delivery of health interventions to people and populations, is often overlooked in enthusiastic discussions of new approaches to the architecture of global health. Indeed, the biggest challenge facing global health today is to reconcile the ongoing global-level transformation with the need to further strengthen and support national-level health systems.

The third article, by Keusch et al. [46], examines how the global health system has evolved to better integrate the research, development, and delivery of health interventions—a core function of the system. We chose the global response to malaria as a good case study because of the long history of global efforts to combat the disease, multiple attempts at institution building in this domain, its recent rise on the global agenda, and the concomitant increase in resources devoted to combating it. Many old and new approaches have evolved and been tested in the field of malaria, including targeted programs like WHO's Malaria Action Programme and the WHO/UNDP/Unicef/World Bank Training in Tropical Diseases (TDR) Programme; governance partnerships like RBM; product development partnerships such as the Medicines for Malaria Venture; and new delivery mechanisms such as GFATM. Goals have oscillated between global eradication, regional and national control, and now perhaps back to global eradication. Exploration of the evolution of institutional arrangements linking malaria research, development, and delivery hold important lessons for understanding the global health system more generally.

The fourth article of the series, by Moon et al. [47], presents conclusions regarding the three central questions raised above and poses questions for further research and recommendations for future action.

Our hope is that this series stimulates debate, encourages further case studies, and provides insights into general principles for the improvement of the global health system.

Author contributions

ICMJE criteria for authorship read and met: NAS BRB DTJ GTK CMM SM WCC. Wrote the first draft of the paper: NAS. Contributed to the writing of the paper: NAS BRB DTJ GTK CMM SM WCC. Co-PI: NAS. Conceptualized the study: NAS WCC. Organized the meetings: BRB WCC. PI on the grant that supported the project: WCC. Chaired the steering group for the project: WCC. Supervised the research: WCC.

Funding

This work was supported by a grant to the Institutional Innovations in Global Health project by the John F. Kennedy School of Government at Harvard University, Cambridge, Massachusetts, United States, under its "Acting in Time" program. Additional support was received from the Burroughs Wellcome

Fund, Research Triangle Park, North Carolina, United States. The funders had no role in the decision to publish or preparation of the manuscript.

Competing Interests

The authors have declared that no competing interests exist.

Abbreviations

GAVI, Global Alliance for Vaccines and Immunization; GFATM, Global Fund to Fight AIDS, Tuberculosis and Malaria; M&E, monitoring and evaluation; R&D, research and development; RBM, Roll Back Malaria Partnership; WHA, World Health Assembly; WHO, World Health Organization.

Provenance

Commissioned, externally peer reviewed.

References

1. Jamison D. T. (2006) Investing in Health. In: Jamison D. T., Breman J. G., Measham A. R., Alleyne G., Claeson M., et al, eds. Disease Control Priorities in Developing Countries. Washington, D.C.: World Bank, pp 3–34.
2. Brundtland G. H. (2002) Address to the 55th World Health Assembly. Geneva: World Health Organization, Available: http://www.who.int/director-general/speeches/2002/english/20020513_addresstothe55WHA.html. Accessed 6 September 2009.
3. Ravishankar N., Gubbins P., Cooley R. J., Leach-Kemon K., Michaud C. M., et al. (2009) Financing of global health: Tracking development assistance for health from 1990 to 2007. Lancet 373: 2113–2124.
4. Keohane R., Martin L. (1995) The Promise of Institutionalist Theory. Int Secur 20: 39–51.
5. McNeil D. G. J. (2008 March 4) Eradicate Malaria? Doubters Fuel Debate The New York Times, Available: http://www.nytimes.com/2008/03/04/health/04mala.html. Accessed: 6 December 2009.
6. The Lancet editors (2009) What has the Gates Foundation done for global health? Lancet 373: 1577.
7. McCoy D., Kembhavi G., Patel J., Luintel A. (2009) The Bill & Melinda Gates Foundation's grant-making programme for global health. Lancet 373: 1645–1653.
8. Black R. E., Bhan M. R., Chopra M., Rudan I., Victora C. G. (2009) Accelerating the health impact of the Gates Foundation. Lancet 373: 1584–1585.
9. Bygbjerg I. C., Meyrowitsch D. W. (2007) Global transition in health – secondary publication. Dan Med Bull 54: 44–45.
10. Mathers C. D., Loncar D. (2006) Projections of global mortality and burden of disease from 2002 to 2030. PLoS Med 3(11): e442. doi:10.1371/journal.pmed.0030442.

11. Bloom B. R., Michaud C. M., La Montagne J. R., Simonsen L. (2006) Priorities for Global Research and Development of Interventions. In: Jamison D. T., Breman J. G., Measham A. R., Alleyne G., Claeson M., et al, eds. Disease Control Priorities in Developing Countries. Washington, D.C: World Bank.

12. Fidler D. P., Drager N., Lee K. (2009) Managing the pursuit of health and wealth: The key challenges. Lancet 373: 325–331.

13. Lee K., Sridhar D., Patel M. (2009) Bridging the divide: Global governance of trade and health. Lancet 373: 416–422.

14. Costello A., Abbas M., Allen A., Ball S., Bell S., et al. (2009) Managing the health effects of climate change: Lancet and University College London Institute For Global Health Commission. Lancet 373: 1693–1733.

15. World Health Organization (2009) Protecting health from climate change: Global research priorities. Available: http://www.who.int/world-health-day/toolkit/report_web.pdf. Accessed 6 September 2009.

16. Koplan J. P., Bond T. C., Merson M. H., Reddy K. S., Rodriguez M. H., et al. (2009) Towards a common definition of global health. Lancet 373: 1993–1995.

17. Frenk J. (2009) Strengthening health systems to promote security. Lancet 373: 2181–2182.

18. Brown T. M., Cueto M., Fee E. (2006) The world health organization and the transition from "international" to "global" public health. Am J Public Health 96: 62–72.

19. World Health Organization (2000) World Health Report 2000—Health Systems: Improving Performance. Available: http://www.who.int/whr/2000/en/whr00_en.pdf. Accessed 6 December 2009.

20. Keohane R. O. (1984) After Hegemony: Cooperation and Discord in the World Political Economy. Princeton (New Jersey): Princeton University Press.

21. Adeyi O., Smith O., Robles S. (2007) Public Policy and the Challenge of Chronic Noncommunicable Diseases. Washington, D.C.: World Bank. 218 p.

22. Beaglehole R., Ebrahim S., Reddy S. (2007) Prevention of chronic diseases: A call to action. Lancet 370: 2152–2157.

23. Evans T. (2004) The G-20 and Global Public Health. In: CIGI/CFGS, The G-20 at Leaders' Level?. Ottawa: IDRC, Available: http://www.120.org/publications/23_fZ_ottawa_conference_report.pdf. Accessed 6 September 2009.

24. Jamison D. T., Breman J. G., Measham A. R., Alleyne G., Claeson M., et al. (2006) Priorities in Health. Washington, D.C.: The World Bank. 221 p.

25. Brugha R., Walt G. (2001) A global health fund: A leap of faith? BMJ 323: 152–154.

26. Cohen J. (2006) Global health. Public-private partnerships proliferate. Science 311: 167.

27. Godal T. (2005) Do we have the architecture for health aid right? Increasing global aid effectiveness. Nat Rev Microbiol 3: 899–903.

28. Hale V. G., Woo K., Upton H. L. (2005) Oxymoron no more: The potential of nonprofit drug companies to deliver on the promise of medicines for the developing world. Health Aff (Millwood) 24: 1057–1063.

29. Kaul I., Faust M. (2001) Global public goods and health: taking the agenda forward. Bull World Health Organ 79: 869–874.

30. Lambert M. L., van der Stuyft P. (2002) Editorial: Global health fund or global fund to fight AIDS, tuberculosis, and malaria? Trop Med Int Health 7: 557–558.

31. Poku N. K., Whiteside A. (2002) Global health and the politics of governance: an introduction. Third World Q 23: 191–195.

32. Schneider C. H. (2008) Global public health and international relations: pressing issues – Evolving governance. AustJ Int Aff 62: 94–106.

33. Gostin L. O. (2007) Meeting the survival needs of the world's least healthy people – A proposed model for global health governance. JAMA 298: 225–228.

34. Lee K. (2006) Global health promotion: How can we strengthen governance and build effective strategies? Health Promot Int 21: 42–50.

35. Tucker T. J., Makgoba M. W. (2008) Public-private partnerships and scientific imperialism. Science 320: 1016–1017.

36. Ellwood D. (2008) Acting in time: overview of the initiative. Available: http://www.hks.harvard.edu/about/admin/offices/dean/ait/overview. Accessed 6 September 2009.

37. Nye J. S., Donahue J. D. (2000) Governance in a globalizing world. Washington, D.C.: Brookings Institution Press. 386 p.

38. Ostrom E. (2005) Understanding institutional diversity. Princeton (New Jersey): Princeton University Press. 355 p.

39. Ruggie J. G. (1982) International Regimes, Transactions, and Change: Embedded Liberalism in the Postwar Economic Order. Int Organ 36(2).

40. Cash D. W., Clark W. C., Alcock F., Dickson N. M., Eckley N., et al. (2003) Knowledge systems for sustainable development. Proc Natl Acad Sci U S A 100(14): 8086–8091.

41. Ruttan V. W., Bell D. E., Clark W. C. (1994) Climate-change and food security—agriculture, health and environmental research. Glob Environ Change 4: 63–77.

42. Clark W. C., Mitchell R. B., Cash D. W. (2006) Global Environmental Assessments: Information and Influence. In: Mitchell R. B., Clark W. C., Cash D. W., Dickson N. M., eds. Evaluating the influence of global environmental assessments. Cambridge (Massachusetts): MIT Press, pp 1–28.

43. Keusch G. T., Medlin C. A. (2003) Tapping the power of small institutions. Nature 422: 561–562.

44. Morel C. M., Acharya T., Bround D., Dangi A., Elias C., et al. (2005) Health innovation networks to help developing countries address neglected diseases. Science 309: 401–404.

45. Frenk J. (2010) The Global Health System: Strengthening National Health Systems as the Next Step for Global Progress. PLoS Med. In press.

46. Keusch G., Kilama W., Moon S., Szlezák N., Michaud C. (2010) The Global Health System: Linking Knowledge with Action – Learning from Malaria. PLoS Med. In press.

47. Moon S., Szlezák N., Michaud C., Jamison D., Keusch G. (2010) The Global Health System: Lessons for a Stronger Institutional Framework. PLoS Med. In press.

96

GLOBAL HEALTH AND MORAL VALUES

Sabina Alkire and Lincoln Chen

Source: *Lancet*, 364:9439 (2004), 1069–74.

Soon after assuming office on July 21, 2003, the new Director-General of WHO, Lee Jong-wook, announced plans to launch several global health initiatives: reenergising primary health care to achieve the Millennium Development Goals (MDGs), launching the ambitious 3 by 5 initiative to expand access to antiretroviral drug treatment to 3 million HIV-positive people by 2005,[1,2] and accelerating country-based action through strengthening human resources. A similar pattern of new global initiatives characterised the opening phase of the previous WHO administration led by Gro Harlem Brundtland, launching programmes such as Roll Back Malaria, Stop TB, tobacco control, polio eradication, and partnerships such as GAVI (Global Alliance for Vaccines and Immunization).[3]

Ethics and moral values are invariably invoked to mobilise support for these global initiatives. Earlier on in May, 2003, Lee used the terms social justice and security in his address to the World Health Assembly.[2] On assuming office, he underscored that "global health work must be guided by an ethical vision". Recently, he wrote: "Both technical excellence and political commitment have no value . . . unless they have an ethically sound purpose."[1]

If ethics are the foundation for global health initiatives, how should moral philosophy guide policy choices and shape the way such programmes are undertaken? In this essay we argue that clarity regarding morality underlying global health initiatives is important, both for why and how programmes should be undertaken. Common moral values might be used to justify new global programmes, suggesting that the programmes might be shaped differently depending on the morals espoused. A rights-based or equity approach, for example, would be expected to differ from a utilitarian or humanitarian approach. Also, an initiative is only partly justified by its moral expediency. Of critical importance are factors shaped by knowledge and by institutional interests. Moral soundness about why particular global programmes should be advanced may need to be balanced against the imperative of achieving consensus among people of many different moral views. Yet, as we argue in the conclusion, moral clarity—as well as knowledge and institutional interests—can usefully shape what, when, and how health initiatives should best proceed.

Schools of moral thought

To stimulate discussion, we have selected four major schools of moral values commonly used to justify global health initiatives: humanitarianism, utilitarianism, equity, and rights. We could have analysed other schools, but these four, we believe, encompass a good range of moral positions. There are, of course, both large and important variations within each school.

Humanitarianism: acting virtuously towards those in need

The appeal for charitable acts to meet pressing humanitarian needs is arguably the most common ethical basis for global health action. Humanitarianism can be a form of virtue ethics but it also often a humanistic response to evident social problems. The ethos of humanitarianism is embedded in nearly all religions. In a humanitarian approach, people respond to human suffering and realise human fulfilment by acting in a virtuous manner based on compassion, empathy, or altruism. The virtues might be specific or broad. Examples of specific acts are charitable tithing among Baptists or zakat (charitable donations) among Muslims. Broadly proscribed virtues encompass such human qualities as generosity, honesty, trustworthiness, integrity, and fairness. Among the wealthy, these virtues might be expressed as philanthropy, which often focuses on health.[4]

Humanitarianism provides the primary ethical basis of voluntary action undertaken by non-governmental organisations (NGOs), and is also an important base of public support for official foreign aid. US president George Bush in announcing US$15 billion in assistance for HIV/AIDS control described the pledge as a "work of mercy". Public opinion polls in the USA consistently show that alleviating world hunger and providing drinking water are worthy of foreign aid from the USA. Emphasis on voluntary generosity and self-expression (rather than on duties or obligations) gives humanitarianism a broad appeal to many social groups, corporations, and governments.

Contemporary appeals to people's humanitarian impulses locus on the giver: who a person becomes by acting well, and how a person realises a sense of accomplishment or fulfilment. There are dangers that those who are helped can be placed in a dependent position, treated as victims not agents. Also, the underlying societal rules and structures that generate the social ills are not necessarily addressed. This approach might be more relevant to

19

humanitarian catastrophes than structural approaches that attempt to correct the root causes of social problems.

Utilitarianism: maximising aggregate subjective happiness

In a utilitarian framework, the value of health is determined by the subjective utility (happiness, pleasure, or desire satisfaction) that it creates for an individual.[5] Across all individuals in a society, the ideal state is one that maximises the aggregate utility. Health could be valued because it generates utility directly, or because good health is instrumental to other utility-generating states, including opulence, or both. Many contemporary health policies are based on a form of utilitarianism in which good health is valued as instrumental to maximising aggregate utility. For example, the WHO Commission on Macroeconomics and Health calculated the costs and benefits of burdens of disease and argued that investing in health would generate economic growth, thereby enhancing incomes and aggregate utility.[6]

The utilitarian approach underscores important interconnections between health and other variables. It can show how improving the health of the deprived can be "in everybody's interest"—including the self-interest of people not inclined to altruism. Its difficulties, however, are several. First, the instrumental valuation of health demeans it as an intrinsically valued goal in all societies. Second, people's self-assessments do not necessarily match their observed health status. For example, the self-reported morbidity rates in the Indian state of Kerala, where life expectancy is 70–75 years, are significantly higher than in Bihar, where life expectancy is significantly lower; and self-reported morbidity in the USA is higher still.[7] Third, it is rather difficult, even theoretically, to aggregate very different kinds of utility together into a single entity. Finally, a utility-maximising approach is not directly sensitive to distributional concerns.

Equity: achieving a fairer distribution of health capabilities

Equity is a relational concept in which ethical assessments are—at least in part—based on distributional features of one or more variable.[8] Fortunately, considerable intellectual work has recently been done on health equity and social justice.[9,10]

Building on the work of political philosopher John Rawls, Amartya Sen has addressed some key features of health equity.[11] First, he poses the question of "equity of what?" Should equity be evaluated with reference to health achievement or access to health care? Sen argues that equity in health should be assessed in terms of health capabilities and achievements rather than healthcare activities. After all, health care is a human activity; what people actually value is the capability to attain good health. He further notes that equitable social processes should inform evaluations of equity in the health space. In some equity domains, such as gender, completely equal distribution of health achievement could be considered unfair because women—whose lifespan in the absence of gender discrimination exceeds that of men—should, under an equity framework, enjoy longer life expectancies.

An equity-based evaluation considers not only allocation of a fixed set of health resources, but also allocation of resources between health and other social objectives. Equitable approaches to health have carried, considerable power in mobilising support for health components of international development. Striking disparities in health achievement and emotively powerful arguments of preventable suffering can animate the public and political leaders. An example is the recent call for public funds to expand antiretroviral treatment to HIV-positive people in poor countries. The disparity between the health of those with access to life-saving drugs and the avoidable deaths among all others evokes the moral imperative to alleviate preventable human suffering caused by the inequitable access to antiretroviral drug therapy.

Rights: fulfilling our obligations so others are dignified

Human rights in health are embedded in several UN declarations, and they have deep and wide moral bases. Legal formulations were created to specify what was argued in the 17th century to be an inalienable moral claim grounded in the ontological dignity of human beings. Human rights can be described as "things which are owed to man because of the very fact that he is man".[12] Some human rights can be expressed in the space of capabilities— for example rights to health, or to inclusion. Yet rights also add to the capability perspective by invoking duties and obligations on the part of others. Because each human being is recognised as an "end", human rights demand obligatory behaviour on the part of the state, firms, groups, and individuals. Obligations may be "perfect" (as enshrined in law) or "imperfect" (a general duty to do what one can to help).[13]

Calls for a rights-based approach to global health have recently grown. Extensions of human rights to children and women both contain references to freedom from preventable suffering and freedom to exercise health choices.[14,15] The application of human rights to good health has drawn attention to the duties and obligations that people and institutions have towards human beings, viewed squarely as an "end" worthy of dignity. A human rights approach often assumes some health minimum that all people should be able to realise for human dignity. The challenge is to implement the corresponding "incomplete obligations" among communities, institutions, and states where good health depends upon resources, knowledge, technologies, and social action.

Knowledge and institutions

These ethical schools do not track precisely to any specific health initiative. None of the schools dominates any specific health action, and several schools are often relevant to any single initiative. At present, whether the 3 by 5 initiative was evaluated according to aggregate utility (increasing the utility of people with HIV/AIDS) or distributional equity (increasing the numbers of people in developing countries who are given antiretroviral treatment), human rights (for health care), or the need for humanitarianism (to alleviate the suffering of those with HIV/AIDS), in all cases action is morally imperative. Ensuring a minimal threshold of health might similarly fit well with human-itarianism and human rights, and equity and justice values will require action on behalf of the most disadvantaged. Beyond moral values, the selection of global health initiatives is shaped by other, often implicit but no less valid, factors. Among these are knowledge and institutions.

To a large degree, ethical assessments will rest not only on the ethical perspective chosen, but also on the information selected for examination.[16] The selection of information is shaped by political and scientific forces as well as by moral theories. Paul Farmer[17] has written eloquently about the selective scrutiny of information that shapes health action. Tuberculosis, especially multidrug-resistant tuberculosis, became recognised as a health crisis when it achieved rapid transmission in New York City. Yet tuberculosis—before, during, and after the New York crisis—kills 2 million people annually, most of whom are poor. Because of informational selectivity, tuberculosis is a silent crisis among the world's poor, invisible to the rich and powerful. Similarly, severe acute respiratory syndrome (SARS) achieved front-page news because of its lethal nature and the paralysing effect it had on global commerce. Yet, "SARS-like" health catastrophes take place daily in thousands of rural villages in low-income countries. These health problems likewise severely affect families and communities, who are invisible to better-off and protected communities.

Scientific knowledge provides the basis for research and development of health technologies, such as vaccines and drugs. Breakthroughs in health research raise moral challenges because they make feasible treatment for conditions that were hitherto incurable—for example, antiretroviral drugs for HIV. Morally, there is a big difference between inevitable human calamity and suffering that can be prevented by modern technology. Growing knowledge gaps between technological potentiality and health realities present huge ethical challenges. Contention is further fuelled if the gap is accentuated by commercial interest. Recent debates over affordable access to life-saving antiretroviral drugs have focused on the fairness of international regimes of intellectual property rights that are perceived to favour commerce over human health.

Global health, like other fields, has a cluster of institutional stakeholders. Governments and intergovernmental agencies like the UN and the World Bank are mandated to play technical, financial, and operational roles. Since health is a major component of the global economy, corporations have interests in profits as well as in protecting their public reputations. Civil society organisations have many roles, ranging from the direct delivery of services to advocacy on public policies. Institutions, like all actors, are endowed with certain capabilities and also seek to advance their bureaucratic, political, and financial agendas. One typical driver of organisational behaviour is to gain command over resources that can translate into more jobs, higher status, and more numerous activities. Tracking of financial flows in global health initiatives can help reveal institutional winners and losers.

Historical studies have examined these institutional motivations in global health. The work of the Rockefeller Foundation overseas, for example, was often linked to corporate interests and political propagation of capitalism.[18] In an excellent historical analysis of tuberculosis control in mid-20th century, Sunil Amrith postulated that the conduct of tuberculosis programmes was primarily shaped by the state of knowledge and the capabilities of global institutions.[19] Field research had shown that directly observed therapy (DOTS) was highly effective in curing tuberculosis in home-based settings. Endowed with new knowledge, yet limited by institutional capacity and scarce funding, WHO decided to pursue tuberculosis control through vertical programmes involving cadres of specifically tasked field workers rather than attempt to build holistic village-based primary services. The latter approach would have been far more demanding institutionally and financially.

Consensus and advocacy

A common usage of moral values is to mobilise public support. Sometimes, however, advocates of global health do not give an accurate representation of distinct ethical schools, simply because they want everyone to agree. Braveman and Groskins,[20] for example, argued that the concepts of equity and rights are essentially identical, and lead to similar strategies. Their aim seems to have been advocacy for certain types of health actions rather than for clarification of distinctive moral schools. De Cock[21] argued that a public health rather than a human rights approach should frame responses to HIV/AIDS in Africa, but again this analysis is based on a very narrow example of both ethical schools. We argue that clarity in thinking is essential, because different moral schools do indeed raise distinct considerations and it can be useful to evaluate these carefully. At the same time, the urge to seek consensus is also valid, and can be sought without either exaggerating differences, or claiming (inaccurately) that differences between moral schools do not exist.

A common usage of moral values is advocacy, often to rich and powerful leaders, institutions, and nation states with the goal of mobilising resources— finance, political will, human motivations—on behalf of particular health action.

But here we run into an apparent paradox: how can one use moral values as advocacy tools, when the moral schools are distinct, and when people argue passionately among them? In order to achieve the support, global health programmes also must build consensus among a diverse constituency of resource-holders as to the central value of the initiative. So when it comes to the language of why support for global health is important, we recognise, with Cass Sunstein,[22] the wisdom of seeking "incompletely theorized agreements" in the moral discourse surrounding global health.[23]

In his 1994 Tanner Lectures in human values, Sunstein[22] argued that in some cases consensus can be achieved if participants refrain from elaborating their moral positions, because if they scrutinised these positions in depth, consensus could fracture. By contrast, he advocates an approach that "enlists silence, on certain basic questions, as a device for producing convergence despite disagreement, uncertainty, limits of time and capacity, and heterogeneity". Sunstein's approach has the advantage of opening space for dialogue, exchange, and discussion, thereby promoting deliberative democracy, political account-ability, and reason-giving. Incompletely theorised agreements satisfy diverse constituencies who might have very different reasons, including incompatible values, for supporting a particular activity.

There is a further point against requiring everyone to agree on only one ethical justification for global health. For not only might different appro-aches appeal to different groups, different people might also have distinct understandings of what the terms "rights", "equity", or "humanitarianism", actually mean. After all, the support base of global health initiatives is diverse, ranging from heads of state to private-sector executives to religious leaders to activists from NGOs to opinion-setters and journalists. It is highly unlikely that these constituencies will share an identical understanding of ethical terms.

A global health initiative can receive emphatic support from people who do not necessarily agree on the ethical foundations for their support, and in fact may very clearly disagree with one another as to why a programme should proceed—ie, its ethical or metaphysical justification. Advocates of global health initiatives would thus do well to proceed with a general appeal to moral concepts such as social justice and compassion, and this generality belies prudence rather than a lack of moral rigour.

Moral clarity

Yet an eclectic appeal to moral values in order to garner support of global health initiatives is not to imply that distinctions among moral values are trivial. Beyond clarifying why an action is important, adopting a particular moral approach can influence health action in other deeply important ways.

First is the scope of health action. An example is the programmatic implication of pursuing access to health care versus equitable distribution of health outcomes. In the former case, the programme would invest heavily in building health clinics and outposts, and perhaps in increasing the ratio of medical personnel per citizen. This sounds very appealing until one recognises that a country may have many rural health outposts, and many doctors on salary role, but if these doctors do not turn up to work, and the outposts do not have adequate pharmaceutical supplies, the population's health outcomes might remain very poor. On the contrary, to achieve an equitable distribution of health outcomes it would be necessary to make sure that the investment in health care results in better health across the population. It would also then be necessary to address broader social determinants of health, such as that raised in Michael Marmot's[24] intriguing research on the under-recognised relation between socioeconomic inequality and health.

Second, different ethical schools (and different groups within them) may shape how global health programmes are undertaken. Charitable acts might treat people as passive recipients of generosity, whereas rights-based approaches would encourage "voice" and participation to strengthen the agency of people for achieving their inherent rights.

Third, advocacy might use moral values to advance a global health agenda—because they are effective in advancing a global agenda. To mobilise a compassionate response, a picture of a feeble, emaciated, and large-eyed child might be used to stir pity among donors. Such advertisements tend to view the poor as helpless victims, rather than people who could be empowered to care for themselves. Arguably, much harm has been done by such dehumanising advocacy techniques. Yet, it could be argued that such moral approaches are legitimate to use because they are more effective in evoking public support than other moral approaches.

When people speak of ethics, the contribution that most readily leaps to mind is motivational: that an appeal to moral values will motivate people to support a set of actions. Yet this is only one of the ways in which moral values can support global health initiatives, and is not necessarily the most powerful. Discussions on whether to frame the objective of global health initiatives in terms of access to health care, or capabilities for good health, or utility maximisation, help to clarify what global health initiatives seek to accomplish. Criteria such as efficiency, or equitable treatment for men and women, clarify which alternative actions to realise similar goals should be selected. Consideration of how health activities contribute to or block non-health objectives such as the support of agency, or the rights to self-determination, clarify the importance of how health initiatives are carried forward. Thus global health may be far easier to achieve if we pause to follow through different moral analyses and thereby clarify what, which, and how global health initiatives can best proceed.

References

1 Lee J. W. Science and the health of the poor. *Bull World Health Organ* 2003; **81**: 473.
2 Lee J. W. Speech at the World Health Assembly. Geneva, Switzerland: May, 2003.

3 Brundtland G. H. Health at the World Summit on sustainable development. XXIV World AIDS Conference, 2002. Barcelona.

4 Rothschild E., Lane M. Philanthropy and health. London: King's College, 2001.

5 Bentham J. Introduction to the principles of morals and legislation. London: The Athlone Press, 1970.

6 WHO Commission on Macroeconomics and Health. Macroeconomics and health: investing in health for development. Geneva: WHO, 2001.

7 Sen A. K. Health: perception vs observation. *BMJ* 2002; **7342**: 860–61.

8 Sen A. K. Inequality reexamined. New York, Cambridge, MA: Russell Sage Foundation, Harvard University Press, 1992.

9 Evans T., Bhuiya A., Wirth M., eds. Challenging inequities in health: from ethics to action. Oxford: Oxford University Press, 2001.

10 Anand S., Peter F., Sen A., eds. Public health, ethics, and equity. Oxford: Clarendon Press, forthcoming 2004.

11 Sen A. K. Why health equity? *Health Econ* 2002; **11**: 659–66.

12 Maritain J., Anson D. C., [from old catalog]. The rights of man and natural law. London: Geoffrey Bles, the Centenary press, 1944.

13 Anand S., Sen A. Human development and human rights: human development report. New York: Oxford University Press for UNDP, 2000.

14 Convention on the Rights of the Child, Nov 20, 1989. New York, general assembly 44/25.

15 Vienna Declaration and Programme of Action, June 25, 1993. Vienna, A/CONF 157/23.

16 Sen A. K. Informational analysis of moral principles. In: Harrison R., ed. Rational action. Cambridge: Cambridge University Press, 1979: 115–132.

17 Farmer P. Infections and inequalities: the modern plague—updated edition with new preface. Berkeley: University of California Press, 2001.

18 Brown R. Rockefeller medicine men: medicine and capitalism in America. Berkeley: University of California Press. 1979.

19 Amrith S. Plague of poverty? The World Health Organization, tuberculosis and international development, c 1945–1980. Centre for History and Economics, Cambridge University: 2002.

20 Braveman P. Gruskin S. Poverty, equity, human rights and health: policy and practice. *Bull World Health Organ* 2003; **80**: 539–45.

21 De Cock K. M., Mbori-Ngacha D., Marum O. Shadow on the continent: public health and HIV/AIDS in Africa in the 21st century. *Lancet* 2002; **360**: 67–72.

22 Sunstein C. R. Legal reasoning and political conflict. New York: Oxford University Press, 1996. PhD thesis. Cambridge, MA: Harvard University, 1998.

23 Ruger J. P. Aristotelian justice and health policy: capability and incompletely theorized agreements: PhD thesis, Cambridge, MA: Harvard University, 1998.

24 Marmot M. Do inequalities matter? in: Daniels N., Kennedy B., Kawachi I., eds. Is inequality bad for our health? Boston: Beacon Press, 2000: 37–41.

CHANGING GLOBAL ESSENTIAL MEDICINES NORMS TO IMPROVE ACCESS TO AIDS TREATMENT

Lessons from Brazil

A. Nunn, E. Da Fonseca and S. Gruskin

Source: *Global Public Health*, 4:2 (2009), 131–49.

Brazil's large-scale, successful HIV/AIDS treatment programme is considered by many to be a model for other developing countries aiming to improve access to AIDS treatment. Far less is known about Brazil's important role in changing global norms related to international pharmaceutical policy, particularly international human rights, health and trade policies governing access to essential medicines. Prompted by Brazil's interest in preserving its national AIDS treatment policies during World Trade Organisation trade disputes with the USA, these efforts to change global essential medicines norms have had important implications for other countries, particularly those scaling up AIDS treatment. This paper analyses Brazil's contributions to global essential medicines policy and explains the relevance of Brazil's contributions to global health policy today.

Introduction

Globally, 33 million people live with HIV/AIDS (UNAIDS 2008). In 2005, the United Nations committed to providing free and universal access to treatment for all people living with HIV/AIDS in need by 2010 (UNGA 2005). Although the global health community still falls far short of this commitment, in the last five years, the number of people estimated to be receiving highly active antiretroviral therapy (HAART) in developing countries has jumped from 400,000 to three million, or approximately 31% of the people in need (WHO 2008b). Global AIDS deaths have also plateaued, in part due to a large increase in the number of people receiving treatment

(UNAIDS 2008). The global commitment to treat all people living with HIV/ AIDS and to build health infrastructure towards that end is unprecedented; never before has the global community committed to and implemented health infrastructure to treat a chronic disease.

Global commitments to AIDS treatment can, to a large extent, be attributed to Brazil's efforts. Brazil was the first developing country to begin offering free treatment to AIDS patients. In the 1990s, Brazil ignored the World Bank's recommendations not to treat AIDS patients, and to focus instead on preventing new infections because that approach was more 'cost-effective' (World Bank 1993, 1998). Brazil began treating AIDS patients in the public sector in the early 1990s, committed to providing free and universal access to HAART in 1996, and has since made AIDS treatment available to over 180,000 people (Nunn *et al.* 2007).

Today, HIV prevalence in Brazil is 0.5%; approximately 600,000 people live with HIV/AIDS in Brazil (UNGASS 2008). AIDS-related mortality and morbidity have declined dramatically as a result of Brazil's AIDS treatment programmes and vertical (mother to child) transmission has been dramatically reduced since the late 1990s (Marins *et al.* 2003, Hacker *et al.* 2004, Souza-Junior *et al.* 2004, Teixeira *et al.* 2004, Campos *et al.* 2005, Dourado *et al.* 2006). However, HIV prevalence rates are considerably higher in several subpopulations such as injecting drug users (IDUs), commercial sex workers and the urban poor (Dourado *et al.* 2006, Fonseca and Bastos 2007). Additionally, although vertical transmission of HIV has declined, the AIDS epidemic increasingly affects Brazilian women and access to important prevention technologies required to prevent vertical transmission of HIV in Brazil (including HIV test kits and antiretroviral (ARV) prophylaxis) remains problematic in some remote regions. Despite these challenges, Brazil's epidemic has generally stabilised as new infections levelled off in the industrialised, urban southeast where the epidemic has historically been concentrated (Dourado *et al.* 2006).

Brazil is signatory to the 1995 World Trade Organization (WTO) Trade-Related Aspects of Intellectual Property Rights (TRIPS) Trade Agreement, which introduced intellectual property rules into the multilateral trading system (WTO 1995). TRIPS allows governments or third parties to issue compulsory licenses, which permit use of intellectual property without the consent of the patent holder in cases of national public health emergency, among other limited circumstances (WTO 1995).

The TRIPS Agreement has profoundly influenced Brazil's AIDS programme. In 2000, facing steadily rising costs for its AIDS treatment programme, Brazil took advantage of the TRIPS compulsory licensing clauses; Brazil began threatening to issue compulsory licenses to produce generic copies of patented drugs if pharmaceutical companies did not lower their prices. Although Brazil did not actually issue a compulsory license for an ARV drug until 2007, the controversy received global media coverage, prompted a 2001 WTO trade dispute with the USA, and sparked global policy dialogue about drug prices. Since 2001, Brazil has continued to publicly challenge multinational pharmaceutical companies about drug prices, produced generic drugs locally, threatened to produce generic copies of patented drugs locally and even imported generic drugs under patent in Brazil (Nunn et al. 2007). Brazil's actions ultimately resulted in pharmaceutical companies lowering their prices for several ARV medicines in Brazil, and saved Brazil over $1 billion (USD) in drug costs since 2001 (Nunn et al. 2007).

Brazil's policies have also had important impacts beyond the country's borders. Brazil proved that treating people living with HIV/AIDS was possible in a developing country context and has become an example for developing countries scaling up AIDS treatment (Marins et al. 2003, Matida et al. 2005, Dourado et al. 2006). Brazil also established an important precedent for challenging pharmaceutical companies about drug prices, a policy some other countries have subsequently adopted (Ford et al. 2007, Nunn et al. 2007). Even as Brazil's policies were met with tremendous opposition from the innovator pharmaceutical industry and several governments, to strengthen its efforts to treat all people living with HIV/AIDS, Brazil also made deliberate and concerted efforts to change global health, human rights and trade policies related to access to essential medicines. (The term 'essential medicines' refers to World Health Organisation guidelines for medications that all health systems should make available to their populations.)

Ongoing global health discussions have been influenced by Brazil's actions in many ways, and Brazil continues to play a role in global policy discussions related to access to medicines. Most recently, in May 2008, the World Health Assembly (WHA) passed a resolution which commits to developing novel strategies for research and development for essential medicines and diagnostics for diseases that disproportionately affect developing countries. Opposed by many developed countries, this resolution can be traced to Brazil's and other developing countries' historical efforts to promote improved access to essential medicines. In this paper, we review the impacts of Brazil's efforts at the United Nations Commission on Human Rights (UNCHR), United Nations General Assembly (UNGA), WHA and WTO between 2000 and the present, and explain their historical links and relevance to related efforts to improve access to medicines today.

This article is grounded in empirical data collected over the last three years, including more than 40 in-depth interviews with key informants; reviews of historical documents related to UNCHR, UNGA and WHA resolutions, as well as WTO agreements from 2000 to 2008; quantitative data about Brazilian and global drug prices; and thousands of newspaper articles. We use a chronological narrative approach to explain how and why Brazil has shaped global health, human rights and trade norms related to essential medicines and highlight their evolving implications for global health policy.

Background

The first AIDS case in Brazil was diagnosed in 1983, and by 1988 Brazil had the second highest number of reported AIDS cases in the world, after the USA (Folha de São Paulo 1991). Brazil's commitment to AIDS treatment can be directly related to the country's transition to democracy, including its 1988 Constitution, which includes a clause guaranteeing a right to health and health services for all Brazilians (Brazil 1988).

During the late 1980s and early 1990s, an AIDS movement mobilised in Brazil demanding that the state provide access to prevention and treatment services. Many non-government organisations (NGOs) established in the late 1980s and in the early 1990s proved overwhelmingly important in pressuring the government to adopt progressive AIDS policies. These NGOs framed the poor public policy response to HIV/AIDS as violations of human and citizenship rights, and publicly demanded that the Brazilian government take steps to reduce HIV-related discrimination, enhance prevention efforts, and offer treatment to people living with HIV/AIDS. In 1990, in response to these demands, the Health Ministry committed to providing AIDS treatment, and began producing generic ARV drugs in 1993. Although the courts interpreted the constitutional right to health to include access to AIDS medicines in the early 1990s, AIDS treatment was available only sporadically until the mid-to-late 1990s, primarily because Brazil's Congress and Health Ministry had not appropriated sufficient funds for treatment and Brazil's health infrastructure was fragmentary (Nunn 2008).

In 1996, Brazil's Congress passed Law 9.313, commonly referred to as 'Sarney's Law', (sponsored by then-Senator and former President José Sarney), which guarantees free and universal access to drugs for AIDS treatment for all people living with HIV/AIDS in Brazil (Lei 9.313 1996). Since the mid-1990s, the World Bank also provided over $500 million in loan support for Brazil's AIDS programmes. The loans forbade spending on drugs for treatment, but Brazil used the loans to subsidise epidemiological surveillance and health infrastructure development, which later facilitated treatment scale up (Nunn 2008). Brazil also began recognising intellectual property rights for pharmaceutical products in 1997, shortly after passing the 1996 Industrial Property Law to comply with WTO intellectual property requirements for middle-income countries (Brazil 1996).

Brazil, obligated by its legal commitments to, on the one hand, provide free and universal access to drugs for AIDS treatment and, on the other, to recognise the intellectual property rights of costly AIDS drugs, faced rapidly rising costs for AIDS treatment in the late 1990s. In 2000, Brazil's Health

Minister José Serra began publicly discussing issuing a compulsory license in order to produce several ARV drugs in Brazil's public drug production facilities. Shortly thereafter, in early 2001, the USA filed a WTO trade dispute against Brazil (Buckley 2001).

Anticipating a trade dispute, Brazil commenced an effort to change global norms related to essential medicines. This strategy was adopted in order to facilitate implementation of Brazil's national efforts and included collaborations with other nation states (Serra 2005, Viana 2005). By working to change global norms in international fora, Brazil was able to help normalise its controversial AIDS treatment policies, including its decisions to challenge multinational pharmaceutical companies about ARV drug prices. We explore the implications of the evolution in global essential medicines norms for global health policy.

Brazil's first forays into changing global policy

During 1999 and 2000, several of Brazil's elected officials and public servants openly discussed the rising costs of AIDS treatment and the possibility of locally issuing a compulsory license in order to produce several patented drugs (Serra 2005, Teixeira 2005, Cardoso 2006). At the 2000 International AIDS Conference in Durban, South Africa, Paulo Teixeira, then Director of Brazil's National AIDS Programme, publicly criticised the US government for pressuring Brazil about its decision to produce generic medicines locally, and alluded to offering African nations assistance with expanding their AIDS programmes (Guedes 2000).

At the same time, other developing countries, including Thailand and South Africa, were facing trade sanction threats from the USA, as well as lawsuits and political pressure from innovator drug companies. In addition, an influential global AIDS movement was emerging that advocated for lowering drug costs and improving access to AIDS treatment for people living in developing countries. The movement also challenged drug companies about their prices while supporting the local production of generic drugs (Smith and Ciplon 2006).

Brazil's efforts to change global health norms related to essential medicines commenced at the WHA[1] in May 2000, when Brazil's delegation introduced a WHA resolution entitled *HIV/AIDS: Confronting the Epidemic*. The proposal sought a WHO-sponsored international price database for essential medicines that would be continuously updated, thereby promoting greater transparency about global drug prices. Also supported by France, Zimbabwe and South Africa, the resolution prompted an aggressive response from the multinational pharmaceutical industry and the US delegation (McNeil 2000, MSF 2000). Although the resolution ultimately failed, it forecasted Brazil's plans to continue to highlight the high costs associated with AIDS treatment in the global policy arena, an effort which escalated in 2001.

2001: a critical year for changing global policy

Brazil's global strategy

In January of 2001, the United States Trade Representative (USTR) launched a formal trade dispute against Brazil at the WTO. The dispute cited Article 68 of Brazil's 1996 Industrial Property Law, which requires that all foreign companies produce their patented products *in Brazil* within three years or else be subject to compulsory license. This clause was initially intended to stimulate development of local industry, but the USA claimed that the Brazilian law was in direct violation of the WTO TRIPS agreement, which guards against protectionist trade measures[2] (Buckley 2001).

The US trade dispute did not directly address Brazil's AIDS treatment programme or its strategies to threaten to issue compulsory licenses to lower the cost of AIDS treatment. One can speculate whether this was because Brazil's threats to issue compulsory licenses had not actually violated the TRIPS agreement and the public relations dangers of trying to undermine an AIDS treatment programme in a developing country. Nonetheless, the dispute drew global attention to Brazil's AIDS treatment policies.

Brazil's public officials knew they were not likely to win a purely economic battle against the USA. It was in this period that they began in earnest to introduce resolutions at the United Nations Commission and Sub-commissions on Human Rights, and the WHA. Former Brazilian President Fernando Cardoso explained why Brazil accelerated its global strategy to promote its AIDS treatment programme:

> At the time, the international political climate was not conducive to AIDS treatment in developing countries. This is why we implemented a Brazilian strategy that included intensive South-South collaboration . . . However, just as our strategy interested developing countries, it prompted strong negative reactions from developed countries and the pharmaceutical industry. It seemed logical then, for Brazil to seek global assistance in protecting our national interests.
>
> (Cardoso 2006)

Brazilian Health Ministry Diplomat José Marcos Viana described the Brazilian strategy to change global norms related to essential medicines:

> We (Brazil) had several pillars in our strategy. One pillar was to defend Brazil's stance on AIDS drugs in several of the UN agencies. We had to defend our position and change international public opinion about these issues, with the press, with NGOs, in every way

possible. The UN agencies were a vehicle for changing public opinion about Brazil's stance on AIDS issues and also for changing the legal frameworks to accomplish our objectives. Normally, all of these issues are reserved for the WTO. We decided our most effective line of defence would be to open the discussion to the Commission on Human Rights and the World Health Organization as well. The idea of moving our resolutions through the UN agencies was important for shaping global public opinion in our favour. So we developed a strategy at the World Health Assembly to introduce medicines resolutions. At the Commission on Human Rights, we pushed through that resolution that documented that access to medicines was a fundamental human right.

Our idea was that the Health Ministry, working with Itamaraty (Brazil's Foreign Affairs Ministry), was going to win over international public opinion. Our strategy was *not* to defeat the US government; the balance of power was not in our favour. The only way to win a trade dispute with the US, to convince the American government to change its policies, is to change the American public's opinion, and the opinion of the world. So that was our strategy, at the WHO, at the Human Rights Commission, at the WTO, with other NGOs, with the New York Times and other countries, to convince the American public to support us . . . We bought ads in the New York Times, the Washington Post, the Los Angeles times, all the big papers in the US.

(Viana 2005)

Shaping global health essential medicines norms through trade policy

Brazil's formal efforts to change essential medicines norms through trade policy began in April 2001, when preparing for the November 2001 WTO round of trade discussions in Doha, Qatar. Zimbabwe, which led a group of African countries in the TRIPS Council, requested the council convene a special session related to access to essential medicines. After several trade and intellectual property disputes related to access to AIDS medicines in Brazil, South Africa and Thailand, the TRIPS council met and outlined a proposal to address conflicts related to trade, intellectual property and access to medicines (Abbott 2002, Cannabrava 2006).

In those meetings, Brazil campaigned for greater 'TRIPS flexibilities', or policies that permit more flexibility or leniency in enforcing the TRIPS agreement in developing countries, particularly regarding public health issues. Diplomat José Marcos Viana sheds light on why Brazil became so vocal about TRIPS flexibilities:

Earlier in 2001, José Serra confronted me and said, 'Now there is a World Trade Organisation dispute against us. I want you to find some way that no one can *ever* file another trade dispute against Brazil, or against any other developing country related to essential medicines'. He was worried that it would happen again. So that was why Brazil got so active at the Doha round of the TRIPS meetings.

(Viana 2005)

Serra aimed to change global institutions to protect Brazil's domestic AIDS treatment policies in order to further trade disputes and conflicts with pharmaceutical companies. There was also consensus among other developing countries of the need for greater TRIPS flexibilities in cases of public health emergency. These discussions continued until the November 2001 Doha round of trade talks.

Using human rights to shape essential medicines policy

In May of 2001, Brazil introduced a resolution to the UNCHR[3] entitled *Access to Medication in the Context of Pandemics such as HIV/AIDS*. The resolution explicitly cites General Comment 14 issued by the UN Committee on Economic, Social and Cultural Rights (CESCR) in 2000, which (CESCR 2000) specifically recognises HIV/AIDS treatment as a fundamental component of the right to the highest attainable standard of physical and mental health and calls on nation states to make HIV treatment available to individuals living with HIV/AIDS. The USA strongly opposed the resolution but abstained from the vote. Nevertheless, the UNCHR overwhelmingly approved the resolution (52-0, with one abstention) (UNCHR 2001). *Access to Medication in the Context of Pandemics such as HIV/AIDS* was the first international human rights resolution to explicitly address the right to access to medicines. It calls on states to promote access to medicines and medical technologies for pandemics such as HIV/AIDS and to recognise that the right to health includes access to medicines, including drugs for AIDS treatment (UNCHR 2001). (Table 1 lists resolutions and agreements that Brazil either sponsored or supported in international fora in order to promote greater access to AIDS treatment and essential medicines. Note the Table excludes resolutions and agreements that were not ultimately accepted and those in which Brazil was not actively engaged.)

This resolution had important impacts on global policy. Beginning to establish the right to AIDS medicines as part of the human right to health within this political forum enabled Brazil to work in partnership with other countries and build upon its key components in other international fora; subsequent resolutions cited and reinforced its content.

One month later in June 2001, the UN High Commissioner on Human Rights issued a report entitled *The Impact of the Agreement on Trade-Related*

Table 1 Brazil's contributions to global essential medicines policy.

Institution	Date	Resolution or agreement	Policy implications
United Nations Commission on Human Rights (UNCHR)[a]	April 2001	Access to medication in the context of pandemics such as HIV/AIDS	Acknowledges that the right to health includes access to medicines, including medicines for HIV/AIDS treatment. Calls on states to promote access to medicines and medical technologies for pandemics such as HIV/AIDS.
World Health Assembly (WHA)	May 2001	WHO medicines strategy	Links human rights and access to medicines at WHA. Encouraged states to implement policies that guarantee access to medicines, including medicines for HIV/AIDS. Led to development of a global drug price monitoring system. WHO added ARVs to the 2002 Essential Medicines List.
World Health Assembly (WHA)	May 2001	Scaling up the response to HIV/AIDS	Endorsed creation of the *Global Fund to Fight HIV/AIDS, TB and Malaria*. Promoted use and distribution of generic drugs for HIV/AIDS treatment.
United Nations High Commission on Human Rights (UNHCHR)	June 2001	The impact of TRIPS agreement on human rights	Commended Brazil's HIV/AIDS treatment policies and programmes. Highlighted dilemmas faced by developing countries to provide access to medicines at affordable prices while acknowledging intellectual property rights.
United Nations General Assembly Special Session (UNGASS)	June 2001	Declaration of commitment on HIV/AIDS	Reaffirmed access to medicines as a fundamental human right. Encouraged governments to address factors related to provision of AIDS drugs, including pricing. Urged provision of the highest attainable standard of treatment for HIV/AIDS. Encouraged development of domestic innovator and generic drug industries, as consistent with international law.

Table 1 (cont'd)

Institution	Date	Resolution or agreement	Policy implications
United Nations Sub-commission on Human Rights	August 2001	Intellectual property and human rights	Reminds governments of the primacy of human rights over other economic policies and agreements.
World Trade Organisation (WTO)	November 2001	Doha Declaration on the TRIPS agreement and public health	Recognised the rights of governments to issue compulsory license in cases of public health emergency. Affirmed governments' right to define what constitutes a national emergency.
World Health Assembly (WHA)	May 2003	Intellectual property rights, innovation and public health	Created an independent commission to investigate the public health implications of intellectual property regulations for developing countries.
World Health Assembly (WHA)	May 2006	Public health, innovation, essential health research and intellectual property rights: towards a global strategy and plan of action	Culminated in a working group to develop strategies and public policies to effectively address the health needs of developing countries. Culminated in creation of the Intergovernmental Working Group on Health (IGWG). IGWG made policy recommendations in 2008 to address the need to develop drugs and diagnostics to address the health needs of developing countries. IGWG's policy recommendations were integrated into the *Global Strategy on Public Health, Innovation and Intellectual Property* resolution of the 2008 WHA.

[a]Renewed and expanded in 2002–2005.

Aspects of Intellectual Property Rights on Human Rights, which, among other things, alludes to the Brazilian case to highlight the dilemmas developing countries face in promoting access to essential medicines at affordable prices (UNHCHR 2001). Brazil was highlighted because of its world-renowned treatment policies and efforts to scale up AIDS treatment, and the report helped further legitimise Brazil's efforts to defend its approach to AIDS treatment and efforts to shape global essential medicines institutions (Elliot 2005, Hunt 2006).

In August 2001, shortly after the events noted above, the UN Sub-Commission on Human Rights[4] approved a resolution entitled *Intellectual Property and Human Rights* without a vote. It's unclear who introduced this resolution, and whether the motivation was actually related to the intellectual property of indigenous populations, but its relevance to Brazils efforts are clear:

> ... (the Sub-Commission on Human Rights) Reminds all governments of the primacy of human rights obligations under international law over economic policies and agreements, and requests them, in national, regional, and international forums, to take international human rights obligation and principles fully into account in international economic policy formation.
>
> (UNSCHR 2001)

Promoting World Health Assembly (WHA) resolutions to encourage generic drug use and transparent pricing

In May 2001, shortly after adoption of Brazil's resolution at the UNCHR, Brazil introduced the *Revised Drug Strategy* at the WHA. The resolution proposed to expand access to essential medicines and controversially called for the WHO to adopt policies to allow for developing countries to expand access to generic drugs. Linking human rights with access to essential medicines, the resolution stated that developing countries should be permitted to use locally produced generics to uphold their commitments to fulfil the human right to health, and reiterated Brazil's previous request for the WHO to develop an international pricing database (Meyer 2005).

Although there was support from a range of countries and Brazilian Health Minister José Serra campaigned vigorously for this resolution, even delivering a speech at the WHA to lobby for support, ultimately the resolution was not adopted (Berlinck 2001). Brazil, Zimbabwe and other developing countries nevertheless used this opportunity to lobby the WHO to provide technical assistance to developing countries that faced challenges with intellectual property and trade issues impacting access to medicines.

A resolution entitled the 2001 *WHO Medicines Strategy*, which superseded the former *WHA Revised Drug Strategy*, was ultimately adopted. The *WHO*

Medicines Strategy outlined a comprehensive approach to promoting access and rational use of medicines. Lobbying from the Brazilian delegation had a profound impact on the final language of this resolution, which highlighted the links between human rights and access to medicines. The resolution also encouraged states to implement policies that guarantee access to medicines, including medicines for HIV/AIDS, and called on the WHO Director-General to develop a global drug price monitoring system.

By acknowledging access to drugs as a fundamental human right and citing the need to expand access to drugs for AIDS treatment, this WHA resolution further legitimised Brazil's AIDS treatment programme. Having public international debate about drug prices relative to per capita health expenditure also lent legitimacy to Brazil's AIDS treatment institutions and provided momentum for Brazil's efforts to challenge multinational pharmaceutical companies about ARV drug prices.

As a result of the resolution and the growing evidence base for treatment in developing countries, the WHO added ARVs to its Essential Medicines List in 2002, establishing ARVs as part of the minimal standard of medicines that should be made available for all health systems (WHO 2002). These changes in global policy highlighted the importance of treating HIV/AIDS, and provided momentum for the movement to encourage greater transparency about drug prices. These resolutions also led to creation of the WHO-sponsored 'prequalification system' for drug manufacturers to be considered for official WHO product endorsement[5] (WHO 2006b). WHO also began financing the Management Sciences for Health's (MSH) International Drug Price Indicator Guide, which is published annually and catalogs online drug pricing information for many types of drugs (McFayden 2005). The guide, coupled with MSF's annual 'Untangling the Web of Price Negotiations' (MSF 2002) promoted transparency and policy dialogue about drug prices. Raising quality standards for generic drugs also promoted more affordable global access to high-quality drugs, which has facilitated scale up of global AIDS treatment.

Brazil also sponsored a second WHA resolution in May 2001 entitled *Scaling up the Response to HIV/AIDS*. Specifically, the resolution called for member states to establish health policies which include promotion and distribution of generic drugs for HIV/AIDS treatment. After Brazil engaged in long discussions with the USA, South Africa, Sweden and Thailand, the resolution was somewhat diminished in substance (Pincock 2001). However, the final resolution does refer to the resolutions previously adopted at the UNCHR and WHA and encourages member states to promote use and access to generic medicines for treating HIV/AIDS. Among other things, these efforts helped jumpstart official WHO policy discussions about the impact of intellectual property rights on access to medicines, and helped fuel global political momentum for creation of the Global Fund to Fight AIDS, Tuberculosis and Malaria, now a multi-billion dollar institution that finances prevention, treatment and care for HIV/AIDS, tuberculosis and malaria programmes.

UN General Assembly Special Session (UNGASS): Brazil and the public stage

Due in part to the legitimacy given to Brazil's treatment policies in international fora since January 2001, there was growing international pressure for the USTR to drop its trade dispute with Brazil (Chade 2001, O Globo 2001). In June 2001, the UNGA held a Special Session (UNGASS) on HIV/AIDS. After much global protest from the global AIDS treatment movement and a strong response from the Brazilian government, on 25 June 2001, the first day of the UNGASS, the USTR formally dropped the WTO trade dispute against Brazil (British Broadcasting Company 2001).

During the Special Session, Brazil promoted its AIDS programme and campaigned for text to encourage changes in global essential medicines policy. Brazil introduced resolution text that mentioned the public health challenges associated with intellectual property rights, drug prices, and access to essential medicines in developing countries. Brazilian Health Minister José Serra's speech highlighted Brazil's dramatic decline in AIDS-related mortality, attributing its success to the country's strategy of producing AIDS drugs locally. He also encouraged pharmaceutical companies to adopt differential pricing policies in developing countries, and urged the General Assembly to commit to providing affordable treatment to all PLWHA (Serra 2001).

The final *Declaration of Commitment on HIV/AIDS* encourages heads of state and government representatives to strengthen health systems and address other factors affecting access to AIDS medicines. Citing the UNCHR resolution *Access to Medication in the Context of HIV/AIDS*, the Declaration of Commitment also reaffirms access to drugs as a fundamental human right. Since this is a political consensus document, it's difficult to tease out Brazil's precise contribution to the final *text* of the resolution. However, it is clear that without Brazil's political actions and evidence base for treatment, this strong global commitment to AIDS treatment would not have occurred. Furthermore, bolstering the legitimacy of Brazil's treatment institutions, the *Declaration of Commitment* fuelled Brazil's ongoing price negotiations with multinational pharmaceutical companies and efforts to change global essential medicines policy.

Promoting Brazil's treatment agenda through the World Trade Organisation (WTO) Doha Declaration on public health

Between the UNGASS session and November 2001, the USA, the European Union (EU) and a group of developing countries,[6] circulated and discussed draft proposals of what would become the *Doha Declaration on the TRIPS Agreement and Public Health*. Brazil played a key role in drafting the developing country position paper that called for greater flexibilities on essential medicines policy in trade regulations. The developing country coalition supported liberal use of compulsory licensing, parallel importation[7] of pharmaceutical products, and differential pricing across markets. The US delegation aligned with multinational pharmaceutical company interests, opposing the developing country positions, including proposals to permit developing countries to locally define what constitutes 'national public health emergency', and TRIPS flexibilities that would permit compulsory license use in cases of national emergency. The EU adopted a middle ground (Abbott 2002, Serra 2005, Cannabrava 2006).

One completely unexpected event changed the course of the Doha negotiations; in September of 2001, after the attack on the US World Trade Center in New York, when the US faced what was thought to be a bio-terror attack with anthrax bacteria, the US Secretary of Health and Human Services threatened to issue a compulsory license for Bayer's Ciprofloxacin, prompting Bayer to lower its prices. Caught in the awkward position of threatening to issue a compulsory license to induce Bayer to lower its drug prices while trying to restrict compulsory license use in developing countries fighting the AIDS epidemic, the USA ultimately moderated its position (Abbott 2002, Cannabrava 2006). According to several diplomats and experts present in Doha, the final text of the Doha Declaration was nego-tiated behind closed doors, primarily between the USA and the Brazilian delegation, with the US altering much of the original developing country coalition proposal (Abbott 2002, Love 2005, Cannabrava 2006). The final Doha Agreement affirmed the right of each nation to declare and define what constitutes a public health emergency (WTO 2001). Health Minister José Serra explained how Brazil was able to garner support for TRIPS flexibilities in Doha:

> Our efforts to change international law were part of Brazil's work as an sovereign nation, and part of my efforts as Health Minister. We were able to push forward the Doha Agenda because the European Union was divided; Spain, France and Italy were more flexible. Germany, England, the UK were all opposed to TRIPS flexibilities. Of course, the rest of the developing world was not difficult to convince. But the EU position was somewhat ambiguous. And Robert Zoellick, the US Trade Representative, ultimately agreed with the flexibilities. Many NGOs helped publicly support our position.
>
> (Serra 2005)

By unambiguously affirming the right of each nation to declare and define what constitutes a public health emergency (WTO 2001), the Doha Declaration clarified some ambiguities of the 1995 TRIPS agreement, which recognised that compulsory licenses can be used in cases of public emergency but did not elaborate on their specific terms of use (WTO 1995). Diplomat Francisco Cannabrava, Brazil's TRIPS negotiator, commented on Brazil's efforts in Doha:

> Our objective was not to do away with TRIPS, but we wanted to preserve TRIPS flexibilities. So that was the very specific objective we pursued in Doha. We knew it wouldn't work to change the TRIPS agreement because that was something that would just take too long. The objective was to avoid very strict interpretation of the TRIPS agreement, to get the WTO to recognise publicly that developing countries had a right to issue compulsory licenses for public health needs . . . Importation is what we fought for at Doha. We promoted clauses to allow for importation of raw materials, which Brazil needed to make its generics . . . We preserved the flexibilities that Brazil needed.
>
> (Cannabrava 2006)

Since adoption of the Doha Declaration, Brazil continued to use the TRIPS flexibilities to threaten to issue compulsory licenses to produce ARV drugs locally. This had important policy impacts; in late 2001, drug companies Merck and Roche both dropped their prices and, since that time, Brazil has negotiated steep price reductions for several additional ARV drugs. These price negotiations are estimated to have saved the country over one billion dollars between 2001 and 2005 (Nunn *et al.* 2007).

In summary, by the end of 2001, Brazil had achieved its objective of preserving its domestic AIDS treatment institutions through strategic use of global policy fora. However, the impacts of these efforts went much further. The US dropped its trade dispute against Brazil. Moreover, by shaping global policy, Brazil's efforts helped pave the way for other developing countries to follow suit in making drugs for AIDS treatment available to their populations.

Brazil's engagement and policy impacts post-2001

Since 2001, Brazil has worked with other countries to continue to shape global norms related to AIDS and access to essential medicines more generally. This has included efforts at the UNCHR and the WHA. Brazil's efforts have also had direct and indirect impacts on global policy and drug prices.

Brazil's impact on human rights policy related to access to essential medicines

In 2002, the UN Sub-Commission on Human Rights renewed the commitments to AIDS treatment with another resolution entitled *Access to Medication in the Context of Pandemics such as HIV/AIDS, Tuberculosis and Malaria.* During 2002–2005, resolutions entitled *Access to Medication in the Context of Pandemics such as HIV/AIDS* and *Access to Medication in the Context of Pandemics such as HIV/AIDS, Tuberculosis and Malaria* were approved by the UNCHR (UNCHR 2002, 2003, 2004, 2005). These resolutions contributed to the development of global human rights standards related to access to essential medicines.

The impact of the Doha Declaration on World Trade Organisation (WTO) policy related to essential medicines

Even in those fora where Brazil has been less engaged since 2001, such as at the WTO, Brazil's previous efforts paved the way for other countries. In the 2003 WTO Cancun negotiations, *Implementation of Paragraph 6 of the Doha Declaration on the TRIPS Agreement and Public Health: Decision of 30 August 2003* expanded on the Doha TRIPS flexibilities by allowing countries with insufficient pharmaceutical production capacity to issue compulsory licenses in order to import generic drugs in cases of national public health emergency (WTO 2003). This decision was reaffirmed in the 2005 Hong Kong round of WTO trade agreements (WTO 2005). Although Brazil was far less active in these discussions, had Brazil not been so influential in Doha, public health TRIPS flexibilities are likely never to have materialised. Since 2003, several countries have used these TRIPS flexibilities to issue compulsory licenses in order to import generic medicines (Love 2007).

Global AIDS treatment access and drug prices

Brazil's resolutions have also directly and indirectly impacted global scale up of AIDS treatment and access to essential medicines. The Global Fund to Fight HIV/AIDS, Tuberculosis and Malaria, which developed in part as a result of the 2001 WHA resolution *Scaling Up the Response to HIV/AIDS* that Brazil introduced, has provided approximately 1.4 million people with AIDS treatment and has also financed hundreds of tuberculosis and malaria programmes (Global Fund 2008). International political momentum for increased global health expenditure also contributed to the creation of the United States' President's Emergency Plan for AIDS Relief (PEPFAR) in 2003, which supplies treatment for another 1.4 million people living with HIV/AIDS in developing countries and supports wide-ranging interventions related to HIV/AIDS (PEPFAR 2008). As a result of these programmes, global AIDS spending expanded from $300 million to $10 billion between 1996 and 2008 and US annual spending for overseas development assistance related to HIV/AIDS grew from $121 million in 1998 to an expected $8 billion in 2008 (CRS 2004, 2005, 2006, UNAIDS 2006, UNAIDS 2007, Nunn 2008, US Public Law No: 110–293 2008). While these changes certainly cannot be attributed to Brazil's efforts alone, these programmes may not have emerged had Brazil not been so vocal about the importance of global AIDS treatment, proved that AIDS treatment was possible in a developing country, and helped to develop the global policy infrastructure to move these programmes forward.

Additionally, Brazil's demand for active pharmaceutical ingredients (APIs) for use in manufacturing generic drugs in Brazil, along with massive global scale up of AIDS treatment as a result of the Global Fund and PEPFAR, have helped stimulate development and competition within the generic ARV drug industry. Competition and Brazil's price negotiations have contributed to large-scale declines in the cost of AIDS drugs globally (MSF 2007, Nunn *et al.* 2007).

Shaping research and development paradigms for essential medicines

Brazil continues its engagement at the WHA to promote greater access to essential medicines. In 2003, Brazil sponsored an important WHA resolution entitled *Intellectual Property Rights, Innovation, and Public Health* and led a delegation of countries who advocated for a WHO mandate to address intellectual property right issues that impact public health. The resolution, approved by the WHA, created an independent commission to investigate the public health implications of intellectual property protection for developing countries called the Commission on Intellectual Property Rights, Innovation and Public Health (WHA 2003). By linking intellectual property rights, innovation and access to a variety of medical technologies for developing countries, Brazil broadened the public policy discussion related to access to medicines.

In April of 2006, the Commission released its report entitled *Intellectual Property Rights, Innovation, and Public Health*, which finds that intellectual property rights have not stimulated development of new technologies to meet public health needs in developing countries. The Commission was not, however, able to reach an agreement on how to effectively address the paucity of affordable technologies for developing countries through public policy (WHO 2006a). Nevertheless, official acknowledgement by this body that current research and development paradigms have not led to development of appropriate medical and diagnostic technologies for the diseases accounting for large disease burdens in developing countries has further legitimised the global AIDS treatment movement and promoted policy changes to stimulate greater access to essential medicines.

The report also brought momentum to the ongoing debate about global research and development paradigms, particularly for diseases primarily affecting developing countries. In May of 2006, Brazil and Kenya co-sponsored a WHA resolution that called for a working group to develop novel ideas and policy recommendations to address the concerns raised in the report.

The resolution, citing all of the aforementioned WHA resolutions sponsored by Brazil since 2001, calls for development of innovative policies for conducting the research and development for drugs and diagnostic products to address the health problems that disproportionately affect developing countries. This resolution created the WHO Intergovernmental Working Group on Innovation, Intellectual Property and Public Health (IGWG), which met in 2006–2008.

Brazil's contributions to global essential medicines policy are ongoing; in December 2007, the IGWG recommended that the WHA establish a needs-driven research and development agenda that responds to the health needs of low- and middle-income countries. In May 2008, IGWG proposed a strategy to finance and implement policies to increase the availability, accessibility and uptake of drugs, diagnostic products and vaccines in developing countries (WHO 2007). In spite of considerable opposition from several developed countries, and with strong support from many developing countries, IGWG's recommendations culminated in the 2008 WHA resolution *Global Strategy on Public Health, Innovation and Intellectual Property*. The resolution committed to developing strategies to finance, coordinate and implement a needs-based research and development agenda to respond to the health needs of developing countries[8] (WHA 2008, WHO 2008a). Although it's difficult to gauge the resolution's long-term policy impacts at this early stage, this WHA resolution may spearhead a fundamental paradigm shift for global research and development for priority diseases in developing countries. This movement, which can be traced to Brazil's 2003 and 2006 WHA resolutions, highlights Brazil's long-term contributions to global essential medicines policy.

Conclusion

Brazil's efforts to preserve its domestic AIDS treatment policies had far-reaching implications for global essential medicines policy. Brazil's reforms improved global transparency about drug prices, affirmed generic drug use to address public health needs, defined access to medicines as a component of the human right to health, promoted incorporation of ARVs into the WHO Essential Medicines List and strengthened TRIPS flexibilities for developing countries. Many of these institutional changes helped pave the way for other countries to begin or expand their national AIDS treatment programmes; today, three million people in developing countries receive drugs for AIDS treatment. Economies of scale for AIDS treatment have also helped stimulate development and competition within the generic ARV drug industry, which has contributed to large-scale declines in the cost of AIDS drugs globally. Perhaps even more importantly, Brazil's efforts have helped shape and promote a global agenda to meet the health needs of developing countries, and these discussions continue to impact global essential medicines policy today. These are important and enduring legacies of Brazil's world-renowned AIDS treatment programme.

Notes

1 The WHA is the World Health Organisation's decision-making body and has 192 member delegates from each of the world's nation states.
2 Article 27:1 of the TRIPS Agreement reads 'Patents shall be available and patent rights enjoyable without discrimination as to the place of invention, the field of technology and whether products are imported or locally produced'.
3 The UN Commission on Human Rights' historical mandate was to examine, monitor and report on human rights situations and violations worldwide. The institution was historically comprised of 53 member states elected each year. The UN Commission on Human Rights (UNCHR) was replaced by the Human Rights Council in 2006.
4 The Sub-Commission on Human Rights was a subsidiary body of the Commission on Human Rights, comprised of 26 experts representing the world's different regions.
5 The prequalification process is a quality assessment and bioequivalence testing process designed to enhance access to high-quality drugs for AIDS, malaria, tuberculosis and reproductive health. To gain official WHO prequalification status and to be used in any programmes funded by UN agencies, both patented and generic drugs must meet bioequivalence, good manufacturing, laboratory and clinical practices.
6 Developing countries included a group of African nations, which called itself the 'Africa Group', Bangladesh, Barbados, Bolivia, Brazil, Cuba, Dominican Republic, Ecuador, Haiti, Honduras, India, Indonesia, Jamaica, Pakistan, Paraguay, Philippines, Peru, Sri Lanka, Thailand and Venezuela.
7 Parallel importation occurs when patented drugs are produced and sold in one market and then imported into a second market without authorisation of the patent holder in the second market.
8 Although several developing countries tried to include clauses stating that the right to health takes precedence over commercial interests into the resolution, the movement ultimately failed.

References

Abbott, F., 2002. The Doha declaration on the TRIPS agreement and public Health: lighting a dark corner at the WTO. *Journal of International Economic Law*, 5, 469–505.

Berlinck, D., 2001. Proposta Brasileira de Remédio Barato Perde Apoio da Índia e da África do Sul. *O Globo*, 17 de Maio, Brazilian proposal for cheap medicines loses support from India and South Africa, pg A1.

Brazil, 1988. Constitution of Brazil.

Brazil, 1996. Lei de Propriedade Industrial Law of Industrial Property.

British Broadcasting Company, 2001. US drops Brazil AIDS drug case. *AIDS Drugs Case*, 25 June.

Buckley, S., 2001. U.S. Brazil clash over AIDS drugs, 'Model' treatment program seen at risk in dispute on patents and pricing. *The Washington Post*, 6 February.

Campos, D. P., Ribeiro, S. R., Grinsztejn, B., Veloso, V. G., Valente, J. G., Bastos, F. I., Morgado, M. G., and Gadelha, A. J., 2005. Survival of AIDS patients using two case definitions, Rio de Janeiro, Brazil, 1986–2003. *AIDS*, 19 (Suppl. 4), S22–S26.

Cannabrava, F., 2006. Interview by Amy Nunn, digital recording.

Cardoso, F. H., President of Brazil, 2006. Interview by Amy Nunn.

CESCR, 2000. *Substantive issues arising in the implementation of the international covenant on economic, social and cultural rights. General comment 14: the right to the highest attainable standard of health.* Geneva, Switzerlands: United Nations Economic and Social Council Committee on Economic, Social and Cultural Rights.

Chade, J., 2001. Patentes: mais de 100 ONGs apoiam 50 countries support Brazilian WTO proposal. *Estado de São Paulo*, 20 de Junio.

CRS, 2004. *HIV/AIDS international appropriations fiscal year 2003–2005*. Washington, DC: Congressional Research Service.

CRS, 2005. *HIV/AIDS international appropriations: fiscal year 2002–2004*. Washington, DC: Congressional Research Service.

CRS, 2006. *AIDS in Africa*. Washington, DC: Congressional Research Service.

Dourado, I., Veras, M. A., Barreira, D., and De Brito, A. M., 2006. Tendências da Epidemia de AIDS no Brasil Após a Terapia anti-retroviral AIDS epidemic trends after the introduction of antiretroviral therapy in Brazil. *Revista de Saúde Público*, 40, 91–97.

Elliot, R., 2005. Interview by Amy Nunn, digital recording.

Folha de São Paulo, 1991. OMS prevê Índice Africano de AIDS no país World Health Organization predicts African-level rates of AIDS in Brazil. *Folha de são paulo*, 6 de Agosto.

Fonseca, M. and Bastos, F., 2007. Twenty-five years of AIDS in Brazil: main epidemiological findings Brazil will help Africa combat AIDS. *Cadernos da Saúde Público*, 23 (Suppl.), S333–S344.

Ford, N., Wilson, D., Costa Chaves, G., Lotrowska, M., and Kijtiwatchakul, K., 2007. Sustaining access to antiretroviral therapy in the less-developed world: lessons from Brazil and Thailand. *AIDS*, 21 (Suppl. 4), S21–S29.

Global Fund, 2008. *The global fund monthly progress update: January 2008*. Geneva, Switzerland: The Global Fund to Fight HIV/AIDS, Tuberculosis and Malaria.

Guedes, C., 2000. Brazil Ajudará Africa a Combater Avanço da AIDS, *O Globo*, 3 de Julio.

Hacker, M., Petersen, M., Enriquez, M., and Bastos, F., 2004. Highly active antiretroviral therapy in Brazil: the challenge of universal access in a context of social inequality. *Revista Panamericana de Salud Pública*, 16, 78–83.

Hunt, P., 2006. Interview by Amy Nunn.

Lei 9.313, 1996. Dispõe sobre a distribuição gratuita de medicamentos aos portadores do HIV e doentes de AIDS. Provision of Free Antiretroviral Medicines for people living with and affected by HIV/AIDS.

Love, J., 2005. Interview by Amy Nunn, digital recording. Consumer Project on Technology, Washington, DC.

Love, J., 2007. *Knowledge ecology international statement on Thailand compulsory licenses* [online]. Washington, DC. Available from: http://www.cptech.Org/ip/health/c/thailand/kei-thaicl-statement.html [Accessed 20 July 2007].

Marins, J. R., Jamal, L., Chen, S., Barros, M., Hudes, E., Barbosa, A., Chequer, P., Teixeira, P., and Hearst, N., 2003. Dramatic improvement in survival among adult Brazilian AIDS patients. *AIDS*, 17, 1675–1682.

Matida, L. H., Da Silva, M. H., Tayra, A., Succi, R. C., Gianna, M. C., Goncalves, A., De Carvalho, H. B., and Hearst, N., 2005. Prevention of mother-to-child transmission of HIV in São Paulo state, Brazil: an Update. *AIDS*, 19 (Suppl. 4), S37–S41.

McFayden, J., ed., 2005. *International drug price indicator guide*. Arlington, VA: WHO and Management Sciences for Health.

McNeil, D., 2000. Patent holders fight proposal on generic AIDS drugs for poor. *The New York Times*, 18 May, A5.

Meyer, F., 2005. Interview by Amy Nunn, digital recording. Mission of Brazil to the United Nations, New York.

MSF, 2000. MSF summary of the 53rd World Health Assembly, 15–21, May 2000. *In*: Médicins Sans Frontières, ed. *Frontières*. Geneva, Switzerland: Médicins Sans Frontières.

MSF 2002. *Untangling the web of price reductions: a pricing guide for the purchase of ARVs for developing countries*. 2nd ed. Geneva, Switzerland: Médicins Sans Frontières.

MSF, 2007. *Untangling the web of price reductions: a pricing guide for the purchase of ARVs for developing countries*. 8th ed. Geneva, Switzerland: Médicins Sans Frontières.

Nunn, A., 2008. *The politics and history of AIDS treatment in Brazil*. New York: Springer International.

Nunn, A. S., Fonseca, E. M., Bastos, F. I., Gruskin, S., and Salomon, J. A., 2007. Evolution of antiretroviral drug costs in Brazil in the context of free and universal access to AIDS treatment. *PLoS Med*, 4, e305.

O Globo, 2001. Brasil defende política anti-AIDS nos EUA. *O Globo*, 21 de Junio.

PEPFAR, 2008. *The power of partnerships: fourth annual report to congress on PEPFAR*. Washington, DC: The President's Emergency Plan for AIDS Relief.

Pincock, S., 2001. WHO to adopt HIV/AIDS resolution. *Reuters*, 18 May.

Serra, J., 2001. *Statement by minister of health Jose Serra at UNGASS. UN General Assembly special session on HIV/AIDS*. New York, NY.

Serra, I, 2005. Interview by Amy Nunn, digital recording. City Hall, São Paulo.

Smith, R. and Ciplon, P., 2006. *Drugs into bodies: a history of AIDS treatment activism*. Westport, CT: Praeger.

Souza-Junior, P., Szwarcwald, C., Barbosa, J. A., Carvalho, M., and De Castilho, Ea, C., 2004. HIV infection during pregnancy: the sentinel surveillance project, Brazil 2002. *Revista de Saúde Pública*, 38, 764–772.

Teixeira, P., 2005. *Interview with Amy Nunn, digital recording*. São Paulo: São Paulo State AIDS Program Headquarters.

Teixeira, P., Vitoria, M. A., and Barcarolo, J., 2004. Antiretroviral treatment in resource-poor settings: the Brazilian experience. *AIDS*, 18 (Suppl. 3), S5–S7.

UNAIDS, ed., 2006. *Report on the global AIDS epidemic*. Geneva: UNAIDS.

UNAIDS, 2007. *Financial resources required to achieve universal access to HIV prevention, treatment, care and support*. Geneva, Switzerland: UNAIDS.

UNAIDS, 2008. *Report on the global AIDS epidemic*. Geneva, Switzerland: UNAIDS.

UNCHR, 2001. *Access to medications in the context of HIV/AIDS*. Geneva, Switzerland: United Nations Commission on Human Rights.

UNCHR, 2002. *Access to medication in the context of pandemics such as HIV/AIDS.* Geneva, Switzerland: UN Commission on Human Rights.

UNCHR, 2003. *Access to medication in the context of pandemics such as HIV/ AIDS, tuberculosis and malaria.* Geneva, Switzerland: UN Commission on Human Rights.

UNCHR, 2004. *Access to medication in the context of HIV/AIDS, tuberculosis and malaria.* Geneva, Switzerland: UN Commission on Human Rights.

UNCHR, 2005. *Access to medications in the context of HIV/AIDS, tuberculosis and malaria.* Geneva, Switzerland: UN Commission on Human Rights.

UNGA, 2005. *2005 World summit outcome.* New York: United Nations General Assembly.

UNGASS, 2008. *Targets and commitments made by the member-states at the United Nation General Assembly special session on HIV/AIDS UNGASS – HIV/AIDS: Brazilian response 2005/2007 country progress report.* New York: UNGASS.

UNHCHR, 2001. *The impact of the agreement on trade-related aspects of intellectual property rights on human rights.* Geneva, Switzerland: United Nations Economic and Social Council.

UNSCHR, 2001. *Intellectual property rights and human rights: subcommission on human rights resolution 2001/21.* Geneva, Switzerland: UN Sub-commission on Human Rights.

US Public Law NO: 110–293, 2008. To authorize appropriations for fiscal years 2009 through 2013 to provide assistance to foreign countries to combat HIV/AIDS, tuberculosis, and malaria, and for other purposes.

Viana, J. M., 2005. Interview by Amy Nunn, digital recording.

WHA, 2003. *Intellectual property rights, innovation and public Health.* Geneva, Switzerland: World Health Assembly.

WHA, 2008. *Global strategy on public health, innovation and intellectual property.* Geneva, Switzerland: World Health Assembly.

WHO, 2002. *WHO takes major steps to make HIV treatment accessible: treatment guidelines and AIDS medicines list announced by WHO.* Geneva, Switzerland: World Health Organisation.

WHO, 2006a. Public health, innovation and intellectual property rights. *In*: I. A. P. H., ed. *The commission on intellectual property rights.* Geneva, Switzerland: World Health Organisation.

WHO, 2006b. *World Health Organisation prequalification system* [online]. Publication of the World Health Organisation. Available from: http://mednet3.who.int/prequal/ [Accessed 29 October 2006].

WHO, 2007. *Draft global strategy and plan of action on public health, innovation and intellectual property. Intergovernmental Working Group On Public Health.* Geneva, Switzerland: World Health Organisation.

WHO, 2008a. *Draft global strategy on public health, innovation and intellectual property.* Geneva, Switzerland: WHO Intergovernmental Working Group on Public Health, Innovation and Intellectual Property.

WHO, 2008b. *Towards universal access: scaling up priority HIV/AIDS interventions in the health sector.* Geneva, Switzerland: World Health Organisation.

World Bank, 1993. *Brazil AIDS and STD control project: world bank staff appraisal report.* Washington, DC: World Bank.

World Bank, 1998. Project appraisal document on a proposed loan in the amount of $165 million to the federative republic of Brazil for a second AIDS and STD control project. *In*: B. C. M., ed. *World Bank human and social development group and unit*. Washington, DC: World Bank.

WTO, 1995. *Agreement on trade-related aspects of intellectual property rights*. Geneva, Switzerland: World Trade Organisation.

WTO, 2001. *Declaration on the TRIPS agreement and public health*. Geneva, Switzerland: World Trade Organisation.

WTO, 2003. Implementation of paragraph 6 of the Doha declaration on the TRIPS agreement and public health: decision of 30 August 2003.

WTO, 2005. Doha world programme, Hong Kong ministerial declaration. WT/MIN(05)/DEC.

UNDERSTANDING CHANGE IN GLOBAL HEALTH POLICY

Ideas, discourse and networks

Andrew Harmer

Source: *Global Public Health*, 6:7 (2011), 703–18.

How is radical change in global health policy possible? Material factors such as economics or human resources are important, but ideational factors such as ideas and discourse play an important role as well. In this paper, I apply a theoretical framework to show how discourse made it possible for public and private actors to fundamentally change their way of working together – to shift from international public and private interactions to global health partnerships (GHPs) – and in the process create a new institutional mechanism for governing global health. Drawing on insights from constructivist analysis, I demonstrate how discourse justified, legitimised, communicated and coordinated ideas about the practice of GHPs through a concentrated network of partnership pioneers. As attention from health policy analysts turns increasingly to ideational explanations for answers to global health problems, this paper contributes to the debate by showing how, precisely, discourse makes change possible.

Introduction

In a 2009 speech, Director General of the World Health Organisation (WHO), Margaret Chan stated that to achieve 'transformational change' in Africa, 'the policies must be right, and the money must be used effectively and efficiently' (Chan 2009). If such radical transformation is possible, *how* is it possible? To answer this question requires a step beyond important, if superficial, statements about getting the policies right: it requires understanding the ideas and discourse, or *ideational factors*, which inform those policies, and the networks through which they travel. As a first step in the application of ideational factors to global public health, I demonstrate how a theoretical framework first developed in the political sciences might usefully be employed to shed light on one particular radical shift in policy – the shift from public and private interaction to public–private global health partnerships (GHPs).

The analysis of discourse that follows is informed by an ideas-based approach to society called Constructivism. Constructivism is beginning to attract interest from global health policy analysts, although it remains on the margins of the discipline (Kickbusch 2003, Harmer 2005, Shiffman 2009). It does, however, have a long pedigree in the political sciences (Adler 1997, Wendt 1999, Hay 2009). I distinguish ideas-based approaches to global health from power-based and interest-based approaches. Whilst the differences between these approaches are complex and nuanced, the most important distinction is that ideas-based approaches – as the name implies – attach much more significance to the role of ideas and discourse.[1] Power-based analyses see ideas as nothing more than functions of power: put crudely, the ideas that shape global health are the ideas of the most powerful actors. Interest-based theories regard ideas as little more than useful tools for maximising self-interest, where ideas act like signalmen diverting a train from one track to another. Ideas-based approaches such as Constructivism argue that ideas rather than material forces structure our lives and *construct* our identities and interests (Wendt 1999, p. 1).

When GHPs first attracted the attention of researchers at the beginning of the twenty-first century, early criticism drew on power-based assumptions to highlight the disparity in power relations between public and private actors and the potential for the most powerful partners to further extend their influence over global health by manipulating the partnership process for their own gain (Karlinger and Bruno 2000, Utting 2000, Richter 2003, 2004). Since that early work, interest-based analyses have dominated the literature on partnerships. In these analyses, the emphasis has predominantly focused on identifying areas for reform (Buse and Walt 2000, Buse and Harmer 2007). There has been little attempt to apply ideas-based insights to analysis of GHPs despite their potential to illustrate how ideational factors construct global health policy, or how the identities and interests of public and private actors might be reconstructed through partnership (Buse and Harmer 2004). This paper seeks to fill that gap – using the phenomena of GHPs to show how ideational factors structure global health policy – whilst also flagging potential areas for future research.

Adopting an ideas-based approach to global health provides theoretical space for researchers to ask a different set of questions from either power-based or interest-based approaches. Numerous studies of GHPs ask *why* questions: *why* did the change from public and private to public–private global health interventions occur? Answers to that question cite changes in ideology, lost legitimacy in international institutions, the monopolistic position of transnational pharmaceutical industries, the growth of non-government organisations (NGO), new technologies, increased support from private foundations and globalisation as causes (Buse and Walt 2000, Reich 2002, Widdus and White 2004). Ideas-based analysis asks a different, *how-possible*, question: how was it possible for such a radical institutional innovation as GHP to be adopted and embraced by the international health community, overcoming entrenched interests, institutional obstacles and cultural barriers in the process? Doty (1993, p. 298) explains the difference between the two questions, thus:

> How meanings are produced and attached to various social subjects/ objects, thus constituting particular interpretive dispositions that create certain possibilities and preclude others. What is explained is not *why* a particular outcome obtained, but rather *how* the subjects, objects, and interpretive dispositions were socially constructed such that certain practices were made possible.

In the following analysis of three GHPs – the Drugs for Neglected Diseases initiative (DNDi), Stop TB Partnership and the TB Alliance – I demonstrate how the practice of GHP was made possible by the meanings produced and attached to a specific health problem. I argue that it was possible for these GHPs to emerge when they did because the 'problem' of tuberculosis and neglected diseases was constructed through the discourse of globalisation, global health governance and global public goods (GPGs). This 'interpretive disposition', to use Doty's phrase, made possible the practice of GHPs.

Before proceeding, it is important to be clear what I am not arguing in this paper. I am not disputing the role of material power: clearly, rich foundations such as the Bill and Melinda Gates Foundation have bankrolled numerous GHPs. Neither am I disputing the existence of strategic self-interests that are no doubt employed by actors when they engage in partnership, though I would argue that partnerships have the potential to re-construct those self-interests. Finally, I do not claim that ideational factors are *more* important than either power or interests, although I would argue that under-standing what ideas and discourse do should precipitate a reconceptualisation of both power and interests – which, sadly, is beyond the scope of this enquiry but warrants further exploration in a public health context.

More modestly, I argue that while power-based and interest-based approaches can, and are, enrolled to explain the historical origins of individual GHPs, only ideational factors provide a satisfactory account of how it was possible for this paradigm shift in public and private relations to take place. The ideas and discourse of GHPs were generated not by the most powerful actors, but by a close network of academics and public health entrepreneurs and advocates; and they had to overcome, not reinforce, institutional self-interest from both public and private spheres hostile to the idea of public–private partnership.

Methods

As noted above, the aim of this analysis is to demonstrate the utility of a theoretical framework, first developed in the political sciences, for understanding the role of discourse in global health policy. In her analysis of European capitalism, Schmidt (2002) presented a set of indicators that demonstrated discourse 'at work' (Table 1). I conducted a comprehensive review of policy documents, transcripts of speeches and minutes of meetings documented on each of the three GHP's websites. The objective of the review was to identify and extract from the documents any instance of each of Schmidt's indicators: technical and scientific arguments, paradigms and frames of reference that defined 'reality', appeals to a deeper core of organising principles and norms, clear associations between the practice of GHP and long-established values, a common language and vision of the practice of GHP, and evidence of the practice of GHP translated into accessible language for public consumption. Once extracted, the instances were collated and common features were identified both within and across GHPs.

In an effort to triangulate findings from the literature review, semi-structured interviews were also conducted with 14 respondents using a pre-designed question guide. The respondents were identified using purposive sampling and 'snowballing' techniques, and were broadly representative of international health organisations, NGO and the pharmaceutical industry. My interviews were conducted either face-to-face or by telephone; each interview was recorded and transcribed and a copy of the transcription sent to each respondent. The interviews lasted from 30 minutes to 2 hours. Close reading of each transcript was conducted with the same objective as the literature review: to identify instances of Schmidt's six indicators of discourse.

Table 1 The roles and indicators of discourse (adapted from Schmidt 2002).

Role of discourse	*'Indicators' of discourse*
Discourse justifies the practice of GHP	• Introduces new technical and scientific arguments. • Depicts paradigms and frames of reference that define 'reality'. • Appeals to a deeper core of organising principles and norms.
Discourse legitimises the practice of GHP	• Associates the practice of GHP with long-established values.
Discourse coordinates the practice of GHP	• Provides a framework for discussion and deliberation through a common language and vision of the practice of GHP.
Discourse communicates the practice of GHP	• Translates the practice of GHP into accessible language for public consumption.

The choice of GHPs was determined not only by their shared interest in neglected diseases, but also their distinct institutional characteristics: Stop TB was hosted by a multilateral organisation; DNDi was managed, initially, by the NGO Médecins sans Frontières (MSF); and the TB Alliance was a legal independent partnership. Given these institutional differences, I hypothesised that different discourses would develop through these partnerships. If a similar discourse was evident, then the challenge would be to provide an explanation that went beyond reference to the institutional setting of the partnership.

The discursive construction of global health partnerships: a review of the literature

Discourse introduced new technical and scientific arguments

All three of the sample GHPs emerged from, and were justified by, scientific and technical arguments developed by working groups comprised of health practitioners, academics and representatives from key international and transnational institutions and organisations. DNDi produced a series of technical papers illustrating the lack of research and development for neglected diseases (MSF 2001, Trouiller *et al.* 2001, 2002), the principal thrust of their argument being that *both* public and private sectors had failed to respond to the problem of neglected diseases, and that a unique public model of partnership was necessary. Both the TB Alliance and Stop TB produced influential reports that presented scientific and technical arguments and data to justify their targets (TB Alliance 2001a, 2001b, WHO 2002). In each example, justification for the move to partnership was grounded in technological and scientific imperatives.

Discourse depicted paradigms and frames of reference that defined reality to justify the idea of global health partnership

It is clear that a policy paradigm for GHP emerged during the late 1990s and early in the twenty-first century *in reaction to* the neo-liberal, market-oriented economic paradigm of the 1980s (Buse and Walt 2000). The call for a new paradigm echoed through the discourse of GHP during this period, although there were differences of opinion as to the precise character of this paradigm. MSF, for example, had long-argued for a 'paradigm shift' in the response to neglected diseases. In 2003, at an international conference organised to consider a global framework for supporting health research and development (R&D) in areas of market and public policy failure, Pecoul (2003) of MSF argued that 'a paradigm shift is needed: changing global rules to prioritise people's health needs over profit'. Pecoul (2003) also identified the principal shift necessary to ensure access to essential medicines: 'withdraw essential drug development from the market logic and build public responsibility to do so'. The DNDi, argued Pecoul, represented a shift away from the market-based development paradigm most strongly associated with neo-liberal economics (Peck and Tickell 2002).

In contrast to DNDi, the TB Alliance and Stop TB did not eschew the market, although they recognised that reliance on the market alone would not achieve their goals. The Alliance provided a cost analysis of the anti-TB drug market in an effort to demonstrate the *potential* of the market to encourage anti-TB drug R&D and also encouraged the industry to invest in that market through various push and pull strategies. The Stop TB Partnership worked closely with one of the chief institutional architects of neo-liberal economic policy – the World Bank – endorsing a key Bank strategy for addressing global poverty – Poverty Reduction Strategy Papers (PRSPs) (Espinal 2004).

Discourse appealed to a deeper core of organising principles and norms to justify the idea of global health partnership

Discourse justified the practice of GHPs first by situating neglected disease in the context of globalisation, which it presented as a 'reality', and second by appealing to a conception of governance (rather than government) as an appropriate organising principle for responding to the crisis in neglected disease. Underpinning the discourse of GHP was also an appeal to an emerging norm that treated neglected disease as a GPG (Table 2).

Globalisation was, and remains, an essentially contested concept (Hirst and Thompson 1999, Lee 2003, Held and McGrew 2008). However, the complexities of the debate were not reflected in speeches communicating the idea of GHP to the global public. Consider, for example, the then Director General of the WHO, G. H. Brundtland's description of the 'global health threat' facing us all: 'In the modern world, bacteria and viruses travel almost as fast as money . . . With globalisation, a single microbial sea washes all of humankind. There are no health sanctuaries' (Brundtland 2001a); or Nils Daulaire's assertion: 'I see globalisation as a morally neutral but nonetheless inevitable force that poses both opportunities and threats' (Hagmann 2001). In these two examples, the discourse presented globalisation as a reality; and thus, a global response – a GHP – was justified.

The practice of neglected disease GHPs was also possible, however, because discourse justified partnership in terms of a global organising principle: global governance. As with globalisation, global governance also remains a contested concept, but by the mid-1990s all of the key international health organisations were talking in global governance terms (World Bank 1994, WHO 1998, United Nations Development Programme [UNDP] 1999). In particular, the search was on for new mechanisms of cooperation that could respond to the challenge of governing globalisation. The discourse of GHPs appealed to

Table 2 How discourse appealed to the 'reality' of globalisation, the organising principle of governance and an emerging norm of health as a global public good.

	The 'reality' of globalisation	Organising principle: global governance	Emerging norm: health as a global public good
Stop TB	'In the days of globalisation, mass migration and cheap air travel, MDR-TB is just a plane ride away'. (Lee 2002) 'In the face of rapid globalization, TB, too, is crossing continents'. (Kochi 2000)	'The development of the global economy has not been matched by a development of the global structures of representative governance'. (Kumaresan et al. 2004) 'As it becomes more commonplace to consider health as one of the prerequisites for development and economic growth, along with such basics as ... good governance, ... I expect we will see a wide variety of new interventions and collaborations'. (Brundtland 2001b)	'The evidence is clear. A world free of TB is a global public good'. (Kochi 2000) 'I am proud to be a sponsor and catalyst of the Global Plan to Stop TB. By supporting the development of this model plan, the Open Society Institute advances its vision of promoting equity and global public good'. (Soros 2002)
TB Alliance	'Because TB anywhere is TB everywhere, we must do better and invest smarter to stop this comeback disease'. (Freire and Dauliere 2002) 'Tuberculosis is Ebola with wings ... and therefore carries a much broader, global threat'. (Raviglione 2001)	'There is also an explosion in intellectual thinking on governance. We should be evolving governments. The markets have evolved much quicker – a lot more, a lot faster. And we should take note of that. So that is the big framework, I think'. (Interview with author, 2nd October 2003)	'The Global Alliance will have an unwavering commitment to global public goods'. (Cape Town Declaration 2000)
DNDi	'The past 30 years have witnessed unprecedented transformations in global health ... however, the benefits of the "global health revolution" have not been distributed evenly'. (MSF 2001)	'In the ongoing process of creating a new world order, the global economy must be structured to address the true needs of society'. (Trouiller et al. 2001)	'Ensuring access to new tubercular drugs means that lifesaving essential medicines cannot be treated like any other commodity, like CDs or cars; they are a global public good'. (Orbinski 2001)

international enthusiasm for global governance and was thus accepted more uncritically than it might have been 10 years earlier.

Finally, discourse justified the practice of GHP by appealing to an emerging norm of health as a GPG. The discourse surrounding all three of the sample GHPs makes repeated reference to this global norm. There is a comprehensive academic literature supporting the argument that health is a GPG (Chen *et al.* 1999, Zacher 1999, Kaul and Faust 2001) and that GHPs provided a governance structure for the provision of health as a GPG (Kaul and Ryu 2001, United Nations Education, Scientific and and Cultural Organisation [UNESCO] 2002).

Discourse associated the practice of global health partnership with long-established values to legitimise that practice

Discourse legitimised the practice of GHP primarily through an appeal to equity. DNDi, for example, described itself as an equitable model of drug development for neglected diseases. Bernard Pecoul, Director of the DNDi, described the Initiative's 'vision' in the following terms: 'To improve the quality of life and the health of people suffering from neglected diseases by using an alternative model to develop drugs for these diseases and ensuring equitable access to new and field relevant health tools' (Pecoul 2003). The Initiative argued that lack of access to drugs for neglected diseases was inequitable because of market failure, and it laid responsibility for the crisis at the feet of both the public and private sectors. Thus not only it became *necessary* to take R&D for neglected diseases away from the market, but also an *appropriate* response for a needs-based initiative where 'monetary gain is inconsequential compared to the cost of human lives' (MSF 2003).

The TB Alliance also presented itself as an equitable response to the crisis in R&D for neglected diseases. A representative from TB Alliance, for example, explained how they first saw the lack of R&D in TB as:

A health equity outrage that somehow we were accepting that in developing countries we could have second-class citizens with second hand drugs that are 50 years old because the disease was not endemic in America or Europe . . . [the Alliance] came from this field where the patients were not being served, and we actually pointed the finger to the complete health equity gap in what is called R&D.

(Interview with author)

The TB Alliance discourse skilfully juxtaposed logics of necessity with logics of appropriateness. This was essential because of the innovative nature of the 'partnership' model (Box 1).

Stop TB (2010) explicitly recognised that 'shared values facilitate achievement of our shared goal'. These values included: urgency, equity, shared

---

Box 1. Examples of discourse juxtaposing logics of necessity with logics of appropriateness

'This partnership demonstrates how it is really possible to combine the fruits of aggressive biotech strategy with a social mission', Maria Freire (TB Alliance 2002).

The Economics of TB Drug Development report 'shows that it not only makes economic sense, but with substantial social returns there is a "moral imperative" to invest in this long neglected area of research', Jacob Kumaresan (TB Alliance 2001c).

'The Alliance is a shining example of public and private sector partnerships to bridge the gap between market opportunities and people's needs . . .' (Brundtland 2001c).

---

responsibility, inclusiveness, consensus, sustainability, and dynamism. They were expressed through the Partnership's commitment 'to act now – for all, through collective action – and into the future' (Stop TB 2010). Partnership provided the most *appropriate* governance mechanism for realising that commitment. Through membership of the Partnership, members were encouraged to make 'efficient, effective, and equitable use of the resources available to them' (Stop TB 2010).

Discourse coordinated the practice of global health partnership by providing a common language and vision

There is evidence across each of the sample GHPs of a common language and vision. I noted above the shared reference to the 'reality' of globalisation, governance as an organising principle and an emerging norm of GPGs. In addition, however, in each of the GHPs there were references to action that was 'needs-driven' and produced 'win–win' outcomes. 'Consensus' was required on technical priorities such as DOTS. Each of the GHPs emphasised the right to healthcare, equity of access, inclusion of developing countries, market failure, drug-based and biomedical responses to neglected disease, generic drug production, TRIPS-compliant safeguards and support for IP rights. Finally, there was an implicit acknowledgement by each of the GHPs that developing countries had the capacity to help themselves and that they should support 'capacity-building' activities; that it was in the interests of both poor and rich to resolve the crisis in R&D; and a shared optimism that the pharmaceutical industry was changing the way it saw its opportunity-cost structure.

That common ideas are shared amongst the GHPs should not be surprising because, as illustrated below in the discussion of the neglected disease

GHP network, there were strong links between various key actors involved in all three of the GHPs. The point to make is simply that given the similar work experiences and environments of many of the key people responsible for establishing these partnerships, it should not be surprising to find that shared ideas first informed and then evolved the practice of GHP. But it should also be noted that key actors involved in the sample GHPs did not always share precisely the same ideas and beliefs – most notably, there were differences in opinion about the most appropriate *model* of partnership.

Discourse communicated the practice of global health partnership by translating it into accessible language for public consumption

In her work on discourse, Schmidt argued that 'the overall outlines of a policy programme are given expression in a "master" discourse by a "master" politician', and that the overall outlines of the policy programme are most clearly articulated through public communication (Schmidt 2002, p. 235).

As early as 1996, at the Habitat II Conference on Human Settlements, the UN made it clear that GHP was a *necessary* guiding principle of its future global governance role, as Noel Brown, former Director of the United Nations Environment Programme, made clear: 'I believe that the future of the United Nations will rest on effective partnering with the private sector – with business and industry' (Veon 1998).

Box 2. The TINA mantra of GHPs

'Partnership with private and public sector actors is not simply a choice. It is the only possible way forward' (J. W. Lee, Director General, WHO).

'Only through new and innovative partnerships can we make a difference . . . Whether we like it or not, we are dependent on the partners' (G. H. Brundtland, former DG, WHO).

'Peace and prosperity cannot be achieved without partnerships involving governments, international organisations, the business community and civil society' (Kofi Annan, UN)

'Public-private partnerships are increasingly seen as the only viable means to solve intractable social and health problems such as poverty and disease eradication, new drug research, access to medicines and improving drug quality' (International Federation of Pharmaceutical Manufacturers Association).

The 'necessity' argument quickly developed into a 'there-is-no-alternative' (TINA) mantra (Box 2). GHPs were presented as 'the only possible' or 'only viable means' of ensuring 'peace and harmony'. The simple but powerful message was that we are 'dependent' on GHPs 'whether we like it or not'; and as noted above, the TINA argument was supported by explicit assumptions about the 'global' character of neglected diseases, the importance of global governance as a coordinating principle and the undisputed value of GPGs. Whilst each of these concepts is contested, the complexities of the debate were never reflected in speeches communicating the idea of GHP to the global public.

Interviewing the partners: a review of findings

As noted in section 'Methods', interviews with individuals working with DNDi, the TB Alliance or Stop TB were conducted to triangulate findings from the literature review. A close reading of the interview transcripts confirmed many of the findings described above as well as providing important insight into the existence of a network of 'partnership pioneers' through which the discourse of GHP travelled.

Only two respondents made explicit and unsolicited reference to either ideas or discourse during the interview, and just one provided a sophisticated analysis of the role that ideas played in defining the operational parameters of partnership, noting: 'the partnership . . . has to be defined, in very clear operational terms to ensure that the ends that that partner or parent partner seeks can be met'. For this respondent, the utility of ideational factors was in their ability to convey information that would ensure that the partnership achieved its agreed purpose. No other respondents provided unsolicited comment on the role of ideational factors and expressed puzzlement when pressed. To the question 'Do you think ideas were important during the early days of the GHP', eight respondents agreed but did not discuss why and four respondents offered cursory answers ('of course', 'ideas are always important') and moved the discussion to another topic.

Common across each of the interviews was repeated reference to other actors' competing interests. The WHO was mentioned by 8 of the 14 interviewees, of which two were complimentary about the role it played and six were critical of the organisation, using terms such as 'inflammatory' or as suffering from a 'dichotomy of thinking' and 'resistant to change'. There were few references to either the private sector or NGO except from interviewees who were representatives of these sectors.

When asked about the context in which GHPs emerged, 11 interviewees made reference to 'globalisation', six to 'governance' and four to 'global governance'. Most made reference to globalisation during their initial description of the development of their respective partnerships. Interestingly, two interviewees working for the WHO, and one independent adviser, argued against the existence of global governance, preferring instead to use the term 'international' to describe relations between actors within the GHP.

As noted in Section 'Introduction', constructivists recognise that ideational factors are more than tools used to maximise self-interest and more than simply an expression of material power: ideas and discourse have the potential to reconstruct actors' identities (Wendt 1999). The literature on GHPs is silent on this potential and barely touches on the possibility that it could be mechanisms within which ideas and discourse reconstruct partners' perceptions of their self-interest (Buse and Harmer 2009). Rather than see GHPs as sites in which social learning can take place, and in which actors' interests are reconstructed through exposure to new ideas and norms, the dominant argument is that actors enter GHPs with predetermined interests, and that these interests do *not* change. There was no indication from any of the interviewees that they *believed* that actors' perceptions of their self-interest were, or could be, reconstructed through exposure to partnerships. No work to date in the field of public health has been done to determine whether such a belief is justified.

Common to all interviewees was an uncritical acceptance of GHPs as a necessary and appropriate response to resolving the problem of neglected diseases. With the exception of two interviewees, who were associated with DNDi, there was no critical commentary about GHPs. Problems associated with GHPs were restricted without exception to problems of effectiveness, cooperation and incentives – in other words, practical problems that could be resolved through reform. This lends weight to the finding noted above that a dominant discourse presented GHPs as a necessary and inevitable development – that there was no alternative.

An unexpected but strong theme that emerged from the interviews was the importance of networks. Although no interviewee made explicit reference to the term 'network', it was evident that the same individuals were cited and referenced by all of the interviewees. This observation prompted a return to the literature and a search for individuals who were linked to each of the three GHPs.

The neglected disease global health partnership network

How ideas are shared is of particular interest to constructivists. Adler (1997, p. 339), for example, argues: 'an evolutionary approach requires that new or changed ideas be communicated and diffused'. Networks are one way in which ideas about partnership could have been diffused. Through interviews with key players involved in my sample GHPs, and a review of key policy documents and grey literature, it quickly became apparent that a small network of actors was instrumental in establishing and maintaining a shared understanding of partnerships for neglected diseases (Figure 1). Network analysis has been usefully applied to global health issues such as health care financing reform (Lee and Goodman 2002). In Lee and Goodman's (2002,

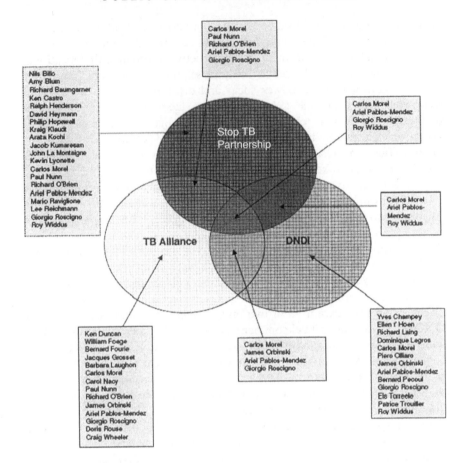

Figure 1 The neglected disease GHP network.

p. 116) analysis, the argument focused on demonstrating that reform had been 'fostered by the emergence of a policy elite rather than a rational convergence of health needs and solutions'. In the case of neglected disease partnerships, however, that argument is less easy to sustain. The idea of partnership was justified in part precisely because it *was* presented as a rational solution to a pressing health need.

What is also striking about the network is the degree of crossover that key players had between public and private sectors. For example, Yves Champey, ex-Director of DNDi, was a former Vice-President of French drug firm Rhone-Poulenc Rorer; Giorgio Roscigno, a key architect of DNDi, the TB Alliance and the Stop TB partnership, originally worked in the pharmaceutical industry, whilst Joelle Tanguy originally worked with MSF, then moved to the TB Alliance as Director of Advocacy and Public Affairs, before moving to the Global Business Coalition on HIV/AIDS.

Given such a highly interconnected network, one should not be surprised to find that a dominant discourse at once informed the development of each of the partnerships and was sustained by the reproduction of the practice of partnership. Constructivists describe this process more formally as having a *structurationist* character (Adler 2005). Thus, collective or *intersubjective* understandings emerged about particular social facts – in this case, GHPs. Crucially, actors engaged in discursive interaction and in so doing generated a structure of ideas about GHP, which in turn influenced the behaviour of agents. Again:

> A cognitive evolutionary theory is structurationist to the extent that individual and social actors successfully introduce innovations that help transform or even constitute new collective understandings, which in turn shape the identities and interests, and consequently the expectations of social actors.
>
> (Adler 1997, p. 339)

From a constructivist perspective, therefore, networks are more than simply an opportunity for the most powerful economic actors to satisfy their interests and more than simply a rational response to ensure more legitimate and effective global health governance.

Conclusion

This paper has argued that ideational factors are important because they help explain how radical shifts in global health policy are possible. As new forms of GHP begin to emerge, understanding how it was possible for them develop, whose ideas informed their development and what discourse predominates is an essential first step in ensuring that these new additions to global health policy-making accord with recognised principles of good governance.

What is most exciting about Constructivism, and where future research would be most productive, is to explore the extent to which new forms of governance such as GHPs do shape the behaviour of actors. Initial findings presented in this paper suggest that behaviour change did not occur, but a more extensive exploration of norm dynamics and logics of appropriateness could yield dividends in understanding how actors behave in partnerships.

For constructivists, how actors behave is inextricably linked to perceptions about who and what they are. It is important to remember that *public–private* partnerships are one model of partnership and alternative models are possible. DNDi, in particular, championed a public partnership model quite different from the public–private partnership model adopted by the TB Alliance and Stop TB. Although the argument that shared ideas have constructed the 'identity' of GHPs has not been explored in this paper, it is likely to find greater purchase in future research as efforts by the international community to develop principles of best practice inevitably strengthen intersubjective under-standings of what global health partnership means to potential new partners.

The role of ideational factors such as discourse and ideas in global health policy, and the application of constructivist insights to help understand that role, is still largely underdeveloped in the literature. The theoretical framework presented in this paper provides the first step in developing a constructivist agenda for global health that starts with the hypothesis that ideas and discourse are about more than self-interest and material power. It is a liberating argument because it cuts through the pessimistic and dispiriting assumption implicit in many public health debates that the strongest states (e.g., the USA) or the richest actors (e.g., the Bill and Melinda Gates Foundation) ultimately shape global health. If it is true, and ideas are no more than tools wielded by the strong to defeat the weak, or do little more than reinforce predetermined self-interests, then it is doubtful whether the radical changes required for global health governance to respond adequately to the 'grand challenges' of global public health (Gostin and Mok 2009) will be achieved.

This paper has only skimmed the surface of the potential of Constructivism to better inform our understanding of ideational factors and their importance for global health. Constructivism provides an optimistic account of the prospects for change in global health: it therefore warrants further exploration.

Acknowledgements

The author would like to thank the Wall Summer Institute for Research for funding the Retreat 'What Difference does the Advent of Civil Society Mean to Global Health Governance?' in London in 2007 where the ideas for this paper were first presented, and to participants at that Retreat for their comments.

Note

1 Neither space nor probable audience render appropriate an extensive discussion of the differences between ideas, power and interest-based approaches within IR (but see Hasenclever *et al.* 1997). I acknowledge that there are different sub-types of Constructivism, ranging from rationalist to reflectivist variants (Wendt 2000, Christiansen *et al.* 2001), which are often described as 'thin' or 'thick' variants in the literature – where thin constructivists give material forces more of a say in explaining the world than thick constructivists, for whom it is 'ideas all the way down'. This paper falls within the 'thin' constructivist camp, and the empirical analysis and interpretive methodology reflect that bias. Constructivist analysis does not compete with Neo-Realist, Neo-Marxist or Liberal-institutionalist theory; indeed, as constructivists are at pains to point out, Constructivism is not a theory but more accurately described as an 'approach'.

References

Adler, E., 1997. Seizing the middle ground: constructivism in world politics. *European Journal of International Relations*, 3 (3), 319–363.

Adler, E., 2005. *Communitarian international relations: the epistemic foundations of international relations.* Oxon: Routledge.

Brundtland, G. H., 2001a. *UN Association Global Leadership Awards.* New York: The United Nations Association of the United States of America and the Business Council for the United Nations.

Brundtland, G. H., 2001b. *Address to Washington International Business Council and Executive Council on Diplomacy.* Washington, DC: Washington International Business Council.

Brundtland, G. H., 2001c. Keynote address. *In: International Conference on Health Research for Development*, 10–13 October 2000, Bangkok.

Buse, K. and Harmer, A., 2004. Power to the partners: the politics of public-private partnerships. *Development*, 47 (2), 49–57.

Buse, K. and Harmer, A., 2007. Seven habits of highly effective global public–private partnerships for health. *Social Science and Medicine*, 64 (2), 259–271.

Buse, K. and Harmer, A., 2009. Global health partnership: the mosh pit of global health governance. *In*: K. Buse, W. Hein, and N. Drager, eds. *Making sense of global health governance: a policy perspective.* Basingstoke: Palgrave Macmillan, 245–267.

Buse, K. and Walt, G., 2000. Global public–private partnerships: part I – a new development in health? *Bulletin of the World Health Organization*, 78, 549–561.

Cape Town Declaration, 2000. The Cape Town Declaration of the Working Alliance for TB Drug Development, Cape Town, South Africa, 8 February.

Chan, M., 2009. *Towards transformational change for health in Africa* [online]. Kigali, Rwanda: World Health Organisation. Available from: http://www.who.int/dg/speeches/2009/afro_regional_committee_20090831/en/index.html [Accessed 6 November 2009].

Chen, L. C., Evans, T. G., and Cash, R. A., 1999. Health as a global public good. *In*: I. Kaul, I. Grundberg, and M. Stern, eds. *Global public goods: international cooperation in the 21st century.* New York: UNDP, 284–304.

Christiansen, T., Jorgensen, K. E., and Wiener, A., 2001. Introduction. *In*, T. Christiansen, K. E. Jorgensen, and A. Wiener, eds. *The social construction of Europe.* London: Sage, 1–22.

Doty, R., 1993. Foreign policy as social construction: a post-positivist analysis of U.S. counterinsurgency policy in the Philippines. *International Studies Quarterly*, 37, 297–320.

Espinal, M., 2004. Keynote address. *In: The Second Stop TB Partners' Forum.* New Delhi, India.

Freire, M. and Dauliere, N., 2002. Join fight against tuberculosis, here and abroad. *The Miami Herald*, 21 March 2002, p. 7B. Available from: http://www.tballiance.org/downloads/inthenews/2002/MiamiHerald_03-21-02.pdf [Accessed 8 September 2010].

Gostin, L. O. and Mok, E., 2009. Grand challenges in global health governance. *British Medical Bulletin*, 90, 7–18.

Hagmann, M., 2001. Globalization – how healthy? *Bulletin of the World Health Organisation*, 79 (9), 902–903.

Harmer, A., 2005. *Understanding the rise of health GPPPs: the role of discourse and ideas.* Thesis (PhD). Southampton University.

Hasenclever, A., Mayer, P., and Rittberger, V., 1997. *Theories of international regimes.* Cambridge: Cambridge University Press.

Hay, C., 2009. Constructivist institutionalism. *In*: R. Rhodes, S. Binder, and B. Rockman, eds. *The Oxford handbook of political institutions*. Oxford: Oxford University Press, 56–74.

Held, D. and McGrew, A., 2008. *Globalisation/anti-globalisation: beyond the great divide*. 2nd ed. Cambridge: Polity Press.

Hirst, P. and Thompson, G., 1999. *Globalization in question*. Cambridge: Polity Press.

Karlinger, J. and Bruno, K., 2000. *Tangled up in blue* [online]. San Fransisco: CorpWatch. Available from: http://www.corpwatch.org/downloads/tangled.pdf [Accessed 25 February 2010].

Kaul, I. and Ryu, G., 2001. Global public policy partnerships seen through the lens of global public goods. *Fourth World Bank conference on evaluation and development – the partnership dimension*, July 23–24, Washington, DC. Available from: http://www.worldbank.org/html/oed/partnershipconference/images/inge-kaul.pdf [Accessed 8 September 2010].

Kaul, I. and Faust, M., 2001. Global public goods and health: taking the agenda forward. *Bulletin of the World Health Organisation*, 79, 869–874.

Kickbusch, I., 2003. Global health governance: some theoretical considerations on the new political space. *In*: K. Lee, ed. *Health impacts of globalization: towards global governance*. London: Palgrave, 192–201.

Kochi, A., 2000. *Tuberculosis and sustainable development*. The Stop TB Initiative 2000 report. Geneva: WHO, p. 4.

Kumaresan, J., Heikamp, P., Smith, P., and Billo, N., 2004. Global partnership to stop TB: a model of an effective public health partnership. *International Journal of Tuberculosis and Lung Disease*, 8 (1), 120–129.

Lee, J. W., 2002. Timebomb: multi-drug resistant TB. *Stop TB News*, Issue 7, Summer, p. 2. Available from: http://www.stoptb.org/assets/.../news/newsletters/Newsletter7_MDR_TB.pdf [Accessed 8 September 2010]

Lee, K., 2003. *Globalization and health: an introduction*. London: Palgrave.

Lee, K. and Goodman, H., 2002. Health care financing reform. *In*: K. Lee, K. Buse, and S. Fustukian, eds. *Health policy in a globalising world*. Cambridge: Cambridge University Press, 97–119.

Médecins Sans Frontières (MSF), 2001. *Fatal imbalance: the crisis in R&D for drugs for neglected diseases*. Geneva: MSF.

Médecins Sans Frontières (MSF), 2003. *DNDi: an innovative solution* (working draft) [online]. Available from: http://www.accessmed-msf.org [Accessed 9 November 2009].

Orbinski, J., 2001. Forging new partnerships to stop TB. *In: Ministerial conference on TB & sustainable development*, 24 March, Amsterdam. Geneva: World Health Organisation. Available from: http://www.stoptb.org/events/meetings/amsterdam_conference/orbinskispeech.asp [Accessed 8 September 2010].

Peck, J. and Tickell, A., 2002. Neoliberalizing space. *Antipode*, 34 (3), 380–404.

Pecoul, B., 2003. Drug R&D for neglected patients: a fatal imbalance. *International meeting on a global framework for supporting health research and development (R&D) in areas of market and public policy failure*, 29 April, Geneva. Geneva: Médecins sans Frontières.

Raviglione, M., 2001. Ebola with wings. *New Scientist*, 29 March. Available from: http://www.newscientist.com/article/dn570-ebola-with-wings.html [Accessed 5 August 2010].

Reich, M., 2002. *Public–private partnerships for public health*. Cambridge: Harvard University Press.

Richter, J., 2003. 'We the Peoples' or 'We the Corporations'? Critical reflections on UN-business 'partnerships'. Geneva: IBFAN.

Richter, J., 2004. Public–private partnerships for health: a trend with no alternatives? Development, 47 (2), 43–48.

Schmidt, V., 2002. The futures of European capitalism. Oxford: Oxford University Press.

Shiffman, J., 2009. A social explanation of the rise and fall of global health issues. Bulletin of the World Health Organization, 87, 608–613.

Soros, G., 2002. Foreword. The global plan to stop TB. Geneva: WHO, p. 8.

Stop TB, 2010. Stop TB partnership: about us [online]. Available from: http://www.stoptb.org/about/default.asp [Accessed 5 August 2010].

TB Alliance, 2001a. The economics of TB drug development. New York: TB Alliance.

TB Alliance, 2001b. Scientific blueprint for TB drug development. New York: TB Alliance.

TB Alliance, 2001c. Praise for the economics report. TB Alliance News: The Newsletter of the TB Alliance, 1 (7).

Trouiller, P., Torreele, E., Olliaro, P., White, N., Foster, S., Wirth, D., and Pecoul, B., 2001. Drugs for neglected diseases: a failure of the market and a public health failure? Tropical Medicine and International Health, 6 (11), 945–951.

Trouiller, P., Torreele, E., Olliaro, P., White, N., Foster, S., Wirth, D., and Pécoul, B., 2002. Drug development for neglected diseases: a deficient market and a public-health policy failure. Lancet, 359, 2188–2194.

United Nations Development Programme (UNDP), 1999. Human development report. New York: UNDP.

United Nations Education, Scientific and and Cultural Organisation (UNESCO), 2002. Genomics and global health. Geneva: UNESCO.

Utting, P., 2000. UN-Business partnerships: whose agenda counts? In: North–South coalition seminar, partnerships for development or privatization of the multilateral system?, 8 November, Oslo. Tromso, Norway: North–South Coalition. Available from: www.unrisd.org/80256B3C005BCCF9/(httpAuxPages)/.../$file/utting.pdf [Accessed 8 September 2010].

Veon, J., 1998. Prince Charles: the sustainable prince. Chap. 2. Oklahoma City: Hearthstone Publishing.

Wendt, A., 1999. Social theory of international relations. Cambridge: Cambridge University Press.

Wendt, A., 2000. On the via media: a response to the critics. Review of International Studies, 26, 165–180.

Widdus, R. and White, K., 2004. Combating diseases associated with poverty: financing strategies for product development and the potential role of public–private partnerships. Geneva: IPPPH.

World Health Organisation (WHO), 1998. Good governance for health. Geneva: WHO.

World Health Organisation (WHO), 2002. The global plan to stop TB. Geneva: WHO.

World Bank, 1994. Governance: the World Bank's experience. Washington, DC: World Bank.

Zacher, M., 1999. Global epidemiological surveillance: international cooperation to monitor infectious diseases. In: I. Kaul, I. Grundberg, and M. Stern, eds. Global public goods: international cooperation in the 21st century. New York: UNDP, 266–283.

Part 16

HUMAN RIGHTS

A HUMAN RIGHT TO HEALTH?

Tony Evans

Source: *Third World Quarterly*, 23:2 (2002), 197–215.

Abstract

A right to health is one of a range of socioeconomic rights for which states accept an obligation under international law. However, the politics of rights has meant that socioeconomic rights are rarely given the same status as liberal freedoms associated with civil and political rights. This article discusses the liberal rationale for rejecting socioeconomic claims as rights and examines the basic rights challenge to liberal arguments. Given the dominance of liberalism, the article concludes with an examination of the potential for promoting a right to health within the context of globalisation.

There is a long and well established tradition of defending human rights in the pages of medical journals, dating from Thomas Wakley, who founded the *Lancet* in 1820 (Kandela, 1998). One of the most recent manifestations of this tradition was seen during 1999 when the *British Medical Journal* (BMJ) provided a forum for a debate between proponents and opponents of a human right to health. Opening the debate, the Tavistock Group offered a draft for a set of ethical principles which affirmed the human right to health. The draft sought to provide a basis for discussion among all branches of medical and health care professions that would finally end in general agreement on the nature of the right to health (Smith *et al.*, 1999). The fundamental principle underscoring the Tavistock Group's proposal was that, while the individual remained the claimant of a right to health, the delivery of the necessary services in response to that claim must be seen in the context of community. Accordingly, as a human right, the right to health cannot be bought and sold in the marketplace like other commodities. Nor can the right to health be limited by the ability to pay. Instead, according to the Tavistock Group, governments have an obligation to fund medical education, training and research, to make provision for sustainable investment in support of health care professionals, and to ensure that knowledge is exchanged freely and without regard for institutional affiliation and claims of ownership.

In response, arguments against a human right to health questioned the definition and extent of both human rights and health care. First, opponents of the Tavistock Group's proposal argued that, while civil and political claims are today generally accepted as human rights, 'it is difficult to find any rational or utilitarian basis for viewing health care in the same way' (Barlow, 1999: 321). Second, according to opponents, even if there were some general agreement on health as a human right, determining exactly who held a duty to provide the necessary resources in fulfilment of the claim remained problematic, even for the provision of basic care. Third, opponents argued that any definition of health care would have to take account of a wide range of social, economic, organisational, scientific and technical issues and relationships before any general agreement on the extent of the right could be reached. Moreover, opponents noted that, even if this difficulty could be resolved, life and death decisions concerning availability and access would still need to be made as demand quickly outstripped supply (Loefter, 1999). It was therefore 'difficult to see how any provision of benefits [could] be termed a human right (as opposed to a legal entitlement) when to meet such a requirement would impose intolerable burdens on others' (Barlow, 1999: 321).

Although debates on health have often emphasised that good health can only be achieved within the context of social organisation, which pays particular attention to poverty, education, housing, economic globalisation and other social factors, this observation has often lacked any basis for justifying greater attention to health. According to some commentators, the human rights movement offers this justification by identifying the 'preconditions for human well-being', which then act as a 'framework for analysis and direct responses to societal determinants of health that is more useful than traditional approaches' (Mann, 1997: 23). This approach seeks to bring together the public health and human rights movements as a single, mutually supportive project said to strengthen at least some claims for social rights. Its success in part might be seen in the Harvard School of Public Health's practice of presenting all graduates with a copy of the Universal Declaration of Human Rights along with their diploma (Mann, 1996). However, the responses to the Tavistock Group's proposal noted above, which are well known within the human rights literature, reflect a liberal understanding of human rights that continues to dominate most 'human rights talk' in both academic and policy circles (Vincent, 1986). Given the dominance of the liberal consensus, the prospects for promoting the cause of health as a human right may therefore be less promising than many would hope. It is the task of this article to examine the potential for linking human rights and health in the current global world order.

Before beginning this task, we should be clearer about what we mean by a right to health. If we take the World Health Organisation's (WHO) definition of health as 'a state of complete physical, mental and social well-being' at face value, and attempt to promote this definition as the basis for a right to health, we might end with absurd claims to outlaw disease, the infirmities brought by aging and even mortality. While the social attitudes to health in many wealthy countries suggest that the idea of infinite mortality is desirable and attainable, proponents of a right to health are more concerned with social, economic and political arrangements that sustain the conditions for health security. Among other things, these include access to health care and the availability of drugs, but also the provision of sewage disposal, housing, education, environmental security and workplace health and safety measures. The right to health is therefore better thought of as '[w]hat we as a society do collectively to ensure the conditions in which people can be healthy' (International Federations of Red Cross and Red Crescent Societies and Francois-Xavier Bagnoud Centre for Health and Human Rights, 1999: 29). Put more formally, and emphasising the non-scientific dimensions, health is concerned with 'the art and the science of preventing disease, promoting health, and extending life through the organised effort of society' (Acheson, 1998). Arguments to do with a right to health are therefore concerned with claims to live in a physical and social environment that does not prejudice the prospects for leading a full and healthy life, including access to health services.

This article will begin with a brief examination of the liberal consensus on universal human rights. This consensus accepts civil and political claims as human rights but relegates socioeconomic claims, including the right to health, to the status of aspirations. Furthermore, the liberal consensus supports this approach by asserting that rights are meaningful only when a duty to fulfil a claim is clearly established, which cannot be achieved in the case of socioeconomic rights. At the centre of this assertion is the argument that, while people clearly need food, shelter and an environment that sustain good health, there is no reason to believe that these needs create an obligation on the part of others to provide them (Bole, 1991). A further defence for rejecting socioeconomic claims as human rights is the scarcity argument, which asserts that, even if it were possible to establish a clear duty on the part of the wealthy to provide basic needs to the poor, fulfilment of such a duty would be too burdensome on the rich. This fear is often expressed as the 'deluge' effect, an emotive term suggesting that the rich would drown in the sea of socioeconomic claims made by the poor. Moreover, liberals claim that, given the pace of technological and scientific change in the field of health, which can never be made available to all, the problem of the 'deluge' is exacerbated. The section finishes with a discussion of the social consequences that follow from the liberal consensus.

The second section offers a brief examination of the basic rights approach to human rights, which seeks to undermine the foundations of the liberal consensus by arguing that civil and political rights and freedoms cannot easily be distinguished from socioeconomic claims, as liberals assert. A third section returns to the health consequences of the liberal consensus in the light of basic rights arguments. In particular, this section will argue that establishing a duty to create the conditions for the fulfilment of socioeconomic rights is possible. However, the prevailing economic orthodoxy, which is seen in the policy formation and practice of the international financial institutions and the World Trade Organization (wTO), offers little hope for those who lack the conditions for good health.

The liberal consensus on universal human rights

One further observation should be made before looking at the liberal consensus on human rights. In contrast to the responses to the Tavistock Group's assertion that there is a right to health, Article 12 of the International Covenant on Economic, Social and Cultural Rights (ICESCR) states that everyone has the right 'to the enjoyment of the highest attainable standard of physical and mental health'. Therefore, if the liberal rejection of socioeconomic rights has any legitimacy, it cannot be within the legal debate, but must instead be found in the philosophical or political debates that together with law form the three branches of human rights talk. The practice of shifting seamlessly between the legal, philosophical and political debates on human rights is a common, if unfortunate, trait found within the literature (Evans, 2001b), and one that often distorts the claims made for human rights. For those who seek to reject the right to health, the propensity to shift among the three debates opens the space for liberals to reject socioeconomic rights, even in the face of the legal obligations most states now accept under international law. This is convenient for the dominant liberal consensus in global politics because it opens the possibility of gaining the moral status that ratifying international human rights law brings while simultaneously denying socioeconomic rights philosophically and politically.

Liberal arguments against accepting a right to health as a human right rest upon the presumption that civil and political rights are qualitatively and significantly different from socioeconomic rights. This distinction is usually expressed as that between 'negative' rights (civil and political) and 'positive' rights (economic and social). Although not expressed explicitly in these terms, disagreements over negative and positive rights are at the heart of the BMJ debate on health and human rights referred to earlier. Following this distinction, negative rights are fulfilled when all members of a community exercise restraint from doing anything that might violate the freedoms of others. Positive rights, on the other hand, require others to provide the material means of life to those unable to provide for themselves: at a minimum, clean water, shelter, food and health care (Plant, 1993). Put simply, the protection of negative rights demands nothing more than forbearance, while the protection of positive rights demands a redistribution of resources.

The defence of negative claims as the limits of universal human rights rests upon several assumptions. First, negative rights can be guaranteed through the simple expedient of passing national laws that guarantee negative freedoms. Negative rights are therefore cost-free in as far as they require restraint rather than a costly redistribution of resources. Second, since all rights are claimed against the state, and positive rights depend upon the level of economic development a country has achieved, setting any universal standards for economic and social rights is impossible. To attempt to do so would demand that some countries acknowledge rights that they could not realistically deliver, effectively asking them to brand themselves as human rights violators. Third, economic and social claims, like the right to a certain standard of living or health care, are culturally determined. To talk of a universal right to 'paid leave' during pregnancy and following childbirth (ICESCR, Art. 10(2)), for example, makes no sense in societies where the concept of 'paid work' or 'leave' has no meaning. Fourth, the correlative duty of forbearance clearly rests with all members of society when negative rights are claimed but this is not so for positive rights. Indeed, the attempt to impose a duty on the wealthy to fulfil positive rights may conflict with negative freedoms, particularly those associated with economic activity, including free market practices and the freedom to own and dispose of property. Fifth, since the right to life is the most basic universal right from which all other claims derive, and the right to life is one of forbearance, negative rights must be ranked above positive rights. Lastly, liberals argue that positive claims cannot be understood as human rights because rights are claimed by the individual, whereas government social policy is concerned with achieving an overall increase in social welfare (Cranston, 1973, 1983; Plant, 1989).

The liberal rejection of positive rights is perhaps less stringent today, although these arguments continue to offer a pertinacious defence of liberal, free market values. Today, liberals are more likely to assert that, while positive claims cannot be universal human rights, nevertheless positive claims are the legitimate *aspirations* of all peoples. According to liberal assertions, the resolution of these aspirations is best achieved by promoting negative freedoms, which provide the conditions for greater economic growth, higher incomes and lower unemployment. The increasing wealth generated through the exercise of negative freedoms therefore promotes the fulfilment of positive aspirations by generating the wealth that allows people to spend more on, for example, health care, nutrition and better housing (McCorquodale & Fairbrother, 1999). Consequently, the fulfilment of socioeconomic claims, including adequate nutrition and health care, are not human rights but 'aspirations that every decent society should strive for' (Staples, 1999).

The liberal consensus on human rights therefore offers a set of rights that emphasise the freedom of individual action, non-interference in the private sphere of economics and the right to own and dispose of property, a set of principles axiomatic to the ideology of the free market. Without any champion for economic and social rights, the liberal consensus, upon which the practices of globalisation are built, has succeeded in establishing the language of civil and political rights as the acceptable voice—indeed, the only voice—of human rights talk. Irrespective of the obligations undertaken in the ICESCR, in the current world order human rights are defined as that set of rights that require government abstention from acts that violate the individual's freedom to innovate, and to invest time, capital and resources in processes of production and exchange (Tetrault, 1988). For liberals, socioeconomic claims are legitimate aspirations, but they can never be rights.

Examples illustrating the dominance of the liberal approach are not hard to find. The spread of free market economics that brings damaging consequences for health and other social needs are reflected in the policies of all the major international organisations, including the WTO and the World Bank. This is nowhere more evident than in the now infamous World Bank memo drafted by Lawrence Summers, which reasoned that the 'measurement of the costs of health-impairing pollution depends on the foregone earnings from increased morbidity and mortality' and that therefore 'a given amount of health-impairing pollution should be done in the country with the lowest wages'. From this analysis, Summers concludes that 'I've always thought that under-polluted countries in Africa are vastly under-polluted: their air quality is probably vastly inefficiently [high] compared to Los Angeles or Mexico City' (Summers, 1992). More recently, many commentators see the aim of talks on the General Agreement on Trade in Services (GATS) as a further attempt to realise liberal freedoms, as transnational corporations (TNCs) press for rules intended to open up health markets to private investment and access to public funds for health services (Loff & Gruskin, 2001). While for liberals this promises to increase the efficiency of health services globally, for others the prospect suggests a further marginalisation of the poor, a reduction in access to health provision, and the appropriation of public funds by powerful TNCs (Price *et al.*, 1999).

Further examples are found in the trend among Western governments during the past two decades to reduce support for all social programmes (Gill, 1995). It is also seen in the conditions attached to aid packages offered by the international financial institutions (Tetrault, 1988). So successful is the liberal consensus that the claim that in 'virtually all regions of the world ... there is broad acceptance of the triad of human rights, free markets and democracy as desirable [and] attainable policy objectives' is common (Conley & Livermore, 1996), with human rights being defined as civil and political claims. Although in achieving these aims liberals accept that some groups will suffer 'high transition costs' (Lee, 1996), including a reduction in expenditure on the factors associated with a healthy environment (education, health care services, potable water, sewage disposal, etc), the prospects for delivering positive aspirations in the future are said to outweigh by far the small sacrifices of the present.

Central to the liberal position is the claim that it is not possible to secure a consensus on how the claims of the poor to rights to food, shelter and health care relate to obligations on the part of others to fulfil them. In the case of negative rights, claimants demand the right to non-interference in the exercise of a range of freedoms that require nothing more than restraint by others. The right to life, for example, is satisfied when we all exercise a duty to refrain from killing others. Understood in this way, the means of fulfilling a right to life is not only costless but also infinite, because restraint is costless and infinite. From the liberal perspective, the 'fact that there is no scarcity consideration makes this right justiciable and capable of being fully respected and implemented because it consists in forbearance rather than action' (Plant, 1989: 6). However, this is not the case when we consider positive rights. For a right to health in particular, the constant development of new technological and scientific discoveries only emphasises the inevitability of scarcity. Thus, according to the liberal consensus, if rights imply 'ought', and duties imply 'can', the attempt to find a duty-bearer with the capabilities to fulfil a right to health will fail (Jones, 2000: 68–71). To add further support to arguments over the impossibility of establishing a clear duty-bearer, liberals might argue that, in any case, 'one's good or ill health is the result of physical and biological processes, and perhaps of social good or ill fortune, but not of actions for which others can be held liable' (Bole, 1991: 4).

Moreover, even if the difficulties of finding a secure moral relationship between a rights claimant and duty-bearer are overlooked, the liberal consensus argues that the problem of the 'deluge' remains. This concerns the question of how much of a particular resource can be claimed legitimately in satisfaction of a positive claim, given the conditions of scarcity. In the case of health, do all individuals have a right to a heart transplant, access to a kidney dialysis machine or the medical technology that allows parents the right to choose the sex of their unborn child? Liberals argue that if positive claims like the right to health are not related to any kind of charge or control on the supply, the demand would be unlimited, effectively creating a right that could never be fulfilled (Veatch, 1991). From the liberal perspective, acknowledging a right to health brings the spectre of demand fast outstripping supply and the impoverishment of all sectors of society in the effort to fulfil socioeconomic duties.

The liberal defence of relegating positive claims to the status of aspirations, rather than universal human rights, is therefore straightforward: satisfying social aspirations is achievable only when the liberal values represented by negative freedoms are promoted and protected, for these freedoms provide the principles of action for creating wealth. Even when the demands of globalisation promote forms of production and exchange that lead to a decline in the health status of populations, poorer nutrition and general standards of living (Evans, 2001b, 2000; UNDP, 1999), liberals remain reluctant to make the connection between the inconvenient facts of human rights violations and the limited conception of human rights they seek to promote and legitimate (Christian Aid, 1996, 1997; HRW, 1996). Indeed, liberals explain the failure to achieve social aspirations as a failure to promote negative freedoms. If liberals do acknowledge the relationship between the practice of negative freedoms and positive claims, the 'high transition costs' are seen as an acceptable price to be borne stoically by the living in the name of future generations. The 'knowledge' that social aspirations will be fulfilled once the protection of negative freedoms is fully implemented means that the prevailing consensus need not be over-concerned by well documented cases that show static or declining social standards, including health standards (UNRISD, 1995). The possibility that this approach to rights might suggest double-standards—egalitarian values in distributing civil and political rights but non-egalitarian values over economic distribution—does not seem to trouble liberals (Beauchamp, 1991).

At first sight the liberal consensus appears compelling, particularly because of the current normative order. If individuals, corporations and international organisations conform to the prevailing norms of conduct, and the only truly universal human rights are negative claims, then no blame can be levelled at those who take advantage of prevailing practices, regardless of the human rights consequences. Put another way, if the principles of the free market are supported by negative freedoms, and the legitimate investment and operational strategies of TNCs bring consequences that displace people, damage their prospects for providing a livelihood, destroy traditional communities and lead to the declining health of populations, no blame can be apportioned to human rights violations.

Countering the liberal consensus

But what if there is no clear distinction between negative and positive rights, as liberals claim? If this were the case, liberal arguments that emphasise the priority of civil and political freedoms, grounded in the need to define a duty-bearer, appear less compelling and the relegation of socioeconomic claims to the status of unsustainable aspirations cannot be sustained (Jones, 2000; Plant, 1989). Some authors have argued, for example, that 'neither rights to physical security nor rights to subsistence fit neatly into their assigned sides of the simplistic positive/negative dichotomy', which remains at the centre of the liberal consensus on human rights (Shue, 1996: 37). According to this criticism, a basic right to food, shelter and the conditions for good health cannot be disaggregated from negative claims nor rights to physical security from positive claims. If this is so, then the liberal claim that civil and political rights are human rights but socioeconomic rights are merely aspirations would be lost. Importantly, if the distinction between negative and positive rights cannot be sustained, it would be possible to identify those who fail to fulfil their duty to protect socioeconomic rights, and to take judicial action in response to violations, just as international society purports to do when individuals fail in their duty to protect civil and political rights.

Opposing the liberal view, some authors have argued that there are basic rights without which no other rights can be enjoyed. These are the rights to life, security and subsistence, where subsistence is understood as the means to sustain physical and social life, including the right to health. None of these claims is wholly negative or positive. For example, while in some cases it is correct to understand physical security as a negative right, in the sense that all members of society undertake a duty of forbearance, this is only a partial description of what we understand by human rights. According to this argument, even liberals accept that the right to security implies something more than forbearance, namely the need to make arrangements actively to protect those whose security is threatened. The demand for civil and political rights is 'not normally a demand simply to be left alone, but a demand to be protected against harm . . . It is a demand for positive action . . . a demand for social guarantees against at least the standard threats' (Shue, 1996: 39). Thus, liberal arguments that negative rights are free of cost overlook the necessity for state intervention in the name of protecting human rights, intervention such as taxation to fund the legislature, police, legal system, courts and prisons. Furthermore, if there are costs attached to both negative and positive rights, and we can reach a consensus on an acceptable level of expenditure for protecting civil and political rights, then why not for socioeconomic rights (Plant, 1989)?

Similarly, it is misleading to label subsistence rights as exclusively positive claims. Just as guaranteeing the negative duty of forbearance can satisfy the right to physical security, so too the right to subsistence can be satisfied by guaranteeing people's access to the means of providing for their own subsistence. Expressed cogently by Shue:

> All that is sometimes necessary is to protect the persons whose subsistence is threatened from the individuals and institutions that will otherwise intentionally or unintentionally harm them. A demand for a right to subsistence may involve not a demand to be provided with grants of commodities but merely a demand to be provided some opportunity for supporting oneself. The request is not to be supported but to be allowed to be self-supporting on the basis of one's own hard work
>
> (1996: 40)

Thus, if TNCs use the free market to invest in ways that deprive people of the means of subsistence, or if the WTO, NAFTA and the EU implement rules, practices and procedures that deprive people of the means to achieve subsistence, this is also a denial of human rights. Consequently, 'those who deny rights can have no complaint when the denial . . . is resisted' (Shue, 1996: 14)

The basic rights argument is not intended to deny that on occasion circumstances may demand a redistribution of resources from the resource rich to those unable to provide for the basic means of life for themselves (Jones, 1994). However, if rights are never wholly positive or negative then correlative duties cannot be wholly positive or negative. For example, the correlative duties associated with civil and political rights include a duty to *avoid* harm, a duty to *protect* from harm, and a duty to *aid* those threatened with harm. Similarly, the right to subsistence includes a duty to *avoid* taking action that deprives others of the means of subsistence, a duty to *protect* others whose only means of subsistence is threatened and a duty to *aid* those unable to provide for their own subsistence. In this way, the means to achieving basic subsistence security could be controlled by 'some combination of the mere restraint of second parties and the maintenance of protective institutions by first and third parties, just as the standard threats that deprive people of their physical security could be controlled by restraint and protection from non-restraint' (Shue, 1996: 41). In similar fashion, the UNDP links civil and political rights to human development, focusing on 'the enhancement of the capabilities and freedoms that the members of a community enjoy', and the conduct of individual and collective agents in the 'design of social arrangements to facilitate or secure these capabilities and freedoms' (UNDP, 2000: 20).

Reflecting the basic rights approach, the United Nations Committee on Economic, Social and Cultural Rights recently issued a report on the right to the highest attainable standards of health for all. The report begins by noting that one should not understand the right to health solely as a set of entitlements; as a set of positive claims, the fulfilment of which depends entirely upon identifying those with an obligation to provide health care and the other conditions for leading a healthy life. Instead, the report argues that the right to health implies both freedoms and entitlements, including 'the right to control one's own body' and 'the right to be free from interference, such as the right to be free from torture, non-consensual medical treatment and experimentation'. Echoing Shue, the report also places an obligation on the state to respect, protect and fulfil the right to health, which cannot be discharged unless non-state actors, like TNCs, are restrained from undertaking actions likely to impair the right to health (Committee on Economic, Social and Cultural Rights, 2000).

From the basic rights perspective it is possible to expose the structural practices that are the cause of many violations of socioeconomic rights (Gill, 1995). These are the practices that the liberal consensus has elevated to the status of 'common sense', legitimate habits that are part of a natural and rational approach to the current world order, to which everyone should subscribe (Muzaffar, 1995). In common with the legal and philosophical traditions, human rights talk often shows a disposition towards 'structural blindness': 'the tendency to focus on phenomena that can be seen as the outcome of actions attributable to concrete juridical persons (including governments), proscribing them and making the actors accountable' (Galtung, 1978: 223). It is the 'naturalisation' of liberalism that provides TNCs, international financial institutions and international organisations with the rationale for denying responsibility for structural violations of human rights. Regular iterations of the liberal consensus have reinforced and promoted these denials in various guises. For instance, in a recent speech to the WTO, US President Bill Clinton asserted that the forces of globalisation were 'not a political choice' but 'a fact' (18 May 1998), a contention reinforced the following day by UK Prime Minister Tony Blair through his own assertion that globalisation was 'irreversible and irresistible' (19 May 1998). Thus, for the liberal consensus, denying responsibility for structural violations of human rights is reasonable, given the 'facts' of the 'natural' world order and the need to identify an empirically verifiable violator.

The basic rights analysis, on the other hand, offers a considerable challenge to the liberal consensus in the context of globalisation, the free market and the dominant conception of universal human rights. In particular, basic rights arguments confront the rules and practices of the global political economy, described by the WTO, NAFTA, EU, IMF, the World Bank and other international organisations. The approach also offers a challenge to TNCs when they seek to defend their decisions, operating procedures and planning with the claim that their obligations extend only to negative responsibilities. Recently, the UNDP has sought to reflect this approach by asserting that adequate nutrition, health care and other social and economic achievements are not merely aspirations:

> They are human rights inherent in human freedom and dignity. But these rights do not mean an entitlement to a handout. They are claims to a set of social arrangements—norms, institutions, laws, an enabling economic environment—that can best secure the enjoyment of these rights. It is thus the obligation of governments and others to implement policies to put these arrangements in place. And in today's more interdependent world, it is essential to recognize the obligations of global actors, who in the pursuit of global justice must put in place global arrangements that promote the eradication of poverty.
>
> (UNDP, 2000: 73)

Several conclusions can be drawn from the basic rights approach, which challenge the liberal consensus. First, for critics of the liberal consensus, socioeconomic rights represent the preconditions for civil and political rights and should be valued equally. When hunger and disease force people into situations where they are totally reliant on others to provide the basic material needs of life, those who profess to promote civil freedoms should be concerned; for without basic rights these freedoms cannot be exercised (Jones, 2000). Second, in response to the 'deluge' argument, basic rights arguments suggest that satisfying a right to health does not require granting universal access to the latest technological and scientific resources for health, but rather a minimum that provides the basis for leading a dignified life. Third, through developing the rationale for defining human rights as exclusively civil and political rights, particularly the arguments on restraint, proponents of basic rights dispel claims about the impossibility of identifying a duty-bearer. Within the terms of liberalism, basic rights arguments suggest that, if we are serious about protecting the rights of others to exercise freedom for self-help, then actions undertaken within the normative ambit of the current world order, which inhibit that freedom, represent a violation of human rights. Fourth, and following from the last point, if basic rights exposes existing practices as the cause of human rights violations, because existing practices deny access to socioeconomic rights, the actors responsible for those acts can be identified.

Globalisation and the right to health

However, despite the basic rights approach, in the age of globalisation the liberal consensus on human rights continues to prevail. The strength of the consensus can be gauged through the many developments within the global political economy that have sought summative reinforcement of liberal values, most notable at the WTO. While the relationship between health and increasing levels of transnational commerce and transportation was first recognised more than 150 years ago, at the International Sanitation Conference held in Paris in 1851 (Toebes, 1999), the scale and intensity of the current phase of globalisation suggests that socioeconomic rights, even as basic rights, are destined to remain mere aspirations at best. In short, the needs of the global political economy will be favoured over the obligations undertaken in international law (Evans & Hancock, 1998).

Although there are several competing versions of globalisation (Spybey, 1996), most accept that we are witnessing a significant shift in the spatial reach of networks of social relations, which are reflected in the growing intensity and complexity of transcontinental, interregional and global interactions. Globalisation is understood as an historic process that both 'stretches' and 'deepens' transnational patterns of economic, political, military, technological and ecological interactions. Together, these processes suggest that events, decisions and activities in one part of the world increasingly affect the economic, social and political well-being of individuals and communities in distant locations, as patterns of interaction and interconnectedness achieve both greater density and intensity (Held et al., 1999; McGrew, 1992). As expressed by

Anthony Giddens, although 'everyone has a local life, phenomenal worlds for the most part are truly global' (Giddens, 1990: 187). The existence of physical, symbolic and normative infrastructures mediates the processes of 'stretching' and 'deepening' through, for example, systems of air transportation, English as the language of business, science and technology, and human rights talk as the only legitimate language of the global normative order. These infrastructures are themselves associated with the development and spread of new technologies, which influence the scale of globalisation and circumscribe social interactions (Buzan, 1993).

While the benefits of globalisation are much vaunted (access to knowledge, availability of a greater range of foods and consumer goods, advances in medical science, etc), these benefits are differentially distributed, both across and within societies, reflecting structural asymmetries in the geometry of global power relations. Patterns of hierarchy and stratification mediate across sites of power while the consequences of globalisation are experienced unevenly and differently. For example, the research and development programmes of the major pharmaceutical companies concentrate on finding products for medical conditions associated with the concerns of the wealthy, like obesity, stress and baldness, rather then life-threatening diseases associated with the poor, like tuberculosis. Of the 1223 chemical products developed for health treatments between 1975 and 1996, only 11 were for the treatment of tropical diseases (WHO, 2001). Similarly, the liberal consensus on human rights, which relegates socioeconomic rights to the status of aspirations, prioritises the interests of those closest to the process of economic globalisation rather than those on the periphery, by emphasising civil freedoms that support values associated with liberty and the free market.

Like many other aspects of security, including health and the environment, the project to protect human rights is not immune from the impact of globalisation. Although there are some attempts in the literature to recontextualise human rights as an important aspect of globalisation, and to argue that globalisation offers the opportunity to realise economic and social aspirations, most of the literature tacitly accepts the liberal consensus. From this perspective, globalisation is presented as an opportunity for promoting 'moral interdependence' parallel to the 'economic interdependence' characteristic of the emerging new order (Donnelly, 1989: 211–213). According to this argument, which rearticulates the notion, promoted by George Washington and later the 19th century parliamentarian Richard Cobden, that trade 'civilises' (Vincent, 1986), the conditions of globalisation provide the context for the emergence of a global civil society, which will, over time, empower the global citizen in the struggle to claim universal human rights. As the conditions of globalisation transform the traditionally held principles of the international system— sovereignty, non-intervention, domestic jurisdiction—greater opportunities are created to implement the standards agreed under international law on human rights (Cassese, 1990), including socioeconomic rights. Today, so the argument goes, the conditions of globalisation provide an opportunity to develop new forms of 'humane governance', including new and more effective ways of securing universal human rights (Clark, 1999).

For the less sanguine, this is a myopic vision of the potential for promoting human rights; a view that highlights future benefits but remains blind to current, potential and future costs. For some critics the uneven consequences of globalisation suggest that economic and moral integration is not indicative of the emergence of a single global moral order. Rather than signalling the 'end of history' (Fukuyama, 1989), an alternative view suggests the emergence of particular forms of class formation and new hierarchies of knowledge and power on a global scale (van der Pijl, 1998, 1997), of which the liberal consensus on universal human rights is part (Stammers, 1999). In this view, 'there is no obvious or unambiguous, let alone, necessary, connection between globalization and freedom' (Scholte, 1996), particularly the freedoms necessary for people to take responsibility for their own economic and social welfare. If a set of values supports the economic globalisation that legitimates free market principles, the prospects for promoting socioeconomic claims under conditions of globalisation may not be as promising as some have suggested. Human rights, as described by the liberal consensus, may therefore gain greater credence than before, while socioeconomic claims may struggle to retain the lesser status of aspirations.

Optimistic speculation on the prospects for promoting the full range of human rights under conditions of globalisation is therefore questionable. In the case of a right to health, there is increasing evidence that globalisation itself will lead to greater levels of disease that is preventable and avoidable, as the movement of people, goods and ideas continues to increase on a global scale. In a recent report, the WHO estimates that nearly a quarter of disease and injury is connected to environmental degradation and decline attributable to globalisation. For example, the report notes that 90% of Malaria deaths (1.5 to 2.7 million annually) are caused by the colonisation of rainforests and the construction of large open-water irrigation schemes, both of which increase human exposure to disease-carrying mosquitoes (WHO, 1997). French observes that more than 30 infectious diseases have been identified in humans for the first time in the past two decades, most of which can be attributed to changes in human behaviour within the framework of globalisation, which alters the established balance between microbes and their hosts (French, 2000). Among these is the HIV/AIDS pandemic, which thrives when economic conditions force many workers to migrate in search of employment, bringing forms of social fragmentation that loosen family ties and the abandonment of traditional sexual mores and taboos (Poku & Cheru, 2001). Similar instances of epidemics associated with sexually transmitted disease during times of socioeconomic upheaval are well known historically (Brandt, 1990; Levine, 1996; Merians, 1998). French also notes that globalisation has enabled some diseases, thought to have been contained for many decades, to re-emerge in epidemic proportions, for example, the Peruvian Cholera epidemic of the early 1990s. Furthermore, some diseases previously associated with particular regions have been reported for the first time in distant locations, providing another indication of the health consequences of globalisation. The outbreak of West Nile virus in New York in 1999 offers an example here (French, 2000).

As with many other social, economic and political issues, the consequences of globalisation for health show both positive and negative attributes. On the positive side, the conditions of globalisation support the development of new technologies, including the provision of improved social conditions that underpin better health, new drugs and new treatments, although many of these are more concerned with addressing the health security of the wealthy, as noted earlier. However, on the negative side, globalisation brings developments in social relations that threaten the health of both rich and poor alike. For example, changing patterns of global trade bring increased exposure to infectious disease and social changes that threaten the health of populations, perhaps through severing family ties, reducing access to nutrition, and unplanned urbanisation (Evans, 1999).

Under international law, the duty to promote and protect health as a human right is assumed to lie with the state, although the liberal expectation is that this duty can only be fulfilled progressively (Gruskin, 2001). However, given the conditions of globalisation, the changing contexts of the social determinants of health are becoming increasingly supranational, as the 'global combination of liberal economic structures and domestic policy constraint promotes socioeconomic inequalities and instabilities' (McMichael & Beaglehole, 2000). This changing context, coupled with the claim commonly found in the globalisation literature that the capacity of the state to provide social protection for populations is eroding (Panitch, 1995), suggests that the state may no longer possess the capabilities to support the social determinants of health. Whereas people once looked to their own state-ordered institutions to provide the infrastructures for organising economic, social and cultural life, today the conditions of globalisation have seen the creation of a global order where corporate and financial interests prevail over the interests of populations. The means of securing these interests in all countries, whether the wealthy North or the impoverished South, is strategic planning at the global level, global management and the creation of global regimes and agreements. Ideological convergence has the effect of homogenising and limiting the policy choices of governments. Global management requires adherence to the rules that ensure all countries conform to a particular model of development so that the 'hidden hand' of the market can operate efficiently (Gill, 1995). Consequently, responsibilities for defining and implementing the rules of action shift away from the state to international institutions and regimes, some of which now have the power to 'strike down particular national interests, even when these are enshrined in law or custom' (George, 1999).

Structural Adjustment Programmes (SAPs) exemplify the redistribution of structural decision-making power away from the state and into global economic institutions, such as the World Bank and the IMF. SAPs packages inevitably include conditionality, which typically demands cuts in government expenditure, including axing or abolishing programmes for education, health, housing and public sector development, like sewage disposal and public housing. The Bank therefore takes responsibility for the economic co-ordination of the state, directing state policy towards addressing the freedoms associated with the market rather than fulfilling socioeconomic rights. In this way socioeconomic claims become meaningless under SAPs, as the human rights to food, health, education and social assistance are abandoned in favour of privileging global financial and corporate interests (Tomasevski, 1993; Gill, 1995).

Locked into an ideology of economic development and growth defined by global institutions, states become involved in a 'Dutch Auction', where countries bid against each other to offer the lowest levels of expenditure and regulation on a wide range of social programmes (environmental, education, health, etc), in the hope of attracting investment (Evans, 2001a). John Carlin's contention that 'on the one hand, multinationals promote the dismantling of government controls [while] on the other, they are busy forging pacts to manage trade privately', free of democratic control and accountability, captures much of the activities of TNCs under conditions of globalisation (Carlin, 1998). In contradiction of the international law assumption that states have a duty to promote and protect human rights, 'development processes (trade agreements, national economic development strategies, and so forth), individuals, organisations (multilateral lenders, multinational and national corporations), and governments, all deny human rights' (Johnston & Button, 1994: 213). Thus, according to the UN's own research, conducted a decade ago, SAPs 'continue to have a significant impact upon the overall realization of economic, social and cultural rights, both in terms of the ability of people to exercise them, and of the capability of government to fulfil and implement them . . . Human rights concerns continue to be conspicuously underestimated in the adjustment process' (Turk, 1992). Since the introduction of SAPs is typically associated with declining incomes and falling levels of public funding for health care, and health is price sensitive, the already inadequate health provision in many countries can only further restrict the poor in their efforts to achieve a dignified life (Simms et al., 2001). If there is a right to health, as international law suggests, then the structures and practices of globalisation seem to deny that right.

Under the current global political economy, the expectation that the state will promote and protect socioeconomic rights therefore seems unrealistic. If the state cannot deliver, and the rules and practices of existing international and transnational organisations and institutions affect the life prospects and health of populations throughout the world, there is a need to promote and protect socioeconomic rights by designing and creating new institutions where rights as 'trumps', trump economic interests (Shue, 1996: 70). To reiterate, within the terms of the liberal defence of negative rights, those who value civil rights cannot but value the necessary preconditions for protecting those rights, including a right to health. Given that more than 800 million people are susceptible to disease through malnourishment, 40,000 people die each day from hunger and related diseases, and one billion people lack access to clean water (UNDP, 1999), many commentators argue that it seems reasonable to expect the one-quarter of the global population that enjoys material resources way beyond their needs to make sacrifices to help the poor. This would require a radical reformation of global institutions and practices in favour of the poor, which the liberal consensus would undoubtedly see as too demanding and unsustainable, overlooking the argument that the current global system cannot be sustained because it is too demanding on the poor (Jones, 2000).

Although this approach has been muted in the past, so far little has been done to develop ways of bringing this transformation about. In the most recent edition of *Basic Rights*, Shue suggests three areas as a guide for creating the context in which socioeconomic rights might emerge. First, if we are to take rights seriously, and there is a greater unity between positive and negative rights than liberals currently allow, we must develop a deeper understanding of the consequences of our actions at all levels, from the local to the global. For example, the recent debate at the WTO on Trade Related Intellectual Property Rights (TRIPS) and GATS offers an opportunity to show that the global community does, in fact, rank health over the profits of drug companies and private health service providers (Oh, 2001). Second, any provision for achieving socioeconomic rights should include a 'division of moral labour'. Shue understands this as 'waves of duties' that roughly mirror the duty to avoid, protect and aid those whose rights are threatened. Each wave should be institutionalised to permit a clear understanding of the circumstances and contexts under which assigned duties should be exercised. Third, while Shue acknowledges that it is no easy task to assign duties, the organisation of institutional arrangements for ensuring the fulfilment of socioeconomic rights must give priority to empowering rights claimants. Empowerment offers people and communities an opportunity to take control of their own lives; an opportunity to enhance their self-esteem rather than suffer the indignity of becoming an object of charity (UNDP, 2000). Whatever institutional arrangements are made for the protection of socioeconomic rights, institutions must be given the powers to restrain TNCs and other actors who persistently pursue policies that prevent people and communities from helping themselves.

Although the prospects for institutionalising a duty to promote and protect human rights seems distant, recently the Committee on Economic, Social and Cultural Rights published a 'General Comment' on Article 12 of the ICESCR, the right to health. Among other things, the Comment presses states to make provision for a reduction in still-births and infant mortality, for the healthy development of children, and to foster improvements in all aspects of environmental and industrial hygiene. The Comment also includes the requirement to provide preventative measures to control epidemic, endemic and occupational diseases, and the creation of medical services accessible to all. Furthermore, the Comment notes that the right to health must also include access to safe water, adequate sanitation systems, education, food, housing and the conditions for a healthy occupational environment. Most importantly, the Comment notes that a right to health cannot be fulfilled simply by providing access to goods and services alone but urges international society to use all legal and political channels to check the activities of third parties, such as multinational corporations, to ensure that their activities do not contribute to the violation of the right to health (Committee on Economic, Social and Cultural Rights, 2000). Whether self-help approach offers a way forward remains unclear, as is the prospect of checking the activities of TNCs when human rights are threatened.

The grip of the liberal consensus remains powerful and may not yield readily to the suggestion that the institutions and organisations that support globalisation need reorientation towards supporting socioeconomic claims. Given the 'irreversible and irresistible' 'facts' of globalisation, as noted earlier, liberals are more likely to see any attempt to reorientate global institutions in favour of socioeconomic rights as futile. The prospects of reorientating global institutions should also be seen in the light of existing techniques for managing the global political economy, which comprise a combination of 'riot control' and 'poor relief' for social control (Cox, 1997). The most tangible evidence of the poor relief element is seen in the growing number and importance of NGOs devoted to humanitarian aid, which parallel the importance that the UN attaches to humanitarian assistance. When this fails in its objective to placate those on the periphery of globalisation, bringing political and economic instability in its wake, powerful governments resort to employing riot control, administered through the military and the police. In this way poor relief and riot control 'help to sustain the emerging social structure of the world by reducing the risk of chaos in the bottom layer' (Cox, 1997: 58). Instead of encouraging empowerment and self-help—values that are contrary to the interests associated with globalisation—current institutional arrangements act to harness and control alternatives. Some commentators are concerned that NGO involvement with humanitarian aid, for example, is little short of co-option, particularly where Western medicine and medical practice is inserted into traditional cultures despite local knowledge and medical networks (Price *et al.*, 1999).

Conclusion

Within the existing literature, it is common to see claims that the protection of human rights has made 'amazing progress' since the creation of the United Nations and the Commission on Human Rights, more than 50 years ago (Opsahl, 1989). Part of this progress is said to include the wide acceptance of human rights norms. However, the discussion here suggests that such statements are founded upon the formal global human rights regime, which focuses on ratifications of international law, overlooking the inconvenient facts of widespread torture, genocide, structural economic deprivation, disappearances, political prisoners, the suppression of trade union and democracy movements and the deaths of tens of thousands from preventable diseases daily (Pasha & Blaney, 1998). As political action, the success of the postwar project to place human rights at the centre of global politics has been very limited, most notably in the attempt to secure acceptance of socioeconomic rights. The dominance of the liberal consensus on human rights remains the single most important factor hindering the establishment of socioeconomic rights as legitimate claims. Although the basic rights approach does offer a challenge to the liberal consensus, the conditions of globalisation suggest that the prospects for human rights are unlikely to improve in the foreseeable future.

By confining human rights to a set of rights that support freedoms associated with free market economics, and redefining socioeconomic rights as 'aspirations', the current global order seeks to establish a set of values that legitimates particular kinds of social behaviour. Importantly, the most powerful actors associated with globalisation seek to free themselves of costs and duties seen as too burdensome and as an unnecessary barrier to the prosecution of their interests. What this seems to overlook is that the processes of globalisation also produce the socioeconomic conditions that increasingly threaten health security in all regions of the world, and both rich and poor alike, while simultaneously producing a decline in social organisation to combat disease. Along with the process of economic exchange, health risk has now been globalized through population movements, and by changes in cultural habit, tourism, diet and trade. This is paralleled by the increasing globalisation of health markets, technologies, science, drugs and the global organisation of business and finance.

If health risk has a 'democratic' dimension, it is in the sense that there is nowhere to hide from the health consequences of globalisation. We are all, rich and poor, confronted by the health risks associated with globalisation (Turner, 2001). Like all other socioeconomic rights, the right to health cannot be realised unless the institutions of the current global order have the capacity to intervene in the activities of those who currently exercise their freedoms to increase their wealth, no matter the social conditions that others must suffer. Since globalisation increasingly exposes us all to health risks, the failure to undertake institutional reform will lead to more epidemics, chronic disease and an environment where the means of leading a dignified and healthy life are less possible.

References

Acheson, D. (1998) *Independent Inquiry into Inequalities in Health* (London: HMSO).
Barlow, P. (1999) Health care is not a human right, *British Medical Journal*, 319, p 321.

Beauchamp, T. L. (1991) The right to health care in a capitalist democracy, in: T. J. Bole & W. B. Bondeson (eds), *Rights to Health Care*, 53–81 (London: Kluwer).

Bole, T. J. (1991) The rhetoric of rights and justice in health care, in: T. J. Bole & W. B. Bondeson (eds), *Rights to Health Care*, pp 1–19 (London: Kluwer).

Brandt, A. (1990) No magic bullet: a social-history of venereal-disease in the United States since 1880, *Community Health Studies*, 14(2), pp 204–5.

Buzan, B. (1993) *The Logic of Anarchy* (New York: Columbia University Press).

Carlin, J. (1998) What's a deal among friends? *Independent on Sunday*, 19 April.

Cassese, A. (1990) *Human Rights in a Changing World* (Oxford: Oxford University Press).

Christian Aid (1997) *A Sporting Chance* (London: Christian Aid).

Christian Aid (1996) *After the Prawn Rush: The Human and Environmental Costs of Commercial Prawn Farming* (London: Christian Aid).

Clark, I. (1999) *Globalization and International Relations Theory* (Oxford: Oxford University Press).

Committee on Economic, Social and Cultural Rights (2000) *The Right to the Highest Attainable Standard of Health* (Geneva: Committee on Economic, Social and Cultural Rights).

Conley, M. & Livermore, D. (1996) Human rights, development and democracy', *Canadian Journal of Development Studies*, XIXI, pp 19–26.

Cox, R. (1997) Democracy in hard times: economic globalization and the limits to liberal democracy, in: A. McGrew (ed), *The Transformation of Democracy*, pp 49–75 (Cambridge: Polity Press).

Cranston, M. (1973) *What Are Human Rights?* (London: Bodley Head).

Cranston, M. (1983) Are there any human rights?, *Daedalus*, 112(4), pp 1–18.

Donnelly, J. (1989) *Universal Human Rights in Theory and Practice* (Ithaca, NY: Cornell University Press).

Evans, T. (1999) Trading human rights, in: A. Taylor & C. Thomas (eds), *Global Trade and Global Social Issues*, pp 31–52 (London: Routledge)

Evans, T. (2000) Citizenship and human rights in the age of globalization, *Alternatives*, 25(4), pp 415–438.

Evans, T. (2001a) If democracy, then human rights?, *Third World Quarterly*, 22(4), pp 623–642.

Evans, T. (2001b) *The Politics of Human Rights: A Global Perspective* (London: Pluto Press).

Evans, T. & Hancock, J. (1998) Doing something without doing anything: international law and the challenge of globalization, *International Journal of Human Rights*, 2(3), p 1021.

French, H. (2000) *Vanishing Borders: Protecting the Planet in the Age of Globalization* (London: Earthscan).

Fukuyama, F. (1989) The end of history, *The National Interest*, Summer, pp 3–18.

Galtung, J. (1978) On the right to mental health: some discussion points, in: R. Dupuy (ed), *The Right to Health as a Human Right*, pp 223–226 (The Netherlands: Suthoff and Noordohoff).

George, S. (1999) *The Lucano Report* (London: Pluto).

Giddens, A. (1990) *Modernity and Self-Identity* (Cambridge: Polity Press).

Gill, S. (1995) Globalization, market civilisation, and disciplinary neorealism', *Millennium: Journal of International Studies*, 24(3), pp 399–423.

Gruskin, S. & Tarantola, D. (2001) *Health and Human Rights* (Boston, MA: Francois-Xavier Bagnoud Center of Health and Human Rights).

Held, D., McGrew, A., Goldblatt, D. & Perraton, J. (eds) (1999) *Global Transformations: Politics, Economics and Culture* (Cambridge: Polity Press).

HRW (1996) *No Guarantee: Sex Discrimination in Mexico's Maquiladora Sector* (: Human Rights Watch, Women's Rights Project).

International Federations of Red Cross and Red Crescent Societies and Francois-Xavier Bagnoud Center for Health and Human Rights (1999) Public health: an introduction, in: J. M. Mann, S. Gruskin, M. A. Grodin & G. J. Annas (eds), *Health and Human Rights*, pp 29–39 (London: Routledge).

Johnston, B. R. & Button, G. (1994) Human environmental rights issues and the multinational corporation: industrial development in the free trade zone, in: B. R. Johnston (ed), *Who Pays the Price?* (Washington, DC: Island Press).

Jones, C. (2000) *Global Justice: Defending Cosmopolitanism* (Oxford: Oxford University Press).

Jones, P. (1994) *Rights* (Basingstoke: Macmillan).

Kandela, P. (1998) Medical journals and human rights, *Lancet*, www.sciencedirect.com

Lee, E. (1996) Globalization and employment, *International Labour Review*, 135(5), pp 485–497.

Levine, P. (1996) Rereading the 1890s: venereal disease as 'constitutional crisis' in Britain and British India, *Journal of Asian studies*, 55(3), pp 585–512.

Loefter, I. J. P. (1999) 'Health care is a human right' is a meaningless and devastating manifesto, *British Medical Journal*, 318, p 1766.

Loff, B. & S. Gruskin (2001) Getting serious about the right to health', www.sciencedirect.com

Mann, J. M. (1996) Health and human rights—protecting human rights is essential for promoting health, *British Medical Journal*, 312, pp 924–925.

Mann, J. M. (1997) Public health: leadership is a global issue, *Lancet*, 350(suppl III), p 23.

McCorquodale, R. & Fairbrother, R. (1999) Globalization and human rights, *Human Rights Quarterly*, 21(3), pp 735–766.

McGrew, A. (1992) A global society, in: S. Hall, D. Held & A. McGrew (eds), *Modernity and Its Futures* (Cambridge: Polity).

McMichael, A. J. & Beaglehole, R. (2000) The changing global context of public health, *The Lancet*, www.sciencedirect.com

Merians, L. E. (1998) *The Secret Malady: Venereal Disease in Eighteenth-Century Britain and France* (London: Professional Scientific Publications).

Muzaffar, C. (1995) From human rights to human dignity', *Bulletin of Concerned Asian Scholars*, 27(4), pp 6–8.

Oh, C. (2001) TWN report on the WTO discussion on TRIPS and public health, Third World Network.

Opsahl, T. (1989) Instruments of implementation of human rights, *Human Rights Law Journal*, 10(1), pp 13–33.

Panitch, L. (1995) Rethinking the role of the state, in: J. Mittelman (ed), *Globalization: Critical Reflections* (Boulder, CO: Lynne Rienner).

Pasha, M. K. & Blaney, D. L. (1998) Elusive paradise: the promise and perils of global civil society, *Alternatives*, 23(1), pp 417–540.

Plant, R. (1989) Can there be a right to health care?, *Institute of Health Policy Studies Occasional Papers* (Southampton: Institute of Health Policy Studies).

Plant, R. (1993) The justification for intervention: needs before contexts, in: I. Forbes & M. Hoffman (eds), *Political Theory, International Relations and the Ethics of Intervention* (Basingstoke: Macmillan).

Poku, N. & Cheru, F. (2001) The politics of poverty and debt in Africa's AIDS crisis. *International Relations*, XV(6) pp 3–55.

Price, D., Pollock, A. M. & Shaoul, J. (1999) How the World Trade Organization is shaping domestic policies in health care, *Lancet*, 254, pp 1889–1892.

Scholte, I. A. (1996) Towards a critical theory of globalization, in: E. Kofman & G. Young (eds), *Globalization in Theory and Practice* (London: Pinter).

Shue, H. (1996) *Basic Rights: Subsistence, Affluence, and US Foreign Policy* (Princeton, NJ: Princeton University Press).

Smith, R., Hiatt, H. & Berwick, D. (1999) Shared ethical principles for everybody in health, *British Medical Journal*, 318, pp 248–251.

Spybey, T. (1996) *Globalization and World Society* (Cambridge: Polity Press).

Stammers, N. (1999) Social movements and the social construction of human rights, *Human Rights Quarterly*, 21(4), pp 980–1008.

Staples, V. J. (1999) What are human rights?, *Lancet*, www.sciencedirect.com

Summers, L. H. (1991) World Bank, office memo, 12 December.

Tetrault, M. A. (1988) Regimes and liberal world order, *Alternatives*, 13(1), pp 5–26.

Toebes, B. C. A. (1999) *The Right to Health as a Human Right in International Law* (Antwerp: Intersentia).

Tomasevski, K. (1993) *Development Aid and Human Rights Revisited* (London: Pinter).

Turk, D. (1992) *The Realization of Economic, Social and Cultural Rights: Final Report* (Geneva: United Nations).

Turner, B. S. (2001) Risks, rights and regulation: an overview, *Health, Risk and Society*, 3(1), pp 9–18.

UNDP (1999) *Human Development Report 1999—Globalization with a Human Face* (Oxford: United Nations Development Programme).

UNDP 2000 *Human Development Report 2000—Human Rights and Human Development* (Oxford: United Nations Development Programme).

UNRISD (1995) *States of Disarray: The Social Effects of Globalization* (Geneva: United Nations Research Institute for Social Development).

van der Pijl, K. (1997) Transnational class formation and state forms, in: S. Gill & J. Mittelman (eds), *Innovation and Transformation in International Studies*, pp 105–133 (Cambridge: Cambridge University Press)

van der Pijl, K. (1998) *Transnational Class and International Relations* (London: Routledge).

Veatch, R. M. (1991) Justice and the right to health care: an egalitarian account, in: T. J. Bole (ed), *Rights to Health Care*, pp 83–102 (London: Kluwer)

Vincent, R. J. (1986) *Human Rights and International Relations* (Cambridge: Cambridge University Press).

WHO (1997) *Health and Environment in Sustainable Development: Five Years After the Earth Summit* (Geneva: World Health Organisation).

WHO (2001) *Globalization, TRIPS and Access to Pharmaceuticals* (Geneva: World Health Organisation).

100

HEALTH AND HUMAN RIGHTS

Jonathan M. Mann, Lawrence Gostin, Sofia Gruskin,
Troyen Brennan, Zita Lazzarini and Harvey V. Fineberg

Source: *Health and Human Rights*, 1:1 (1994), 6–23.

Abstract

Health and human rights are complementary approaches for
defining and advancing human well-being. This article presents
a three-part provisional framework for exploring potential
collaboration in health and human rights. The first relationship
involves the impact (positive and negative) of health policies,
programs and practices on human rights; the goal is to negotiate
an optimal balance between public health goals and human rights
norms. The second relationship posits that violations of rights have
important health effects, thusfar generally unrecognized, that
must be described and assessed. The third and most fundamental
relationship proposes that promotion and protection of health
are inextricably linked to promotion and protection of human
rights and dignity. The interdependence of health and human rights
has substantial conceptual and practical implications. Research,
teaching, field experience and advocacy are required to explore
this intersection. This work can help revitalize the health field,
contribute to enriching human rights thinking and practice,
and offer new avenues for understanding and advancing human
well-being in the modern world.

Health and human rights have rarely been linked in an explicit manner. With
few exceptions, notably involving access to health care, discussions about
health have rarely included human rights considerations. Similarly, except
when obvious damage to health is the primary manifestation of a human
rights abuse, such as with torture, health perspectives have been generally
absent from human rights discourse.

Explanations for the dearth of communication between the fields of health and human rights include differing philosophical perspectives, vocabularies, professional recruitment and training, societal roles, and methods of work. In addition, modern concepts of both health and human rights are complex and steadily evolving. On a practical level, health workers may wonder about the applicability or utility ("added value"), let alone necessity of incorporating human rights perspectives into their work, and vice versa. In addition, despite pioneering work seeking to bridge this gap in bioethics,[1,2] jurisprudence,[3] and public health law,[4,5] a history of conflictual relationships between medicine and law, or between public health officials and civil liberty advocates, may contribute to anxiety and doubt about the potential for mutually beneficial collaboration.

Yet health and human rights are both powerful, modern approaches to defining and advancing human well-being. Attention to the intersection of health and human rights may provide practical benefits to those engaged in health or human rights work, may help reorient thinking about major global health challenges, and may contribute to broadening human rights thinking and practice. However, meaningful dialogue about interactions between health and human rights requires a common ground. To this end, following a brief overview of selected features of modern health and human rights, this article proposes a provisional, mutually accessible framework for structuring discussions about research, promoting cross-disciplinary education, and exploring the potential for health and human rights collaboration.

Modern concepts of health

Modern concepts of health derive from two related although quite different disciplines: medicine and public health. While medicine generally focuses on the health of an individual, public health emphasizes the health of populations. To oversimplify, individual health has been the concern of medical and other health care services, generally in the context of physical (and, to a lesser extent, mental) illness and disability. In contrast, public health has been defined as, ". . . (ensuring) the conditions in which people can be healthy."[6] Thus, public health has a distinct health-promoting goal and emphasizes prevention of disease, disability and premature death.

Therefore, from a public health perspective, while the availability of medical and other health care constitutes one of the essential conditions for health, it is not synonymous with "health." Only a small fraction of the variance of health status among populations can reasonably be attributed to health care; health care is necessary but clearly not sufficient for health.[7]

The most widely used modern definition of health was developed by the World Health Organization (WHO): "Health is a state of complete physical, mental and social well-being and not merely the absence of disease or infirmity."[8] Through this definition, WHO has helped to move health thinking beyond a limited, biomedical and pathology-based perspective to the more positive domain of "well-being." Also, by explicitly including the mental and social dimensions of well-being, WHO radically expanded the scope of health, and by extension, the roles and responsibilities of health professionals and their relationship to the larger society.

The WHO definition also highlights the importance of health promotion, defined as "the process of enabling people to increase control over, and to improve, their health." To do so, "an individual or group must be able to identify and realize aspirations, to satisfy needs, and to change or cope with the environment."[9] The societal dimensions of this effort were emphasized in the Declaration of Alma-Ata (1978), which described health as a ". . . social goal whose realization requires the action of many other social and economic sectors in addition to the health sector."[10]

Thus, the modern concept of health includes yet goes beyond health care to embrace the broader societal dimensions and context of individual and population well-being. Perhaps the most far-reaching statement about the expanded scope of health is contained in the preamble to the WHO Constitution, which declared that "the enjoyment of the highest attainable standard of health is one of the fundamental rights of every human being."[11]

Modern human rights

The modern idea of human rights is similarly vibrant, hopeful, ambitious and complex. While there is a long history to human rights thinking, agreement was reached that all people are "born free and equal in dignity and rights"[12] when the promotion of human rights was identified as a principal purpose of the United Nations in 1945.[13] Then, in 1948, the Universal Declaration of Human Rights was adopted as a universal or common standard of achievement for all peoples and all nations.

The preamble to the Universal Declaration proposes that human rights and dignity are self-evident, the "highest aspiration of the common people," and "the foundation of freedom, justice and peace." "Social progress and better standards of life in larger freedom," including the prevention of "barbarous acts which have outraged the conscience of mankind," and, broadly speaking, individual and collective well-being, are considered to depend upon the "promotion of universal respect for and observance of human rights."

Several fundamental characteristics of modern human rights include: they are rights of individuals; these rights inhere in individuals because they are human; they apply to all people around the world; and they principally involve the relationship between the state and the individual. The specific rights which form the corpus of human rights law are listed in several key documents: foremost is the Universal Declaration of Human Rights (UDHR), which, along with the United Nations Charter (UN Charter), the International Covenant on Civil and Political Rights (ICCPR)—and its Optional Protocols—and the International Covenant on Economic, Social and Cultural Rights (ICESCR), constitute what is often called the "International Bill of Human Rights." The UDHR was drawn up to give more specific definition to the rights and freedoms referred to in the UN Charter. The ICCPR and the ICESCR further elaborate the content set out in the UDHR, as well as setting out the conditions in which states can permissibly restrict rights.

Although the UDHR is not a legally binding document, nations (states) have endowed it with great legitimacy through their actions, including its legal and political invocation at the national and international level. For example, portions of the UDHR are cited in numerous national constitutions, and governments often refer to the UDHR when accusing other governments of violating human rights. The Covenants are legally binding, but only on the states which have become parties to them. Parties to the Covenants accept certain procedures and responsibilities, including periodic submission of reports on their compliance with the substantive provisions of the texts.

Building upon this central core of documents, a large number of additional declarations and conventions have been adopted at the international and regional levels, focusing upon either specific populations (such as the International Convention on the Elimination of All Forms of Racial Discrimination, entry into force in 1969; the Convention on the Elimination of All Forms of Discrimination Against Women, 1981; the Convention on the Rights of the Child, 1989) or issues (such as the Convention Against Torture and Other Cruel, Inhuman or Degrading Treatment or Punishment, entry into force in 1987; the Declaration on the Elimination of all Forms of Intolerance and of Discrimination Based on Religion or Belief, 1981).

Since 1948, the promotion and protection of human rights have received increased attention from communities and nations around the world. While there are few legal sanctions to compel states to meet their human rights obligations, states are increasingly monitored for their compliance with human rights norms by other states, nongovernmental organizations, the media and private individuals. The growing legitimacy of the human rights framework lies in the increasing application of human rights standards by a steadily widening range of actors in the world community. The awarding of the Nobel Peace Prize for human rights work to Amnesty International and to Ms. Rigoberta Menchu symbolizes this extraordinary level of contemporary interest and concern with human rights.

Since the late 1940s, human rights advocacy and related challenges have gradually extended the boundaries of the human rights movement in four related ways. First, the initial advocacy focus on civil and political rights and certain economic and social rights is expanding to include concerns about the environment and global socioeconomic development. For example, although the right to a "social and international order in which (human rights) can be fully realized" (UDHR, Article 28) invokes broad political issues at the global level, attention to this core concept as a right has only grown in recent years.

Second, while the grounding of human rights thinking and practice in law (at national and international levels) remains fundamental, wider social involvement and participation in human rights struggles is increasingly broadening the language and uses of human rights concepts.

Third, while human rights law primarily focuses on the relationship between individuals and states, awareness is increasing that other societal institutions and systems, such as transnational business, may strongly influence the capacity for realization of rights, yet they may elude state control. For example, exploitation of natural resources by business interests may seriously harm rights of local residents, yet the governmental capacity to protect human rights may be extremely limited, or at best indirect, through regulation of business practices and laws which offer the opportunity for redress. In addition, certain individual acts, such as rape, have not been a traditional concern of human rights law, except when resulting from systematic state policy (as alleged in Bosnia). However, it is increasingly evident that state policies impacting on the status and role of women may contribute importantly, even if indirectly, to a societal context which increases women's vulnerability to rape, even though the actual act may be individual, not state-sponsored.

Finally, the twin challenges of human rights promotion (hopefully preventing rights violations; analogous to health promotion to prevent disease) and protection (emphasizing accountability and redress for violations; analogous to medical care once disease has occurred) have often been approached separately. Initially, the United Nations system highlighted promotion of rights, and the nongovernmental human rights movement tended to stress protection of rights, often in response to horrific and systematic rights violations. More recently, both intergovernmental and nongovernmental agencies have recognized and responded to the fundamental interdependence of rights promotion and protection.

In summary, despite tremendous controversy, especially regarding the philosophical and cultural context of human rights as currently defined, a vocabulary and set of human rights norms is increasingly becoming part of community, national and global life.

A provisional framework: linkages between health and human rights

The goal of linking health and human rights is to contribute to advancing human well-being beyond what could be achieved through an isolated health- or human rights-based approach. This article proposes a three-part framework for considering linkages between health and human rights; all are interconnected, and each has substantial practical consequences. The first two are already well documented, although requiring further elaboration, while the third represents a central hypothesis calling for substantial additional analysis and exploration.

First, the impact (positive and negative) of health policies, programs and practices on human rights will be considered. This linkage will be illustrated by focusing on the use of state power in the context of public health.

The second relationship is based on the understanding that human rights violations have health impacts. It is proposed that all rights violations, particularly when severe, widespread and sustained, engender important health effects, which must be recognized and assessed. This process engages health expertise and methodologies in helping to understand how well-being is affected by violations of human rights.

The third part of this framework is based on an overarching proposition: that promotion and protection of human rights and promotion and protection of health are fundamentally linked. Even more than the first two proposed relationships, this intrinsic linkage has strategic implications and potentially dramatic practical consequences for work in each domain.

The first relationship: the impact of health policies, programs and practices on human rights

Around the world, health care is provided through many diverse public and private mechanisms. However, the responsibilities of public health are carried out in large measure through policies and programs promulgated, implemented and enforced by, or with support from, the state. Therefore, this first linkage may be best explored by considering the impact of public health policies, programs and practices on human rights.

The three central functions of public health include: assessing health needs and problems; developing policies designed to address priority health issues; and assuring programs to implement strategic health goals.[14] Potential benefits to and burdens on human rights may occur in the pursuit of each of these major areas of public health responsibility.

For example, assessment involves collection of data on important health problems in a population. However, data are not collected on all possible health problems, nor does the selection of which issues to assess occur in a societal vacuum. Thus, a state's failure to recognize or acknowledge health problems that preferentially affect a marginalized or stigmatized group may violate the right to non-discrimination by leading to neglect of necessary services, and in so doing, may adversely affect the realization of other rights, including the right to "security in the event of . . . sickness (or) disability . . ." (UDHR, Article 25), or to the "special care and assistance" to which mothers and children are entitled (UDHR, Article 25).

Once decisions about which problems to assess have been made, the methodology of data collection may create additional human rights burdens. Collecting information from individuals, such as whether they are infected with the human immunodeficiency virus (HIV), have breast cancer, or are genetically predisposed to heart disease, can clearly burden rights to security of person (associated with the concept of informed consent) and of arbitrary interference with privacy. In addition, the right of non-discrimination may be threatened even by an apparently simple information-gathering exercise. For example, a health survey conducted via telephone, by excluding households without telephones (usually associated with lower socioeconomic status), may result in a biased assessment, which may in turn lead to policies or programs that fail to recognize or meet needs of the entire population. Also, personal health status or health behavior information (such as sexual orientation, or history of drug use) has the potential for misuse by the state, whether directly or if it is made available to others, resulting in grievous harm to individuals and violations of many rights. Thus, misuse of information about HIV infection status has led to: restrictions of the right to work and to education; violations of the right to marry and found a family; attacks upon honor and reputation; limitations of freedom of movement; arbitrary detention or exile; and even cruel, inhuman or degrading treatment.

The second major task of public health is to develop policies to prevent and control priority health problems. Important burdens on human rights may arise in the policy-development process. For example, if a government refuses to disclose the scientific basis of health policy or permit debate on its merits, or in other ways refuses to inform and involve the public in policy development, the rights to "seek, receive and impart information and ideas . . . regardless of frontiers" (UDHR, Article 19) and "to take part in the government . . . directly or through freely chosen representatives" (UDHR, Article 21) may be violated. Then, prioritization of health issues may result in discrimination against individuals, as when the major health problems of a population defined on the basis of sex, race, religion or language are systematically given lower priority (e.g., sickle cell disease in the United States, which affects primarily the African-American population; or more globally, maternal mortality, breast cancer and other health problems of women).

The third core function of public health, to assure services capable of realizing policy goals, is also closely linked with the right to non-discrimination. When health and social services do not take logistic, financial, and socio-cultural barriers to their access and enjoyment into account, intentional or unintentional discrimination may readily occur. For example, in clinics for maternal and child health, details such as hours of service, accessibility via public transportation and availability of daycare may strongly and adversely influence service utilization.[15]

It is essential to recognize that in seeking to fulfill each of its core functions and responsibilities, public health may burden human rights. In the past, when restrictions on human rights were recognized, they were often simply justified as necessary to protect public health. Indeed, public health has a long tradition, anchored in the history of infectious disease control, of limiting the "rights of the few" for the "good of the many." Thus, coercive measures such as mandatory testing and treatment, quarantine, and isolation are considered basic measures of traditional communicable disease control.[16]

The principle that certain rights must be restricted in order to protect the community is explicitly recognized in the International Bill of Human Rights: limitations are considered permissible to "(secure) due recognition and respect for the rights and freedoms of others and of meeting the just requirements of morality, public order and the general welfare in a democratic society." (UDHR, Article 29). However, the permissible restriction of rights is bound in several ways. First, certain rights (e.g., right to life, right to be free from torture) are considered inviolable under any circumstances. Restriction of other rights must be: in the interest of a legitimate objective; determined by law; imposed in the least intrusive means possible; not imposed arbitrarily; and strictly necessary in a "democratic society" to achieve its purposes.

Unfortunately, public health decisions to restrict human rights have frequently been made in an uncritical, unsystematic and unscientific manner. Therefore, the prevailing assumption that public health, as articulated through specific policies and programs, is an unalloyed public good that does not require consideration of human rights norms must be challenged. For the present, it may be useful to adopt the maxim that health policies and programs should be considered discriminatory and burdensome on human rights until proven otherwise.

Yet this approach raises three related and vital questions. First, why should public health officials be concerned about burdening human rights? Second, to what extent is respect for human rights and dignity compatible with, or complementary to public health goals? Finally, how can an optimal balance between public health goals and human rights norms be negotiated?

Justifying public health concern for human rights norms could be based on the primary value of promoting societal respect for human rights as well as on arguments of public health effectiveness. At least to the extent that public health goals are not seriously compromised by respect for human rights norms, public health, as a state function, is obligated to respect human rights and dignity.

The major argument for linking human rights and health promotion is described below. However, it is also important to recognize that contemporary thinking about optimal strategies for disease control has evolved; efforts to confront the most serious global health threats, including cancer, cardio-vascular disease and other chronic diseases, injuries, reproductive health, infectious diseases, and individual and collective violence, increasingly emphasize the role of personal behavior within a broad social context. Thus, the traditional public health paradigm and strategies developed for diseases such as smallpox, often involving coercive approaches and activities which may have burdened human rights, are now understood to be less relevant today. For example,

WHO's strategy for preventing spread of the human immunodeficiency virus (HIV) excludes classic practices such as isolation and quarantine (except under truly remarkable circumstances) and explicitly calls for supporting and preventing discrimination against HIV-infected people.

The idea that human rights and public health must inevitably conflict is increasingly tempered with awareness of their complementarity. Health policy-makers' and practitioners' lack of familiarity with modern human rights concepts and core documents complicates efforts to negotiate, in specific situations and different cultural contexts, the optimal balance between public health objectives and human rights norms. Similarly, human rights workers may choose not to confront health policies or programs, either to avoid seeming to under-value community health or due to uncertainty about how and on what grounds to challenge public health officials. Recently, in the context of HIV/AIDS, new approaches have been developed, seeking to maximize realization of public health goals while simultaneously protecting and promoting human rights.[17] Yet HIV/AIDS is not unique; efforts to harmonize health and human rights goals are clearly possible in other areas. At present, an effort to identify human rights burdens created by public health policies, programs and practices, followed by negotiation towards an optimal balance whenever public health and human rights goals appear to conflict, is a necessary minimum. An approach to realizing health objectives that simultaneously promotes—or at least respects — rights and dignity is clearly desirable.

The second relationship: health impacts resulting from violations of human rights

Health impacts are obvious and inherent in the popular understanding of certain severe human rights violations, such as torture, imprisonment under inhumane conditions, summary execution, and "disappearances." For this reason, health experts concerned about human rights have increasingly made their expertise available to help document such abuses.[18] Examples of this type of medical-human rights collaboration include: exhumation of mass graves to examine allegations of executions;[18] examination of torture victims;[20] and entry of health personnel into prisons to assess health status.[21]

However, health impacts of rights violations go beyond these issues in at least two ways. First, the duration and extent of health impacts resulting from severe abuses of rights and dignity remain generally under-appreciated. Torture, imprisonment under inhumane conditions, or trauma associated with witnessing summary executions, torture, rape or mistreatment of others have been shown to lead to severe, probably life-long effects on physical, mental and social well-being.[22] In addition, a more complete understanding of the negative health effects of torture must also include its broad influence on mental and social well-being; torture is often used as a political tool to discourage people from meaningful participation in or resistance to government.[23]

Second, and beyond these serious problems, it is increasingly evident that violations of many more, if not all, human rights have negative effects on health. For example, the right to information may be violated when cigarettes are marketed without governmental assurance that information regarding the harmful health effects of tobacco smoking will also be available. The health cost of this violation can be quantified through measures of tobacco-related preventable illness, disability and premature death, including excess cancers, cardiovascular and respiratory disease. Other violations of the right to information, with substantial health impacts, include governmental withholding of valid scientific health information about contraception or measures (e.g., condoms) to prevent infection with a fatal virus (HIV).

As another example, the enormous worldwide problem of occupation-related disease, disability and death reflects violations of the right to work under "just and favorable conditions" (UDHR, Article 23). In this context, the World Bank's identification of increased educational attainment for women as a critical intervention for improving health status in developing countries powerfully expresses the pervasive impact of rights realization (in this case to education, and to non-discrimination on the basis of sex) on population health status.[24]

A related, yet even more complex problem involves the potential health impact associated with violating individual and collective dignity. The Universal Declaration of Human Rights considers dignity, along with rights, to be inherent, inalienable and universal. While important dignity-related health impacts may include such problems as the poor health status of many indigenous peoples, a coherent vocabulary and framework to characterize dignity and different forms of dignity violations are lacking. A taxonomy and an epidemiology of violations of dignity may uncover an enormous field of previously suspected, yet thusfar unnamed and therefore undocumented damage to physical, mental and social well-being.

Assessment of rights violations' health impacts is in its infancy. Progress will require: a more sophisticated capacity to document and assess rights violations; the application of medical, social science and public health methodologies to identify and assess effects on physical, mental and social well-being; and research to establish valid associations between rights violations and health impacts.

Identification of health impacts associated with violations of rights and dignity will benefit both health and human rights fields. Using rights violations as an entry point for recognition of health problems may help uncover previously unrecognized burdens on physical, mental or social well-being. From a human rights perspective, documentation of health impacts of rights violations may contribute to increased societal awareness of the importance of human rights promotion and protection.

The third relationship: health and human rights—exploring an inextricable linkage

The proposal that promoting and protecting human rights is inextricably linked to the challenge of promoting and protecting health derives in part from recognition that health and human rights are complementary approaches to the central problem of defining and advancing human well-being. This fundamental connection leads beyond the single, albeit broad mention of health in the UDHR (Article 25) and the specific health-related responsibilities of states listed in Article 12 of the ICESCR, including: reducing stillbirth and infant mortality and promoting healthy child development; improving environmental and industrial hygiene; preventing, treating and controlling epidemic, endemic, occupational and other diseases; and assurance of medical care.

Modern concepts of health recognize that underlying "conditions" establish the foundation for realizing physical, mental and social well-being. Given the importance of these conditions, it is remarkable how little priority has been given within health research to their precise identification and understanding of their modes of action, relative importance, and possible interactions.

The most widely accepted analysis focuses on socioeconomic status; the positive relationship between higher socioeconomic status and better health status is well documented.[25] Yet this analysis has at least three important limitations. First, it cannot adequately account for a growing number of discordant observations, such as: the increased longevity of married Canadian men and women compared with their single (widowed, divorced, never married) counterparts;[26] health status differences between minority and majority populations which persist even when traditional measures of socioeconomic status are considered;[27] or reports of differential marital, economic and educational outcomes among obese, compared with non-obese women.[28]

A second problem lies in the definition of poverty and its relationship to health status. Clearly, poverty may have different health meanings; for example, distinctions between the health-related meaning of absolute poverty and relative poverty have been proposed.[29]

A third, practical difficulty is that the socioeconomic paradigm creates an overwhelming challenge for which health workers are neither trained nor equipped to deal. Therefore, the identification of socioeconomic status as the "essential condition" for good health paradoxically may encourage complacency, apathy and even policy and programmatic paralysis.

However, alternative or supplementary approaches are emerging about the nature of the "essential conditions" for health. For example, the Ottawa Charter for Health Promotion (1986) went beyond poverty to propose that, "the fundamental conditions and resources for health are peace, shelter, education, food, income, a stable eco-system, sustainable resources, social justice and equity."[9]

Experience with the global epidemic of HIV/AIDS suggests a further analytic approach, using a rights analysis.[30] For example, married, monogamous women in East Africa have been documented to be infected with HIV.[31] Although these women know about HIV, and condoms are accessible in the marketplace, their risk factor is their inability to control their husbands' sexual behavior, or to refuse unprotected or unwanted sexual intercourse. Refusal may result in physical harm, or in divorce, the equivalent of social and economic death for the woman. Therefore, women's vulnerability to HIV is now recognized to be integrally connected with discrimination and unequal rights, involving property, marriage, divorce and inheritance. The success of condom promotion for HIV prevention in this population is inherently limited in the absence of legal and societal changes which, by promoting and protecting women's rights, would strengthen their ability to negotiate sexual practice and protect themselves from HIV infection.[32]

More broadly, the evolving HIV/AIDS pandemic has shown a consistent pattern through which discrimination, marginalization, stigmatization and, more generally, a lack of respect for the human rights and dignity of individuals and groups heightens their vulnerability to becoming exposed to HIV.[33,34] In this regard, HIV/AIDS may be illustrative of a more general phenomenon in which individual and population vulnerability to disease, disability and premature death is linked to the status of respect for human rights and dignity.

Further exploration of the conceptual and practical dimensions of this relationship is required. For example, epidemiologically-identified clusters of preventable disease, excess disability and premature death could be analyzed to discover the specific limitations or violations of human rights and dignity which are involved. Similarly, a broad analysis of the human rights dimensions of major health problems such as cancer, cardiovascular disease and injuries should be developed. The hypothesis that promotion and protection of rights and health are inextricably linked requires much creative exploration and rigorous evaluation.

The concept of an inextricable relationship between health and human rights also has enormous potential practical consequences. For example, health professionals could consider using the International Bill of Human Rights as a coherent guide for assessing health status of individuals or populations; the extent to which human rights are realized may represent a better and more comprehensive index of well-being than traditional health status indicators. Health professionals would also have to consider their responsibility not only to respect human rights in developing policies, programs and practices, but to contribute actively from their position as health workers to improving societal realization of rights. Health workers have long acknowledged the societal roots of health status; the human rights linkage may help health professionals engage in specific and concrete ways with the full range of those working to promote and protect human rights and dignity in each society.

From the perspective of human rights, health experts and expertise may contribute usefully to societal recognition of the benefits and costs associated with realizing, or failing to respect human rights and dignity. This can be accomplished without seeking to justify human rights and dignity on health grounds (or for any pragmatic purposes). Rather, collaboration with health experts can help give voice to the pervasive and serious impact on health associated with lack of respect for rights and dignity. In addition, the right to health can only be developed and made meaningful through dialogue between health and human rights disciplines. Finally, the importance of health as a pre-condition for the capacity to realize and enjoy human rights and dignity must be appreciated. For example, poor nutritional status of children can contribute subtly yet importantly to limiting realization of the right to educa-tion; in general, people who are healthy may be best equipped to participate fully and benefit optimally from the protections and opportunities inherent in the International Bill of Human Rights.

Conclusion

Thus far, different philosophical and historical roots, disciplinary differences in language and approach, and practical barriers to collaboration impede recognition of important linkages between health and human rights. The mutually enriching combination of research, education and field experience will advance understanding and catalyze further action around human rights and health. Exploration of the intersection of health and human rights may help revitalize the health field as well as contribute to broadening human rights thinking and practice. The health and human rights perspective offers new avenues for understanding and advancing human well-being in the modern world.

References

1. Beauchamps D. E., "Injury, Community and the Republic," *Law, Medicine and Health Care* 17, no. 1(Spring 1989):42–49.
2. Ronald Bayer, Arthur L. Caplan and Norman Daniels, eds., *In Search of Equity: health needs and the health care system*, from The Hastings Center series in ethics (New York: Plenum Press), 1983.
3. Ronald Dworkin, *Taking Rights Seriously* (Cambridge: Harvard University Press), 1978.
4. Scott Burris, "Rationality Review and the Politics of Public Health," *Villanova Law Review* 34(1989):1933.
5. Lawrence Gostin, "The Interconnected Epidemics of Drug Dependency and AIDS," *Harvard Civil Rights-Civil Liberties Law Review* 26, no. 1, (Winter 1991):113–184.
6. Institute of Medicine, *Future of Public Health*, (Washington DC: National Academy Press) 1988.

7. The International Bank for Reconstruction and Development, *World Development Report 1993: Investing in Health* (NY: Oxford University Press), 1993.
8. World Health Organization, *Constitution*, in *Basic Documents*, 36th ed. (Geneva, 1986).
9. *Ottawa-Charter for Health Promotion*, presented at first International Conference on Health Promotion (Ottawa, November 21, 1986).
10. *Declaration of Alma-Ata*, "Health for All" Series No. 1 (Geneva: World Health Organization, September 12, 1978).
11. *Supra* note 8.
12. *Universal Declaration of Human Rights*, adopted and proclaimed by UN General Assembly Resolution 217A(III) (December 10, 1948).
13. *United Nations Charter*, signed at San Francisco, 26 June 1945, entered into force on 24 October, 1945.
14. *Supra* note 6.
15. Emily Friedman, "Money Isn't Everything," *Journal of the American Medical Association* 271, no. 19. (May 18, 1994):1535–1538.
16. American Public Health Association, *Control of Communicable Disease in Man*, 15th ed., (Washington, D.C.: APHA), 1990.
17. International Federation of Red Cross and Red Crescent Socities, *AIDS, Health and Human Rights: A manual*, (in press).
18. Geiger H. J., and Cook-Deegan R. M., "The role of physicians in conflicts and humanitarian crises: Case studies from the field missions of Physicians for Human Rights, 1988–1993," *JAMA* 270(1993):616–620.
19. Physicians for Human Rights, *Final Report of UN Commission of Experts*. UN document #S/1994/674 (May 27, 1994).
20. Mollica R. F. and Caspi-Yavin Y., "Measuring torture and torture-related syndromes," *Psychological Assessment* 3, no. 4(1991): 1–7.
21. Timothy Harding, "Prevention of Torture and Inhuman or Degrading Treatment: Medical Implications of a New European Convention," *The Lancet* 1, no. 8648 (May 27, 1989):1191–1194.
22. Anne E. Goldfield, Richard F. Mollica, Barbara H. Pesavento, et. al., "The physical and psychological sequelae of torture; symptomatology and diagnosis," *JAMA* 259, no. 18(May 13, 1988):2725–2730.
23. Metin Basoglu, "Prevention of Torture and Care of Survivors: An integrated approach," *JAMA* 270, no. 5(August 4, 1993):607.
24. *Supra* note 7.
25. Dutton D. B. and Levine S., "Overview, methodological critique, and reformulation," in J. P. Bunker, D. S. Gomby and B. H. Kehrer, eds., *Pathways to Health. The role of social factors* (Menlo Park, CA: Henry J. Kaiser Family Foundation), 1989.
26. J. Epp, *Achieving Health for All: a framework for health promotion*, (Ottowa: Health and Welfare Canada, 1986)
27. Schoendorf K. C., Hogue C. J., Kleinman J. C., and Rowley D., "Mortality among infants of black as compared with white college-educated parents," *NEJM* 326(1992):1522–6.
28. S. Gortmaker, A. Must, J. M. Perrin et. al., "Social and economic consequences of overweight in adolescence and young adulthood," *NEJM* 329(1993): 1008–1012.

29. Ichiro Kawachi et. al., "Income Inequality and Life Expectancy: Theory, Research and Policy," *Society and Health Working Paper Series* May 1994, no. 94-2, (Boston: The Health Institute, New England Medical Center and Harvard School of Public Health), 1994.

30. Global AIDS Policy Coalition, "Towards a New Health Strategy for AIDS: A Report of the Global AIDS Policy Coalition," (Cambridge, MA: Global AIDS Policy Coalition, June 1993).

31. Said H. Kapiga, et. al., "Risk Factors for HIV Infection among Women in Dar-er-Salaam, Tanzania" *JAMA* 7, no. 3(1994):301–309.

32. Jacques du Guerny and Elisabeth Sjoberg, "Inter-relationship between gender relations and the HIV/AIDS epidemic: some considerations for policies and programmes," *AIDS* 7 (1993): 1027–1034.

33. *Supra* note 30.

34. Jonathan M. Mann, Daniel J. M. Tarantola and Thomas W. Netter, *AIDS in the World*, (Cambridge: Harvard University Press), 1992.

101

TOWARDS AN IMPROVED UNDERSTANDING OF THE INTERNATIONAL HUMAN RIGHT TO HEALTH

Brigit Toebes

Source: *Human Rights Quarterly*, 21:3 (1999), 661–79.

I. Introduction

In the context of international human rights, economic, social, and cultural rights are generally distinguished from civil and political rights. Although it is often asserted that both sets of rights are interdependent, interrelated, and of equal importance,[1] in practice, Western states and NGOs, in particular, have tended to treat economic, social, and cultural rights as if they were less important than civil and political rights.[2] Civil and political rights, for example, are frequently invoked in national judicial proceedings, and several complaint mechanisms are designed to protect these rights at the international level. In contrast, economic, social, and cultural rights are often considered non-justiciable and are regarded as general directives for states rather than rights.

Another serious obstacle to the implementation of economic, social, and cultural rights is their lack of conceptual clarity. An economic and social right that is characterized by particular vagueness is the international human right to health. It is by no means clear precisely what individuals are entitled to under the right to health, nor is it clear what the resulting obligations are on the part of states. Given these difficulties, this article seeks to further clarify the scope and implications of the right to health in order to contribute to an improved implementation of this specific right. This article will address some definitional problems when it comes to the right to health, as well as its international codification and current implementation practice. Finally, this article will outline the scope of the right to health and the ensuing state obligations.

II. The problem of definition

When it comes to health as a human right, there is an initial problem with regard to its definition. Specifically, there is confusion and disagreement over what is the most appropriate term to use to address health as a human right. Due to this disagreement, different terms are used by various authors. The terms that most commonly appear in human rights and health law literature are: the "right to health," the "right to healthcare" or to "medical care," and to a lesser extent, the "right to health protection."[3]

It has been argued that the term "right to health" is awkward because it suggests that people have a right to something that cannot be guaranteed, namely perfect health or to be healthy. It has also been noted that health is a highly subjective matter, varying from person to person and from country to country.[4] It is argued, therefore, that the terms "right to healthcare" or "right to health protection" are more realistic.[5]

At the international level, however, the term "right to health" is most commonly used. This term best matches the international human rights treaty provisions that formulate health as a human right. These provisions not only proclaim a right to healthcare but also a right to other health services such as environmental health protection and occupational health services. The term "healthcare" would accordingly not cover this broader understanding of health as a human right. Thus, in practice the term "right to health" is generally used as a shorthand expression for the more elaborate treaty texts.[6] Using such shorthand expressions is rather common in human rights discourse; terms such as the rights to life, privacy, a fair trial, and housing have all obtained a very specific practical connotation, as has the right to health.

III. International codification of the right to health

The right to health is firmly embedded in a considerable number of international human rights instruments. The right to health as laid down in the preamble to the Constitution of the World Health Organization (WHO) constitutes the point of departure on which most of the provisions in these instruments are based.[7] The preamble formulates the "highest attainable standard of health" as a fundamental right of everyone and defines health as a "state of complete physical, mental and social well-being and not merely the absence of disease or infirmity."[8] In the same vein, most treaty provisions stipulate a right to the highest attainable standard of (physical and mental) health and include a number of government obligations as well. These government undertakings usually include commitments regarding healthcare and also mention a number of underlying preconditions for health, such as occupational health, environmental health, clean drinking water, and adequate sanitation.

In addition to specific treaty provisions addressing the right to health, there are a number of general treaty provisions that stipulate that there is a universal right to health. The most well-known and influential of these provisions is Article 12 of the International Covenant on Economic, Social and Cultural Rights (ICESCR).[9] In addition to Article 12 of the ICESCR, there are a number of other treaty provisions that stipulate a right to health for particular vulnerable groups, such as women,[10] children,[11] racial minorities,[12] prisoners,[13] migrant workers,[14] and indigenous populations.[15]

The documents produced during several UN World Conferences, including the Vienna Declaration,[16] the Programme of Action of the Cairo Conference,[17] and the Beijing Declaration and Programme of Action,[18] have also elaborated on the meaning and scope of the international human right to health, and of international health issues generally. In fact, during the Fourth World Conference on Women, considerable attention was paid to a number of aspects relating to the health of women.[19]

Finally, a great number of national constitutions include a right to health (care) or stipulate states' duties with regard to the health of their people. Some of these provisions existed before the international human right to health was formulated.[20]

IV. Implementation practice of the right to health

In view of the above, it becomes clear that the problem with the right to health is not so much a lack of codification but rather an absence of a consistent implementation practice through reporting procedures and before judicial and quasi-judicial bodies, as well as a lack of conceptual clarity. These problems are interrelated: a lack of understanding of the meaning and scope of a right makes it difficult to implement, and the absence of a frequent practice of implementation in turn hampers the possibility of obtaining a greater understanding of its meaning and scope.

A. Reporting procedures

International treaty monitoring bodies do not have a very clear understanding of how they should implement the right to health. Under the heading of the "right to health," these bodies deal with a great number of health-related issues in a somewhat haphazard fashion. The treaty monitoring body of the ICESCR, the Committee on Economic, Social and Cultural Rights ("the Committee"), for example, addresses the following broad range of topics within the framework of the right to health: the national health policies adopted, issues related to healthcare, issues related to environmental health, accessibility of clean drinking water and adequate sanitation, availability of health-related information, occupational health, and the accessibility of health services for various vulnerable groups. One may divide the aggregate of these issues into four larger parts: (1) general issues, (2) healthcare, (3) underlying preconditions for health, and (4) vulnerable groups and health-specific subjects.[21] In spite of the somewhat inconsistent attitude of the Committee with regard to these four topics, one can draw important insights from an analysis of the ICESCR reporting procedure.

1. General issues

Included within the category of general issues is the overall requirement that state parties make certain commitments in the area of public health. First, state parties are required to devote a sufficient percentage of their CNP to health.[22] If, for example, military spending is high as compared to health expenditure, the Committee assumes that the country concerned should have spent its budget otherwise.[23] Second, this health commitment entails an obligation to adopt a national health policy, including the adoption of the Primary Health Care strategy (PHC) of WHO.[24] Also, state parties have to ensure that no disparities exist between the standard of health services offered in the private and public sectors.[25] The Committee opines that, although the right to health may be satisfied through whatever mix of public and private sector services is appropriate in the national context, state parties are responsible for the equality of access to healthcare services, whether privately or publicly provided. Plans to privatize and decentralize healthcare services do not in any way relieve state parties of their obligation to use all available means to promote adequate access to healthcare services, particularly for the poorer segments of the population.[26] The health legislation adopted by states is discussed;[27] however, the type of legislation state parties must adopt is not further spelled out by the Committee.

2. Healthcare

As far as the provision of healthcare services is concerned, a distinction between availability, accessibility, affordability, and quality of healthcare services proves useful in order to scrutinize the Committee's approach. With regard to the *availability* of healthcare services, the Committee assesses the aggregate of hospital beds and the population per nurse and per doctor.[28] In order to guarantee the availability of healthcare facilities, the Committee notes that state parties should encourage health personnel to stay and practice in the country.[29] Regarding the *accessibility* of healthcare services, the Committee focuses on the most vulnerable groups, who are generally minority and indigenous populations, women, children, the elderly, disabled persons, and persons with HIV/AIDS. In addition, the Committee expresses its concern about the accessibility of healthcare facilities in remote, rural areas.[30] State parties are to make efforts to institute rural health subcenters and to stimulate doctors and nurses to set up practice in rural areas.[31] An important aspect of the accessibility of healthcare facilities is the *affordability* of the available services.[32] State parties are to ensure that healthcare services are affordable for the economically underprivileged in general and for the elderly and low-income women in particular. As part of the affordability requirement, state parties must make sure that privatization does not constitute a threat to the affordability of healthcare services.[33] Finally, state parties must ensure that the available healthcare services are of good *quality*. This requires that doctors and nurses are skilled[34] and that equipment and drugs are adequate.[35]

3. Underlying preconditions for health

When it comes to the underlying preconditions for health there is some overlap with other rights. In particular, there is overlap with those rights contained in Article 11 of the ICESCR: food, housing, and clothing. Of these, the most explicitly health related are food-related issues.[36] Additional preconditions for health that are not covered by other rights but are discussed within the framework of Article 12 are access to safe water and the provision of adequate sanitary facilities, environmental hygiene, occupational hygiene, and health education. State parties have to make sure that their population has sufficient access to safe water and adequate sanitation.[37] In particular, they have to ensure that people living in remote, rural areas have sufficient access to these facilities.[38]

The Committee is also interested in environmental policies. However, it seeks to address environmental issues only in as far as they affect, or may affect, human health.[39] For example, state parties have to take safety measures for the protection against radioactive radiation.[40] The area of occupational health requires the implementation and monitoring of health and safety measures in the workplace.[41] Finally, health education requires that measures be taken to provide education concerning prevailing health problems, as well as the measures that are necessary for preventing and controlling them.[42]

4. Vulnerable groups and health-specific subjects

With regard to vulnerable groups and health-specific subjects, multiple topics have emerged in the reporting procedure. When the inhabitants of remote, rural areas are concerned, state parties must ensure that there is not an imbalance between rural and urban areas when it comes to access to health services.[43] With regard to indigenous populations, state parties are required to both guarantee respect for the cultural identity of those populations (for example, their use of traditional medicine) and to improve their health status.[44] State parties are also required to improve poor sanitary and hygiene conditions prevailing in penal institutions.[45] With respect to women, state parties are expected to combat maternal mortality,[46] to provide medical assistance to low-income women,[47] and to combat "traditional practices," including female circumcision.[48] Moreover, state parties are to reduce infant mortality[49] and to ensure that the rising costs of healthcare do not disadvantage the elderly.[50]

Other important issues include the policies and practices concerning abortion. The Committee has found that the circumstances under which such practices take place are more relevant under Article 12 of the ICESCR than the legal status of abortion.[51] Nevertheless, the legal status of abortion is an issue under discussion because the prohibition of abortion may lead to illegal and unsafe abortions.[52] Still another area of concern for the Committee is HIV/AIDS. State parties are urged to take measures to reduce the spread of HIV/AIDS, to set up information campaigns, to adopt laws to prevent discrimination against HIV-positive persons, and to endeavor to avoid measures that discriminate against people with HIV/AIDS.[53] These measures are in response to some states' adoption of coercive measures, including transit restrictions to minimize the risk of the spread of AIDS, mandatory testing, and control of prostitution.[54] Regarding drug abuse, state parties are to remain vigilant on the question of human rights violations and the means used to punish abuses. It has been observed that the drug problem cannot be solved solely by resorting to repressive measures without recognizing other serious problems, such as extreme poverty or inequality.[55] For example, drug addicts should not necessarily be regarded as delinquents but rather as victims or patients.[56] Finally, state parties are to take measures to combat alcoholism and to discourage minors from having access to alcoholic beverages and tobacco products.[57]

In a more general sense, it seems that Committee members disapprove of coercive policies relating to the health of the population. Forcing people to undergo certain treatment, such as psychiatric treatment, treatment for drug addiction, HIV/AIDS testing, or forcing indigenous populations to abandon traditional healing, is generally rejected by the Committee, which emphasizes the adverse effects that such policies may have. Committee members have expressed concern that these practices give rise to violations of economic, social, and cultural rights, as well as violations of civil and political rights. In this regard, it is noteworthy to observe that some of the issues addressed by the Committee within the framework of the right to health overlap with civil and political rights.

B. Justiciability of the right to health

At the United Nations, as well as the regional and national levels, very few examples exist where courts have reviewed the right to health; however, there are some sources of inspiration for judicial review of the right to health. At the UN level there are no specific complaint procedures in force to make health rights and other economic, social, and cultural rights justiciable. Given this fact, some attempts have been made to introduce health issues in other international procedures. For example, within the context of the 1235 procedure of the UN Sub-Commission, issues related to environmental health have been brought up; however, no decision has been made.[58] In addition, WHO requested an Advisory Opinion from the International Court of Justice concerning the right to health and the legality of the use of nuclear weapons, but this was to no avail.[59] A final example is the World Bank, which recently introduced a special Inspection Panel before which health issues, among other things, may be addressed.[60] Although there is perhaps a slight tendency towards attention for health issues within UN bodies, the situation is altogether not very promising.

At the regional level the situation is somewhat more encouraging. For example, the development of complaint procedures for economic, social, and cultural rights has proceeded somewhat further at the regional levels than at the United Nations. In principle, the right to health as contained in the African Charter[61] is susceptible to invocation before and review by the African Commission, although this procedure has not often been used.[62] The Organization of American States has adopted a limited complaints procedure, however it has yet to come into force. However, given the limited scope of the Inter-American Protocol of San Salvador,[63] the right to health would not be susceptible to judicial review. Nevertheless, it is possible to submit complaints to the Inter-American Commission on Human Rights (IACHR) on the basis of the right to health as provided for in the American Declaration.[64] This, in fact, was tried in the case of the Yanomani Indians,[65] where the IACHR declared that the right to health in Article XI of the American Declaration was violated. The Government of Brazil was held to have failed to protect the Yanomani against the exploitation of the rainforest and the detrimental health effects that could be caused.[66] Finally, with the adoption of a complaint procedure under the European Social Charter (ESC) of the Council of Europe, the right to protection of health in the ESC will become susceptible to (quasi-) judicial review. This procedure will, however, only allow specific organizations to submit complaints, not individuals.[67]

Inspiration for the justiciability of the right to health can be derived from the national level. In some countries either the constitutional or the international right to health has been given effect before domestic courts. Whereas some of these cases involve a right to certain healthcare facilities, others concern a right to environmental health. With regard to healthcare, a 1992 Colombian case that concerned the terminal illness of an AIDS patient is worth mentioning. In that case the Colombian Supreme Court ruled that the state was required, by the right to health in Article 13 of the Colombian constitution, to provide special protection when the lack of economic resources "prevents a person from decreasing the suffering, discrimination, and social risk involved in being afflicted by a terminal, transmissible, and incurable illness."[68] To this end, the Court decided that the hospital was required to provide the AIDS patient the necessary services.[69] With regard to environmental health, the well-known 1993 Philippine *Minors Oposa*[70] case is significant. In that case the Philippine Supreme Court ruled that the state should stop providing logging licences in order to protect the health of present and future generations. The decision was based on Article II of the Declaration of Principles and State Policies of the 1987 Philippine constitution, which sets forth the rights to health and ecology.[71]

Finally, one may derive inspiration from the justiciability of civil and political rights. On some occasions, civil and political rights have offered protections similar to that of the right to health. Again, such protections may concern access to a certain healthcare facility or protection against environmental health threats. A case indirectly involving a right to access to healthcare services has been brought before the Human Rights Committee (HRC). This body has adopted the practice of considering Article 26 ICCPR (nondiscrimination) as an autonomous provision that may include the prohibition of discriminatory actions with relation to social rights.[72] In *Hendrika S. Vos v. the Netherlands*,[73] the HRC considered whether the denial of a disability benefit constituted a violation of Article 26 of the ICCPR. Although the HRC held that there was no violation of the nondiscrimination clause in Article 26, the fact that the HRC tested the denial of the sickness benefit against Article 26 shows its willingness to read social rights into the nondiscrimination clause.[74] Also worth mentioning is a decision by the Indian Supreme Court where the Court ruled that on the basis of the right to life contained in the Indian constitution, the claimant had a right to the available emergency medical treatment.[75] It explained that:

> [p]roviding adequate medical facilities for the people is an essential part of the obligations undertaken by the Government in a welfare State. . . . Article 21 imposes an obligation on the State to safeguard the right to life of every person. Preservation of human life is thus of paramount importance. . . . Failure on the part of a Government hospital to provide timely medical treatment to a person in need of such treatment results in a violation of his right to life guaranteed under Article 21.[76]

Regarding environmental health, a case on point is *López Ostra v. Spain*,[77] which concerned the nuisance caused by a waste treatment plant and its effects on the applicant's daughter's health in the town of Lorca, Spain. The Spanish court opined that "severe environmental pollution may affect individuals' well-being and prevent them from enjoying their homes in such a way as to effect their private and family life adversely. . . ."[78] It concluded that the municipality of Lorca had failed to take steps to respect the applicant's right to respect for her home and for her private life under Article 8 of the European Convention on Human Rights and that Article 8 had accordingly been violated.[79]

V. The creation of conceptual clarity with regard to the right to health

A. In search of its scope and core content

On the basis of the above findings, one can clarify further the meaning of the right to health and delineate its scope and core content. Whereas the scope constitutes the general content of the right to health, the core content consists of those elements that a state has to guarantee under any circumstances, irrespective of its available resources.

Regarding the scope, it is important to recognize the broad character of the right to health and not recognize a right to "healthcare" only. The right to health can be said to embrace two larger parts: (1) elements related to "healthcare," and (2) elements concerning the "underlying preconditions for health" (these may include a healthy environment, safe drinking water and adequate sanitation, occupational health, and health-related information). Simultaneously, it is important to demarcate limits on the right to health and not allow it to include everything that might involve health. For example, with a few minor exceptions, the right to health does not include a prohibition against torture or inhuman and degrading treatment, nor does it include protection against arbitrary killing or medical or scientific experimentation. The right to health also does not include regular education at schools nor a right to adequate housing. It offers protection against environmental pollution only if there are clear health risks, and it is related to the right to work only if it concerns the safeguarding of industrial hygiene and the prevention, treatment, and control of occupational diseases. On the other hand, it is important to recognize that there is a certain overlap with several civil and political as well as other economic, social, and cultural rights, in that on some occasions the right to health may offer protection similar to that of other rights. For example, the right to health may overlap with other human rights where it concerns prevention of infant mortality (right to life), the safeguarding of adequate prison conditions, measures to combat "traditional practices" (prohibition of torture and inhuman and degrading treatment), and access to healthy foodstuffs (right to food).

Secondly, there is a trend among scholars and activists towards delineating a certain core in the right to health. This so-called core content consists of a set of elements that states have to guarantee immediately, irrespective of their available resources.[80] The core content stands in contrast to some elements of the right to health that are to be realized "progressively."[81] This core content includes those elements without which the right loses its significance; it refers to those elements that encompass the essence of the right.[82] For the definition of the core content of the right to health, one may derive inspiration from the Primary Health Care strategy (PHC) of WHO.[83] The core content of the right to health accordingly consists of a number of basic health services.

Irrespective of their available resources, states are to provide access to: maternal and child healthcare (including family planning), immunization against the major infectious diseases, appropriate treatment for common diseases and injuries, essential drugs, and an adequate supply of safe water and basic sanitation. In addition, they should ensure freedom from serious environmental health threats.

Finally, in addition to the scope and core content, a number of guiding principles constitute the framework of the right to health. States should safeguard the availability, equality, accessibility (financial, geographic, and cultural), and quality of the above mentioned health services.

B. Obligations resulting from the right to health

For further clarification of the normative content of the right to health, it is helpful to approach it from the angle of (state) obligations. A useful concept in this regard is the tripartite typology of duties, which assumes that obligations to respect, protect, and fulfill can be derived from each human right.[84] An analysis of the right to health on the basis of this typology demonstrates that the right to health not only gives rise to positive obligations to protect[85] and to fulfill[86] but also embraces negative obligations to respect. Obligations to respect the right to health include, for example, the obligation to respect equal access to health services and to refrain from health-harming activities, as in the sphere of environmental health.[87] The fact that an economic and social right embraces negative obligations underlines the interdependence and interrelatedness of civil and political rights with economic, social, and cultural rights. In effect, both sets of rights—civil and political, and economic, social, and cultural—require state abstention.

In the chart presented in this section, thirty-two obligations to respect, to protect, and to fulfill are derived from the right to health. It is assumed that the right to health contains two larger parts: healthcare and underlying preconditions for health.

VI. Conclusion

It will take a long time for economic, social, and cultural rights to obtain the same status and impact as civil and political rights. States will continue to fear the financial commitments of guaranteeing such rights. A conceptual clarification of the separate economic, social, and cultural rights may nevertheless contribute to their recognition and implementation. In addition, this clarification reveals that economic, social, and cultural rights, equal to civil and political rights, may require state abstention, a commitment that requires no financial resources on the part of states. Simultaneously, the fact that civil and political rights may embrace positive obligations underlines the interdependence and interrelatedness of both sets of rights. If positive

	Healthcare		Underlying Preconditions for Health		
	healthcare	family planning and pre- and post-natal care	water and sanitation	environmental and industrial health	physical integrity
RESPECT	1) respect for equal access to healthcare 2) no interference with the provision of healthcare 3) no interference with the provision of healthcare related information	4) respect for equal access to family planning services and pre- and post-natal care 5) no interference with the provision of such services by others 6) no interference with the provision of information on such services	7) respect for equal access to water and sanitation 8) no interference with the provision of water and sanitation 9) no interference with the provision of information on water and sanitation	10) abstention from environmental and industrial policies detrimental to health 11) no interference with environmental and industrial health-related information	12) abstention from traditional practices 13) no interference with information about harmful effects of such practices
PROTECT	14) adoption of legislation and other measures in order to assure adequate access to healthcare provided by third parties 15) adoption of legislation and other measures in order to assure that adequate information on healthcare is provided by third parties	16) adoption of legislation and other measures in order to assure adequate access to family planning and pre- and post-natal care provided by third parties 17) assurance of adequate provision of information on such services by third parties	18) adoption of legislation and other measures in order to assure adequate access to water and sanitation provided by third parties 19) assurance of adequate provision of information on such services by third parties	20) adoption of legislation and other measures for protection against environmental and industrial health infringements by third parties, particularly in the field of environmental health 21) assurance of adequate dissemination of information of environmental health risks by third parties	22) adoption of legislation and other measures for protection against traditional practices 23) assurance of adequate provision of information on such practices by third parties
FULFILL	24) provision of healthcare services 25) provision of healthcare related information	26) provision of family planning services and pre- and post-natal care, the latter free of charge if necessary. 27) provision of information on such services	28) provision of water and sanitation 29) provision of information on water and sanitation	30) measures to ensure and promote a healthy environment 31) provision of information about environmental health issues	32) measures to ensure and promote freedom from traditional practices 33) provision of information on such practices

obligations are derived from civil and political rights, why not recognize similar obligations with regard to economic, social, and cultural rights?

As to the right to health, it has become clear that it concerns a broad right that is difficult to pinpoint. Therefore, the adoption of a General Comment on the right to health in Article 12 of the ICESCR is of the utmost importance. It is also important that reliable indicators be developed to measure states' progress in the field of health and that states, UN Specialized Agencies, and NGOs make efforts and cooperate in this regard. For the further development of the justiciability of the right to health, one may keep in mind that justiciability is a fluid concept, which implies that it may further develop in the future.[88] Frequent application of the right to health may further enhance its justiciability.

Notes

1 *See* Vienna Declaration and Programme of Action, U.N. CAOR, World Conf. on Hum. Rts., 48th Sess., 22d plen. mtg., part I, ¶ 5, U.N. Doc. A/CONF.157/23 (1993), *reprinted in* 32 I.L.M. 1667 (1993).

2 Many other states, notably those belonging to the so-called Second and Third Worlds, on the other hand, have been more prominent in promoting economic, social, and cultural human rights.

3 The right to healthcare is often used in discussions on access to healthcare services at the national level. Article 11 of the European Social Charter (ESC) stipulates the "right to protection of health." European Social Charter, *opened for signature* 18 Oct. 1961, art. 11, Europ. T.S. No. 38 (*entered into force* 26 Feb. 1965), *reprinted in* HUMAN RIGHTS DOCUMENTS 212 (Committee on Foreign Affairs ed., 1983). *See also* Ruth Roemer, *The Right to Health Care, in* THE RIGHT TO HEALTH IN THE AMERICAS 17 (Pan American Health Org. 1989) (arguing in favor of the term "right to health protection"). In addition, the term "right to health security" has recently been applied by WHO. *See* WORLD HEALTH ORGANIZATION, THE RIGHT TO HEALTH SECURITY AS A BASIC HUMAN RIGHT: A PRELIMINARY ANALYSIS (draft) (1996). And finally, the term "health rights" is occasionally used. *See, e.g.,* Katarina Tomaševski, *Health Rights, in* ECONOMIC, SOCIAL AND CULTURAL RIGHTS, A TEXTBOOK 125–43 (Asbørjn Eide et al. eds., 1995).

4 *See* Joseph M. Boyle, Jr., *The Concept of Health and the Right to Health,* 3 Soc. THOUGHT, Summer 1977, at 5, 6 (quoting Leon R. Kass, *Regarding the End of Medicine and the Pursuit of Health,* 40 PUB. INTEREST 39 (1975)).

5 *See* H.D.C. ROSCAM ABBING, INTERNATIONAL ORGANIZATIONS IN EUROPE AND THE RIGHT TO HEALTH CARE 104–05 (1979); Roemer, *supra* note 3, at 17.

6 *See* Virginia A. Leary, *Implications of a Right to Health, in* HUMAN RIGHTS IN THE TWENTY-FIRST CENTURY 481, 485 (Kathleen E. Mahoney & Paul Mahoney eds., 1993).

7 Constitution of the World Health Organization, 14 U.N.T.S. 186, 22 July 1946 (*entered into force* 7 April 1948), *reprinted in* BASIC DOCUMENTS OF THE WHO (32d ed. Geneva, 1981).

8 *See id.* at 186.

9 International Covenant on Economic, Social and Cultural Rights, art. 12, *adopted* 16 Dec. 1966, G.A. Res. 2200 (XXI), U.N. GAOR, 21st Sess., Supp. No. 16, U.N. Doc. A/6316 (1966), 993 U.N.T.S. 3 (*entered into force* 3 Jan. 1976) [hereinafter ICESCR]. *See also* European Social Charter, *supra* note 3, art. 11; Additional Protocol to

the American Convention on Human Rights in the Area of Economic, Social and Cultural Rights ("Protocol of San Salvador"), *signed* 17 Nov. 1988, O.A.S.T.S. No. 69, *reprinted in* ORGANIZATION OF AMERICAN STATES, BASIC DOCUMENTS PERTAINING TO HUMAN RIGHTS IN THE INTER-AMERICAN SYSTEM, O.A.S. Doc. OEA/Ser.L.V/II.82, doc. 6, rev. 1, at 67 (1992) [hereinafter Protocol of San Salvador].

10 *See* Convention on the Elimination of All Forms of Discrimination Against Women, art. 12, *adopted* 18 Dec. 1979, G.A. Res. 34/180, U.N. CAOR, 34th Sess., Supp. No. 46, U.N. Doc. A/34/46 (1980) (*entered into force* 3 Sept. 1981), *reprinted in* 19 I.L.M. 33 (1980).

11 *See* Convention on the Rights of the Child, art. 24, *adopted* 20 Nov. 1989, G.A. Res. 44/25, U.N. GAOR, 44th Sess., Supp. No. 49, U.N. Doc. A/44/49 (1989) (*entered into force* 2 Sept. 1990), *reprinted in* 28 I.L.M. 1448 (1989).

12 *See* International Convention on the Elimination of All Forms of Racial Discrimination, art. 5(e)(iv), *adopted* 21 Dec. 1965, 660 U.N.T.S. 195 (*entered into force* 4 Jan. 1969), *reprinted in* 5 I.L.M. 352 (1966).

13 *See* Standard Minimum Rules for the Treatment of Prisoners, *adopted* 30 Aug. 1955, First U.N. Congress on the Prevention of Crime and the Treatment of Offenders, U.N. Doc. A/CONF/6/1, annex I, A (1956), *approved* 31 July 1957, E.S.C. Res. 663(c), U.N. ESCOR, 24th Sess., Supp. No.1, at 11, U.N. Doc. E/3048 (1957), amended 13 May 1977, E.S.C. Res. 2076, U.N. ESCOR, 62d Sess., Supp. No. 1, at 35, U.N. Doc. E/5988 (1977), *reprinted in* INTERNATIONAL HUMAN RIGHTS INSTRUMENTS 450.1 (Richard B. Lillich ed., 2d ed. 1990).

14 *See* International Convention on the Protection of the Rights of All Migrant Workers and Members of Their Families, *adopted* 18 Dec. 1990, G.A. Res. 45/158, U.N. GAOR, 45th Sess., Agenda Item 12, art. 28, U.N. Doc. A/RES/45/158 (1991) (*opened for signature* 2 May 1991), *reprinted in* 30 I.L.M. 1517 (1991).

15 *See* Convention Concerning Indigenous and Tribal Peoples in Independent Countries (ILO No. 169), *adopted* 27 June 1989, art. 25, 72 ILO OFFICIAL BULL. 59 (*entered into force* 5 Sept. 1991), *reprinted in* 28 I.L.M. 1382 (1989).

16 Vienna Declaration and Programme of Action, *supra* note 1.

17 *Programme of Action of the International Conference on Population and Development: Report of the International Conference on Population and Development*, U.N. GAOR, 29th Sess., U.N. Doc. A/CONF.171/13 (1994).

18 *Action for Equality, Development, and Peace: Beijing Declaration and Platform for Action*, U.N. GAOR, Fourth World Conf. on Women, U.N. Doc. A/CONF.177/20 (1995), *reprinted in* REPORT OF THE FOURTH WORLD CONFERENCE ON WOMEN (1995) (recommended to the UN General Assembly by the Committee on the Status of Women on 7 Oct. 1995). Paragraph 30 of the Beijing Declaration sets the objective to "Ensure equal access to and equal treatment of women and men in education and healthcare and enhance women's sexual and reproductive health as well as education." *Id.* ¶ 30. In Chapter III of the Platform for Action, the inadequate and unequal access to healthcare and related services is mentioned as a critical area of concern. *Id.* ch. III.

19 *See id.* ¶ 30.

20 For example, Article 10 of the Chilean constitution of 1925 stipulates that "[i]t is the duty of the state to oversee the public health and hygienic well-being of the country. Each year a sufficient sum of money should be earmarked in order to maintain a national health service." CHILE CONST. (1925) art. 10. Article 19 of the present Chilean constitution of 1980 stipulates that the right to health protection is guaranteed to all persons and that "[t]he State protects free and equal access to activities for the promotion, protection and recovery of health and for rehabilitation of the individual." CHILE CONST. (1980) art. 19.

21 The Committee has not yet adopted a General Comment on the right to health in Article 12.

22 *The Nature of States Parties Obligations*, General Comment No. 3, U.N. ESCOR, Comm. on Econ., Soc. & Cult. Rts., 5th Sess., Supp. No. 3, at 104 qstn. 3, U.N. Doc. E/1991/23-E/C.12/1990/8 (1991) [hereinafter *Guidelines on Reporting*].

23 *See, e.g., Summary Record of the 13th Meeting*, U.N. ESCOR, Comm. on Econ., Soc. & Cult. Rts., ¶ 25, UN Doc. E/C.12/1988/SR.13 (1988) (Committee member making a remark regarding Chile); *Summary Record of the 22nd Meeting*, U.N. ESCOR, Comm. on Econ., Soc. & Cult. Rts., ¶¶ 5, 17, U.N. Doc. E/C.12/1987/SR.22 (1987) (Committee member making a remark regarding North Korea).

24 *See Guidelines on Reporting, supra* note 22, at 104 qstn. 2.

25 *See Summary Record of the 2nd Meeting*, U.N. ESCOR, Comm. on Econ., Soc. & Cult. Rts., ¶ 61, U.N. Doc. E/C.12/1990/SR.2 (1990) (Committee member Mr. Rattray making a remark regarding Cyprus) [hereinafter *1990 Summary Record of the 2nd Meeting*].

26 *See, e.g., Concluding Observations on Philippines*, U.N. ESCOR, Comm. on Econ., Soc. & Cult. Rts., ¶ 20, U.N. Doc. E/C.12/1995/7 (1995).

27 *See, e.g., Initial Reports Submitted by States Parties Under Articles 16 and 17 of the Covenant: Iran*, U.N. ESCOR, Comm. on Econ., Soc. & Cult. Rts., ¶¶ 110–29, U.N. Doc. E/1990/5/Add.9 (1992); *Second Periodic Reports Submitted by States Parties to Covenant: Netherlands*, U.N. ESCOR, Comm. on Econ., Soc. & Cult. Rts., ¶ 85, U.N. Doc. E/1986/4/Add.24 (1988); *Third Periodic Reports Submitted by States Parties Under Articles 16 and 17 of the Covenant: Russian Federation*, U.N. ESCOR, Comm. on Econ., Soc. & Cult. Rts., ¶ 223, U.N. Doc. E/1994/104/Add.8 (1995).

28 *See Summary Record of the 12th Meeting*, U.N. ESCOR, Comm. on Econ., Soc. & Cult. Rts., 12th Sess., ¶ 52, U.N. Doc. E/C.12/1995/SR.12 (1995) [hereinafter *1995 Summary Record of the 12th Meeting*]; *Summary Record of the 19th Meeting*, U.N. ESCOR, Comm. on Econ., Soc. & Cult. Rts., 1st Sess., ¶ 55, U.N. Doc. E/C.12/1987/SR.19 (1987) (Representative of the Federal Republic of Germany) [hereinafter *1987 Summary Record of the 19th Meeting*].

29 *See 1995 Summary Record of the 12th Meeting, supra* note 28, ¶ 52 (Committee member Mr. Grissa making a remark regarding the Philippines). For response of the Philippine representative, *see id.* ¶ 53.

30 *Guidelines on Reporting, supra* note 22, ¶ 4(f). *See also id.* ¶ 5(b)–(d), (i).

31 *See, e.g., Summary Record of the 38th Meeting*, U.N. ESCOR, Comm. on Econ., Soc. & Cult. Rts., 5th Sess., ¶ 16, U.N. Doc. E/C.12/1990/SR.38 (1990) (Committee member Mr. Simma posed question to Ecuador) [hereinafter *1990 Summary Record of the 38th Meeting*]. For remarks made by the representative of Ecuador with respect to this matter, see *Summary Record of the 37th Meeting*, U.N. ESCOR, Comm. on Econ., Soc. & Cult. Rts., 5th Sess., ¶ 23, U.N. Doc. E/C.12/1990/SR.37 (1990) [hereinafter *1990 Summary Record of the 37th Meeting*]. *See also Summary Record of the 39th Meeting*, U.N. ESCOR, Comm. on Econ., Soc. & Cult. Rts., 5th Sess., ¶ 11, U.N. Doc. E/C.12/1990/SR.39 (1990).

32 *See Concluding Observations of the Committee on Economic, Social and Cultural Rights*, U.N. ESCOR, Comm. on Econ., Soc. & Cult. Rts., ¶ 5, U.N. Doc. E/C.12/1994/7 (1994) (containing the Committee's concluding observations regarding Belgium).

33 *See Summary Record of the 12th Meeting*, U.N. ESCOR, Comm. on Econ., Soc. & Cult. Rts., 2d Sess., ¶ 57, U.N. Doc. E/C.12/1988/SR.12 (1988) (Committee Member Mr. Neneman remark regarding Chile).

34 *Guidelines on Reporting, supra* note 22, indicators 4(f)–(h) ("Proportions of population/pregnant women/infants having access to trained personnel for care").

35 *See Summary Record of the 5th Meeting*, U.N. ESCOR, Comm. on Econ., Soc. & Cult. Rts., 3d Sess., ¶ 45, U.N. Doc. E/C.12/1989/SR.5 (1989) (Representatives of Poland); *1995 Summary Record of the 12th Meeting, supra* note 28, ¶ 55 (the Philippines); *Second Periodic Reports Submitted by States Parties to Covenant: Mongolia*, U.N. ESCOR, Comm. on Econ., Soc. & Cult. Rts., at 9, U.N. Doc. E/1986/4/Add.9 (1986); *Initial Reports Submitted by States Parties Under Articles 16 and 17 of the Covenant: Morocco*, U.N. ESCOR, Comm. on Econ., Soc. & Cult. Rts., ¶ 107, U.N. Doc. E/1990/5/Add.13 (1990).

36 *See 1987 Summary Record of the 19th Meeting, supra* note 28, ¶ 69 (question posed by Committee member to the Federal Republic of Germany). For reply of the representative of the Federal Republic of Germany, see *Summary Record of the 20th Meeting*, U.N. ESCOR, Comm. on Econ., Soc. & Cult. Rts., 1st Sess., ¶ 60, U.N. Doc. E/C.12/1987/SR.20 (1987). *See also Summary Record of the 6th Meeting*, U.N. ESCOR, Comm. on Econ., Soc. & Cult. Rts., 2d Sess., ¶ 54, U.N. Doc. E/C.12/1988/SR.6 (1988) (representative of Romania).

37 *Guidelines on Reporting, supra* note 22, at 104 qstns. 4(b)–(c).

38 Pursuant to the Guidelines, the provided data have to be desegregated by urban/rural. *Id.*

39 *See 1987 Summary Record of the 19th Meeting, supra* note 28, ¶ 44 (Committee member Mr. Alston regarding the Federal Republic of Germany).

40 *See Summary Record of the 9th Meeting*, U.N. ESCOR, Comm. on Econ., Soc. & Cult. Rts., 1st Sess., ¶ 30, U.N. Doc. E/C.12/1987/SR.9 (1987) (regarding the Ukrainian Soviet Socialist Republic); *Summary Record of the 10th Meeting*, U.N. ESCOR, Comm. on Econ., Soc. & Cult. Rts., 1st Sess., ¶¶ 4, 34, U.N. Doc. E/C.12/1987/SR.10 (1987). With regard to the measures taken by the Russian Republic, see *Summary Record of the 14th Meeting*, U.N. ESCOR, Comm. on Econ., Soc. & Cult. Rts., 16th Sess., ¶ 10, U.N. Doc. E/C.12/1997/SR.14 (1997) [hereinafter *1997 Summary Record of the 14th Meeting*].

41 *See, e.g., Concluding Observations of the Committee on Economic, Social and Cultural Rights*, U.N. ESCOR, Comm. on Econ., Soc. & Cult. Rts., ¶ 18, U.N. Doc. E/C.12/1995/12 (1995) (remark made by the Committee). *See also Concluding Observations of the Committee on Economic, Social and Cultural Rights: Russian Federation*, U.N. ESCOR, Comm. on Econ., Soc. & Cult. Rts., ¶ 18, U.N. Doc. E/C.12/1997/1/Add.13 (1997) [hereinafter *Concluding Observations: Russian Federation*].

42 *Guidelines on Reporting, supra* note 22, at 105. *See also List of Issues to be Taken Up in Connection with the Consideration of the Initial Report of Suriname Concerning the Rights Covered by Articles 1 to 15 of the International Covenant on Economic, Social and Cultural Rights (E/1990/5/Add.20)*, U.N. ESCOR, Comm. on Econ., Soc. & Cult. Rts., 11th Sess., U.N. Doc. E/C.12/1994/WP.14 (1994).

43 *See Guidelines on Reporting, supra* note 22, ¶ 4(f). *See also id.* ¶ 5(b)–(d), (i). Some countries admitted to an imbalance between rural and urban areas where access to medical services is concerned. *See Initial Reports Submitted by States Parties to the Covenant: Philippines*, U.N. ESCOR, Comm. on Econ., Soc. & Cult. Rts., ¶ 664, U.N. Doc. E/1986/3/Add.17 (1986); *Summary Record of the 7th Meeting*, U.N. ESCOR, Comm. on Econ., Soc. & Cult. Rts., 3d Sess., ¶ 47, U.N. Doc. E/C.12/1989/SR.7 (1989) (Representative of Cameroon) [hereinafter *1989 Summary Record of the 7th Meeting*].

44 *See Summary Record of the 16th Meeting*, U.N. ESCOR, Comm. on Econ., Soc. & Cult. Rts., 1st Sess., ¶ 14, U.N. Doc. E/C.12/1987/SR.16 (1987) (regarding the USSR) [hereinafter *1987 Summary Record of the 16th Meeting*]; *Summary Record of the 13th Meeting*, U.N. ESCOR, Comm. on Econ., Soc. & Cult. Rts., 4th Sess.,

¶ 46, U.N. Doc. E/C.12/1990/SR.13 (1990) (regarding Colombia) [hereinafter *1990 Summary Record of the 13th Meeting*]; *Summary Record of the 7th Meeting*, U.N. ESCOR, Comm. on Econ., Soc. & Cult. Rts., 6th Sess., ¶ 52, U.N. Doc. E/C.12/1991/SR.7 (1991) (regarding Syria). *See also Concluding Observations of the Committee on Economic, Social and Cultural Rights: Uruguay*, U.N. ESCOR, Comm. on Econ., Soc. & Cult. Rts., ¶ 12, U.N. Doc. E/C.12/1994/3 (1994). Finally, for a useful remark made by the Representative of Colombia, see *Summary Record of the 14th Meeting*, U.N. ESCOR, Comm. on Econ., Soc. & Cult. Rts., 4th Sess., ¶ 35, U.N. Doc. E/C.12/1990/SR.14 (1990) [hereinafter *1990 Summary Record of the 14th Meeting*].

45 Although prison inmates are not singled out as a specific category in the Guidelines, on some occasions Committee Members have asked questions about this subject matter. *See, e.g., 1997 Summary Record of the 14th Meeting, supra* note 40, ¶ 8 (Committee member Mr. Ceville). *See also Concluding Observations: Russian Federation, supra* note 41, ¶ 39; *1997 Summary Record of the 14th Meeting, supra* note 40, ¶ 13 (reply of the Russian Representative).

46 *See, e.g., Concluding Observations of the Committee on Economic, Social and Cultural Rights: Mali*, U.N. ESCOR, Comm. on Econ., Soc. & Cult. Rts., ¶ 13, U.N. Doc. E/C.12/1994/17 (1994) [hereinafter *Concluding Observations: Mali*]. *See also Initial Reports Submitted by States Parties to the Covenant: Uruguay*, U.N. ESCOR, Comm. on Econ., Soc. & Cult. Rts., ¶ 206, U.N. Doc. E/1990/5/ Add.7 (1990) [hereinafter *Initial Reports: Uruguay*]; *Initial Reports Submitted by States Parties to the Covenant: Suriname*, U.N. ESCOR, Comm. on Econ., Soc. & Cult. Rts., ¶ 109, U.N. Doc. E/1990/5/Add.20 (1990).

47 *See 1990 Summary Record of the 13th Meeting, supra* note 44, ¶ 17 (question on the list of issues for the Representative of Colombia).

48 *See Concluding Observations: Mali, supra* note 46, ¶ 14; *Concluding Observations of the Committee on Economic, Social and Cultural Rights: Gambia*, U.N. ESCOR, Comm. on Econ., Soc. & Cult. Rts., ¶ 16, U.N. Doc. E/C.12/1994/9 (1994). Mali and the Gambia have not submitted their initial report yet.

49 *Guidelines on Reporting, supra* note 22, at 104 qstns. 4(a), 4(d).

50 *Id.* at 105. *See also Report on the 12th and 13th Sessions*, U.N. ESCOR, Comm. on Econ., Soc. & Cult. Rts., Supp. 2, ¶¶ 34, 35, U.N. Doc. E/1996/22 (1996).

51 *See Summary Record of the 5th Meeting*, U.N. ESCOR, Comm. on Econ., Soc. & Cult. Rts., 4th Sess., ¶ 2, U.N. Doc. E/C.12/1990/SR.5 (1990) (Committee member Mr. Simma regarding Cyprus).

52 *See 1989 Summary Record of the 7th Meeting, supra* note 43, ¶ 56 (Representative of Cameroon noting an exception when the life of the mother is in danger); *1990 Summary Record of the 2nd Meeting, supra* note 25, ¶ 43 (representative of Cyprus noting an exception for medical reasons and in cases of rape); 1990 *Summary Record of the 37th Meeting, supra* note 31, ¶ 23 (representative from Ecuador noting an exception in cases where the mother's life could only be saved by an abortion and when the consent of the woman or her husband or close relatives was given, and in case of the rape of a mentally deficient woman). *See also 1990 Summary Record of the 38th Meeting, supra* note 31, ¶ 20 (containing remark that the Ecuadorian constitution went beyond the CRC in stipulating that the State safeguarded the child from the time of conception).

53 *See, e.g., Concluding Observations: Russian Federation, supra* note 41, ¶¶ 27, 40–41.

54 *See 1987 Summary Record of the 19th Meeting, supra* note 28, ¶ 52 (Representative of the Federal Republic of Germany regarding transit restrictions, which were imposed by the Bavarian State Government); *1997 Summary Record of the 14th Meeting, supra* note 40, ¶ 9 (Representative of the Russian Federation in

response to a question of Committee member Mr. Riedel); *Initial Reports: Uruguay, supra* note 46, ¶ 207(g) (regarding mandatory testing).

55 *See 1990 Summary Record of the 14th Meeting, supra* note 44, ¶ 51 (Committee member Mr. Texier regarding Colombia).

56 *See 1987 Summary Record of the 16th Meeting, supra* note 44, ¶ 16 (Committee member Ms. Taya regarding the USSR).

57 *See 1997 Summary Record of the 14th Meeting, supra* note 40, ¶ 6 (Committee member Mr. Ceausu regarding the Russian Republic). *See also 1987 Summary Record of the 16th Meeting, supra* note 44, ¶ 38 (Committee member Mr. Muterahejuru regarding the former USSR).

58 The first case involved aerial fumigation programs carried out jointly by Guatemala and the United States. *See* Melissa Thorme, *Establishing Environment as a Human Right,* 19 DENVER J. INT'L L. & POL'Y 305, 306 (1991). The second case challenged a proposal by a US oil company to build an access road in Yasuni National Park in Ecuador. *See* Beth Gammie, *Human Rights Implications of the Export of Banned Pesticides,* 25 SETON HALL L. REV. 558, 611–12 (1994). The Sub-Committee responded to these interventions by adopting a draft decision on the subject of the environment and its relation to human rights at the end of the session and by appointing Mrs. Fatma Ksentini as a Special Rapporteur to monitor the relation between the environment and human rights. *See Final Report Prepared by Mrs. Fatma Zohra Ksentini, Special Rapporteur,* Comm'n on Hum. Rts., 46th Sess., ¶¶ 176–80, U.N. Doc. E/CN.4/Sub.2/1994/9 (1994).

59 International Court of Justice, *Legality of the Use by a State of Nuclear Weapons in Armed Conflict,* Request for an Advisory Opinion, 13 Sept. 1993, General List No. 93 (based on WHO Resolution 46/40 of 14 May 1993). *See also* Virginia A. Leary, *The Right to Complain: The Right to Health, in* THE RIGHT TO COMPLAIN ABOUT ECONOMIC, SOCIAL AND CULTURAL RIGHTS 87 (A.P.M. Coomans & G.J.H. van Hoof eds., 1995).

60 Inspection Panel of the International Bank for Reconstruction and Development and International Development Association ("The World Bank Inspection Panel"), International Bank for Construction and Development Res. 93-10, International Development Association Res. 93-6 (1993). *See* Daniel D. Bradlow, *International Organizations and Private Complaints: The Case of the World Bank Inspection Panel,* 34 VA. J. INT'L L. 553 (1994). *See, e.g.,* World Bank Inspection Panel, Nepal: Arun III, Recommendation sent to the Executive Directors, 16 Dec. 1994; World Bank Inspection Panel, Nepal: Arun III, Investigation Report: Proposed Hydroelectric Project & Restructuring of IDA Credit-2029, Summary sent to the Executive Directors, 21 June 1995.

61 African Charter on Human and Peoples' Rights, art. 16, *adopted* 26 June 1981, O.A.U. Doc. CAB/LEG/67/3 Rev. 5 (*entered into force* 21 Oct. 1986), *reprinted in* 21 I.L.M. 58 (1982).

62 A communication has recently been submitted to the African Commission by two nongovernmental organizations regarding the actions of the Nigerian Government involving the "widespread contamination, the destruction of homes, the burning of crops and killing of farm animals and the climate of terror visited upon the Ogoni communities." The communication bases its complaint on the alleged violations of the right to health in Article 16 of the African Charter, Article 12 of the ICESCR, Article 24 of the CRC, and Article 12 of CEDAW. The communication was submitted by the Social and Economic Rights Action Center (SERAC) in Lagos and the Center for Economic and Social Rights (CESR) in New York (date unknown). During its 22nd session held in Banjul, The Gambia, from 2–11 November 1997, the African Commission was unable to take a decision on the merits.

63 Protocol of San Salvador, *supra* note 9.

64 American Declaration of the Rights and Duties of Man, *signed* 2 May 1948, OEA/Ser.L/V/II.71, at 1 7 (1988), *reprinted in* BASIC DOCUMENTS ON HUMAN RIGHTS 488 (Ian Brownlie ed., 3rd ed. 1993).

65 *See* Case 7615, Inter-Am. C.H.R. 12/85, O.A.S. Doc. OEA/Ser.L/V/II.83, doc. 14, corr. 1, at 33, ¶ 1 (1985).

66 *See id.* at 33, ¶ 3(a), (c).

67 Additional Protocol to the European Social Charter Providing for a System of Collective Complaints, *opened for signature* 9 Nov. 1995, Europ. T.S. No. 158 (*entered into force* 1 July 1998), *reprinted in* 34 I.L.M. 1453 (1995); *Social Rights = Human Rights*, NEWSL. ON EUR. SOC. CHARTER (Council of Eur., Strasbourg, France), Sept. 1996. *See also* R. Brillat, *A New Protocol to the European Social Charter Providing for Collective Complaints*, 1 EUR. HUM. RTS. L. REV. 52 (1996); A. W. Heringa, *The European Social Charter: New Initiatives for the Improvement of Basic Social Rights Protection Within the Framework of the Council of Europe*, *in* THE INCREASING IMPORTANCE OF ECONOMIC, SOCIAL AND CULTURAL RIGHTS 30 (A.P.M. Coomans et al. eds., 1994). A first complaint has been submitted by the International Commission of Jurists concerning the alleged violation of Article 7(1) of the ESC (minimum age of admission to employment) by Portugal. The Complaint was declared admissible. See Complaint No. 1/1998, Eur. Comm'n Soc. Rts. (Decision on Admissibility, 12 Oct. 1998).

68 Constitutional Court, *Judgment No. T-505 of 28 August 1992, in* 21 REVISTA MENSUAL, JURISPRUDENCE Y DOCTRINA 1101 (1992).

69 *See id.*

70 Minors Oposa v. Factoran [1993] Supreme Court of Philipines, G.R. No. 101083, *reprinted in* 33 I.L.M. 173 (1994).

71 PHIL. CONST. art. II, §§ 15–16.

72 *See* Leary, *supra* note 59, at 116.

73 Hendrika S. Vos v. The Netherlands, Communication No. 218/1986, *adopted* 29 Mar. 1989, U.N. GAOR, Hum. Rts. Comm., 44th Sess., Supp. No. 40, at 232, U.N. Doc. A/44/40 (1989).

74 *See id.* at 232–40. *See also* F. H. Zwaan-de Vries v. The Netherlands, Communication No. 182/1984, *adopted* 9 Apr. 1987, U.N. GAOR, Hum. Rts. Comm., 42d Sess., Supp. No. 40, at 160, U.N. Doc. A/42/40 (1987), *reprinted in* 2 Selected Decisions of the Human Rights Committee under the Optional Protocol 213, U.N. Doc. CCPR/C/OP/2 (1990). This case involved Article 26 of the ICCPR and discrimination with regard to unemployment benefits. It referred to Article 9 of the ICESCR. *See also* Leary, *supra* note 59, at 116. *See also* Feldbrugge v. The Netherlands, 99 Eur. Ct. H.R. (ser. A) at 16–18 (1986), *reprinted in* 7 HUM. RTS. L.J. 353 (1986) (on the right to a fair trial in Article 6 ECHR and the right to a sickness allowance); Leary, *supra* note 6, at 96–97.

75 *See* Samity v. State of West Bengal, A.I.R. 1996 S.C. 2426, 2429 (India). The claimant had suffered serious head injuries and brain hemorrhage as a result of having fallen off a train.

76 *Id.*

77 López Ostra v. Spain, 303 Eur. Ct. H.R. (ser. A) at 41, 47 (1995).

78 *Id.* at 54.

79 *Id.* at 55–56. Concerning the right to the disclosure of health information and Article 8 of the ECHR, see Anna Maria Guerra and 39 Others v. Italy, Rep. J. & Dec. 1998-I (Eur. Ct. H.R.) (*decided* 19 Feb. 1998); McGinley and Egan v. the United Kingdom, Rep. J. & Dec. 1998-III (Eur. Ct. H.R.) (*decided* 9 June 1998); L.C.B. v. the United Kingdom, Rep. J. & Dec. 1998-III (Eur. Ct. H.R.) (*decided* 9 June 1998).

80 *See* A.P.M. Coomans, *Clarifying the Core Elements of the Right to Education, in* THE RIGHT TO COMPLAIN ABOUT ECONOMIC, SOCIAL AND CULTURAL RIGHTS, *supra* note 59, at 17.

81 Article 2(1) of the ICESCR allows state parties to realize the rights set forth in the Covenant "progressively." ICESCR, *supra* note 9, art. 2(1).

82 *See Guidelines on Reporting, supra* note 22, ¶ 7. *See also* Coomans, *supra* note 80.

83 *See* WORLD HEALTH ORGANIZATION, PRIMARY HEALTH CARE: REPORT OF THE INTERNATIONAL CONFERENCE ON PRIMARY HEALTH CARE, ALMA ATA CONFERENCE, USSR, 6–12 SEPTEMBER 1978 (1978).

84 This typology was developed by Henry Shue. *See* HENRY SHUE, BASIC RIGHTS, SUBSISTENCE, AFFLUENCE AND U.S. FOREIGN POLICY (1980). Later, it was further developed by Eide. See *The New International Economic Order and the Promotion of Human Rights*, Comm'n on Hum. Rts., 39th Sess., UN Doc. E/CN.4/Sub.2/1987/23 (1987). *See also* C. J. H. van Hoof, *The Legal Nature of Economic, Social and Cultural Rights: A Rebuttal of Some Traditional Views, in* THE RIGHT TO FOOD 97 (Philip Alston & Katarina Tomaševski eds., 1984) (dividing the fourth obligation to fulfill into obligations to "ensure" and to "promote").

85 Examples of cases include López Ostra, *supra* note 77; Minors Oposa, *supra* note 70; and Yanomani, *supra* note 65.

86 *See* Constitutional Court, *supra* note 68.

87 For example, the request of WHO for an Advisory Opinion of the ICJ concerned states' negative obligation to refrain from the use of nuclear weapons. *See* International Court of Justice, *supra* note 59.

88 *See* Craig Scott & Patrick Macklem, *Constitutional Ropes of Sand or Justiciable Guarantees?: Social Rights in a New South African Constitution*, 141 U. PA. L. REV. 1, 17 (1992).

THE PROLIFERATION OF HUMAN RIGHTS IN GLOBAL HEALTH GOVERNANCE

Lance Gable

Source: *Journal of Law, Medicine & Ethics* (Winter, 2007), 534–44.

As our world becomes increasingly interconnected, threats to global public health continue to proliferate. New and novel risks to health have emerged consistently over the past 30 years.[1] Moreover, our shrinking world now allows health threats to spread more quickly than ever before.[2] Given these realities, efforts to protect and improve global health must be expansive, flexible, and able to take into account the variety of circumstances that may imperil good health. These efforts also must consider the multiple levels and varying contexts in which laws, policies, and other factors govern global health and affect health outcomes.

Human rights play an integral, and perhaps underappreciated, role in the global governance of health. Indeed, the continued proliferation of human rights in many settings has resulted in the expanded application of human rights in global health governance. This symposium on global health law provides an excellent opportunity to explore the ways in which human rights contribute to global health governance. Governance has been well-defined elsewhere as "the management of the course of events in a system."[3] In the context of global health, governance involves the structural and normative aspects of managing the determinants and outcomes of global health.

The existing structural and normative components of human rights have continually evolved over time, resulting in a broader and more expansive conception of human rights as applied to health, particularly when compared with older understandings. More recently, however, the application of human rights to health has begun to proliferate at an even greater rate across multiple levels and within multiple contexts. Human rights proliferation is likely to have a positive impact on the governance of global health because it can expand the avenues through which a human rights framework or human rights norms may be used to address and improve health.

This article first describes two types of governance where health and human rights overlap in multiple systems and contexts around the world. Next, the article uses a case study to assess the structural and normative proliferation of human rights in the context of the new United Nations Convention on the Rights of Persons with Disabilities. Finally, I offer several observations about the potential implications of human rights proliferation on the future of global health governance, while recognizing the inherent interdependency of approaches to governance.

Part I. Structural and normative aspects of human rights governance

The human rights paradigm is powerful because it is simultaneously global and individualistic. Under human rights theory, individuals possess a universal claim to certain rights regardless of their nationality, location, or health status. Human rights transcend normal state sovereignty and impose obligations on states to respect, protect, and fulfill the human rights of all persons.[4] The human rights paradigm, therefore, provides a compelling approach to understanding and protecting health from both global and local perspectives. Jonathan Mann, Larry Gostin, and their colleagues famously framed the connection between health and human rights as an "inextricable linkage."[5] The model linking health and human rights, based on Mann's work of applying human rights to combat HIV/AIDS during his time at the World Health Organization, recognized that efforts to enforce human rights were synergistic with efforts to improve health in most cases.[6] Without good health, people may have great difficulty advocating for and benefiting from their human rights. Without adequate human rights protections, harmful conditions and practices that undermine health may persist. Thus the advancement of health and human rights can and should occur contemporaneously.[7] It is important to note that the intersection of human rights and health goes beyond the right to health and implicates a number of other rights (life, liberty, judicial redress, privacy, education, etc.) that have an impact on the ability of a person to achieve good health.

The interaction of health and human rights depends on structural and normative components that comprise human rights systems and applications. The structural and normative components of human rights as applied to health are derived from essentially the same sources, but serve different functions. Structural components control where rights are found and how they are applied and enforced. Normative components, by contrast, confer substance to human rights, influencing the content and context of rights – in other words, determining to whom rights apply and under what circumstances. As these structural and normative components have evolved over time, the relationship between human rights and health governance has similarly progressed.

The structural aspects of human rights can be defined as the institutions or mechanisms in place at the international, regional, national, local, and nongovernmental levels that allow for the protection and fulfillment of human rights. Structural human rights institutions include international human rights monitoring bodies, regional human rights commissions and courts, and national oversight mechanisms, whether judicial, administrative, or otherwise. Structural components of human rights also can exist within non-institutional and non-governmental settings. For example, many non-governmental organizations (NGOs), civil society organizations, and policy programs incorporate a human rights approach in their efforts to improve health. Altogether, the structural aspects of human rights can facilitate the recognition of human rights in the context of health; establish the procedural and jurisdictional contours of monitoring, oversight, and enforcement that uphold these rights; and delineate specific mechanisms to support and uphold human rights that affect health.

The normative components of human rights also may affect the relationship between health and human rights. I define the normative aspects of human rights as the substantive content, scope, and applicability of human rights principles. Human rights norms include the substantive rights set out in international and regional human rights systems and national laws, as well as the interpretive understandings of these rights that subsequently have been developed in multiple fora. Normative development can occur through the enactment of new human rights frameworks, the promulgation of standards and explanatory guidance, the decisions of courts, or the practical interpretation and implementation of rights. This suggests that human rights norm development related to health can be undertaken by a multitude of actors, some with greater influence than others. While the normative content of human rights related to health certainly has not reached universal consensus, the proliferation of normative interpretations within multiple systems and contexts potentially could have a cumulative and reiterative effect. Additionally, normative interpretations in one system may influence other systems, resulting in a harmonization or equivalency across jurisdictions of human rights norms relevant to health.[8]

The structural and normative aspects of human rights manifest themselves at many levels and in various contexts. Thus, it is useful to categorize the human rights governance of health into two groups: (1) formal human rights regimes that impact health and (2) health institutions, mechanisms, or actors that adopt a human rights paradigm.

Formal human rights regimes

Formal human rights regimes exist on the international, regional, and national levels. These regimes are complex and evolving, encompassing multiple, overlapping human rights frameworks and numerous interpretations of human rights at each level. Formal regimes are often hierarchical and premised on agreements or frameworks based in law. The structure of these human rights frameworks dictates the scope and applicability of human rights in a particular jurisdiction, as well as the methods of oversight and enforcement of human rights. A variety of legal sources may govern human rights within these frameworks, including treaties, legislation, regulations, and case law.

The United Nations human rights system

At the international level, the United Nations human rights system arose 60 years ago in the aftermath of World War II. This system – comprised of conventions, declarations, recommendations, and guidelines – has established an extensive international legal regime that binds signatory states. Three general human rights instruments form the foundation of the United Nations system: the Universal Declaration of Human Rights (UDHR),[9] the International Covenant on Civil and Political Rights (ICCPR),[10] and the International Covenant on Economic, Social and Cultural Rights (ICESCR).[11] The UDHR, adopted in 1948, enumerates the fundamental human rights applicable to all persons and contains a broad assortment of human rights. Some of these rights include the right to life, liberty, and security of person; the prohibition of torture and cruel, inhuman and degrading treatment; the prohibition of arbitrary arrest and detention; freedom of movement; the right to participate in government; and the right to a standard of living adequate for health and well-being.[12] While the UDHR laid the groundwork for all subsequent human rights treaties, it does not legally bind member states or provide mechanisms to enforce the rights it incorporates, although some have argued that the UDHR may be considered universally binding under customary international law.[13]

The subsequent enactment of the ICCPR[14] and the ICESCR[15] advanced the structural and normative evolution of human rights. The Covenants, which came into force in 1977, have been widely ratified and bolster the structural aspects of human rights by providing a legally binding framework. States parties who fail to comply with enumerated rights may face rebuke from oversight committees established under the Covenants. The Covenants also expand the normative context of human rights as applied to health, articulating these rights in more detail than the UDHR. For instance, the ICESCR requires states to uphold "the right of everyone to the enjoyment of the highest attainable standard of physical and mental health."[16]

Additional human rights conventions have been enacted under the United Nations system to protect the rights of racial minorities,[17] women,[18] children,[19] victims of torture or other cruel, inhuman, or degrading treatment,[20] migrants, and most recently, persons with disabilities.[21] Each of these conventions expanded the human rights protections applicable to these specific groups beyond those offered in the International Covenants. In essence, these topical human rights conventions add to the structural protections available to covered groups through the creation of new oversight mechanisms and enforcement bodies, which could serve as alternative venues for protecting human rights. Furthermore, each convention contributes to the normative development of human rights, within its specific contexts, by more clearly rendering the contours of these rights.

Beyond international conventions, the United Nations system has also generated significant guidance regarding the application of human rights to health through other instruments, such as declarations, explanations, reports, resolutions, general comments, and other guidance materials. For example, the United Nations system has promulgated declarations on the rights of mentally retarded[22] and disabled[23] persons. These Declarations enunciate a specific interest in applying human rights protections to these groups. The Committee on Economic, Social, and Cultural Rights (CESCR) formed by the ICESCR has drafted a series of General Comments to develop the normative content of the rights in the ICESCR. General Comment 14, which addresses the right to health, conceives of an expansive right to health that encompasses individual and population health services and efforts to improve the determinants of health.[24] The United Nations also has appointed Special Rapporteurs to study disability issues[25] and the right to health.[26]

These examples provide further evidence of the structural and normative development of human rights by the United Nations system. The CESCR – a structural institution created by international treaty – drafted General Comment 14, which in turn provided the conceptual, normative explication of the right to health contained in Article 12 of the ICESCR. Likewise, the appointment of a Special Rapporteur on the right to health is an example of an institutional position being created through structural mechanisms, with the explicit objective of defining the normative contours of the right to health. The Rapporteurs have helped to develop practical understandings of human rights in the context of health. For example, Paul Hunt, the current Special Rapporteur on health, has created a more thorough and persuasive explication of the scope of the right to health through his investigations and reports.[27]

Taken together, these developments and other related efforts demonstrate a multilayered and evolving structural and normative framework for health and human rights in the United Nations system. However, this system has significant shortcomings with regard to human rights interpretation and enforcement. The covenants and conventions establish legally binding rights and discrete monitoring bodies to oversee state compliance with human rights obligations, yet individuals cannot bring specific human rights claims before these bodies for consideration, adjudication, or redress under many of these systems (although some conventions have taken steps to recognize individual claims).[28] Moreover, the sanctions available to monitoring committees are scant: they may issue scathing indictments of a state's rights violations, but they cannot directly force changes in law or policy. Not all states have signed and ratified these treaties, and even those that have done so may not comply with their obligations. In addition, these systems are charged with the monumental task of protecting human rights around the world, a prospect that goes beyond the capabilities of organizations with relatively modest funding and staffing and minimal enforcement powers. The drafting of declarations and guidance principles serves a role in building a consensus for rights and providing explanations and persuasive guidelines, but as "soft law," these guidelines and principles do not legally bind states or enable any direct oversight to ensure state compliance in a way that protects or improves health.[29] Given these shortcomings, it is imperative that proponents of human rights systems engage in efforts to collect empirical data regarding their effectiveness and replicate models that are shown to be effective in implementation.

Regional human rights systems

Three regional human rights systems have been created, including one in Europe, the Americas, and Africa, respectively. These regional systems also utilize international agreements (conventions and treaties) and interpretive standards (declarations, recommendations, guidelines) to delineate human rights. Regional human rights systems differ from the United Nations in two significant ways. First, compared with the United Nations system that includes most of the world, the regional systems cover only certain countries, and therefore their application is limited to those countries. Second, while the regional systems exist based upon international human rights agreements[30] that contain many of the same human rights as the United Nations system, the regional systems are structurally quite different from the United Nations system. The regional systems establish stronger mechanisms for oversight and enforcement of human rights. All three systems have created adjudicatory bodies (commissions or courts) that provide for judicial oversight and allow individuals or groups to bring claims directly to the commissions or courts.[31] Consequentially, regional systems have had more success in enforcing human rights through binding court decisions that may directly sanction governments for violations.

Regional human rights commissions and courts serve both structural and normative purposes. The judicial processes create a structural mechanism for individuals to directly seek redress for violations of their human rights. The reports and decisions of these judicial bodies interpret and apply the human rights implicated in a case, and therefore contribute to the normative development of case law interpreting human rights. For example, the European human rights system in particular has created an extensive body of case law precedent addressing health issues, including rulings upholding clear human rights protections for persons with disabilities.[32] In addition, regional human rights systems occasionally have been receptive to incorporating human rights standards and precedents from other systems.[33] For example, in the case of *Victor Rosario Congo v. Ecuador*, the Inter-American Commission on Human Rights favorably cited precedents and interpretations from the United Nations System and the European Human Rights System.[34]

However, regional systems have limitations because the systems apply only to specific countries. Thus, the application of human rights under these systems is confined to these countries, and not to some parts of the world, such as Asia and the Middle East, that do not have a regional human rights system. Moreover, despite the judicial mechanisms present in these systems, human rights enforcement is still subject to national acquiescence.

National human rights laws

The integration of human rights norms into national laws is an important strategy for protecting health through human rights. From a structural perspective, national laws typically are more enforceable and more accessible than international treaties. Violations of national human rights laws may be addressed directly by national level judicial enforcement or other interventions. National level provisions can advance the normative content of human rights by developing more detailed laws and policies to implement rights in the context of health.

Human rights related to health may find their way into national law through constitutional provisions, national health or disability legislation, or the incorporation of international human rights standards into national law. First, many countries protect human rights through constitutional or legislative provisions that guarantee basic rights and fundamental freedoms. For example, the United States Constitution guarantees many civil and political rights such as rights to a fair trial,[35] personal liberty,[36] and due process and equal protection under the law.[37] South Africa and Brazil, for instance, also provide constitutional protection for economic, social, and cultural rights, including rights to education[38] and health.[39]

Second, some countries have incorporated human rights norms into national health laws or disability legislation. Disability rights legislation, which has been promulgated in approximately 40 countries, provides the emblematic example of this approach. Quite a few national disability rights laws use a human rights approach;[40] the Americans with Disabilities Act (ADA), passed in the United States in 1990, is one of them.[41] The ADA incorporates many human rights principles, including prohibiting discrimination against persons with disabilities and facilitating reasonable accommodations to allow full participation in employment and other areas of public life.[42] The United States Supreme Court has narrowed its interpretation of the ADA in recent years and defendants have won a substantial majority of disability discrimination cases, leading to scrutiny of the ADA's effectiveness as a statute protecting persons with disabilities from discrimination.[43] However, empirical research has suggested that the disability protections prescribed by the ADA do influence employers to make reasonable accommodations for their employees in many situations.[44] Additionally, the disability rights approach first articulated in the ADA continues to influence other national disability rights laws, with approximately 40 other states subsequently adopting some of its structural and normative provisions.[45]

Finally, some national governments have adopted international human rights standards directly into national law. The Human Rights Act of 1998 in the United Kingdom, for instance, incorporated the decisions of the European Court of Human Rights into national law.[46] While residents of the U.K. previously could bring human rights claims directly under the European human rights system, the passage of the Human Rights Act allowed challenges in U.K. courts based on the European system's human rights norms and decisions. Pursuant to this Act, for example, psychiatric patients have been able to challenge their confinement under U.K. law, using the precedents of the European Court of Human Rights.[47]

At the national level, however, human rights are not ubiquitous, especially in the context of health. Many countries have not incorporated human rights provisions or norms into their national laws and policies. Even when countries recognize human rights provisions in national law, it does not always translate into enforcement of human rights in the context of health. Countries with broad constitutional and legislative protections for human rights may not enforce these rights until challenged by individuals or groups in society. In South Africa, despite broad constitutional provisions protecting the right to health, it took substantial pressure from civil society groups and a legal decision by the Supreme Constitutional Court to force the government to provide pregnant women with access to anti-retroviral treatment to prevent mother to child transmission of HIV.[48]

Health organizations that adopt human rights

The proliferation of human rights extends beyond the international and regional human rights systems and national efforts to incorporate human rights into law. A second major category of human rights governance related to health involves health institutions, mechanisms, and actors that adopt human rights principles or methods. This category encompasses a wide variety of organizations, from international health institutions to non-state actors in the public and private sectors. The following illustrates the common threads between these organizations: (1) they are not created pursuant to human rights laws or agreements; (2) they directly or indirectly influence health; and (3) they explicitly or impliedly use human rights methods or norms to achieve their objectives. Thus, the category is broad enough to include international institutions such as the World Health Organization

(WHO), World Bank, and Pan American Health Organization (PAHO); NGOs such as Human Rights Watch and Mental Disability Rights International (MDRI); and public health organizations at the national level. I will discuss separately the international organizations and the other non-state actors.

International and regional organizations

International organizations play an increasingly vital role in making law.[49] In addition, several prominent international organizations, besides the formal human rights institutions, have a significant impact on health. Many of these organizations have adopted the language and methods of human rights to assist in their health-related objectives. The inclusion of human rights in multiple United Nations documents outside of the traditional human rights structure, on behalf of official efforts to mainstream human rights in the United Nations, has been an important catalyst.[50]

Notably, the WHO, the primary health agency in the United Nations system, has embraced the human rights model for addressing a number of health concerns.[51] Although human rights are referenced in older WHO documents (including the 1948 WHO Constitution),[52] the meaningful incorporation of specific human rights structures and norms into WHO programs and guidance documents is a more recent development. The most recent Global Programme of Work, which plans health strategy for WHO for the next ten years, uses a human rights model and demonstrates a commitment by WHO to the linkage between health and human rights.[53] Recent initiatives have explicitly invoked a human rights strategy in programs targeted at mental disability.[54]

WHO's newly adopted version of the International Health Regulations (IHRs) provide another prominent example of the incorporation of human rights principles into health governance document.[55] Countries subject to the IHRs must coordinate efforts to stop the spread of public health emergencies of international concern.[56] In implementing the IHRs, countries are required to ensure "full respect for the dignity, human rights and fundamental freedoms of persons" and "shall treat travelers with respect for their dignity, human rights and fundamental freedoms and minimize any discomfort or distress associated with such measures [taken to prevent the spread of disease]."[57] The inclusion of human rights language in the IHRs, however cursory, recognizes the importance of human rights considerations in health governance and helps to further solidify the connection between health and human rights.[58]

Other international, regional, and national entities have embraced human rights norms in both broad and targeted health initiatives. At the international level, organizations such as the United Nations Joint Programme on HIV/ AIDS (UNAIDS) and United Nations Development Program (UNDP) have recognized the impact of human rights on health and have explicitly adopted human rights norms into their health strategies and policy guidance.[59] Likewise, PAHO has long advocated the inclusion of human rights in regional and national efforts in the Americas.[60] This concern has translated into numerous efforts by PAHO to expand the normative connection between health and human rights. For example, the Montreal Declaration on Intellectual Disabilities, drafted in 2004 by PAHO and a number of partners, is a broad statement of support for human rights of persons with intellectual disabilities: it reaffirms that these persons possess the same rights and freedoms as all other human beings while promoting openness and non-stigmatization.[61] Although this declaration is not legally binding, it represents yet another instance of human rights norm development by health institutions and their partners. PAHO has recently embarked on an ambitious human rights education and training program in the Americas as well.[62]

Other non-state actors

Non-state actors are entities that often use the language and orientation of human rights to advance health. These entities were not included in the traditional paradigm of international human rights law. Scholars have described this traditional model as "Westphalian," based on the 1648 Peace of Westphalia that first solidified a state-based approach to international law.[63] The increasing participation of non-state actors in health governance has precipitated an emerging post-Westphalian model in which human rights norms have been advanced globally by NGOs, charitable funders, private businesses, and other non-state actors.[64]

Human rights have increasingly appeared in multiple contexts, including outside traditional legal structures. The inclusion of human rights models or norms in programs run by NGOs or local health organizations spreads the impact of human rights into new settings. These entities typically have the most impact in discrete locations where they provide health services, education, or financial support. For example, organizations such as Physicians for Human Rights expressly use human rights models to achieve improvements in health, especially in developing countries.[65] Other organizations such as Human Rights Watch generally are not focused on health issues, but occasionally have used their human rights expertise to highlight health concerns such as HIV/AIDS.[66] The efforts of these organizations often provide advocacy for improving the structural enforcement of human rights at the local or national levels to achieve better health. The reports issued by these organizations also may advance the normative interpretation of human rights related to health by documenting violations and explaining the applicability of human rights obligations. These efforts are obviously not legally binding, but they may increase pressure on governments to remedy human rights violations. Another vital human rights intervention furthered by advocacy organizations is assisting individuals in bringing human rights cases in front of national courts or regional human rights bodies. MDRI has an excellent track record of advocacy for the human rights of persons with mental disabilities in the Americas[67] and Central Europe.[68] In one case, for example, MDRI was able to utilize the threat of litigation in front of the Inter-American Court of Human Rights to encourage the Paraguayan government to change their policies and procedures in a psychiatric hospital to comply with human rights principles.[69]

As human rights have helped inform the goals and strategies of non-state actors, these actors have likewise played an increasingly prominent role in influencing the development of human rights structures and norms that impact health. NGOs and other non-state actors were heavily involved in the recent negotiations and drafting of international instruments, including the Framework Convention on Tobacco Control[70] and the United Nations Convention on the Rights of Persons with Disabilities (CRPD).[71] During the drafting of CRPD, NGOs and other specialized organizations participated in the process and the negotiations, along with state representatives.[72] The heightened prominence of non-state actors in international and national fora facilitates the inclusion of health perspectives into the human rights debate, advancing the development of human rights norms in the process.[73]

Part II. Structural and normative proliferation of human rights in the context of health: the U.N. Convention on the Rights of Persons with Disabilities

The structural and normative developments of human rights in the context of health often have progressed in tandem. The creation of new structural frameworks to protect human rights has resulted in the explication of the normative content of these newly articulated rights. Likewise, the need to explain and apply human rights norms across a variety of situations has fostered the expansion and utilization of existing and new human rights frameworks at all levels.

The newly drafted United Nations Convention on the Rights of Persons with Disabilities (CRPD) provides an interesting case study for examining how the human rights model can support health governance.[74] CRPD – which was finalized in late 2006 and opened for signature on March 30, 2007 – creates a new human rights framework, establishing stronger protections for persons with physical, mental, and intellectual disabilities. For many years, the human rights of persons with disabilities have been seriously neglected around the world. This treaty represents the culmination of many years of negotiations at the international level by multiple parties. The resulting convention provides an important extension of human rights as applied to persons with disabilities. The CRPD exemplifies the potential impact of human rights proliferation in the context of health through structural augmentation and normative development. The following section explores these developments and their possible impact on health governance in light of this convention.

Structural augmentation

As described above, the structural frameworks available for protecting human rights in the context of health have expanded substantially over the years. This structural evolution of international human rights law has changed the legal landscape available for protecting the rights of persons with mental and intellectual disabilities.

The newly drafted CRPD represents the most significant recent structural augmentation of health and human rights at the international level. The Convention includes several structural innovations that support the newly articulated rights. First, the enactment of the Convention is itself a structural augmentation. It explicitly recognizes the importance of the human rights of persons with disabilities in a distinct international legal instrument, and it creates obligations for signing states "to promote, protect, and ensure the full and equal enjoyment" of these rights.[75] Article 34 of the Convention provides for the creation of a standing committee with monitoring and oversight responsibilities.[76] Signatory states must set up their own monitoring bodies and compile reports to the international committee detailing their compliance with the terms of the Convention.[77] The international committee is also required to collect statistics and data on violations of the Convention.[78] The Convention requires states to seek close consultation and active involvement by persons with disabilities in the development and implementation of the rights established by the Convention, although it is not clear what level of consultation is required.[79] An Optional Protocol, if enacted, would permit individuals or groups to claim violations directly to the committee.[80] Each of these structural innovations contributes to a more substantial recognition of the importance of health and human rights, and establishes systems and mechanisms to protect and fulfill these rights.

Normative development

The promulgation of the CRPD also contributes to the normative development of human rights in the health context. The Convention develops the normative content and subsequent application of many fundamental human rights as they apply to persons with disabilities. This recognition of these rights at the treaty level does more than create new obligations or monitoring mechanisms; it also advances the recognition of human rights as they apply to persons with disabilities, essentially expanding the normative scope of these rights through their inclusion in the Convention.

The CRPD expounds a broad definition of disability,[81] and then sets out a long list of specific substantive rights, which include the following: guarantees of equality and non-discrimination, accessibility, and rights to life; equal recognition before the law; access to justice; and liberty and security of person.[82] The Convention also protects fundamental rights, such as freedom from torture and cruel, inhuman or degrading treatment or punishment; freedom from exploitation, violence, and abuse; as well as freedom of expression, opinion, and access to information.[83] The integrity of the person; liberty of movement and nationality; the right to live independently, community inclusion; and personal mobility are all covered, as well as respect for privacy, home, and the family.[84] Also protected are rights to education; health; habitation and rehabilitation; work and employment; an adequate standard of living and social protection; and participation in political, public, and cultural life, as well as recreation, leisure, and sport.[85] This extensive list of rights reflects, but is not identical to, similar rights included in previous international human rights conventions. Nevertheless, the reiteration of these rights in this convention solidifies the link between longstanding human rights principles and their application to persons with disabilities. The language of the convention frames the rights in context and the structure of the convention facilitates further development of these rights over time.

Impact on health

The structural and normative provisions of the CRPD represent an ambitious effort to expand human rights protections for persons with disabilities at an international level. Consequently, the CRPD presents both opportunities and challenges. International conventions can be extremely influential in establishing consensus and proliferating new norms and practices throughout the world. Nevertheless, conventions have inherent limitations due to their structural lack of legal enforceability and need for normative generalization. Within the context of the CRPD, advocates will have stronger tools and arguments to advance the human lights of persons with disabilities. However, it is too soon to predict whether the new Convention will have a measurable impact on the daily lives or health of persons with disabilities. Even if the treaty is widely ratified, which initial indications support, different states will incorporate disability rights norms into practice with varying rapidity and effectiveness. Often the acculturation of new lights into a state's law and practice takes time.[86] Some commentators have expressed skepticism at the likelihood that the Convention will attain sufficient international consensus to be enforceable[87] while others remain more optimistic about the eventual effectiveness of the Convention's oversight mechanisms.[88] Other observers have questioned whether the normative guidance granted by the CRPD is detailed enough to achieve universal standards.[89] Some countries, such as the United States, will almost certainly not ratify the treaty. However, even without universal ratification, widespread adoption of the norms advanced may still be possible. Ultimately, the effectiveness of this disability rights paradigm will hinge on a multitude of factors, including the extent of the recognition of the link between human rights, disability, and health.[90]

Admittedly, the impact that the CRPD will have on health is impossible to predict prospectively so assessments above are largely conceptual. It is therefore imperative to continue to collect empirical information on the link between health and human rights and to monitor the effect that the structural and normative components of the CRPD have on the lives of persons with disabilities going forward. Only with such data will we be able to definitively assess the influence of the CRPD.

Implications of the proliferation of human rights in the context of global health: a future agenda

Sorting through the intricacies of global health governance suggests two interrelated conclusions. First, no ideal, singular method of global health governance exists, so multilevel governance is inevitable and necessary. Threats to global public health come in many varieties and often require the coordinated efforts of many actors including governments, international organizations, non-governmental organizations, and private organizations. Since a multiplicity of actors and structures from the global to local levels may exert influence on public health outcomes, multilevel and compatible health governance is vital to good health outcomes, even when a coordinated effort is not required. Second, the proliferation of the structural and normative aspects of human rights throughout these multiple levels creates important opportunities to use human rights to improve health governance. Multilevel human rights governance may actually result in better health outcomes due to expanded opportunities for interventions to protect and improve health, although this conclusion will require more evaluation of empirical evidence of the link between human rights and health governance. The multiple options created by the redundancy in these systems may be particularly helpful in countries that are reluctant to comply with human rights systems at one or more of levels.

In order to adequately assess the ultimate impact of human rights on health governance, several problematic areas demand further attention and study. First, determining the effects of human rights on health requires sophisticated analysis of law and practice. Despite the rich and developing literature in health governance theory,[91] the place of human rights within global health governance remains under-explored. Likewise, the impact of human rights on health currently lacks empirical evaluation; thus, additional studies that empirically assess the impact of human rights proliferation on health outcomes and health governance should be pursued. Such an effort could help to solidify or discredit the link between human rights and health outcomes. Finally, the proliferation of human rights related to health should be accompanied by sustained efforts to study, and if effective, augment the coverage and effects of human right systems and principles as they apply to health.

The proliferation of human rights can provide useful structural and normative guidance for global health governance. Since human rights pervade so many levels of health governance, multiple interpretations and applications of human rights abound in relation to health. Many institutions, entities, and actors participate in the interpretation of human rights norms that impact health. Thus, greater attention should be paid to the potentially positive synergy between health and human rights. This will require systematic, concerted, and ongoing efforts to expand the recognition and acceptance of human rights in the context of health. Though barely explored here, the proliferation of structural and normative human rights outside formal human rights settings may be a promising avenue for the expansion of human rights in health governance. The existence of multiple levels of governance should not suggest that any level should remain static. Each level and system should be consistently improved to incorporate human rights norms that improve health outcomes. Additional research and transparency among systems will likely facilitate this goal.

Despite the limitations discussed above, this multi-layered framework of human rights that has evolved is probably good for health in the aggregate. Ultimately, success in respecting, protecting, and fulfilling human rights requires the adoption of many strategies, which should be pursued simultaneously and vigorously.

Acknowledgements

I would like to thank my diligent research assistants Bruce Bielawa, Tamar Dolcourt, Delia Johnson, and Nicole Rowley who helped immensely on the research for this article. I would also like to thank Susan Cancelosi and an anonymous reviewer for helpful comments.

References

1. Committee on International Science, Engineering, and Technology, *Infectious Disease a Global Threat: Report of the National Science and Technology Council*, Washington, D.C., 1995.
2. D. P. Fidler, *International Law and Infectious Diseases* (New York: Oxford University Press, 1999): at 5.
3. S. Burris, "Governance, Microgovernance and Health," *Temple Law Review* 77, no. 2 (2004): 335–61, at 336.
4. L. O. Gostin and L. Gable, "The Human Rights of Persons with Mental Disabilities: A Global Perspective on the Application of Human Rights Principles to Mental Health," *Maryland Law Review* 63, no. 1 (2004): 20–121.
5. J. M. Mann et al., "Health and Human Rights," *Journal of Health and Human Rights* 1, no. 1 (1994): 6–23, at 19; L. O. Gostin and Z. Lazzarini, *Human Rights*

and Public Health in the AIDS Pandemic (New York: Oxford University Press, 1997): at 1; L. O. Gostin, *The AIDS Pandemic: Injustice, Complacency, Unfulfilled Expectations* (Chapel Hill: University of North Carolina Press, 2004): at 67.

6. J. M. Mann, "Medicine and Public Health, Ethics and Human Rights," *Hastings Center Report* 27, no. 1 (1997): 6–13, at 9: S. Gruskin, "Is There a Government in the Cockpit: A Passenger's Perspective, or Global Public Health: The Role of Human Rights," *Temple Law Review* 77, no. 2 (2004): 313–33, at 314.

7. See Mann, *supra* note 5.

8. D. P. Fidler, "A Globalized Theory of Public Health," *Journal of Law, Medicine & Ethics* 30, no. 2 (2002): 150–61.

9. Universal Declaration of Human Rights. General Assembly Resolution 217A (III), U.N. Doc. A/810, Preamble (1948), adopted December 10, 1948 [hereinafter cited as UDHR].

10. International Covenant on Civil and Political Rights, General Assembly Resolution 2200A (XXI), 21 U.N. GAOR Supp. (No. 16) at 52, UN. Doc. A/6316 (1966), 999 U.N.T.S. 171, entered into force Mar. 23, 1976 [hereinafter cited as ICCPR].

11. International Covenant on Economic, Social and Cultural Rights, General Assembly Resolution 2200A (XXI), 21 U.N. GAOR Supp. (No. 16) at 59, U.N. Doc. A/6316 (1966), 999 U.N.T.S. 302, entered into force March 23, 1976 [hereinafter cited as ICESCR].

12. *Id.*, at art. 3–28.

13. H. Hannum, "The Status and Future of the Customary International Law of Human Rights: The Status of the Universal Declaration of Human Rights in National and International Law," *Georgia Journal of International and Comparative Law* 25, no. 2 (1995): 287–398.

14. See ICCPR, *supra*, note 10.

15. See ICESCR, *supra* note 11.

16. *Id.*, at art. 12.

17. International Convention on the Elimination of All Forms of Racial Discrimination, 660 U.N.T.S. 195, entered into force January 4, 1969 [hereinafter cited as CERD].

18. Convention on the Elimination of All Forms of Discrimination Against Women, General Assembly Resolution 34/180, 34 U.N. GAOR Supp. (No. 46) at 193, U.N. Doc. A/34/46, entered into force September 3, 1981 [hereinafter cited as CEDAW].

19. Convention on the Rights of the Child, General Assembly Resolution 44/25, annex, 44 U.N. GAOR Supp. (No. 49) at 167, U.N. Doc. A/44/49 (1989), entered into force September 2, 1990 [hereinafter cited as CRC].

20. Convention Against Torture and Other Cruel, Inhuman or Degrading Treatment or Punishment, General Assembly Resolution 39/46, annex, 39 U.N. GAOR Supp. (No. 51) at 197, U.N. Doc. A/39/51 (1984), entered into force June 26, 1987.

21. Convention on the Rights of Persons with Disabilities, General Assembly Resolution A/61/611 (2006) [hereinafter cited as CRPD].

22. Declaration on the Rights of Mentally Retarded Persons, General Assembly Resolution 2856 (XXVI), 26 U.N. GAOR Supp. (No. 29) at 93, U.N. Doc. A/8429 (1971).

23. Declaration on the Rights of Disabled Persons, General Assembly Resolution 3447 (XXX), 30 U.N. GAOR Supp. (No. 34) at 88, U.N. Doc. A/10034, (1975).
24. General Comment 14, Committee on Economic, Social, and Cultural Rights, 22nd Session, April 25–May 12, 2000.
25. See B. Lundquist, *Monitoring the Implementation of the Standard Rules on the Equalization of Opportunities for Person with Disabilities, Annex – Final Report of the Special Rapporteur of the Commission for Social Development on Monitoring and Implementation of the Standard Rules on the Equalization of Opportunities for Persons with Disabilities on His Second Mission, 1997–2000*, U.N. Doc. E/CN.5/2000/3 (2000), paras. 111–16, 152. See also, *Report of the Special Rapporteur of the Commission for Social Development on Monitoring and Implementation of the Standard Rules on the Equalization of Opportunities for Persons with Disabilities on His Third Mandate, 2000–2002*, U.N. Doc. E/CN.5/2002/4, paras. 29–37, 84–90.
26. Commission on Human Rights resolution, U.N. Doc. E/CN.4/RES/2002/31, adopted April 22, 2002; Economic and Social Council Resolution, U.N. Doc. E/DEC/2002/259, adopted July 25, 2002.
27. See P. Hunt, *Report of the Special Rapporteur on the Right of Everyone to the Enjoyment of the. Highest Attainable Standard of Physical and Mental Health*, Commission on Human Rights, 4th Sess., U.N. Doc. A/HRC/4/28 (2007). See also, P. Hunt, *Report of the Special Rapporteur on the Right of Everyone to the Enjoyment of the Highest Attainable Standard of Physical and Mental Health*, General Assembly, Commission on Human Rights, 61st Sess., U.N. Doc. A/61/338; P. Hunt, *Report of Paul Hunt, Special Rapporteur on the Right of Everyone to the Enjoyment of the Highest Attainable Standard of Physical and Mental Health*, Commission on Human Rights, 61st Sess., U.N. Doc. E/CN.4/2005/51.
28. Individuals can submit claims under Optional Protocols to the ICCPR and CEDAW. Optional Protocol to the International Covenant on Civil and Political Rights, General Assembly Resolution, 2200A (XXI), 21 U.N. GAOR Supp. (No. 16) at 59, U.N. Doc. A/6316 (1966), 999 U.N.T.S. 302, entered into force March 23, 1976; Optional Protocol to the Convention on the Elimination of Discrimination against Women, General Assembly Resolution 54/4, annex, 54 U.N. GAOR Supp. (No. 49) at 5, U.N. Doc. A/54/49 (Vol. I) (2000), entered into force December 22, 2000.
29. See Fidler, *supra* note 8.
30. European Convention for the Protection of Human Rights and Fundamental Freedoms, (ETS 5), 213 U.N.T.S. 222, entered into force September 3, 1953, as amended by Protocols Nos. 3, 5. and 8, which entered into force September 21, 1970, December 20, 1971, and January 1, 1990, respectively [hereinafter cited as ECHR]; Inter-American Convention on Human Rights, O.A.S. Treaty Series No. 36, 1144 U.N.T.S. 123, entered into force July 18, 1978, reprinted in Basic Documents Pertaining to Human Rights in the Inter-American System, OEA/Ser. L.V/II.82 doc.6 rev.1 at 25, 1992 [hereinafter cited as IACHR].
31. See ICCPR, *supra* note 10, at arts. 28–45 and Optional Protocol, at arts. 1–6; CEDAW, *supra* note 18, at arts. 17–22 and Optional Protocol, arts. 1–14; CRC, *supra* note 19, at arts. 43–45; CERD, *supra* note 17, at arts. 8–15; CRPD, *supra* note 21, at arts. 34–39 and Optional Protocol, arts. 1–9.

32. L. O. Gostin and L. Gable, "The Human Rights of Persons with Mental Disabilities: A Global Perspective on the Application of Human Rights Principles to Mental Health," *Maryland Law Review* 63, no. 1 (2004): 20–121.

33. L. Gable et al., "Mental Health and Due Process in the Americas: Protecting the Human Rights of Persons Involuntarily Admitted to and Detained in Psychiatric Institutions," *Pan American Journal of Public Health* 18, no. 4/5 (2005): 366–73.

34. *Victor Rosario Congo v. Ecuador*, Case 11.247 (Inter-American CHR 63/99, 1999).

35. U.S. Constitution, amends. 5, 6, and 7.

36. U.S. Constitution, amends. 1 and 4.

37. U.S. Constitution, amend. 14.

38. Constitution of the Federative Republic of Brazil, at arts. 6, 205–14 (1988); Constitution of the Republic of South Africa, at art. 29 (1996).

39. Constitution of the Federative Republic of Brazil, at arts. 6, 196–200 (1988); Constitution of the Republic of South Africa, at art. 27 (1996).

40. A. Kanter, "The Globalization of Disability Rights Law," *Syracuse Journal of International Law and Commerce* 30, no. 2 (2003): 241–70, at 241.

41. 42 USCS § 12101 (2007).

42. S. R. Bagenstos, "The Future of Disability Law," *Yale Law Journal* 114, no. 1 (2004): 1–84.

43. *Id.*

44. S. Hoffman, "Settling the Matter: Does Title I of the ADA Work?" *Alabama Law Review*, forthcoming, *available at* <http://ssrn.com/abstract=978198> (last visited September 10, 2007).

45. T. Degener and G. Quinn, "A Survey of International, Comparative and Regional Disability Law Reform," in M. L. Breslin and S. Yee, eds., *Disability Rights Law and Policy: International and National Perspectives* (New York: Transnational Publishers, 2002): at 3–128; see Kanter, *supra* note 40.

46. *Human Rights Act*, 1998, c. 42.

47. J. Bindman et al., "The Human Rights Act and Mental Health Legislation," *British Journal of Psychiatry* 182, no. 2 (2003): 91–94.

48. *Minister of Health v. Treatment Action Committee*. Constitutional Court of South Africa, 2002 (10) BCLR 1033 (CC) (S.Afr.); L. Forman, "The Imperative to Treat. The South African State's Constitutional Obligations to Provide Antiretroviral Medicines," *Health Law Review* 12, no. 1 (2002): 9–15.

49. J. E. Alvarez, *International Organizations as Law-Makers* (New York: Oxford University Press, 2005): at 650.

50. Report of the Secretary-General, *In Larger Freedom: Towards Development*, Security and Human Rights for All, U.N. Doc. A/59/2005 (2005), at 37.

51. World Health Organization, *25 Questions and Answers on Human Rights*, Geneva, 2002.

52. Constitution of the World Health Organization (1948), *available at* <http://www.who.int/entity/governance/eb/constitution/en/index.html> (last visited September 10, 2007).

53. World Health Organization, *Engaging for Health: The 11th Global Programme of Work, 2006–2015: A Global Health Agenda*, Geneva, 2006.

54. World Health Organization, *WHO Resource Book on Mental Health, Human Rights, and Legislation*, Geneva, 2005.

55. World Health Assembly, *International Health Regulations*, Geneva, 2005, entered into force June 15, 2007, *available at* <http://www.who.int/gb/ebwha/pdf_files/WHA58/WHA58_3-en.pdf> <last visited September 10, 2007) [hereinafter cited as IHR].

56. *Id.*, at art. 6.

57. *Id.*, at arts. 3, 32.

58. L. O. Gostin, "International Infectious Disease Law: Revision of the World Health Organization's International Health Regulations," *JAMA* 291, no. 21 (2004): 2623–27.

59. UNAIDS, *International Guidelines on HIV/AIDS and Human Rights*, Geneva, 2006; UNAIDS, *Handbook for Legislators on HIV/AIDS, Law, and Human Rights*, Geneva, 1999; UNDP, *Supporting National HIV/AIDS Responses*, Geneva, 2004; UNDP, *Human Development Report 200: Human Rights and Human Development* (New York: Oxford University Press, 2000).

60. Pan American Health Organization, *The Right to Health in the Americas*, Washington, D.C., 1989.

61. *The Montreal Declaration on Intellectual Disabilities*, adopted October 6, 2004, *available at* <http://www.declarationmontreal.com/english/declaration.htm> (last visited September 10, 2007).

62. See, e.g., Pan American Health Organization, *Understanding and Responding to HIV/AIDS-related Stigma and Stigma and Discrimination in the Health Sector*, Washington D.C., 2003.

63. D. P. Fidler, *SARS, Governance, and the Globalization of Disease* (New York: Palgrave Macmillan, 2004): at 21–22.

64. *Id.*

65. Physicians for Human Rights, *Epidemic of Inequality: Women's Rights and HIV/AIDS in Botswana and Swaziland*, Cambridge, MA, 2007.

66. Human Rights Watch, *Rhetoric and Risk: Human Rights Abuses Impeding Ukraine's Fight against HIV/AIDS*, March 2006; Human Rights Watch, *Locked Doors: The Human Rights of People Living with HIV/AIDS in China*, August 2003.

67. Mental Disability Rights International, *Human Rights and Mental Health in Peru*, 2004, and *Human Rights and Mental Health: Uruguay*, 2004.

68. Mental Disability Rights International, *Not on the Agenda: Human Rights of People with Mental Disabilities in Kosovo*, 2002, and *Human Rights and Mental Health: Hungary*, 1997.

69. A. Hillman, "Protecting Mental Disability Rights: A Success Story in the Inter-American Human Rights System," *Human Rights Briefs* 12, no. 3 (2005): 25–28.

70. *WHO Framework Convention on Tobacco Control*, entered into force February 27, 2005.

71. See CRPD, *supra* note 21.

72. A. A. Dhir, "Human Rights Treaty Drafting through the Lens of Mental Disability: The Proposed International Convention on Protection and Promotion of the Rights and Dignity of Persons with Disabilities," *Stanford Journal of International Law* 41, no. 2 (2005): 181–216.

73. See Fidler, *supra* note 8.

74. See CRPD, *supra* note 21.

75. *Id.*, at arts. 1, 4(1).

76. *Id.*, at art. 34.
77. *Id.*, at art. 35.
78. *Id.*, at art. 31.
79. *Id.*, at art. 4(3).
80. Optional Protocol to the International Convention on the Rights of Persons with Disabilities.
81. See CRPD, *supra* note 21, at art 1.
82. *Id.*, at arts. 5, 9, 10, 12, 13, 14.
83. *Id.*, at arts. 15, 16, 21.
84. *Id.*, at arts. 18–20, 22, 23.
85. *Id.*, at arts. 24–30.
86. R. Goodman and D. Jinks, "How to Influence States: Socialization and International Human Rights Law," *Duke Law Journal* 74, no. 3 (2004): 621–703.
87. M. Jones, "Can International Law Improve Mental Health? Some Thoughts on the Proposed Convention on the Rights of People with Disabilities," *International Journal of Law and Psychiatry* 28, no. 2 (2005): 183–205.
88. T. J. Melish, "The U.N. Disability Convention: Historic Process, Strong Prospects, and Why the U.S. Should Ratify," *Human Rights Brief* 14, no. 2 (2007): 37–46.
89. See Dhir, *supra* note 72; T. R. Justesen and T. R. Justesen, "An Analysis of the Development and Adoption of the United Nations Convention Recognizing the Rights of Individuals with Disabilities: Why the United States Refuses to Sign This U.N. Convention," *Human Rights Brief* 14, no. 2 (2007): 36–41.
90. M. A. Stein, "Disability Human Rights," *California Law Review* 95, no. 1 (2007): 75–121.
91. See Burris, *supra* note 3; N. D. Hunter, "'Public-Private' Health Law: Multiple Directions in Public Health," *Journal of Health Care Law & Policy* 10, no. 1 (2007): 101–132; O. Lobel, "The Renew Deal: The Fall of Regulation and the Rise of Governance in Contemporary Legal Thought," *Minnesota Law Review* 89, no. 2 (2004): 342–470; L. G. Trubek, "New Governance and Soft Law in Health Care Reform," *Indiana Health Law Review* 3, no. 1 (2006): 137–170.

SWINE FLU VACCINE

What is fair?

Lawrence O. Gostin

Source: *Hastings Center Report*, 39:5 (2009), 9–10.

A novel strain of influenza A (H1N1)—so-called swine flu—spread through Mexico in April 2009, and by June 11th, the World Health Organization raised the alert level to a full-blown pandemic.[1] The virus spread widely during the Southern hemisphere's regular flu season, with the Northern hemisphere bracing for its peak flu season. The United States continues to report the largest number of cases of any country worldwide.

The surprisingly rapid global transmission has focused political attention on developing an effective vaccine. Australia initiated the first vaccine trials in July, followed by Europe and the United States. Finding a medical solution to this threat is attractive but also raises questions of fundamental fairness.

Cost comparisons

In 2009 Congress authorized $7.65 billion in spending for the Department of Health and Human Services, the vast majority of which is for therapeutic interventions such as vaccine development and distribution and stockpiling of the antiviral Tamiflu. This funding, together with private spending and the more than $7 billion federal authorization for research and development on and medical interventions for influenza A (H5N1)—avian flu—amounts to a windfall for the pharmaceutical industry. Roche has reported that sales of Tamiflu have tripled, and GlaxoSmithKline predicts huge profits from a vaccine.[2]

Politicians on all sides of the spectrum support large expenditures, but it is not obvious that novel influenza should be such a high resource priority. Human-to-human transmission of H5N1 is rare, with only a small number of human cases and deaths worldwide.[3] Although H1N1 is widespread, the first wave was not highly pathogenic; it caused far fewer deaths than seasonal

147

influenza, which kills some thirty-six thousand Americans and up to five hundred thousand globally each year. And even the number of deaths pales in comparison to those caused by chronic diseases such as diabetes, coronary heart disease, and respiratory disease.[4] But while government falls over itself to fund therapeutic interventions for exotic infections such as anthrax, SARS, and novel strains of influenza, it continues to chronically underfund more cost-effective public health services. Approximately 2 percent of total health expenditures goes to prevention and population-based services.

The political dilemma, of course, is that H1N1 could mutate—through re-assortment with H5N1, for example—rendering it much more lethal. We should recall that the first wave of the 1918 Spanish flu, which killed some fifty million people in a much less populated world, was relatively benign. It is that slight but serious potential that has the public and health officials concerned.

Research: detecting adverse events

Clinical trials of swine flu vaccine have enrolled relatively few human subjects and are being conducted in a compressed time frame. In Australia and Europe, there are calls to truncate the research even further and to fast-track the vaccine. In the United States, initial trials are being conducted on healthy adult volunteers, including the elderly, followed by children as young as six months and pregnant women, who are at higher risk. The problems of obtaining informed consent among participants with limited capacity can probably be managed. More worrying is the inability of small trials to detect rare but serious adverse effects that cannot be fully understood until the vaccine is rolled out to a mass population. Although the first trials did not use adjuvants that stimulate the immune system, these may be necessary to stretch the vaccine supply, even though they cause more side effects.

For its part, the Food and Drug Administration will be under public and political pressure to quickly approve vaccines without large clinical trials for safety and effectiveness. Also, the FDA has never approved a human vaccine containing adjuvants, which could increase the complexity of its decision.[5]

When the vaccine is marketed, key issues involving liability protection for manufacturers and fair compensation for patients will become paramount. The industry will insist on protection, as well as economic incentives from government. And patient groups will call for inclusion in the no-fault vaccine compensation system.

Just allocation

Effective vaccines will almost certainly be scarce—the antigen yield for candidate vaccines may be much lower than expected, trials may not conclusively demonstrate safety and effectiveness, and the virus may mutate. What factors determine which countries will gain greater access to available vaccine stocks? The United States is vulnerable because most manufacturers are based in Europe. In times of extreme shortage, industry is more likely to supply the markets where they are located. Still, rich countries in general will probably use their vastly superior spending power to acquire vaccines. Stockpiling by the rich, of course, leaves poor countries in Africa, Asia, and Latin America much more vulnerable. President Obama plans to spend a miniscule $350 million of swine flu resources for global health and child survival, and two-thirds of that sum will go to surveillance, which benefits rich countries more than poor.[6] Serious questions of global social justice arise when wealth, rather than need, becomes the primary allocation criterion. The maldistribution of vaccines in the face of a global health crisis will only widen the already large health gap between rich and poor.

Just allocation within a country, of course, is mostly—although not exclusively—driven by politics. The United States gives priority to children and the elderly for seasonal influenza, and the HHS avian influenza plan preferences health care and emergency professionals among others. The Centers for Disease Control and Prevention assigned top priority for the swine flu vaccine to a group comprising 160 million people and five populations: pregnant women, household contacts of children under six months old, health care and emergency medical services workers, everyone six months to twenty-four years old; and people twenty-five to sixty-four who have conditions that put them at higher risk of serious illness and death.[7] Unlike virtually all flu vaccine plans, the CDC will not grant priority to the elderly; they appear to have some immunity because of past exposure to related flu strains. CDC's allocation appears justified by current need and vulnerability. However, the private market may still privilege the rich and politically connected in gaining access, particularly if the virus becomes more pathogenic and consumer demand is strong.

Mass prophylaxis capabilities

During the late autumn and winter, seasonal and H1N1 viruses will circulate simultaneously, and both will require vaccines. The H1N1 vaccine schedule, moreover, may require two inoculations. The vaccine also requires cold storage, handling, and transportation. This all raises the question of how to handle distribution and delivery, particularly to the most vulnerable people.[8] Individuals who lack mobility or mental capacity, for example, may be unable to attend vaccination clinics. Public health departments, clinics, and hospitals will have to gear up for fair and efficient distribution, with a sophisticated tracking system. And this will be on top of the expected surge in demand for their services—both from those with swine flu and the many others who are fearful and seek medical attention.

The 1976 swine flu affair

Inevitably, the current situation will be compared to the 1976 swine flu scare, when the media fanned fears of a catastrophic epidemic that never emerged. Pharmaceutical companies lobbied Congress hard, and successfully, for resources and liability protection. After the director of the CDC advised President Ford to support a mass immunization campaign, surveillance revealed an increased incidence of a neurological disorder called Guillain-Barré syndrome.[9] The president halted the campaign by mid-December of that year, after forty-five million Americans had been vaccinated. When the federal government changed hands in January 1977, the CDC director was fired and the Victoria flu program (a component of the larger swine flu program) was restarted for high-risk individuals only. By some accounts, the swine flu affair cost Gerald Ford the election.

In 1976 as now, the media made swine flu salient in the public mind; the drug industry insisted on being held harmless against lawsuits while profiting from a massive vaccination program; and politicians wanted to gain credit for a successful public health program. But the swine flu affair still fails to tell us whether, in the face of scientific uncertainty, it is better to err on the side of caution or aggressive intervention.

A fair and prudent course today would be to conduct careful clinical trials with due scientific deliberation; phase in vaccinations as evidence of safety and effectiveness becomes clearer; and conduct rigorous postmarket surveillance for adverse effects. Liability protection and just compensation should be part of a comprehensive evaluation involving all vaccines, with no special arrangements for novel diseases that capture the public's attention. Domestic distribution of vaccines should, as the Obama administration has made clear, focus on those at greatest risk. Above all, the international community, and rich countries in particular, should pay attention to the most disadvantaged. It is politically tempting to hoard vaccines for American citizens, but the urgent needs of the world's poor should not be ignored. Swine flu is largely innocuous for otherwise healthy people but potentially deadly for those with the compounding health problems likely in poor, minority, and indigenous populations. The response to swine flu is quintessentially a problem of social justice.

References

1. L. O. Gostin, "Influenza A (H1N1) and Pandemic Preparedness Under the Rule of International Law, "*Journal of the American Medical Association* 301 (2009): 2376–78.
2. A. Padlock, "Sales of Flu Drug Improve Results at Roche," *New York Times*, July 24, 2009.
3. World Health Organization, "Avian Influenza Factsheet," at http://www.who.int/mediacentre/factsheets/avian_influenza/en/#humans.

4. Centers for Disease Control and Prevention, "FASTATS," at http://www.cdc.gov/nchs/FASTATS/deaths.htm.
5. D. McNeill, "Clinical Trials for Flu Vaccine Are to Begin Soon," *New York Times*, July 23, 2009.
6. Supplemental Appropriations Act 2009, Pub. L. 111 PL 32, 123 Stat 1859.
7. D. Brown, "Flu Vaccine Panel Creates Priority List: Pregnant Women, Caregivers Are First," *Washington Post*, July 30, 2009.
8. "CDC Recommendations for State and Local Planning for a 2009 Novel H1N1 Influenza Vaccination Program," July 8, 2009, at http://www.cdc.gov/h1n1flu/vaccination/start elocal/planning.htm.
9. R. E. Neustadt and H. Fineberg, *The Epidemic That Never Was: Policy-Making and the Swine Flu Affair* (New York: Vintage Books, 1983).

104

WHEN TO START ANTIRETROVIRAL THERAPY IN RESOURCE-LIMITED SETTINGS

A human rights analysis

Nathan Ford, Alexandra Calmy and Samia Hurst

Source: *BMC International Health and Human Rights*, 10:6 (2010), 9 pp.

Abstract

Background: Recent evidence from developed and developing countries shows clear clinical and public health benefit to starting antiretroviral therapy (ART) earlier. While discussions about when to start ART have often focused on the clinical risks and benefits, the main issue is one of fair limit-setting. We applied a human rights framework to assess a policy of early treatment initiation according to the following criteria: public-health purpose; likely effectiveness; specificity; human rights burdens and benefits; potential for less restrictive approaches; and fair administration.

Discussion: According to our analysis, a policy of earlier ART initiation would better serve both public health and human rights objectives. We highlight a number of policy approaches that could be taken to help meet this aim, including increased international financial support, alternative models of care, and policies to secure the most affordable sources of appropriate antiretroviral drugs.

Summary: Widespread implementation of earlier ART initiation is challenging in resource-limited settings. Nevertheless, rationing of essential medicines is a restriction of human rights, and the principle of least restriction serves to focus attention on alternative measures such as adapting health service models to increase capacity, decreasing costs, and seeking additional international funding. Progressive realisation using well-defined steps will be necessary to allow for a phased implementation as part of a framework of short-term targets towards nationwide policy adoption, and will require international technical and financial support.

Background

Highly active antiretroviral therapy (ART) has transformed HIV/AIDS from a death sentence into a manageable, chronic disease. Today, an adult 20 years of age diagnosed with HIV/AIDS in the developed world can expect to live at least 23 years [1,2]. In the developing world, fewer therapeutic options are available for patients; nevertheless current treatment approaches are effective at reducing mortality, with studies demonstrating similar survival outcomes compared to western countries, at least in the short term [3].

Among the different strategies for improving long-term survival for people with HIV/AIDS in resource-limited settings, the question of when to start ART is gaining increasing attention. Studies from developed and developing country settings conclude that early initiation results in substantial gains in survival and reduced incidence of opportunistic infections, in particular tuberculosis (TB). However, a number of concerns have been put forward against starting treatment earlier, namely increased costs, potential toxicity of treating more patients longer, and increased burden on health systems.

One approach to disentangling competing policy goals in a manner supportive of patient need is through a human rights analysis [4]. Human rights analysis frameworks provide a methodology for assessing health policy from a range of different perspectives, and thus provide a broader analysis that draws on a range of disciplines, in contrast to more conventional research methods such as systematic reviews or cost-effective analyses. Such analyses have been applied to a number of different issues of importance to public health, such as the prevention of mother-to-child transmission of HIV [5] and management of drug-resistant TB [6]. This paper applies such an analysis to the question of when to start antiretroviral treatment.

When to start antiretroviral treatment

HIV infection progresses to AIDS disease as the virus replicates in cells of the immune system (CD4 cells), destroying a patient's immune defence and allowing opportunistic infections to take hold. ART works by preventing viral replication.

The decision of when to start ART is generally made according to clinical or immunological criteria. Clinical decisions are based on the presence of one or more severe opportunistic infections, categorised by the World Health Organisation (WHO) as stage III and IV AIDS-defining illnesses. Developed and developing country guidelines all recommend starting ART if a patient presents with a stage III or IV infection, though decisions based on such clinical criteria alone are generally only used in resource-limited settings where laboratory capacity is limited. More commonly, the decision to start ART is based on immunological criteria, as defined by the level of CD4 cells.

Until recently, the level of CD4 indicating ART differed between developed and developing countries. European and US guidelines recommend ART initiation at a CD4 cell threshold of 350 cells/µL (moderate immunodeficiency). A policy of deferred initiation (200 cells/µL) was originally based on concerns related to the accumulative risks of toxicity and drug resistance [7]. Such concerns have diminished in recent years as newer medicines have become available with fewer toxicities and better potency (reducing the chance of resistance development). The availability of these newer medicines, together with studies that have increased the understanding of the risks of developing life-threatening illnesses over time if ART is initiated at a low CD4 count, have shifted the risk-benefit equation [7]. Recent evidence from European cohorts showed that starting ART earlier (at least 350 cells/µL) results in significant survival gains [8].

Guidelines for developing countries have recently been revised in line with developed world recommendations. Treatment guidelines issued by the International AIDS Society in August 2008 state that "the core principle underlying these guidelines, namely pathogenesis-directed therapy with regimens designed to achieve full virologic suppression with minimal toxicity and maximal simplicity, is applicable to the developing world" [9], and the latest WHO antiretroviral treatment guidelines for resource-limited settings released at the end of 2009 recommend a move towards earlier initiation at CD4 count <350 cells/µL [10].

However, these recommendations have for the most part yet to be translated into country-level policy, and most national guidelines in developing countries continue to recommend "deferred" ART initiation at CD4 <200 cells/µL (severe immunodeficiency). The main concern for developing countries is that providing treatment earlier, for longer, would increase overall drug expenditure costs [11]. In addition, other significant health systems costs are associated with ART provision to large numbers of people when there are already too few doctors and hospitals are saturated [12]. Finally, given that most people present at ART services with an even lower CD4 count of around 100 cells/µL [13], the issue of early initiation has been argued to be a moot point. These issues have led some to voice concern that earlier initiation "may end up doing more harm than good" by weakening already strained ART programmes [14].

Discussion

A number of frameworks have been developed to assess the impact of public health policy on human rights. We chose the Mann-Gostin Framework [4] because it is well suited to the analysis of policies that involve a restriction of rights, which can be considered to be the case when ART is deferred. This framework interrogates policy according to the following questions: what is the public-health purpose of the policy? What is the likely effectiveness of the policy in relation to its purpose? Is the policy well targeted? What are the human rights burdens and benefits? Is there a less restrictive policy to achieve the same objective? Are there fair administrative procedures in place? These considerations are discussed below and summarised in Additional File 1, Table S1.

What is the public-health purpose?

When analysing the public health purpose of a given policy, the objectives of the policy should be assessed independently of the methods chosen to reach them. The three main reasons for establishing a restrictive threshold for initiating ART are: (i) to treat people who need ART; (ii) to minimise harms caused by prolonged exposure to toxicity; and (iii) to ration care.

The primary goal of ART is to decrease HIV-related morbidity and mortality. The benefits of starting ART in terms of reduced mortality and morbidity are clear, and these are most immediately evident when a patient's immune system is severely compromised, although a patient's immunological nadir – how low their CD4 count is allowed to drop – is predictive of how successfully future ART will benefit them [15].

A related health concern, which was the principal reason for delaying ART in developed countries, is the risk of accumulated drug toxicities. The main drugs used in Africa for first-line ART – stavudine, zidovudine, lamivudine, efavirenz, and nevirapine [16] – all have associated toxicities, including nausea, diarrhoea, and headache; more severe adverse effects such as acute hepatitis, anaemia, neuropathy, lipodystrophy, hypersensitivity, and pancreatitis; and life-threatening toxicities such as fulminant hepatitis and lactic acidosis [17].

However, the overriding purpose of maintaining a more restrictive threshold for initiation is unstated in policy: it acts as a form of rationing treatment. Rationing can be defined as "any implicit or explicit mechanisms that allow people to go without beneficial services" [18].

What is the likely effectiveness of the policy?

With lower CD4 count comes higher risk of mortality and morbidity. In untreated patients with a high viral load, the risks of developing AIDS within 6 months are approximately 40%, 10%, and 3% for CD4 cell count groups <200, 200–349, and >350 cells/μL, respectively [19]. Similarly, the long-term prognosis for patients on ART is determined by immune status at initiation: patients starting ART at a lower CD4 count have a lower chance of long-term survival [20].

A recent randomised trial conducted in Haiti comparing patients who started ART early (<350 cells/μL) and those who were deferred (<200 cells/μL) found a 4-fold increase in mortality and a 2-fold increase in incident TB in the deferred group [21]. This reduction in TB incidence also suggests a public health benefit to starting earlier where high coverage can be achieved. These data reinforce evidence from trials in Africa suggesting a greater survival benefit of starting therapy earlier [22].

While the focus to date has been on opportunistic infections that are most frequent at CD4 <200 cells/μL, recent studies have raised concern about the risk of death from liver, renal, and heart diseases, as well as from "non-AIDS" cancers; incidence of these diseases is increased at lower CD4 counts, with significant differences seen between those with CD4 <350 cells/μL and those with CD4 >350 cells/μL [23]. Therefore, if reducing mortality and morbidity is the main objective, then on the basis of the latest clinical evidence the 350 cells/μL threshold should be adopted everywhere. HIV-positive pregnant women should be provided with ART regardless of CD4 count.

Furthermore, models have indicated a public health benefit in terms of reduced transmission. A modelling study from South Africa found a 54% reduction of HIV transmission when therapy is initiated at CD4 <350 cells/μL as compared to <200 cells/μL [24]. The potential for broader access to reduce HIV transmission was suggested by subsequent studies [25].

Concerns about long-term toxicity and drug resistance have been lessened in the developed world as more potent and less toxic medicines became available [26–28]. These concerns are still justified in developing countries, where older drugs with less favourable side-effect profiles still form the backbone of therapy, but would be largely overcome with the wider availability of less-toxic drugs. Withholding medicines is certainly an effective way of preventing the development of toxicity and resistance in the short term, but in the long term everyone will eventually be eligible. Delaying treatment until the CD4 count has fallen below 300–350 cells/μL carries greater risks than does starting treatment earlier, provided that less toxic drugs are available [7].

Rationing care can be viewed as having two legitimate aims: getting more benefit from available resources by giving priority to more cost-effective interventions over less cost-effective ones targeting the same condition, and allocating available health resources as fairly as possible. In the first sense, using a low CD4 count as a means to ration ART could be counterproductive. Symptomatic patients place the greatest burden on health systems, as they require multiple doctor consultations and hospitalisation. In the same way that provision of ART led to massive cost savings in terms of avoided hospitalisations and opportunistic infections [29], the cost savings made by delaying ART initiation are at least partly offset by the cost of treating opportunistic infections among those who present sick (with low CD4). A cost-effectiveness simulation from South Africa found that earlier initiation would be cost-effective over a 5-year period [30]. This means that a restrictive CD4 threshold for treatment initiation will also be counterproductive in attempting to allocate resources fairly; "doing less with more" in this area also implies depriving others of needed interventions towards which these resources could otherwise have been channelled.

Moreover, even at the lower cut-off of CD4 <200 cells/µL, still less than half of those eligible for treatment in the developing world are receiving ART. It must therefore be acknowledged that CD4 count is not the only criterion, or even the main one, by which care is currently being rationed. Lack of capacity within health systems and poor proximity to health-care entry points play much greater roles [31].

Is the policy well targeted?

Deferred treatment initiation prioritises those patients in greatest clinical need of ART, but still excludes substantial numbers of patients at risk. Given that the latest evidence supports initiating treatment at CD4 <350, a cut-off below that level is a decision to treat some, but not all, of the patients who would substantially benefit. Therefore, a policy of deferred initiation can at best be considered to be moderately well targeted.

In terms of limiting toxicity, the policy is poorly targeted. Although it limits the overall person-time exposure to ART, not all toxicities are cumulative. As everyone who is HIV-positive will eventually need to be put on treatment and so will be exposed, the policy only delays exposure to toxicity, but does not address the underlying causes: the fact that toxic drugs are being provided when less toxic alternatives exist.

A major challenge for ART programmes in resource-poor settings is pre-ART defaulting: patients diagnosed as HIV-positive but not yet eligible for treatment fall out of care because they have little reason to visit the clinic. One recent study from South Africa reported that almost three-quarters of patients defaulted pre-ART [32]. While an argument in favour of a lower CD4 threshold could be that these individuals would be eligible for ART once their CD4 count has descended to below 200 cells/µL, the reality is that many of these patients are not seen again until they are very sick. Raising the threshold could support this goal by providing more opportunities to enrol people into treatment and retain them in care before they become sick.

What are the human rights benefits and burdens?

The United Nations Commission on Human Rights explicitly recognised "that access to medication in the context of pandemics such as HIV/AIDS is one fundamental element for achieving progressively the full realisation of the right of everyone to the enjoyment of the highest attainable standard of physical and mental health" [33]. This right is subject to both progressive and immediate realisation. Article 2 (1) of the International Covenant on Economic, Social and Cultural Rights (ICESCR) stipulates the right to the highest attainable standard of health, including access to medicines, is subject to progressive realisation and resource availability [34]. At the same time, General Comment 14 of the UN Committee on Economic, Social and Cultural Rights (CESCR) declares that states have an immediate obligation to make essential medicines available and accessible throughout their jurisdiction [35]. Antiretroviral drugs are defined as essential medicines [36].

Rationing of ART brings into consideration a number of human rights principles that are articulated by international and regional human rights instruments. The most relevant concerns covered by these instruments include the right to life [34,36–38], access to health care [34,36–38], access to medicines [33,34,37], non-discrimination [34], protection of the most vulnerable [34], and restriction of rights [37,39,40].

A number of benefits and burdens are associated with the policy of using a restrictive CD4 count to determine ART eligibility. The main issues are outlined below.

Benefits

As a general point, from a human rights perspective, rationing of ART could bring a benefit if it led to broader access, and thus to greater overall implementation of the rights to life, access to health care, and access to medicine. This, however, would only be the case if limiting indications enabled health systems to provide access more extensively to persons who would otherwise be deprived of it. For example, this could apply if rationing was required to make ART available to everyone who met a lower CD4 threshold, even in rural areas, rather than to all who presented with the higher threshold, but exclusively at urban centres. Moreover, such a benefit could only ever be said to exist in circumstances where full access for all was not feasible. More specifically, one of the most important aspects of employing medical criteria, as opposed to other forms of rationing such as occupation or social worth [41], is that it meets the criteria of non-discrimination [42]: everyone meeting the criteria is given a chance to access treatment via the consistent application of the same criteria in an objective and transparent manner.

There is, however, a concern regarding the fact that eligibility based on laboratory investigations requires access to those investigations. While clinical criteria would determine that a certain proportion of patients should start treatment, those who would be eligible on immunological but not clinical grounds would be denied care. They are in any case likely to be among the most vulnerable, and in some cases this difference in treatment will even amount to a form of inequity in settings where CD4 is poorly available [41]. However, this applies equally to any CD4-based initiation strategy, whether early or deferred. Certainly, CD4 counts provide a more objective threshold than clinical criteria.

Burdens

The main human rights burden of limiting ART is that it denies treatment to people who, in other (wealthier) parts of the world, would be considered eligible. If access to ART is subject to immediate realisation, and the latest evidence suggests that ART should be provided earlier, then from a human rights perspective every effort should be made to ensure this happens and happens for all. Higher CD4 count at treatment initiation gives a greater chance of escaping symptomatic disease. Crudely put, the current policy is one that lets people progress from having a 10% chance of developing AIDS illness within 6 months to a 40% chance. This is in clear conflict with the human right to the highest attainable standard of health [34].

Finally, the issue of stigma is important. The common symptoms of AIDS-defining illnesses are well-known within communities, and allowing people with HIV to develop symptoms may increase their risks of being stigmatised [43]. This represents a violation of the right to non-discrimination [34]. Stigma can also act as a barrier to uptake of HIV services [44] and as such goes against the right to access to health care.

Is there a less restrictive policy to achieve objective?

Human rights doctrine recognises the need to limit certain human rights, usually in times of public health emergency when certain individual rights are temporarily restricted over concern for the common good. The most commonly cited example of such a trade off is the isolation of individuals to prevent the spread of infectious diseases. A core principle of such restrictions is that they are legitimate, non-arbitrary, and necessary. The Siracusa Principles on the Limitation and Derogation of Provisions in the International Covenant on Civil and Political Rights state that: "Public health may be invoked as a ground for limiting certain rights in order to allow a state to take measures dealing with a serious threat to the health of the population or individual members of the population. These measures must be specifically aimed at preventing disease or injury or providing care for the sick and injured" [45].

Human rights considerations require that where different policy options may be pursued to reach the same objective, the less-restrictive policy should be applied. In terms of meeting the stated public health objectives of reducing mortality and morbidity, increasing the threshold to 350 cells/μL would be less restrictive. In regards to limiting exposure to toxic drugs, a number of medicines are available today with a better toxicity profiles than those most widely used in the developing world. One of the most severe side effects, lactic acidosis, can be largely avoided by replacing one drug (stavudine) with less toxic alternatives (tenofovir or abacavir). However, these drugs are currently more expensive and widespread adoption will likely require a reduction in price [46]; of note, mechanisms which have been successful in influencing drug prices and encouraging generic competition also include the use of public health safeguards [47–49]]. Thailand and Brazil, for example, have both issued compulsory licenses to enable them to purchase generic versions of tenofovir, which is more affordable than the patented version [48]. The Indian patent office recently rejected the patent on tenofovir, allowing generic production [49]. The global price for tenofovir has fallen commensurate with an increase in generic production [28].

Any policy to ration essential care is by definition restrictive, and such restrictions are a feature of health care across the world. However, policies that restrict essential health services on the basis of limited resources have been challenged elsewhere. In the UK for example, a high court decision regarding the rationing of leukaemia chemotherapy ruled that the health authorities' power to refuse treatment on grounds of resource shortage were severely limited, and that the authorities had to prove that the money saved by rationing was being better placed elsewhere [50]. Although made in a developed country, this ruling makes the general point that if rationing is being employed, it is incumbent on the state to demonstrate that resources saved in one area are meeting important priorities elsewhere.

Recent cuts in the HIV/AIDS budgets in some developing countries suggest that this is not the case [51]. In the case of HIV/AIDS treatment, a substantial portion of funding comes from the international community, notably developed countries who do not themselves apply such limiting criteria. Although most human rights documents address the duties of states towards their own citizens only, this is a case where, arguably, this limitation does not fully apply. As pointed out by UN Committee on Economic, Social and Cultural Rights "... given that some diseases are easily transmissible beyond the frontiers of a State, the international community has a collective responsibility to address this problem. The economically developed States parties have a special responsibility and interest to assist the poorer developing States in this regard" [29]. HIV/AIDS clearly falls into this category. It is therefore also incumbent on donor countries to justify why they do not support a policy of earlier initiation.

Part of the justification for rationing is based on the fact that current ART sites are overburdened. Much could be done to increase capacity by increasing efficiency, which would be a less restrictive alternative to rationing. Various national and international guidelines recommend ways of doing this. One such measure is the task-shifting of clinical responsibilities from doctors to nurses and the deployment of community health workers to overcome severe human resource shortages [52]. There are also emerging decentralised models of how to manage "stable" patients out-of-facility [53]. Such approaches provide alternative ways of improving cost savings and increasing access despite bottlenecks due to doctor shortages, and are consistent with health-systems approaches supporting the right to the highest attainable standard of health [54].

Finally, international financing already supports a substantial part of the AIDS response [55]. This is not mere charity on the part of wealthier countries, but is consistent with their obligation under international human rights law to provide resources to support the realisation of "core and other obligations," which includes access to ART [56].

Are fair administrative procedures in place?

A human rights-based approach to HIV care means ensuring transparency and accountability for how policies and programmes are carried out. This relates to a state's duty to promote human rights by providing rights holders with sufficient information to realise their rights [57]. The requirement for fair administrative procedures means that the policy – in this instance, to ration ART by CD4 count, or relying on clinical criteria where CD4 measures are not possible – is based on adequate assessment of all relevant evidence and that safeguards are in place to provide opportunities for appeal and review, and that all parties understand the reasons behind the decisions taken [58]. Most national guidelines in developing countries do not adequately reflect the latest evidence regarding the clinical and public health benefits of initiating therapy at the higher threshold of CD4 <350 cells/μL. Moreover, it is unlikely that the decision to ration treatment in this way is properly understood by health providers and recipients (patients). In particular, the high rate of defaulting among HIV-positive patients who are not yet eligible for ART suggests that many do not understand the need to remain in care until eligibility requirements are met.

Overall, is the policy the optimal approach to the problem?

From this analysis, the policy is suboptimal in terms of addressing the public health and human rights issues in terms of reducing mortality and morbidity, limiting toxicity, supporting public health goals, and rationing.

Alternative frameworks for assessing rationing decisions

It has been argued that "No single analytical framework – whether grounded in economics, social sciences, ethics or human rights – can determine to everyone's satisfaction who should benefit from services first, second or last." [57]

Human rights principles of restriction of rights have most often been looked at from a perspective of restriction of movement [5] but could also be employed to analyse rationing decisions. Ethics and human rights are interconnected; both are based on the core principles of the respectful and dignified

161

treatment of persons [58]. Since the inclusion of a right to health within the Human Rights framework, both also recognise a right to health care. Currently, the most influential ethical defence of such a right is based on the fact that health is a prerequisite if we are to have access to the life choices which should be open to everyone [59–61]. Although a full discussion is beyond the scope of this paper, this is arguably particularly relevant to access to ART, as without it patients are vulnerable to stigma, disability, and death All three effectively close options that these patients should have, and which treatment can reopen. Inasmuch as stigma compounds other sources of vulnerability, this may even constitute a reason to give a degree of priority to ART in health care resource allocation [62].

Discussions of ethical aspects of rationing have focused on individual-level access and decisions, as well as institutional or national priorities in resource allocation [63]. These discussions have however tended to focus less on public-health interventions than on clinical or other health policy decisions. Two recent examples from the US – oseltamivir and influenza vaccine – have looked at rationing from a public health perspective. In the case of oseltamivir (an antiviral drug for the treatment of influenza) it was argued that while, in general, doctors should defer to patients' requests for a treatment that provided a modicum of benefit, where the drug is limited in quantity, physicians should be guided by principles of public-health ethics (maximising the health of the population while minimising infringements on individual liberty) [64]. Public discussions about rationing were limited for fear of evoking panic, allowing "invisible" rationing decisions to be made [65]. Similar considerations were brought to bear in the case of influenza vaccine, where rationing was accepted by health professionals and doctors as a necessary way to manage limited resources [66]. However, broader decisions about resource allocation were based on prioritising key personnel that by definition excluded those who were unemployed or in "nonessential" jobs. While this can ensure greater protection for a broader public, it can also exclude the most disenfranchised populations, thereby promoting social injustice [67].

Both of these issues – lack of discussion and the choice of prioritisation criteria – are ethically problematic. The main point emphasised in both these examples is the need for public discourse to ensure transparency in decision-making. This has become an increasing focus of ethical discussions as attempts to identify generally justifiable criteria for allocation failed, and has led to the development of philosophical frameworks for procedural justice in resource allocation [68]. This need is broadly recognised: when the recent trial data showed the benefits of earlier initiation, patient groups in South Africa immediately demanded a change in guidelines [69]. Nevertheless, the involvement of people with HIV/AIDS in such decisions is at best limited to public advocacy; they are rarely invited to the policy table. Thus, a need exists to explicitly frame and debate the main issues at stake by engaging key stakeholders from all sides – government, providers, civil society, and patients. Such debate should not be limited to narrow cost concerns but should consider broader principles that apply to rationing policies such as justice, reciprocity, consistency, explicitness, and revisability [70]. Public debate is also needed to gain political support for moving towards a policy that would effectively result in a drop in ART coverage as the number of people in need of treatment will increase.

Summary

The latest evidence on risks to health for people with HIV at CD4 counts above 200 cells/μL, together with the availably of newer, less toxic drugs, support the raising of the threshold of ART initiation from public health, ethical, and human rights perspectives. Guidelines for developed countries have adopted a higher cut-off for ART eligibility, and international guidelines for developing countries have recently been amended to support earlier initiation. However, most national-level guidelines continue to recommend deferring treatment to 200 cells/μL, a policy that, in human rights terms, falls into the category of "impermissible under-inclusiveness" [4].

This paper aims to show that a human rights analysis can contribute to more considered deliberation regarding the way forward, from which concrete policy options can emerge (Additional File 2, Table S2). The framework used here serves to clarify a number of important issues. The first step was to clarify the public health purpose. Clearly no medical reason exists for why deferred ART initiation should be preferred. Rather, the principal purpose of starting treatment later is to ration care. Rationing of essential medicines is a restriction of human rights, and the principle of least restriction serves to focus attention on alternative measures such as implementing policies that would increase capacity and decrease costs of care, and seeking additional funding to support ART expansion. Finally, where resources remain insufficient to provide early treatment for all, different views exist among governments, academia, civil society, and donors, and the principal of fair administration highlights the need to discuss these issues in a transparent manner involving all relevant stakeholders.

More data are needed on the cost-effectiveness of starting ART earlier, including not only the costs associated with treating opportunistic infections but also the costs of delaying ART [30]. Such evidence could be gained through the gradual adoption of an earlier threshold for initiation in pilot sites. This would also allow for important lessons to be learnt in terms of training staff, educating patients, and scaling up services. Such cost effectiveness data will be critical given that a shift towards earlier initiation will require both affected-country governments and the international community to provide additional funding to support expansion of care, even if long-term savings can be anticipated. Finally, implementation of these new recommendations is challenging. Progressive realisation using well-defined steps will be necessary to allow for a phased implementation as part of a framework of short-term targets towards nationwide policy adoption.

In conclusion, we believe that instead of continuing a policy of rationing ART based on medical criteria that have been abandoned elsewhere, governments should revise the initiation threshold in line with international recommendations, adopt a treatment policy that includes the use of less-toxic drugs, and implement cost-effective policies such as task-shifting and sourcing of more affordable medicines on the international market. Such measures require clear technical and financial support from donor governments that are currently applying a double standard by supporting ART care with restrictions to access that they themselves would not accept. Indeed, it is their duty under international law to provide such assistance.

Competing interests

The authors declare that they have no competing interests.

Authors' contributions

NF conceived of the study and wrote the first draft. All authors contributed to subsequent drafts. All authors have read and approved the final manuscript.

Acknowledgements

The authors would like to thank Leslie London for useful discussions, and Oliver Yun for editorial support.

Appendix

Table S1 Human rights analysis of when to start antiretroviral therapy.

Human rights analysis	Public Health Purpose		
	Reduce mortality and morbidity	Limit toxicity	Rationing
What is its likely effectiveness?	**Moderate** – targets those at greatest risk of mortality – promotes the development of opportunistic infections, including TB evidence supports an increase to CD4 <350: i) higher likelihood of treatment success if ART initiated earlier ii) illnesses develop even at CD4 >200	**Moderate** – delays number of people exposed to ART-related toxicities but does not address primary cause (the use of toxic drugs)	**Low** – Other mechanisms dominate
Is the policy well targeted?	**Yes/No** – applies to all HIV+ people – excludes some patients who would benefit from treatment – misses opportunities to enrol patients who may become eligible in the future (ie does not address pre-ART defaulting)	**Yes/No** – limits person-time exposure to ART – exposure delayed but not avoided	**No** – selects sicker patients who place greater demands on health services
What are the human rights benefits?	– promotes access to care and treatment for those at greatest risk of illness	– Limits harm of exposure to toxic drugs	– all individuals <200 are equally eligible – supports progressive realization (all patients will eventually meet criteria) – unclear whether rationing in this way leads to community (health system) benefits

Table S1 (cont'd)

	Public Health Purpose		
	Reduce mortality and morbidity	Limit toxicity	Rationing
What are the human rights burdens?	– allows the development of stigmatizing illnesses – poor availability of CD4 in rural areas may lead to discrimination by delaying ART initiation for the poorest	– unfavourable harm/benefit trade-off between limiting toxicity and treatment – does not address causes of toxicity: all people will eventually be exposed	– inconsistent with the duty to immediately provide access to essential medicines – places some patients at risk of disease (by allowing immune deterioration) – blanket policy that rations care even in places that could enrol more patients – may exhaust resources, and therefore limit access to health care, by focusing on the sickest
Are there less restrictive means to achieve the same objective?	**Yes** – Raise threshold to <350	**Yes** – provide less-toxic drugs (eg TDF)	**Yes** – decrease need to ration by increasing available resources – reduce HIV programme spending by reducing costs elsewhere (drugs, lab investigations, human resources) – increase capacity by adapting the model of delivery (out-of-clinic care or stable patients, nurse initiation of therapy) – limit long-term need by scaling up prevention – seek additional (international) resources to fund ART expansion
Are fair administrative procedures in place?	**No** – inadequate assessment of latest evidence	**No** – inadequate assessment of latest evidence	**No** – rationale implied rather than stated – public consultation lacking
Overall, is the policy the optimal approach to the problem?	**No** Policy restricts treatment for those who could benefit, misses opportunities to minimize defaulting, and may promote stigma	**No** Using less toxic drugs (TDF) would limit toxicity without limiting access to treatment. This would require a policy to procure less-expensive (generic) sources of TDF.	**No** Reasons for rationing should be addressed

Table S2 Recommendations for policy.

Promote transparency in decision-making
- *Public discourse involving relevant stakeholders*

Move towards increased threshold for initiation (350 cells/µl)
- *Phased implementation to build support and learn lessons*
- *Clear, short-term targets for nationwide polity adoption*

Implement supportive policies to improve efficiency in expanded access to care
- *Task-shifting*
- *Decentralized care to clinic level*

Pilot new models of delivery
- *fast-track procedures and out-of-facility care for stable patients*

Reduce drug prices
- *Use policy measures such as compulsory licensing to secure more affordable sources of antiretrovirals*

Make available less toxic drugs
- *Include less-toxic regimens in EDL and national guidelines*

Promote human rights considerations in public health decision-making

---

References

1. Antiretroviral Therapy Cohort Collaboration: Life expectancy of individuals on combination antiretroviral therapy in high-income countries: a collaborative analysis of 14 cohort studies. *Lancet* 2008, 372:293–9.

2. Lewden C., Chene G., Morlat P., *et al.*: HIV-infected adults with a CD4 cell count greater than 500 cells/mm3 on long-term combination antiretroviral therapy reach same mortality rates as the general population. *J Acquit Immune Defic Syndr* 2007, 46:72–7.

3. Braitstein P., Brinkhof M., Dabis F. F., *et al.*: Mortality of HIV-1-infected patients in the first year of antiretroviral therapy: comparison between low-income and high-income countries. *Lancet* 2006, 367:817–24.

4. Gostin L., Mann J.: Towards the development of a human rights impact assessment. In *Health and Human Rights: A Reader* Edited by: Mann J., Gruskin S., Grodin M., Annas G. New York: Routledge; 1999:54–71.

5. London L.: Human rights and public health: dichotomies or synergies in Developing countries? Examining the case of HIV in South Africa. *J Med Law Ethics* 2002, 30:677–91.

6. London L.: Confinement in the management of drug-resistant TB: The unsavoury prospect of balancing individual human rights and the public good. *SAJBL* 2008, 1:11–19.

7. Phillips A., Gazzard B., Clumeck N., *et al.*: When should antiretroviral therapy for HIV be started? *BMJ* 2007, 13:76–78.

8. When To Start Consortium: Timing of initiation of antiretroviral therapy in AIDS-free HIV-1-infected patients: a collaborative analysis of 18 HIV cohort studies. *Lancet* 2009, 373:1352–63.

9. Hammer S., Eron J., Reiss P., *et al.*: Antiretroviral Treatment of Adult HIV Infection 2008 Recommendations of the International AIDS Society-USA Panel. *JAMA* 2008, 300:555–570.

10. World Health Organisation: Rapid advice: antiretroviral therapy for HIV infection in adults and adolescents – November 2009. World Health Organisation, Geneva, Switzerland; 2009.

11. Badri M., Geary S., Maartens G., *et al.*: When to initiate highly active antiretroviral therapy in sub-Saharan Africa? A South African cost-effectiveness study. *Antiviral Therapy* 2006, 11:63–72.

12. MSF: *Help wanted: health worker shortages limits access to HIV/AIDS treatment in southern Africa* 2007 [http://www.msf.org.za/docs/Help Wanted FINAL.pdf]. MSF, Johannesburg.

13. The ART-LINC Collaboration of the International Databases to Evaluate AIDS (IeDEA): Antiretroviral therapy in resource-limited settings 1996 to 2006: patient characteristics, treatment regimens and monitoring in sub-Saharan Africa, Asia and Latin America. *TMIH* 2008, 13:870–879.

14. Cullinan K.: What's good for the individual might crash the system. *Health-E News* 2008 [http://www.health-e.org.za/news/article.php?uid=20032045].

15. Miller V., Mocroft A., Reiss P., *et al.*: Relations among CD4-lymphocyte count nadir, antiretroviral therapy, and HIV-1 disease progression: results from the EuroSIDA study. *Ann Intern Med* 1999, 130:570–7.

16. Renaud-Théry F., Nguimfack B., Vitoria M., *et al.*: Use of antiretroviral therapy in resource-limited countries in 2006: distribution and uptake of first- and second-line regimens. *AIDS* 2007:S89–95.

17. Carr A., Amin J.: Efficacy and tolerability of initial antiretroviral therapy: a systematic review. *AIDS* 2009, 23:343–53.

18. Ubel P.: Pricing Life: Why It's Time for Health Care Rationing. Cambridge, Massachusetts, MIT Press; 2001.

19. Phillips A., Cascade Collaboration: Short-term risk of AIDS according to current CD4 cell count and viral load in antiretroviral drug-naïve individuals and those treated in the monotherapy era. *AIDS* 2004, 18:51–8.

20. Egger M., May M., Chêne G., *et al.*: ART Cohort Collaboration. Prognosis of HIV-1-infected patients starting highly active antiretroviral therapy: a collaborative analysis of prospective studies. *Lancet* 2002, 360:119–129.

21. Ford N.: Highlights of the International AIDS Society Conference. *Lancet Infectious Diseases* 2009, 9:528.

22. Danel C., Moh R., Minga A., *et al.*: CD4-guided structured antiretroviral treatment interruption strategy in HIV-infected adults in west Africa (Trivacan ANRS 1269 trial): a randomised trial. *Lancet* 2006, 367:1981–9.

23. Strategies for Management of Antiretroviral Therapy (SMART) Study Group, El-Sadr W., Lundgren J., *et al.*: CD4+ count-guided interruption of antiretroviral treatment. *N Engl J Med* 2006, 355:2283–96.

24. Auvert B., Males S., Puren A., *et al.*: Can highly active antiretroviral therapy reduce the spread of HIV?: A study in a township of South Africa. *J Acquir Immune Defic Syndr* 2004, 36:613–21.

25. Granich R., Gilks C., Dye C., *et al.*: Universal voluntary HIV testing with immediate antiretroviral therapy as a strategy for elimination of HIV transmission: a mathematical model. *Lancet* 2009, 373:48–57.

26. Boyd M.: Improvements in antiretroviral therapy outcomes over calendar time. *Curr Opin HIV AIDS* 2009, 4:194–9.

27. Gill V., Lima V. D., Zhang W., *et al.*: Improved Virological Outcomes in British Columbia Concomitant with Decreasing Incidence of HIV Type 1 Drug Resistance Detection. *Clin Infect Dis* 2010, 50:99–105.

28. Ford N., Calmy A.: Improving first-line antiretroviral therapy in resource-limited settings. *Curr Opin HIV AIDS* 2010, 1:38–47.

29. Galvao J.: Access to antiretroviral drugs in Brazil. *Lancet* 2002, 360:1862–65.
30. Walensky R., Wolf L., Wood R., *et al.*: When to start antiretroviral therapy in resource-limited settings. *Ann Intern Med* 2009, 151:157–66.
31. Boulle A., Bock P., Osier M., *et al.*: Antiretroviral therapy and early mortality in South Africa. *Bull World Health Organ* 2008, 86:678–87.
32. Maponyane M., Jaffer A., Meyer-Rath G., *et al.*: 2-year follow up of patients attending ART clinics in Gauteng & North West province: results of a systematic review of 12,987 patient files. *Third South African AIDS Conference, Durban* 2007. Abstract 326
33. United Nations. Access to medication in the context of pandemics such as HIV/AIDS: commission on human rights, resolution 2001/33. [http://www.temple.edu/lawschool/drwiltext/docs/UN%20Commission%20on%20Human%20Rights%20Res%202001_22.pdf].
34. International Covenant on Economic, Social and Cultural Rights (ICESCR), UN. 1976.
35. UN Committee on Economic, Social and Cultural Rights (CESCR). General Comment 14, paras 43–44 [http://www2.ohchr.org/english/bodies/cescr/comments.htm]
36. WHO Model List of Essential Medicines 2007 [http://www.who.int/medicines/publications/08_ENGLISH_indexFINAL_EML15.pdf].
37. Universal Declaration of Human Rights (UDHR). UN, Paris; 1948.
38. International Covenant on Civil and Political Rights (ICCPR) 1976 [http://www2.ohchr.org/english/law/ccpr.htm].
39. African Charter on Human and People's Rights 1981 [http://www.hrcr.org/docs/Banjul/afrhr.html].
40. Patients' rights charter [http://www.doh.gov.za/docs/legislation/patientsright/chartere.html]
41. McGough L., Reynolds S., Quinn T., *et al.*: Which Patients First? Setting Priorities for Antiretroviral Therapy Where Resources AreLimited. *AJPH* 2005, 95:1173–80.
42. Hunt P., Khosla R.: The human right to medicines. *Sur Int J Human Rights* 2008, 8:99–117.
43. Boulle A., Hilderbrand K., Menten J., Coetzee D., Ford N., Matthys F., Boelaert M., Stuyft P. Van der: Exploring HIV risk perception and behaviour in the context of antiretroviral treatment: results from a township household survey. *AIDS Care* 2008, 20:771–81.
44. Mahajan A., Sayles J., Patel V., *et al.*: Stigma in the HIV/AIDS epidemic: a review of the literature and recommendations for the way forward. *AIDS* 2008, 22:S67–79.
45. United Nations, Economic and Social Council, UN Sub-Commission on Prevention of Discrimination and Protection of Minorities *Siracusa principles on the limitation and derogation of provisions in the International Covenant on Civil and Political Rights, Annex* 1984 [http://hei.unige.ch/~clapham/hrdoc/docs/siracusa.html].
46. Rosen S., Long L., Fox M., *et al.*: Cost and Cost-Effectiveness of Switching From Stavudine to Tenofovir in First-Line Antiretroviral Regimens in South Africa. *JAIDS* 2008, 48:334–344.
47. Ford N., Gray A., Venter F.: Tough choices: Tenofovir, tenders and treatment. *Southern African J HIV Med* 2008:8–10.
48. Ford N., Wilson D., Costa Chaves G., *et al.*: Sustaining access to antiretroviral therapy in developing countries: lessons from Brazil and Thailand. *AIDS* 2007, 21:S21–29.

49. Jack A.: India overturns drug patents. *Financial Times* 2009.
50. Dickenson D.: Can Medical Criteria Settle Priority-Setting Debates? The Need for Ethical Analysis. *Health care Anal* 1999, 7:131–7.
51. Anon: Frustration over South African AIDS budget cuts. *Afrol News* 2008.
52. World Health Organisation: "Treat train retain. Task shifting: Global recommendations and guidelines" Geneva. 2007 [http://www.who.int/healthsystems/task_shifting/en]. Accessed 9 April 2009.
53. Jaffar S., Amuron B., Foster S., Birungi J., Levin J., Namara G., Nabiryo C., Ndembi N., Kyomuhangi R., Opio A., Bunnell R., Tappero J. W., Mermin J., Coutinho A., Grosskurth H., on behalf of the Jinja trial team: Rates of virological failure in patients treated in a home-based versus a facility-based HIV-care model in Jinja, southeast Uganda: a cluster-randomised equivalence trial. *Lancet* 2009, 374(9707):2080–9.
54. Hunt P., Backman G.: Health systems and the right to the highest attainable standard of health. *Health and Human Rights* 2008, 10:81–92.
55. Bristol N.: US Senate passes new PEPFAR bill. *Lancet* 2008, 372:277–8.
56. Ooms G., Derderian K., Melody D.: Do we need a world health insurance to realise the right to health? *PLoS Med* 2006, 3:1271 –6.
57. Gruskin S., Tarantola D.: Universal Access to HIV prevention, treatment and care: assessing the inclusion of human rights in international and national strategic plans. *AIDS* 2008, 22:S123–S132.
58. Singer P., Benatar S., Bernstein M., *et al.*: Ethics and SARS: lessons from Toronto. *BMJ* 2003, 327:1342–1344.
59. Baldwin-Ragaven L., de Gruchy J., London L.: An Ambulance of the wrong colour. Health professionals, human rights and ethics in South Africa. UCT Press, Cape Town; 1999.
60. Daniels N.: Just Health Care. Cambridge, New York: Cambridge University Press; 1985.
61. Mann J.: Medicine and public health, ethics and human rights. In *Health and Human Rights: A Reader* Edited by: Mann J., Gruskin S., Grodin M., Annas G. New York: Routledge; 1999:54–71.
62. Hurst S.: "Vulnerability in Research and Health Care: Describing the Elephant in the Room?". *Bioethics 22, S.A* 2008:191–202.
63. London L.: A case for integrating human rights in public health policy. *SAMJ* 2006, 96:302–3.
64. Coulter A., Ham C.: The global challenge of health care rationing. Oxford, Oxford University Press; 2000.
65. Brett A., Zuger A.: The Run on Tamiflu – Should Physicians Prescribe on Demand? *NEJM* 2005, 353:2636–2637.
66. DeCoster B.: Avian Influenza and the Failure of Public Rationing Discussions. *J Med Law Ethics* 2006, 3:620–623.
67. Lee T.: Rationing Influenza Vaccine. *NEJM* 2004, 351:2365–2366.
68. Gostin L., Powers M.: What Does Social Justice Require For The Public's Health? *Health Affairs* 2008, 25:1053–1060.
69. Daniels N., Sabin J.: Limits to health care: fair procedures, democratic deliberation, and the legitimacy problem for insurers. *Philos Public Aff* 1997, 26:303–50.
70. Anon: TAC calls on National Health Council to adopt SANAC proposals. 2009 [http://www.tac.org.za/community/node/2726].

105

HIV/AIDS IN CUBA

A rights-based analysis

Tim Anderson

Source: *Health and Human Rights*, 11:1 (2009), 93–104.

Abstract

The common assertion that Cuba's achievements in HIV/AIDS control have come at a cost in human rights is reinforced by US hostility toward its small neighbor. Nevertheless, a rights-based analysis may be one useful way of examining the actual Cuban experience. By reference to the United Nation's Guidelines on HIV/AIDS and Human Rights, this paper examines the Cuban experience as it relates to the themes of quarantine and personal freedom; privacy in testing and tracing; education, participation, and non-discrimination; and the availability of AIDS treatment. The paper concludes that Cuba's quarantine period was unnecessarily prolonged in the late 1980s but that this prolonged quarantine did not target men who have sex with men. Testing and tracing procedures in Cuba follow a standard protocol, but they are more thorough than elsewhere. Cuba has strengthened participation in education programs, and treatment is now the best in the Caribbean region. The human rights implications of HIV programs must be considered in an integrated way. Selective criticisms of the Cuban program have not improved international understanding of HIV/AIDS treatment in Cuba.

Introduction

Cuba has achieved the lowest rate of HIV infection and the highest level of AIDS treatment in the Caribbean region.[1] Yet the Cuban HIV program — part of its famous health system — has been subjected to many criticisms, usually linked to the themes of "freedom" and "rights." These criticisms must be seen in the broader context of demands for economic "freedoms" in Cuba and in the context of US demands for the dismantling of Cuban socialism and for widespread privatization, including privatization of the public health system. Outside understandings of the Cuban health system are further undermined by the US economic blockade of Cuba, roundly condemned each year by the United Nations General Assembly, which prevents normal scientific and cultural exchange between the US and Cuba.

In view of the global search for lessons on best practices for containing the HIV/AIDS pandemic, particular criticisms of the Cuban HIV program deserve closer attention. A rights-based analysis could be one useful way of examining the Cuban experience. Such an approach might address some of the criticisms directed at Cuba, whether through a selective focus on particular rights issues or through general, utilitarian notions that Cuba has forced "trade offs" between personal liberties and the protection of public health.[2]

This paper introduces the Cuban experience with HIV/AIDS by reference to historical developments and recent Cuban perspectives. It draws on data from interviews with a number of Cuban peer educators and HIV professionals in 2005–2006. Following discussion of these interviews, the paper then uses the United Nations International Guidelines on HIV/AIDS and Human Rights to apply a rights-based analysis to several themes in the way Cuba approaches HIV/AIDS treatment: quarantine and personal freedom; privacy in testing and tracing; education, participation, and non-discrimination; and the availability of AIDS treatment. It concludes with a rights-based assessment of the Cuban program.

Achievements and criticism

UNAIDS notes that "Cuba's epidemic remains the smallest in the [Caribbean] region," with a sexually active adult infection rate of around 0.1%.[3] Table 1 shows infection rates and antiretroviral therapy (ART) coverage rates for Cuba and many of its closest neighbors. The Caribbean region has the second highest HIV infection rate in the world, and Cuba, often advertised in tourism literature as a "sexually permissive" society, appears particularly exposed to risk as it has been receiving more than two million tourists per year since 2004.[4] Although there has been a steady increase in newly reported HIV infections since the late 1990s, mostly in men who have sex with men (MSM), Cuba's epidemic remains relatively small.

Nevertheless, by late 2008, Cuba's infection rate had risen (see Table 2) and may now approach 0.15% of sexually active adults. This is still a significantly lower rate than that of Cuba's neighbors, but it represents an ongoing challenge. After universal and free coverage of patients with antiretroviral treatment began in 2001, the death rate fell markedly.[5] The HIV infection prevalence is slowly rising, but AIDS is being controlled.

In the face of these achievements, there has been a series of predominantly US-based criticisms of the Cuban methods, mostly in the popular media but reinforced by some academic material. The first criticism was over the 1986–1989 use of a mandatory quarantine period in health resorts (called *sanatorios*,

Table 1 HIV infection rates and ART coverage: Cuba and her neighbors.

	Haiti	Domin. Republic	Honduras	Jamaica	USA	Costa Rica	Colombia	Mexico	Cuba
Infection rates, adults age 15–49 (%), 2007	1.9–2.5	0.9–1.2	0.4–1.1	1.1–2.1	0.4–1.0	0.2–0.6	0.4–0.8	0.2–0.5	<0.1–0.2
ART coverage of HIV-positive persons (%), 2006	41	38	47	43	NA	>95	38	57	>95

Sources: For HIV infection rates: UNAIDS, *2008 Report on the Global AIDS Epidemic* (Geneva: United Nations Programme on HIV/AIDS and World Health Organization, 2008), p. 230. Available at http://data.unaids.org/pub/GlobalReport/2008/jc1510_2008_global_report_pp211_234_en.pdf; and for ART coverage: "Annex 1: Estimated numbers of people receiving and needing antiretroviral therapy and coverage percentages, 2006–2007," in World Health Organization, *Towards universal access: Scaling up priority HIV/AIDS interventions in the health sector* (Geneva: World Health Organization, 2008). Available at http://www.who.int/hiv/pub/2008progressreport/en/.

Table 2 Cumulative HIV/AIDS cases in Cuba from 1986 to 2008.

National data from 1986 to:	November 22, 2005	August 28, 2007	November 18, 2008
Total seropositive	6,827	8,873	10,454
Total AIDS cases	2,782	3,387	3,910
Total deaths	1,405	1,534	1,721
Seropositive males	5,468 (80.1%)	7,159 (80.7%)	8,363 (80%)
Men who have sex with men	4,707 (68.9%)	6,025 (67.9%)	7,119 (68.1%)
Seropositive females	1,339 (19.6%)	1,714 (19.3%)	2.090 (20%)

Source: Compiled from Vice-Ministerio de Higiene Epidemiologica, "VIH/SIDA: Datos fecha de cierre" (Centro Nacional de Prevención de las ITS/VIH/SIDA, Havana) 22 Nov. 2005/28 Aug. 2007/18 Nov. 2008.

or sanatoria) for the first persons infected with HIV. A *Los Angeles Times* report from 1988 noted that a US delegation visiting a sanatorium described it as "pleasant but frightening."[6] The following year, a US medical report noted wide-scale testing but claimed that "Cuba has not made education the key focus of its anti-AIDS strategy."[7] Such criticisms were not always well-informed. Education has been central to the Cuban HIV/AIDS programs from the beginning, though the emphases of education efforts have changed (discussed further below).

Programs similar to Cuba's experiment with quarantine were also proposed in many parts of the US in the 1980s. Between 1987 and 1990, for example, "more than a dozen states" brought AIDS within the scope of state quarantine statutes.[8] However, modernization of these laws generally included provisions for "the least restrictive alternative."[9] In Cuba's case, patients began to come and go from sanatoria in 1989. In 1993, an alternate non-sanatoria-based day care program was introduced.[10] Some US medical reports took the Cuban approach seriously, studied it in some detail, and noted the phasing-out of quarantine in the late 1980s.[11] Nevertheless, attacks in the popular media continued long after the removal of quarantine, even though advances in HIV education were also noted.[12]

These attacks have used examples — from individual cases and from the testing regime as a whole — in their efforts to reinforce the theme that Cuban patients with HIV/AIDS were being deprived of their freedom as a way to explain Cuba's relative success. Some Cuban professionals, however, do not consider the early quarantine period to have been a significant part of their program's success.[13] One 2003 medical report, for example, noting that Cuba had an HIV infection rate "nearly eleven times lower than [that of] the United States," suggested that this could be due to Cuba being "politically and socially isolated," to Cubans being less susceptible to risk factors such as poverty and social inequality, and to "aggressive HIV screening and subsequent contact tracing of infected individuals."[14] Yet "aggressive" seems an inappropriate word and "isolated" improbable since, by the time of the report, there had been nearly a decade of mass tourism to Cuba.

A rights-based analysis

In view of the polemics over Cuba and their extension into discussions of the Cuban HIV program, it seems useful to complete a more systematic rights-based analysis of the Cuban program in historical perspective.[15] This can be done by reference to the UN's human rights guidelines, which call on states "to implement an effective, rights-based response" to the HIV pandemic.[16] I will do this by addressing the major relevant themes of quarantine and personal freedom; privacy through the testing and tracing regimes; the rights of education, participation and non-discrimination; and finally the right to access AIDS treatment.

Quarantine and personal freedom

The quarantine period that was enforced as a standard procedure for HIV/AIDS treatment in Cuba between 1986 and 1989 is probably the most controversial practice associated with Cuban health care. As it relates to human rights, the issue here is the personal freedom of movement, a cost borne by every person subject to any quarantine regime; such a denial of freedom may also have discriminatory implications.[17] However, two misunderstandings persist about the Cuban quarantine period. First, it is sometimes suggested that the practice persisted into the 1990s, when the virus and its treatment were better understood.[18] Second, it has been suggested that quarantine predominantly targeted men who have sex with men (MSM).[19] In response to these criticisms on quarantine, Cuban authors argue that it was an emergency response that took place when little was known about the disease and that the practice has since changed.[20] Cuban respondents also argue that the initial (quarantine) period gave health care workers a useful "space" to prepare a more considered response.[21] Nancy Scheper-Hughes was told that the early use of sanatoria was not about quarantine but rather "aggressive medical treatment, research, testing of new drugs and epidemiological vigilance"; Scheper-Hughes concluded that she was left with "contradictory impressions" but mostly admiration for the achievements of the Cuban program.[22] Most visitors to the sanatoria have commented favorably on their environment, food, and general conditions. A smaller group of patients remains in sanatoria voluntarily, to this day, because of the favorable conditions and support or because of problems at home. Yet some relationship between the initial quarantine and issues of stigmatization and fear of the disease has also been acknowledged.[23]

A National AIDS Commission was set up in Cuba in 1983 with the aim of developing a complete prevention and treatment program. In that same year, Fidel Castro charged the Instituto Pedro Kourí with the responsibility of ensuring that this epidemic "does not constitute a health problem for Cuba."[24] The first Cuban AIDS case was not diagnosed until 1985, and the first death occurred in 1986; the decision to proceed with sanatoria was based on a 1982 law set up to allow for the isolation of those carrying an infectious disease that might be a danger to the public.[25] The first sanatorium was in Havana Province; soon others on the island followed. Cuba has more recently used quarantine to prevent dengue fever victims from infecting the broader population.[26]

The Cuban quarantine of HIV-positive persons has raised concerns about the likelihood of unjust discrimination against gay and bisexual men in light of Cuba's traditionally "macho" culture and the emerging trend of the 1980s to associate HIV/AIDS with MSM. In the 1980s, Cuban analysts recognized that the groups most at risk for HIV infection in Western countries were MSM, intravenous drug users, and those receiving blood transfusions. Yet the association of HIV infection with gay and bisexual men was not a global tendency, since those at risk in Africa were young sexually active hetero-sexuals, children, sex workers, and those receiving blood transfusions.[27] Cuba in the 1980s was strongly linked to Africa through various aid missions, particularly through its deployment of thousands of troops in Angola. AIDS in Africa was and remains a disease primarily affecting heterosexual persons, with almost equal numbers of HIV-positive women and men. Initial evidence suggested that Cuba had a pattern of HIV infection similar to that of Africa, though there were signs of an emerging hybrid infection pattern toward the Western one of a largely MSM epidemic. By 1988, Cuba had 190 HIV-positive cases and seven deaths. By the late 1980s, MSM were substantially over-represented in the HIV-positive population in Cuba but were still a minority of cases (39 cases or 21%); these numbers were identical to those for infected women.[28] MSM were thus a minority of those quarantined for HIV/AIDS. This may suggest that the stigmas associated with HIV infection and against homosexuality (in a culture with significant homophobia) did not necessarily coincide. The initial quarantine measure therefore did not suggest a regime of discrimination against gay and bisexual men, since they did not constitute a majority of infected persons until later in the mid-1990s.

From 1989 onward, patients could come and go from the sanatoria, and at the end of 1993, the day care program (*sistema de atención ambulatoria* or SAA) was opened for all those who did not want to live in a sanatorium. However, all newly infected patients were (and are) required to attend a course called "Living with HIV." Those in the SAA program live at home but attend clinics daily. They receive the same treatment as those at the sanatoria, including a diet supplemented with milk, fiber, and vegetables.[29] After the first few months of close observation at the sanatoria, patients are monitored as outpatients by their family doctor.[30] In January 1998, the "Hospital for a Day" system was opened. This provided morning sessions in the sanatoria as part of an eight-week program.[31] Some of these programs were later taken over by support teams, and since the year 2000, many newly-diagnosed patients do not use sanatoria at all, opting instead to participate in the "Living with HIV" program. This program is directed and operated by peer educators (who are often also HIV-positive) in a community-based "Line of Support" for those living with HIV/AIDS.[32]

By the mid-2000s, those voluntarily in the sanatoria appeared to be a shrinking minority; in Plaza Municipality, for example, seven times more HIV-positive individuals were in day care than in sanatoria.[33] Nevertheless, the expansion in day care seems to have resulted in sanatoria populations composed of a disproportionately high percentage of socially marginalized individuals. In 2002–2003, for example, 80% of the 267 patients at Los Cocos had some family dysfunction, 66% had been unemployed, over 40% had some type of psychiatric disturbance, and over 50% had received only basic secondary schooling (a low level for Cubans).[34] These statistics have been cited in Cuba as evidence of the need to further develop integrated systems of social support to prevent isolation of marginalized people.[35]

Social integration rather than isolation remains a strong priority of the Cuban system. A specialist nurse with nine years of experience in Cuba's HIV/AIDS programs puts it this way:

> From the time a person is diagnosed, it is the responsibility of the state to put that person back in society to resume their normal life. So public health, workplaces, mass organizations, all have a role in the well-being of the patient, so that they don't feel rejected, so they know this is a person living with a virus, or an illness, but that this is nothing to be ashamed of.[36]

An important structural part of this policy of social inclusion is that by law all HIV-positive patients maintain their job entitlements and 100% of their salary when they have to be absent from work for programs or treatment.[37] Despite this law, some Cuban employers have tried to remove HIV-positive people from their jobs. In a survey of 80 patients who had left Los Cocos sanatorium for ambulatory care, 16 had faced attempts to exclude them from their work. For 12 patients who had permanent jobs, these attempts failed, except in the case of one individual who became discouraged and abandoned his appeal. However, four individuals who had been on temporary contracts lost their jobs, even though they had been considered good workers. Some health workers have also faced pressures, for example, to move their place of work to an HIV patient care facility, such as a sanatorium. This had led to calls for greater clarity in anti-discrimination procedures and for more social support consistent with "the principles of solidarity of Cuban society."[38]

Although the early quarantine practice was a result of a strong directive to protect public health, it seems that fear of the disease, including fear among some professionals, may have led to the prolonging of the quarantine period.[39] This extension was an unreasonable deprivation of liberty, but there is no evidence that the early quarantine period was directed at gay and bisexual men — or more broadly, MSM — who formed a minority of the HIV-positive population at that time.

Privacy: testing and tracing

The second main theme of the rights-based criticism of the Cuban quarantine system for HIV/AIDS relates to privacy concerns over the regimes for testing and contact tracing. The UN has called for law and practice to "ensure privacy and confidentiality" of HIV-infected people and their families.[40] Here criticism of Cuba has been anecdotal and weak. While the Cuban practice of testing and contact tracing is thorough, its basic principles appear similar to those of many other countries with effective testing regimes. Scheper-Hughes described early Cuban testing as part of "the classical public health tradition — routine testing with contact tracing and partner notification," yet also as "the most comprehensive . . . of any nation."[41] Testing is neither universal nor aggressive but is targeted at high-risk groups. Patient consent is required for any personal procedure, such as a blood test, and privacy laws to protect patient confidentiality are said to be taken seriously.[42]

Testing began in 1986, and by the following year, testing included vulnerable groups such as pregnant women, health workers, blood donors, and those who had traveled to areas with a high incidence of the disease.[43] By February 1988, around 25% of the sexually active Cuban population had been tested. There was mandatory testing of blood donors, pregnant women, those with other sexually transmitted diseases (STDs), all hospital admissions, and the sexual contacts of those already infected. Some critics of the Cuban system complained about its sexual contact tracing and requests for testing.[44] However, this practice is hardly unique to Cuba. Some invasion of the privacy of the contact group would seem to be justified on public health grounds; indeed measured breaches of privacy occur in most forms of epidemiological surveillance. In 1988, there were positive results in almost 4% of contact trace testing in Cuba, a far higher level than any of the other groups (pregnant women, and so forth) undergoing targeted testing.[45]

By 2003, there were approximately 1.5 to 1.6 million tests per year.[46] While MSM came to be the largest infected group in the mid-1990s, women still constitute 21% of infected Cubans, and they are the fastest growing HIV-positive group.[47] All testing is done through the family doctor or anonymously through a Policlinic (Cuban treatment centers that carry out most procedures and lie between the basic community health centers and the hospital system). Blood tests require patient consent, a fundamental element of Cuban medical practice.[48] Sexual contacts are traced with some sensitivity but also with thoroughness. There is a fair degree of moral persuasion in the Cuban system, generally, but our interviews suggested that there is also a respect for rights in the professional procedure. When there is a positive HIV finding, for example, the person is asked, as part of a structured interview, for all of their sexual contacts in recent years. These contacts are followed up with privately by the family doctor and often assisted by a nurse.[49] HIV cases and some other listed diseases (such as leprosy) are confidentially registered with the National Center for Epidemiology. This information is protected by law, with penalties for breaches of the privacy of patients' records.[50]

The November 2005 data for Plaza Municipality (which, by Cuban standards, has a high rate of infection), covering 1985–2005, gives a more detailed picture of the Cuban HIV-positive population and the testing system. Over the previous twenty years in Plaza Municipality, 57 HIV-positive individuals died, and the remaining 223 of the 280 HIV-positive persons were classified as "people living with HIV." Of these, 187 were day care patients, 25 were in a sanatorium, 19 had gone overseas, and several were in a specialist hospital or under private care.[51] The major methods of discovery of the 280 infections were by normal family doctor consultations (74), tracing the sexual contacts of infected persons after an interview (55), hospital in-patient tests (43), STD tests (36), self-reports (31), blood donor tests (29), and prisoner tests (9). A little over 15% of the group members were female and 75% were MSM. This proportion varies only slightly from the national average (see Table 2 on page 95).[52]

These findings seem to suggest that Cuba's privacy and confidentiality practices in testing and tracing are standard in that laws provide penalties for breaches of the privacy rules. Cuba is distinct, however, for the moral persuasion that puts particular pressure on individual choices across a range of issues in Cuban society. Because of this moral persuasion, patients requested to disclose sexual contacts might feel a stronger sense of obligation to do so. But a strong sense of obligation to certain behaviors does not, in our view, in and of itself constitute a breach of the United Nations standards as they relate to HIV/AIDS and human rights.

Education, participation, and non-discrimination

Education on rights (to medical care and social treatment) and participation in HIV programs are important principles stressed by the UN's human rights guidelines.[53] These principles must in turn be linked to the basic right to non-discrimination. Cuba's social policy has always stressed education and popular involvement, but the structure of the HIV program, including the education and participation components, has undergone several changes.

The National Program for the Prevention and Control of STDs and HIV/AIDS was established in Cuba in 1986, with the primary aim of "ensuring that the process of infection-illness does not become an important health

Table 3 Key themes in the Cuban HIV/AIDS strategic principles, 1986 and 1998.

1986	1998
epidemiological vigilance	information
medical assistance	capacity building
epidemiological and clinical research	education
education	research
	communication
	counseling

Source: R. Ochoa Soto, J. Sánchez Fuentes, M. Villalón Oramas, et al., *Manual para Médicos de Familia Sobre ITS/VIH/SIDA* (Havana: Ministerio de Salud Pública, Centro Nacional de Prevención de las ITS/VIH/SIDA, 2003), p. 9.

problem for the Cuban population."[54] This preventive approach was very soon challenged by the international shift to a focus on health promotion. Committed to developing and prioritizing their health system, Cuba took seriously the discussions at the 1986 First International Health Promotion Conference in Ottawa, Canada, and began to elevate the notion of "health as a source of the richness of life," regarding programs of prevention as "doors of entry" to health promotion.[55] This principle was well established by the time Cuba revised their policy on AIDS in 1998, which was issued by the newly formed National Center for the Prevention of STDs/HIV/AIDS. This revised policy put into place a stronger emphasis on social support and participation, and this shift in emphasis is reflected in Table 3 on page 99.

Several booklets provide a foundation for patient education in the new policy. The educational text "Living with HIV" covers clinical information, HIV and the social environment, information on mutual help, nutrition and hygiene, sexuality, and some legal considerations.[56] It explains the details of drug therapy, the development of mutual aid groups and self help strategies, and the rights and duties of HIV-positive persons, as well as work, social security, health, and confidentiality law. A second booklet, "Living together with HIV" is designed for the families of HIV-positive individuals; this booklet discusses topics such as the social, familial, and work implications of HIV/AIDS in addition to discussing HIV/AIDS treatment and HIV/AIDS-related concerns as they pertain to biosecurity, nutrition and hygiene, death, pregnancy, children, and where to get help.[57] It explains infection and the disease, treatment regimes, and how to support family members living with the disease. When Dr. Byron Barksdale told the American Association for the Advancement of Science that the US could learn lessons from Cuba, he pointed in particular to Cuba's six-week "Living with AIDS" program, noting that six weeks "is certainly a longer time than is given to people in the US who receive such a diagnosis. They may get about 5 minutes worth of education."[58] Indeed, the "Living with AIDS" program appears to meet several of the UN's educational and rights requirements.[59] A family doctor manual on HIV and STDs, another educational resource available in Cuba, provides parallel, detailed information to local health workers.[60]

Since the 1990s, when the Cuban HIV epidemic became one characterized as being most prevalent among MSM, the question of public education — in particular dealing with the compound issue of homophobia in a macho Latino culture and of public stigmatization of and discrimination against HIV patients — has required greater focus. Campaigns in support of sexual diversity, considered a part of the "social inclusion" policy, are first introduced to children through the school system, which begins sex education (including sexual diversity education) at grade five. The national program, including a TV soap opera with gay and lesbian individuals as well as characters who are HIV-positive, is led by the National Center for Sex Education (CENESEX). The Federation of Cuban Women (FMC) began sex education programs in the early 1970s and set up CENESEX in 1989. Led by Mariela Castro (daughter of Raul Castro and the late Vilma Espín, a founder of the FMC), CENESEX stresses acceptance of sexual diversity and has attracted international attention in recent years for its campaigns for the rights of transgender persons, including the recognition of an individual's gender identity, regardless of birth sex, and provision of state-funded sexual reassignment surgery.[61]

Cuba's National Center for the Prevention of STDs and HIV/AIDS, with international support (for example, from the United Nations Development Programme [UNDP]), hosts training programs, assessment, and research in-person and helpline telephone counseling, networking, condom distribution, help for mutual support groups, nutrition education, and support for vulnerable groups. An "Afroache" program trains educators and develops specially focused educational materials for addressing the issues from that religious perspective as it is practiced in Cuba.[62] Although churches appear to have no great influence on the educational campaign or the use of condoms, some of the material developed by the National Center includes the basic information that safe sex includes abstinence and that this is the only form of safe sex endorsed by the Catholic Church. Nevertheless, most materials provide an overwhelming emphasis on the use of condoms, which are distributed freely, in the millions, through the National Center.

Education programs must be periodically reviewed. The manual for groups working in HIV/AIDS prevention refers to a method developed by US academic Dr. David Kolb. This method is a teaching and learning process that emphasizes a circular relationship among concrete experience, observation and reflection, conceptualization, and practice.[63] Long-term cooperation was also developed with some international agencies, in particular the World Health Organization and the UNDP. The National Center for the Prevention of STDs and HIV/AIDS, for example, was created in 1998 with support from the UNDP and Doctors without Borders (Holland) to help expand HIV education.[64]

Many of the health promotion pamphlets that this author observed in use during 2005–2006 were aimed at the general population, with some material aimed more directly at men who have sex with men (for example, "Siempre conmigo/Always with me" and "Hablando entre nosotros/Speaking amongst ourselves") or addressing the male responsibility for condom use (for example, "Los hombres marcan la diferencia/Men make the difference"). Another national pamphlet addressed cultural attitudes, urging, "Judge your friends by their qualities, not by their sexual orientation," and stressing acceptance of sexual diversity to counter prejudices and stigmas. This pamphlet states that lesbian, gay, bisexual, and transgender identities are all valid forms of sexuality and gender identity and that "understanding and accepting people as they are, will make you grow as a better person" (for example, a pamphlet titled, "He is also one of us"). Local music stars have been enlisted to help promote safe sex, for example in the national HIV magazine *Lazo Adentro*.[65]

International polemic has sometimes argued that homophobia in Cuba is a matter of official policy. Some outside commentators argue that homophobia was "institutionalized," at least prior to the 1980s.[66] Nevertheless, Cuban activists for sexual diversity seem to regard homophobia these days as mostly a cultural problem.[67] One activist who is transgender rejects the idea that violence against people for their sexual orientation or gender identity exists in Cuba, as it does in some other parts of Latin America.[68] Fidel Castro accepts that "homosexuals were victims of discrimination" in Cuba in the past but adds that "in the more cultured sectors there was less prejudice against homosexuals. . . . [D]iscrimination and machismo are today inversely proportional to the level of culture and knowledge. . . . I would like to think that discrimination against homosexuals is a problem that is being overcome."[69]

Participation of HIV-positive persons in HIV/AIDS programs, less evident in the early phase when programs were led by professionals, has increased since the 1998 reforms. Following the growth of the post-1993 day care program, a community-based "Line of Support" for people living with HIV/AIDS has been developed, and this program has been increasingly populated by HIV-positive peer educators. This changing trend in program leadership has also helped to separate much of the "Living with AIDS" program from its earlier association with the sanatoria.[70] The peer educators/health promoters are volunteers, with paid time out from their employment. The number of HIV-positive educators/health promoters is not disclosed for privacy reasons, but HIV-positive workers can disclose their own status. After pressure from "Line of Support" groups, the government began to pay many of the municipal coordinators full-time salaries. Health promoters have created pressure for more resources to support the expansion of the day care program, but they have been told that this allocation of resources had to compete in the health budget with, for example, programs for children with cancer or those with diabetes.[71] Both the National Center and the Line of Support have been fostering mutual support groups, some of which are very small and want to remain anonymous. Another more recent shift in health promotion campaigns has been to redirect some attention to the 25+ age group, where there have been higher than average infection rates.[72]

Cuba has thus taken some significant steps toward developing levels of participation in its HIV programs, as well as cooperating effectively with international agencies, as is urged by the UN guidelines.[73] In the two decades since the creation of CENESEX in 1989, Cuba has made some significant advances in popular education on sexual diversity. In the HIV/AIDS program, the expanded role of peer educators in the 2000s is noteworthy, when considering the right to education and participatory programs.

AIDS treatment

With full treatment coverage of patients, Cuba's commitment to equal and universal access to treatment is arguably ahead of the "widespread availability" of treatment measures suggested by the UN.[74] However, full treatment coverage took time to implement. Drugs for antiretroviral treatment were in short supply in the 1990s, but, since 2001, 100% of Cuba's HIV-positive patients have had access to a relatively full cocktail of ART drugs, free of charge. As a result, the death rate from HIV/AIDS has been falling rapidly, and most HIV-positive Cubans are able to avoid secondary infections. Treatment for those with opportunistic infections associated with HIV/AIDS has been coordinated through the Instituto Pedro Kourí, which specializes in tropical medicine.[75]

The use of immune system-boosting drugs was recommended in Cuba from 1986 onward. In 1987, zidovudine (ZDV) was recommended for all those who developed AIDS. With limited drugs available, Cuban experts stressed the need for an "intense educational campaign" designed to lower the risk of infection, emphasizing reduced "sexual promiscuity" and promoting stable relationships.[76] Later literature would caution against pejorative use of the term "promiscuous."[77] In 1996, after the Worlds AIDS conference and the recommendation of highly active antiretroviral treatment (HAART), Cuba bought ART drugs for all children with AIDS and their mothers, at a cost of US$14,000 per person per year. This was a strain on resources, especially as this occurred just after Cuba's deep economic crisis in the mid-1990s. At the same time, between 1998 and 2001, 100 Cuban AIDS patients were treated with ART drugs donated by NGOs.[78] Because of these serious resource constraints, not every patient who needed it received treatment in the 1990s.

However, from 1998, with economic recovery and the gradually growing number of HIV cases, generic drugs began to be developed. Cuba was well-placed for this due to its biomedicine industry.[79] The first drug produced was zidovudine. Then in 2001, lamivudine (3TC), stavudine (D4T), zalcitabine

(DDC), didanosine (DDI), and indinavir (IDV) were produced. Bioequivalence was assessed and those drugs were registered for use. Production of nevirapine (NVP), abacavir (ABC), efavirenz (EFV), and nelfinavir (NFV) was then assessed. The full "cocktail" was made available to all Cubans, and after 2001 there was no further foreign assistance to purchase any HIV treatment drugs or materials except for the purchase of Western blot test materials, which supplement the Cuban ELISA test materials.[80]

With removal of the economic constraints and the widespread availability of ART drugs, Cuba's treatment regime has become "pre-emptive," unlike some health systems where initiating treatment requires an immune system below a certain level *plus* an opportunistic infection. Indeed, in the first years of treatment, Cuba required a CD4 cell count below 350, a viral load above 55,000 copies per milliliter, and an opportunistic infection before HAART treatment was begun.[81] However, a health promoter involved in monitoring adherence to treatment programs reports that, as of late 2005, the practice had shifted to administering treatment when the cell count was low, without an additional infection required.[82] This treatment plan might indeed produce better results through earlier treatment regimes. The nutritional supplements provided to HIV-positive patients most likely also assist recovery.

Final comments: HIV/AIDS and rights in Cuba

This paper has sought to apply a rights-based analysis, in light of the UN's International Guidelines on HIV/AIDS and Human Rights, to several themes in Cuba's approach to HIV/AIDS: quarantine and personal freedom; privacy, testing, and tracing; education, participation and non-discrimination; and AIDS treatment.

Under the Cuban constitution, the state guarantees "that every sick person will have medical attention" and that "[a]ll have the right to attention and protection of their health . . . [including] free medical and hospital attention."[83] The Cuban system appears to have made substantial steps to deliver on this promise to HIV/AIDS patients. It has also taken important steps in law and in practice consistent with the UN's human rights guidelines, in particular on freedom of movement, privacy, and education.

The early quarantine practice followed a strong political directive to protect public health and was the result of uncertainty over the nature of the disease. However, it seems that fear of the disease, including among professionals, may have unnecessarily prolonged this quarantine period.[84] This extension was an unreasonable deprivation of liberty. However, the early period and its privations do not appear to have been directed at gay and bisexual men, who formed a minority of the HIV-positive cohort at that time.

Outside suggestions that the early quarantine period traded personal liberties for public health achievements have little support in Cuba. Cuban health professionals suggest that the concerted and "intersectoral" approach to health problems, combined with strong epidemiological vigilance, extensive education campaigns, a free public health system, and social solidarity are central to the relative success of the Cuban program. The quarantine system of the 1980s is not thought to have been an important factor.[85]

Cuba's privacy and confidentiality practices in testing and tracing appear to follow routine practices, though they are more thorough than in other countries, and there are penalties for breaches of privacy. Target groups have been tested from the beginning of the epidemic, and normal patient consent is required for tests. The moral persuasion that is common in Cuban culture might generate a stronger sense of obligation for patients to disclose sexual contacts, but this is not in itself a breach of UN standards.

From the 1990s onward, Cuba took significant steps toward developing participation and non-discrimination. Since this time, the country has actively promoted respect for sexual diversity. In the late 1990s, Cuba developed and backed an important peer educator campaign. There were problems in providing access to antiretroviral treatment in the 1990s, aggravated by the economic crisis and by the US economic blockade. However, the extension of full treatment to all HIV-positive patients in 2001 puts Cuba ahead of the entire region with respect to widespread availability of treatment.

It is important to consider human rights in an HIV/AIDS program in an integrated way. Selective attacks on and caricatures of the Cuban program have not helped understanding and have deprived others of the lessons that can be learned from the Cuban experience. The Cuban system has made mistakes, developed its own practices, learned from the international experience, and effectively built its capacity to meet the needs and the rights of patients, families, and the community.

References

1. Joint United Nations Programme on HIV/AIDS (UNAIDS), *Caribbean: AIDS epidemic update, Regional Summary* (Geneva: Joint United Nations Programme on HIV/AIDS and World Health Organization, 2008), p. 8. Available at http://data.unaids.org/pub/Report/2008/jc1528_epibriefs_ caribbean_en.pdf.
2. See, for example, E. Michelson, "Individual freedom or collective welfare? An analysis of quarantine as a response to global infectious disease," in M. Selgelid, M. Battin, and C. Smith (eds), *Ethics and Infectious Disease* (Blackwell: Melbourne, 2006), pp. 53–69.
3. UNAIDS (see note 1), p. 8.
4. UNAIDS (see note 1), pp. 215, 230; Oficina Nacional de Estadisticas, *Anuario Estadistico de Cuba 2008: 15.2 Visitantes por mes* (Havana, 2008). Available at http://www.one.cu/aec2008/esp/15_ tabla_cuadro.htm.
5. J. Pérez, *SIDA: Confesiones a un Médico* (Havana: Centro Nacional de Prevención de las ITS/VIH/SIDA, 2006).
6. V. Zonana, "Cuba's AIDS quarantine center called 'frightening,'" *Los Angeles Times* (November 4, 1988), p. 1, col 5.

7. R. Bayer and C. Healton, "Controlling AIDS in Cuba: The logic of quarantine," *New England Journal of Medicine* 320/15 (1989), pp. 1022–1024.

8. Pérez (see note 5).

9. R. Bayer, "AIDS, public health, and civil liberties: Consensus and conflict in policy," in F. G. Reamer (ed), *AIDS and Ethics* (New York: Colombia University Press, 1991), pp. 26–49.

10. Pérez (see note 5).

11. R. Granich, B. Jacobs, J. Mermin, and A. Pont, "Cuba's national AIDS program: The first decade," *Western Journal of Medicine*, 163/2 (1995), pp. 139–144.

12. For attacks in the media, see, for example, V. Bauza and T. Collie, "HIV-positive Cubans get care but live in quarantine," *South Florida Sun-Sentinel* (July 7, 2001), p. A4; For advances in HIV education that were noted at this time, see, for example, E. Pérez-Stable, "Cuba's response to the HIV epidemic," *American journal of Public Health* 81/5 (1991), pp. 563–567.

13. T. Vilacha (Vice-director of epidemiology at La Rampa Policlinic, Havana), interview with the author, Havana, December 21, 2005; and C. Segredo (specialist nurse in HIV treatment centers, previously at Los Cocos Sanatorium and in 2006 at the Instituto Pedro Kourí), interview with the author, Havana, January 3, 2006.

14. H. Hansen and N. Groce, "Human immunodeficiency virus and quarantine in Cuba," *Journal of the American Medical Association* 290 (2003), p. 2875.

15. Hansen and Groce (see note 14).

16. UNAIDS, *International Guidelines on HIV/AIDS and Human Rights, 2006 Consolidated Version* (Geneva: UNAIDS, 2006), p. 17. Available at http://data.unaids.org/Publications/IRC-pub07/jc1252-internguidelines_en.pdf.

17. UNAIDS, *International Guidelines* (see note 16), pp. 17, 19, guidelines 3, 5, and 11.

18. A. Yera (Coordinator of the People Living with HIV/AIDS Program in the Plaza Municipality), interview with the author, Vedado, Havana, December 22, 2005.

19. D. W. Johnston, "Cuba's quarantine of AIDS victims: A violation of human rights," *Boston College International and Comparative Law Review*, 15 (1992), p. 189, citation 12.

20. Yera (see note 18).

21. L. Oliva, "Modelos de salud en Cuba," *Temas* 47 (2006), pp. 35–43 (interview with Dr. Francisco Rojas Ochoa on p. 39).

22. N. Scheper-Hughes, "AIDS, public health and human rights in Cuba," *Lancet*, 342 (1993), p. 966.

23. Pérez (see note 5).

24. Pérez (see note 5), p. 12.

25. A. R. Socarrás, "Derechos de las personas que viven con VIH en Cuba: Legalidad y perjuicios sociales" (paper presented at El Foro en VIH/SIDA/ITS de América Latina y el Caribe 2003, Havana, Cuba, April 7–8, 2003). Available at http://www.foro2003.sld.cu/recursos/ver.php/Rosabal%20Socarrás?id=349.

26. Oliva (see note 21), p. 38.

27. E. García, N. de Quesada Ramírez, and A. Cádiz Lahens, *Programa de entrenamiento sobre el SIDA 3: Epidemiología* (Havana: Editorial Ciencias Medicas, 1989), p. 18.

28. García et al. (see note 27), p. 51.
29. Yera (see note 18).
30. J. Pérez, D. Pérez, I. Gonzalez, et al., "Approaches to the management of HIV/AIDS in Cuba: Case study, Perspectives and Practice in Antiretroviral Treatment" (Geneva: World Health Organization, 2004), p. 3. Available at http://www.who.int/hiv/amds/case1.pdf.
31. Socarrás (see note 25).
32. Yera (see note 18).
33. Centro de Higiénico y Epidemiología, *Personas infectadas en Municipio Plaza: 1986–2005*, (Municipio Plaza, Vedado: Centro de Higiénico y Epidemiología, November 2005).
34. Socarrás (see note 25).
35. Ibid.
36. Segredo (see note 13).
37. Socarrás (see note 25); Yera (see note 18).
38. Socarrás (see note 25).
39. Pérez (see note 5), pp. 21–32.
40. UNAIDS (see note 16), pp. 17–18, guideline 5.
41. Scheper-Hughes (see note 22), p. 965.
42. Vilacha (see note 13); Segredo (see note 13).
43. Pérez et al. (see note 30), p. 2.
44. Bayer and Healton (see note 7); A. C. d'Adesky, "Cuba fights AIDS its own way," (New York: The Foundation for AIDS Research [AMFAR], 2003). Available at http://www.thebody.com/amfar/cuba_aids.html.
45. García et al. (see note 27), pp. 49—50.
46. Pérez et al. (see note 30), p. 2.
47. Yera (see note 18); Pérez et al. (see note 30), p. 1.
48. Vilacha (see note 13).
49. Ibid.
50. Segredo (see note 13).
51. Centro de Higiénico y Epidemiología (see note 33).
52. Ibid.
53. UNAIDS (see note 16), pp. 17–19, guidelines 1, 2, 5, 7, 8, 9, and 12.
54. R. Soto, J. Fuentes, M. Oramas, et al., *Manual para médicos de familia sobre ITS/VIH/SIDA*, (Havana: Ministerio de Salud Pública, Centro Nacional de Prevención de las ITS/VIH/SIDA, 2003), p. 9.
55. Soto et al. (see note 54), pp. 13–15.
56. A. González, M. Oramas, G. González, et al., *Viviendo con VIH: Manual para las personas que viven con VIH/SIDA en Cuba*, second edition (Havana: Centro Nacional de Prevención de ITS/VIH/SIDA, Havana, 2004).
57. A. de la Torre, O. Carro, and I. Carro, *"Conviviendo con VIH: Manual dirigido a las familias de las personas que viven con VIH/SIDA en Cuba* (Havana: Centro Nacional de Prevención de ITS/VIH/SIDA, 2003).
58. T. Fawthrop, "Cuba: Is it a model in HIV-AIDS battle?" (New York: Global Policy Forum, December 2003). Available at http://www.globalpolicy.org/component/content/article/211/44946.html.
59. See, for example, UNAIDS (see note 16), pp. 17–19, guidelines 5, 7, 8, and 9.
60. Soto et al. (see note 54).

61. M. Castro (Director of Cuba's CENESEX), Presentation on sexual diversity and inclusion in Cuba, World Social Forum, Caracas, Venezuela (January 28, 2006).
62. Ministerio de Salud Pública, "Centro Nacional de Prevención de las ITS/HIV/SIDA" (brochure) (Havana: Ministerio de Salud Pública, 2005).
63. R. Soto, I. Santana, M. Fernández, et al., *Manual metologo: trabajo de prevención de la ITS/VIH/SIDA* (Havana: Ministerio de Salud Pública, Centro Nacional de Prevención de las ITS/VIH/SIDA, 2004).
64. Ministerio de Salud Pública (see note 62).
65. English translations of pamphlet titles and messages by the author.
66. See, for example, I. Lumsden, *Machos, maricones and gays: Cuba and homosexuality* (Philadelphia: Temple University Press, 1996).
67. Yera (see note 18).
68. Presentation on sexual diversity and inclusion in Cuba by Daniela, Cuban transgender spokesperson to the World Social Forum, Caracas, Venezuela (January 28, 2006).
69. I. Ramonet, *Cien Horas con Fidel: Conversaciones con Ignacio Ramonet*, 2nd edition (Havana: Oficina de Publicaciones del Consejo de Estado, 2006), pp. 253–256.
70. Yera (see note 18).
71. R. Cruz (Coordinator Provincial of the Line of Support for HIV/AIDS in Vedado, Havana), interview with the author, Havana, Cuba, (January 4, 2006).
72 Yera (see note 18).
73. UNAIDS (see note 16), pp. 17–19, guidelines 1, 8, 9, and 12.
74. Ibid., pp. 17–19, guideline 6.
75. Of note, the Policlinics (Vilacha, see note 13) do not deal with HIV or with diseases (such as malaria, for example) that are considered to no longer exist in the country.
76. García et al. (see note 27), p. 60.
77. Soto et al. (see note 54), pp. 27–48.
78. Pérez et al. (see note 30), pp. 3–6.
79. Ibid., p. 3.
80. No further foreign assistance: Ibid., p. 2; Western blot tests: Segredo (see note 13).
81. Pérez et al. (see note 30), p. 4.
82. Yera (see note 18).
83. *Constitución de la República de Cuba (1976)* (Havana: Editora Política, 2005), Art. 9b, Art. 50, translation by the author.
84. Pérez (see note 5), pp. 21–32.
85. Granich et al. (see note 11); Vilacha (see note 13); Segredo (see note 13).

106

PARTICIPATION AND THE RIGHT TO HEALTH

Lessons from Indonesia

Sam Foster Halabi

Source: *Health and Human Rights*, 11:1 (2009), 49–59.

Abstract

The right to participation is the "the right of rights" — the basic right of people to have a say in how decisions that affect their lives are made. All legally binding international human rights treaties explicitly recognize the essential role of participation in realizing fundamental human rights. While the substance of the human right to health has been extensively developed, the right to participation as one of its components has remained largely unexplored. Should rights-based health advocacy focus on participation because there is a relationship between an individual's or a community's active involvement in health care decision-making and the highest attainable standard of health? In the context of the human right to health, does participation mean primarily political participation, or should we take the right to participation to mean more specifically the right of persons, individually and as a group, to shape health care policy for society and for themselves as patients? Decentralization of health care decision-making promises greater participation through citizen involvement in setting priorities, monitoring service provision, and finding new and creative ways to finance public health programs. Between 1999 and 2008, Indonesia decentralized health care funding and delivery to regional governments, resulting in substantial exclusion of its poor and uneducated citizens from the health care system while simultaneously expanding the opportunities for political participation for educated elites. This article explores the tension between the right to participation as an underlying determinant of health and as a political right by reviewing the experience of Indonesia ten years after its decision to decentralize health care provision. It is ultimately argued that rights-based advocates must be vigilant in retaining a unified perspective on human rights, resisting the persistent tendency to separate and prioritize the civil and political aspects of participation over its social component.

Introduction

The right to participation is the "the right of rights" — the basic right of people to have a say in how decisions that affect their lives are made.[1] All legally binding international human rights treaties recognize the essential role of participation in realizing fundamental human rights. The United Nations Committee on Economic, Social and Cultural Rights, in its 2000 General Comment No. 14, *The Right to the Highest Attainable Standard of Health*, provides that participation of the population in all health-related decision-making at the community, national, and international levels is an important aspect of the right to health.[2] Paragraph 43(f) of General Comment No. 14 directs states to use participatory methods to adopt and implement a national public health strategy and implement a plan of action to achieve it. Article 4 of the 1978 Declaration of Alma-Ata on Primary Health Care states that "people have the right and duty to participate individually and collectively in the planning and implementation of their health care."[3]

Within the literature on the right to health, there is no conceptual clarity about the role that participation plays for individuals in attempting to obtain the highest attainable standard of health, as human rights law mandates.[4] Should rights-based health advocacy focus on participation because there is a relationship between an individual's or a community's active involvement in health care decision-making and the highest attainable standard of health? In the context of the human right to health, does participation mean primarily political participation, or should we take the right to participation to mean more specifically the right of persons, individually and as a group, to shape health care policy for society and for themselves as patients? As Neil Popovic phrased it, "[D]oes [the right to participate] matter for its own sake (the elemental model), or as a means to protect . . . other cherished values (the instrumental model)?"[5]

In the context of the right to health, these two types of participation are best understood with reference to 1) General Comment 14, which, along with food, nutrition, housing, healthy occupational and environmental conditions, and access to health-related education and information, lists participation as an "underlying determinant[ ] of health"; and 2) the 1993 Vienna Declaration and Programme of Action, which calls for "the freely expressed will of the people to determine their own political, economic, social and cultural systems."[6] With the former approach, participation occurs under the direction of health providers to "reduce individual illness or improve the individual's environment."[7] Under the latter, citizens are decision-making stakeholders who have a say at every level, from where resources are allocated to logistical planning.[8] The right to participation has traditionally been researched only in the political context, that is, involvement in decision-making, planning, and implementation processes ranging from community organization to electoral politics. That argument has been extended to health care policies. Proponents say that participatory politics are necessary to ensure participation in health care and public health planning, via elected officials and a responsive, transparent government. However, in this article, I show that the two approaches to participation are quite distinct and can be unrelated or even follow opposing trends.

Juxtaposing participation as an elemental right versus an instrumental right does not necessarily entail any contradictions. When effective community participation can contribute to improvements in individual and community health, then the elemental and instrumental approaches converge. Yet the evidence as to the relationship between community participation and health outcomes is relatively thin.[9] Practitioners often adopt an idea of community based on spatial and social factors and political ideas that may not correspond to local understandings or circumstances.[10] Advocates of rights to participatory health care may overlook key challenges to meaningful participation in health care decision-making, mistaking idealized notions of "inclusion" for effective health care planning and provision.[11] This apparent contradiction is easily resolved when taking both approaches into consideration, not discarding participation if its benefits are not immediately obvious, and not insisting on participation at all costs where such costs are considerable.

Politicians, scholars, and civil society groups have advanced decentralization of health care decision-making as a possible solution to achieving the right balance between increasing opportunities for decision-making participation and involving interested stakeholders in a way that would improve individual and community health.[12] Decentralization of health care decision-making promises greater participation by involving citizens in setting priorities, monitoring service provision, and finding new and creative ways to finance public health programs.[13] The theory, informed largely by political science and public choice literature, is simple: citizens understand their ability to shape health care outcomes, within parameters of general policy, if given the opportunity.[14] The more local the decisions, the greater the participation. This theory depends, of course, on a careful assessment of local circumstances; decentralization without deliberation risks burdening resource-poor regions or municipalities with expensive responsibilities but insufficient information, personnel, or technology.

This article explores the realization of the right to participation as a component of the right to health, and as a political right, by reviewing the experience of Indonesia ten years after its decision to decentralize health care provision. I argue that the two perspectives on the right to participation are distinct and can run contrary to one another. Indonesia embraced the 1978 Alma-Ata principles and pushed its planning agenda through a centralized system of building health centers and training local workers. In 1995, the Indonesian Ministry of Health first studied decentralizing the public health system, and in 1999 took steps to do so within broader efforts to decentralize administrative authority. Three major factors led the Indonesian government to decentralize authority over public services, including health care, to regional governments. First, international lending institutions imposed restrictive conditions on loans made in the wake of the 1997 Asian financial crisis. Second, secessionist movements in Indonesia's peripheral provinces surged during this time period. Third, diminished public revenue in the wake of the financial crisis pushed officials to identify budget items, such as the centralized health care system, for which alternative financing arrangements could be developed.[15]

Indonesia adopted Law No. 22/1999 on regional governance and Law No. 25/1999 on fiscal balance, devolving powers to the regions.[16] The laws gave provinces, districts, subdistricts, and villages authority over public affairs — including health — while the central government retained control over foreign policy, defense, security, the judiciary and fiscal policy, and religious affairs.[17] The move to localize service sectors boosted rights-based health advocates' call for local participation. At the same time, the diminishing role of the central government eroded the previous commitment to a model of health care as a public good.[18]

Participation as a human right

Human rights are comprised of civil, cultural, economic, political, and social rights made binding as part of customary international law and at least two major international covenants: the International Covenant on Economic, Social and Cultural Rights (ICESCR), and the International Covenant on Civil and Political Rights (ICCPR). In the context of the ICCPR, the right to participation has generally been taken to mean the right to organize a political party, to vote, or to freely express political opinions.[19] Other treaties define participation as the right to participate in cultural life or, the right of children to participate in decision-making processes affecting their interests.[20]

The ICESCR casts participation as part of the right to health both as an "underlying determinant[] of health" and as a right to have a say in health matters, generally. The UN Committee on Economic, Social and Cultural Rights interpreted the right to health, as defined in article 12.1, as an inclusive right comprised of:

> access to safe and potable water and adequate sanitation, an adequate supply of safe food, nutrition and housing, healthy occupational and environmental conditions, and access to health-related education and information, including on sexual and reproductive health. A further important aspect is the participation of the population in all health-related decision-making at the community, national and international levels.[21]

On one hand, the Committee's interpretation suggests that, like potable water or a safe workplace, participation is an underlying factor contributing to health. On the other hand, the Committee separated its discussion of participation from its list of underlying factors and framed it as a "decision-making" or political aspect of the right to health.

Rights-based practitioners and scholars have focused on this latter interpretive option, analyzing participation within the meaning of the ICCPR. In her analysis of the right to health under international human rights law, Virginia Leary adopted the perspective of the Vienna Declaration, writing that:

> Participation of individuals and groups in matters that affect them is essential to the protection of all human rights. Democracy and human rights are frequently linked in current rights discourse — and democracy means more than merely voting: it requires provision of information and informed participation.[22]

Celebrating the thirtieth anniversary of the Alma-Ata Declaration, one set of contributors to *The Lancet*'s special issue noted that the primary health care movement focused on "putting the 'public' into public health":

> The inherent focus on equity, the necessity of reaching the unreached and involving them not only in the benefits of health care, but more importantly, in the decisions and actions that collectively make health, was at once novel and revolutionary.[23]

Yet both the fundamental documents and scholars discussing the right to health have emphasized its substance, that is, the basic needs the state must address that constitute factors necessary to attain the highest attainable standard of health.[24] Furthermore, they stressed that health is key to participating in all other aspects of life.

Based in part on building enthusiasm for broader models of participation, other scholars elaborated detailed mechanisms for advancing participation. These include regional and national conferences and permanent or temporary forums that include providers, patients, and decision makers; localized health teams; and public meetings and focus groups to discuss policy changes.[25] Under these mechanisms, citizens participate as policy-makers and as policy-reviewers. Such mechanisms assume a public sufficiently informed to make policy suggestions and demand accountability. To do so, they would need to have access to basic information to propose and monitor how the state fulfills its rights obligations. For many developing and middle-income countries, that assumption is highly unrealistic. Implementing ill-conceived mechanisms for participation may result, for example, in multiple forums in which participants cannot meaningfully voice their interests or participate in policy development for lack of knowledge or information. Such a scenario highlights the ambiguity of pursuing participation within a rights-based approach to health for its own sake.

Participation as a determinant of health:
the example of Indonesia

During the Suharto regime (1965–1998), Indonesia was centrally governed, with little authority or autonomy granted to regional and local governments. Under authoritarian rule, the right to health care was one of the few core rights retained in the Indonesian Constitution and supported financially and politically.[26] The Indonesian government embraced the 1978 Alma-Ata principles, embarking on a far-reaching plan to provide access to basic health care services for all citizens. The central government supplied nearly 80% of total public expenditure at the regional level. Grants from the central government for development projects, including roads, irrigation, schools, and public health, made up the remaining 20% of local public expenditure.[27]

As Indonesia's Ministry of Health understood participation, its core function was to expand available resources under a national development strategy that aimed at local access to an "essential health care package" that would raise the national standard of living, particularly that of the rural poor who faced higher levels of social and economic exclusion.[28] *Gotong royong*, "mutual burden sharing," aimed to match local volunteer labor with central government transfers.[29] Mutual burden sharing activities included providing expanded access to toilets, maintaining common gathering places, and cleaning the floors of houses.[30] These basic sanitation schemes brought about reductions in mortality at low cost.[31] The central government also trained teams of villagers in preventive strategies dedicated to nutrition, family planning, and immunization.[32] By 1996, approximately 1.25 million volunteers, mostly women, were involved in these initiatives. The proportion of births attended by skilled health personnel increased from 40.7% in 1992 to 68.4% in 2002.[33] Although the literature on *gotong royong* contains many warnings as to its cooption for government propaganda purposes, the basic success of this participatory aspect of Indonesian policy is well supported.[34] For example, in their study of Indonesian women's participation in local networks, Jenna Nobles and Elizabeth Frankenberg found a positive and statistically significant relationship between participation and child health, particularly among mothers with little or no education.[35]

These participatory strategies complemented Suharto's program to establish community health centers (*puskesmas*) throughout the country in the 1970s and 1980s.[36] The program realized full national health care coverage by the late 1980s, and encompassed 900 general hospitals and 7000 *puskesmas* by 1998.[37] These centers charged low user fees with the intention of thus ensuring access to basic health care. A requirement for physicians to provide public service increased access to health care providers through an incentive scheme: more remote assignments required less public service time. The results were gains in health outcomes, such as declining infant mortality and incidence of communicable diseases like polio.[38] Although Indonesia continued to lag behind other countries in the Asia-Pacific region in achieving better health metrics, *gotong royong, puskesmas,* and public service requirements contributed significantly to improving access to health care in Indonesia and raising health outcomes.[39] Between 1980 and 1997, child mortality for children under the age of five dropped 30–40%.[40] For the period 1990–1996, infant mortality rates improved in each of Indonesia's 26 regions by about 20%.[41] Between 1985 and 1997, vaccination coverage increased from 28% to 70%.[42] Like food, water, and sanitation, participation was viewed as an underlying component of improving the basic health profile of communities.

Political participation

Driven by the financial pressures of the 1997 financial crisis and the demands of international lenders, the Indonesian Ministry of Health modified this view of participation as burden sharing to instead emphasize community consensus and planning as a way for regions to "implement development . . . in the health sector, to accelerate even distribution and justice according to local problems, potential, and diversity."[43] In a report titled "Healthy Indonesia 2010," the Indonesian government, with the support of international lenders and Western aid agencies, reshaped the state's role in health care provision under three interrelated objectives: 1) advocacy; 2) health promotion/demand generation; and 3) community participation.[44] Instead of mobilizing community resources toward the common objectives of basic health care access and enhanced community health, "community participation" in the new idiom could be defined as:

> village-based certification program[s] [in which] local stakeholders agree on a limited number of priority health issues, develop standards for those selected issues, and then publicly recognize and reward families that achieve and maintain those standards. These families act as models for other families to adopt new health behaviors.[45]

In order to realize this new vision of participation, the Ministry of Health partnered with the Coalition for Health Indonesia (*Koalisi untuk Indonesia Sehat,* or KUIS), which is comprised of government agencies and prominent Western and Indonesian NGOs. These NGOs held workshops and training sessions aimed at encouraging the formation of participatory bodies and setting common agendas.[46] Preliminary results from these sessions showed that few medical personnel or community members knew of KUIS's activities; that when they did know of them, community members showed indifference; and that suggested preventive practices were already commonplace.[47]

While administrative decentralization provided opportunities for Indonesians to play a role in local health care decision-making, the quality of the available health care deteriorated, particularly for Indonesia's poor.[48] Instead of playing a major role in setting standards, providing personnel and funding, and monitoring outcomes, the national Ministry of Health established minimal standards for services and public health provision with inadequate corresponding ability to secure or implement them.[49] Rather than viewing health care as a public good, administrations in regions, districts, and sub-districts viewed health care as a private good that was increasingly accessible on the basis of affordability. The number of private hospitals steadily grew under the decentralized regime, while doctors increasingly used their position in community health centers to "attract patients to their own private and more expensive services."[50] Without the distribution of physicians under the public service requirement, local governments paid large sums to attract physicians, or paid for their education at the University of Indonesia. Increased local outlays on health care providers corresponded with a reduction in spending for environmental or preventive measures, and "principles of universal access and solidarity in health services [yielded] to a market-based ideology and an increasing role of private insurance companies."[51] District parliaments, empowered to set user fees, focused on the more profitable curative approach to health.

Following these changes, preventable diseases that were in abatement — like dengue hemorrhagic fever, leprosy, and tuberculosis — reemerged.[52] Between 1995 and 2005, childhood immunization rates fell from 70% to 60% before climbing again.[53] Between 2000 and 2006, the number of births in Indonesia that were attended by skilled health personnel averaged 66% even as the number of village midwives serving poor Indonesians was decreasing.[54]

The picture that emerges is one of community residents no longer participating in building community health centers or maintaining water and sanitation schemes because 1) the community health centers could not provide necessary care, and 2) the alternatives were prohibitively expensive. As Hasbullah Thabrany of the University of Indonesia's School of Public Health noted:

> Devolving authority and obligation of health functions to the local governments poses threats to public health. Since the local government, including the local parliament, is an elected body, the chances of elected officials not having an understanding or commitment to public health are greater than in the previous "less democratic" government.[55]

The deterioration in Indonesia's commitment to providing health care coincided with increasing opportunities for participation in how local decisions were made. Yet as an economic and social matter, the uneducated poor have seen their ability to participate decline, as many households are at risk of impoverishment from the high cost of care.[56]

The threat of eroding health standards is demonstrated by Indonesia's medical card program to secure access to health care during the 1997 financial crisis. In that period, the World Bank and the Asian Development Bank partnered with the Indonesian central government to distribute health care access cards (*kartu sehat*) to protect poor citizens' access to health care. The health card entitled the owner and his or her family members to free services from public health care providers; these services consisted of outpatient and inpatient care, contraceptives for women of child-bearing age, prenatal care, and assistance at birth. Health cards were usually distributed through local health centers and village midwives and were based on a list of criteria that reflected need for assistance. Local leaders were given considerable discretion and distributed health cards according to their own views on local need. Distribution at the local level should have ensured that the poorest citizens would be identified and provided with medical cards. Yet the program failed to achieve many of its objectives because 1) many of the poorest citizens did not know about the cards, and 2) many cardholders did not believe they would actually receive services covered by the cards.[57]

The right to participation: lessons from Indonesia

The two interpretations of participation as a political right and as a determinant of health are not mutually exclusive. Indonesia's central government could have retained its centralized financing structure, albeit perhaps not at pre-1997 levels, together with its commitment to providing health care as a public good while at the same time establishing local, regional, and national participatory forums. Yet prominent organizations committed to a rights-based approach energetically worked in communities attempting to "put the 'public' back into public health," while overlooking that decentralization entailed jettisoning health as a public good. What are the lessons to be drawn for a rights-based approach?

Rights-based advocates must be vigilant in maintaining a unified perspective on human rights, resisting the persistent tendency to separate and prioritize civil and political rights over economic, cultural, and social rights. Political participation alone is no panacea for improving other rights, such as the highest attainable standard of health. Within the literature on participation, rights-based scholars and practitioners have consistently focused on the political right to participation, neglecting its other relevant aspects. As UN Special Rapporteur on the Right to Health Anand Grover recently noted, scholars and practitioners are creating an artificial dichotomy in Article 12 when they focus on "physical" determinants of health like adequate food and water to the detriment of "social" determinants like education and social inclusion.[58]

A rights-based approach views participation according to the "sensitivity" of local capacity, that is, to issues where locals have sufficient information and an individual stake, and a direct link to effecting health care outcomes. John D. Montgomery, for example, suggests that local participation makes sense for improving the diet of preschool children (where local knowledge and circumstances can have a significant effect), but not for building city sanitary systems (where local knowledge is not uniquely helpful).[59] In the Indonesian context, the central government's commitment to building nationwide health infrastructure, while communities complemented the central effort with low-cost burden-sharing, generated significant gains for both access and improved health.

Yet a rights-based approach must also remain committed to what is known as the "progressive realization" of the right to health. The concept of progressive realization is used by rights-holders or their advocates to delineate incremental obligations of duty-bearers to fulfill the right to health through, for example, increased access to essential medicines, emergency care, and pre- and post-natal care.[60] In the Indonesian context, the efforts of KUSI to expand participation did not explicitly aim to increase the capacity of community members to hold their government accountable for the "essential health care package" available before decentralization and to build essential health care into the Indonesian Constitution.[61] Since 1945, the Indonesian Constitution has promised some degree of access to health care, and, since 2000, that guarantee has been explicit.[62] Indonesia ratified the International Covenant on Social, Economic and Cultural Rights and implemented domestic enacting legislation in 2005.[63] The deterioration of the central government's commitment to provide health care raises the urgency of incorporating human rights into the regular and professional conduct of providers.[64]

A rights-based approach requires a dialogue between practitioners, policy makers, and participants with the aim of educating and providing participants with information, not only about health or sanitation, but also about their rights to quality care. KUIS is one example of practitioners who define successful participation in health care provision merely as participants' contributions to prioritize their own needs; rates of voluntarism; utilization; and financial contribution.[65] Similarly, many advocates practice a narrow interpretation of the kind of information they must share with patients and community members. A rights-based approach to health requires not only participation via these types of solicited information contributions, but also an interactive campaign of promotion and education about human rights.

The failure of the *kartu sehat* scheme (which still operates despite known, persistent weaknesses) mirrors the underlying state of Indonesians' knowledge of their human rights. In his recent survey of efforts to litigate social and economic rights in Indonesia, Brvitri Susanti noted that 97% of Indonesians with no formal education were unable to name a single basic human right to which they were entitled.[66] Although anthropologists, lawyers, and human rights-activists have studied the awareness of human rights in both rural and urban populations, similar studies in the right-to-health literature are scarce.[67]

Addressing the gaps in information faced by local participants and reaching across areas of human rights activism will play fundamental roles in realizing the human right to participation as both an end and a means. Citizens armed with knowledge of human rights are better equipped to demand action from local government and hold it accountable. Rights-based advocates are well-positioned to encourage the incorporation of human rights curricula into Indonesia's growing number of educational institutions for public health professionals. Because institutions are being established rapidly (although perhaps not thoughtfully, as they are driven largely by the promise of tuition revenues), the comprehensive nature of this essential education is currently being compromised.[68]

Besides holding local governments accountable, informed citizens may also be able to force governmental accountability through legal action, although that promise is distant. In the words of A. Patra M. Zen, "[economic and social] rights in principle have become constitutional rights, but they have not become rights. That is to say, they cannot be enforced using the domestic legal framework."[69] While the Indonesian judiciary continues to confront serious corruption and bureaucratic challenges, civil society organizations are increasingly effective at using the courts to vindicate rights or draw attention to public health threats.[70] In 2003, a Jakarta court ordered the government to take "necessary concrete measures" to feed, shelter, and provide medical care to migrant laborers who had been expelled from Malaysia.[71]

Whether through local activism or through the national judiciary, health professionals are uniquely positioned to provide local residents with important information regarding their health, including human rights. On a day-to-day basis, these professionals are already actively translating traditionally conceived "health information" into the local vernacular. Rights-based public health professionals are aware of the major conventions establishing fundamental rights and can communicate that understanding to their patients as well as to other individuals in the community.[72]

Conclusion

While the Vienna Declaration officially ended the indivisibility of political rights and social rights, the distinction persists in important scholarly and policy-making circles. The right to participation presents a unique challenge for the effective realization of the Vienna Declaration's unifying aim.[73] In the Indonesian context, the expansion of political participation occurred contemporaneously with a diminishing commitment to access to basic health care.[74] Civil society groups committed to the environment, public health, and the rule of law supported not only the downfall of Suharto but the decentralization of political authority in the name of political participation.[75] However, the result of decentralization has not improved health outcomes or bolstered political participation among Indonesia's poorest and most marginalized citizens.

Participation as a component of the right to health requires a commitment to the idea set forth by the UN Committee on Social, Economic and Cultural Rights that "[h]ealth is a fundamental human right indispensable for the exercise of other human rights."[76] In his essay challenging public health orthodoxies in health and human rights, Paul Farmer phrased it this way:

> In short, I advocate, as a public health activist, reversing the present priority which places civil and legal rights first and adjourns substantive rights for another day. It is when people are able to eat and be well that they have the chance to build democratic institutions.[77]

We must recognize, first, that access to health care is and must be a public good from which no person can be excluded as a matter of right. We must also recognize that participation as a component of the right to health is different from, yet works in partnership with, participation as political inclusion; and that "health information" and "human rights information" are equally important to realizing the highest attainable standard of health. Until we recognize all three of these principles, the existing commitment to *political* participation remains one that is misdirected, since it may not only fail to achieve improved health for communities, but may delay the more meaningful ability to have a say in how decisions are made that affect their lives.

Acknowledgments

The author wishes to thank Crystal Johnson for assistance in understanding the Indonesian environmental movement's use of litigation, and Jenelle Beavers and Christoph Wilcke for their helpful comments.

References

1. J. Waldron, "Participation: The right of rights," *Proceedings of the Aristotelian Society* 98 (1998), pp. 307–337.
2. Committee on Economic, Social and Cultural Rights, General Comment No. 14, The Right to the Highest Attainable Standard of Health (Art. 12), U.N. Doc. No. E/C.12/2000/4 (2000). Available at http://www.unhchr.ch/tbs/doc.nsf/(symbol)/E.C.12.2000.4.En.
3. Available at http://www.who.int/hpr/NPH/docs/declaration_almaata.pdf.
4. V. A. Leary, "The right to health in international human rights law," *Health and Human Rights: An International Journal* 1 (1994), p. 32.
5. N. Popovic, "The right to participate in decisions that affect the environment," *Pace Environmental Law Review* 10 (1993), pp. 684–685.
6. Committee on Economic, Social and Cultural Rights, General Comment No. 14, (see note 2), para. 4, 11; United Nations, World Conference on Human Rights: Vienna Declaration and Programme of Action, Vienna, June 14–25, 1993, UN

Doc. No. A/CONF.157/24 (1993), Art. 8. Available at http://www.unhchr.ch/huridocda/huridoca.nsf/(Symbol)/A.CONF.157.23.En?OpenDocument.

7. J. Church et al., "Citizen participation in health decision-making: Past experience and future prospects," *Journal of Public Health Policy* 23/1 (2002), p. 13.

8. Ibid.

9. C. Wayland and J. Crowder, "Disparate views of community in primary health care: Understanding how perceptions influence success," *Medical Anthropology Quarterly* 16/2 (2002), pp. 231–232.

10. Ibid; D. Zakus and C. Lyzack, "Revisiting community participation," *Health Policy and Planning* 13/1 (1998), pp. 1, 6.

11. This is especially true in Indonesia, where ethnic diversity has a significantly negative effect on efforts at community participation; see C. Okten and U. Okonkwo Osili, "Contributions in heterogeneous communities: Evidence from Indonesia," *Journal of Population Economics* 17/4 (2004), p. 603.

12. R. Lakshminarayanan, "Decentralisation and its implications for reproductive health: The Philippines experience," *Reproductive Health Matters* 11/21 (2003), p. 102.

13. S. Lieberman, J. Capuno, and H. Van Minh, "Decentralizing health: Lessons from Indonesia, the Philippines and Vietnam," in World Bank, *East Asia decentralizes: Making local government work* (Washington, D.C: World Bank: 2005), pp. 155–157.

14. B. C. Smith, "The decentralization of health care in developing countries: organizational options," *Public Administration and Development* 17 (1997), p. 399.

15. S. Kristiansen and P. Santoso, "Surviving decentralization? Impacts of regional autonomy on health service provision in Indonesia," *Health Policy* 77/3 (2006), pp. 247–259.

16. G. Bell, "The new Indonesian laws relating to regional autonomy: Good intentions, confusing laws," *Asia-Pacific Law & Policy Journal* 2 (2001), p. 1.

17. B. Susanti, "The implementation of the right to health care and education in Indonesia," in D. Brinks and V. Gauri (eds), *Courting social justice* (Cambridge: Cambridge University Press, 2008), p. 232.

18. From a rights-based perspective, access to basic health care is a "public good" — that is, no one can be denied access on the basis of ability to pay; see L. Rubenstein, "The right to health care," (remarks at "Human Rights in the United States: Domestic Application of International Human Rights Law," November 12, 2008). According to orthodox economic theory, a public good is one that is non-rivalrous and non-excludable. A non-rivalrous good is one that may be consumed by one consumer without preventing consumption by another, and a non-excludable good may not be denied because one has not paid for it; see T. Cowen, *The concise encyclopedia of economics.* Available at http://www.econlib.org/library/Enc/PublicGoods.html.

19. M. Nowak, *UN Covenant on Civil and Political Rights: CCPR Commentary.* (Kehl am Rhein: N. P. Engel, 1993), p. 445.

20. Convention on the Rights of the Child (CRC), G.A. Res. 44/25 (1989). Available at http://www2.ohchr.org/English/law/crc.htm.

21. Committee on Economic, Social and Cultural Rights, General Comment No. 14 (see note 2), para. 11.

22. Leary (see note 4).

23. J. Lawn, J. Rohde, S. Rifkin, et al., "Alma-Ata 30 years on: Revolutionary, relevant, and time to revitalise," *Lancet* 372/9642 (2008), pp. 917–920.
24. S. D. Jamar, "The international human right to health," *Southern University Law Review* 22 (1994), pp. 1–68.
25. F. Scutchfield, C. Ireson, and L. Hall, "The voice of the public in public health policy and planning: The role of public judgment," *Journal of Pubic Health Policy* 25/2 (2004), pp. 197–205; H. Potts, "Participation and the right to the highest attainable standard of health" (presentation at The UN Special Rapporteur on the Right to the Highest Attainable Standard of Health: Looking Back and Moving Forward, September 25–27, 2008). Available at http://www.ifhhro.org/files/Helen%20Potts%20-%20WG10.ppt#272,6.
26. Susanti (see note 17).
27. A. Booth, "Intergovernmental relations and fiscal policy in Indonesia: The national impact of equity and inequality in provinces" in C. Fletcher (ed), *Equity and development across nations: Political and fiscal realities* (New York: St. Martin's Press, 1996), pp. 180–206.
28. M. El-Naggar, "More than twenty years of community action for health," *Regional Health Forum* 1/2 (1996), p. 3.
29. C. Okten and U. Okonkwo Osili, "Contributions in heterogeneous communities: Evidence from Indonesia," *Journal of Population Economics* 17/4 (2004), pp. 603–626.
30. B. Mitchell, "Sustainable development at the village level in Bali, Indonesia," *Human Ecology* 22/2 (1994), p. 206.
31. Kristiansen and Santoso (see note 15).
32. El-Naggar (see note 28).
33. WHO, *The Millennium Development Goals for Health: A review of the indicators.* (Jakarta: WHO Indonesia, 2002).
34. R. van Niel, "Review," *Journal of Asian Studies* 56/4 (1997), pp. 1153–1155.
35. J. Nobles and E. Frankenberg, "Mothers' community participation and child health," *California Center for Population Research On-Line Working Paper Series.* Available at http://www.ccpr.ucla.edu/ccprwpseries/ccpr_016_06.pdf.
36. P. van Eeuwijk, "Health care from the perspective of Minahasa villagers, Indonesia," in L. Whiteford and L. Manderson (eds), *Global health policy, local realities: The fallacy of the level playing field* (Boulder, CO, and London: Lynne Rienner, 2000), p. 90.
37. A. Thind, "Analysis of health services use for respiratory illness in Indonesian children: Implications for policy," *Journal of Biosocial Science* 37/2 (2005), pp. 129–142.
38. C. Simms and M. Rowson, "Reassessment of health effects of the Indonesian economic crisis: Donors versus the data," *Lancet* 361/9366 (2003), pp. 1382–1385.
39. Ibid.
40. BAPPENAS, BPS, and United Nations Development Programme, *Towards a new consensus: democracy and human development in Indonesia: Indonesia human development report* (Jakarta: United Nations Development Programme, 2001), pp. 6, 31. Available at http://www.undp.or.id/pubs/ihdr2001/ihdr2001_full.pdf.
41. Ibid.
42. USAID, *Country health statistical report Indonesia* (Washington, DC: AIM 2008), p. 11.

43. Ministry of Health, Republic of Indonesia, *Health development plan towards healthy Indonesia* 2010 (Jakarta: Ministry of Health, 1999), p. 13.

44. Available at http://www.jhuccp.org/asia/indonesia/2010int.shtml.

45. Ibid.

46. D. Storey, A. Ambar, and M. Lediard, *Summary monitoring & evaluation report: Healthy Indonesia 2010 initiatives July 2000–December 2002* (Jakarta: Johns Hopkins University Center for Communication Programs Indonesia Country Office, 2003), pp. 17–22.

47. Ibid.

48. Kristiansen and Santoso (see note 15). There is a general consensus around this issue, although the Asian Development Bank (ADB) and the World Bank have published conflicting data. In their essay assessing data provided by international lending institutions, Chris Simms and Mike Rowson have cast doubt as to the data: "The inconsistencies that we report suggest that the ADB's and World Bank's conclusions did not incorporate data that contradicted the notion that the social safety net provided [for the health sector, a plan known by the acronym JPS-BK] had successfully mitigated effects of the economic crisis on the health of Indonesia's poor citizens. Because the donor process was neither transparent nor consultative, the reasons for this optimistic assessment are unclear." (Simms and Rowson [see note 38], p. 1385).

49. Kristiansen and Santoso (see note 15), pp. 250–251.

50. Ibid.

51. Kristiansen and Santoso (see note 15), p. 256.

52. I. Kandun, "Emerging diseases in Indonesia: Control and challenges," *Tropical Medicine and Health* 34/4 (2006), pp. 141–147.

53. USAID (see note 42); Center for Data and Information, Indonesian health map (Jakarta: Ministry of Health Republic of Indonesia 2007), pp. 37–39.

54. Available at http://www.globalhealthfacts.org/country.jsp?c=107&i=77&cat=6; see also United Nations Development Program, *Indonesia, Indonesia Progress Report on the Millenium Development Goals. Goal 5: Improving Maternal Health* (Jakarta: United Nations Development Program, 2004). Available at http://www.undp.or.id/pubs/imdg2004/English/MDG-IDN_English_Goal5.pdf.

55. H. Thabrany, "Human resources in decentralized health systems in Indonesia: Challenges for equity," *Regional Health Forum* 10/1 (2006), p. 77.

56. L. P. Freedman, W. J. Graham, E. B. Brazier, et al., "Practical lessons from global safe motherhood initiatives: Time for a new focus on implementation," *Lancet* 370/9595 (2007), p. 1386.

57. International Labour Organization, *Indonesia: Providing health insurance for the poor* (Jakarta: ILO, 2008). Available at http://www.ilo.org/public/english/region/asro/bangkok/events/sis/download/paper25.pdf.

58. A. Grover, "Key Note" (remarks at Second Human Rights and Tobacco Control Convention, Tata Institute of Social Sciences, Mumbai, India, March 13, 2009).

59. J. D. Montgomery, "When local participation helps," *Journal of Policy Analysis and Management* 3/1 (1983), p. 99.

60. *Minister of Health v. Treatment Action Campaign* (2002) 5 SA 721 (CC).

61. An accompanying principle is the requirement of "nonregression." The UNC-ESCR has stated: "Moreover, any deliberately retrogressive measures in that regard would require the most careful consideration and would need to be fully

justified by reference to the totality of the rights provided for in the Covenant and in the context of the full use of the maximum available resources." Committee on Economic, Social and Cultural Rights, General Comment No. 3, The Nature of States Parties Obligations (para. 9), UN Doc. E/1991/23 (1990). Available at http://www.unhchr.ch/tbs/doc.nsf/(symbol)/CESCR+General+comment+3. En?OpenDocument.

62. Susanti (see note 17), p. 233.
63. Ibid.
64. L. London, "What is a human rights-based approach to health and does it matter?" *Health and Human Rights: An International Journal* 10/1 (2008), p. 68.
65. Wayland and Crowder (see note 9).
66. Susanti (see note 17), p. 226.
67. C. Mahler, A. Mihr, and R. Toivanen (eds), *The United Nations decade for human rights education and the inclusion of national minorities* (Frankfurt am Main: Peter Lang, 2008); M. A. Ogunlayi, "An assessment of the awareness of sexual and reproductive rights among adolescents in south western Nigeria," *African Journal of Reproductive Health / La Revue Africaine de la Santé Reproductive* 9/1 (2005), pp. 99–112.
68. Thabrany (see note 55).
69. Susanti (see note 17), p. 228.
70. General Comment 14 adds that "any person or group victim of a violation of the right to health should have access to effective judicial or other appropriate remedies at both national and international levels [and] . . . should be entitled to adequate reparation. Committee on Economic, Social and Cultural Rights, General Comment No. 14 (see note 2).
71. Susanti (see note 17), pp. 250–252.
72. S. E. Merry, "Transnational human rights and local activism: Mapping the middle," *American Anthropologist* 108/1 (2006) pp. 38–51.
73. London (see note 64).
74. L. Rieffel, "Indonesia's quiet revolution," *Foreign Affairs* 83/5 (2004), pp. 100–103, 106–109.
75. H. Antlöv, R. Ibrahim, and P. van Tuijl, "NGO governance and accountability in Indonesia: Challenges in a newly democratizing country," in L. Jordan and P. van Tuijl (eds), *NGO accountability: Politics, principles and innovations* (London and Sterling, VA: Earthscan, 2006), pp. 4–5. Available at http://www.justassociates. org/associates_files/Peter_NGO%20accountability%20in%20Indonesia%20 July%2005%20version.pdf; J. Gordon, "NGOs, the environment and political pluralism in new order Indonesia," *Explorations in Southeast Asian Studies* 2/2 (Fall 1998), pp. 47–68.
76. Committee on Economic, Social and Cultural Rights, General Comment No. 14 (see note 2).
77. P. Farmer, "Challenging orthodoxies in health and human rights" (American Public Health Association 134th Annual Meeting and Exposition Keynote Address, November 5, 2006). Available at http://www.pih.org/inforesources/essays/ APHA_2006_keynote-Paul_Farmer.pdf.

107

RESTRICTIONS ON UNDOCUMENTED IMMIGRANTS' ACCESS TO HEALTH SERVICES

The public health implications of welfare reform

Jeffrey T. Kullgren

Source: *American Journal of Public Health*, 93:10 (2003), 1630–3.

The Personal Responsibility and Work Opportunity Reconciliation Act of 1996 greatly restricts the provision of many federal, state, and local public services to undocumented immigrants. These restrictions have prompted intense debates about the provision of free and discounted primary and preventive health care-services and have placed significant burdens on institutions that serve large undocumented immigrant populations. Intended to serve as a tool for reducing illegal immigration and protecting public resources, federal restrictions on undocumented immigrants' access to publicly financed health services unduly burden health care providers and threaten the public's health. These deleterious effects warrant the public health community's support of strategies designed to sustain provision of health services irrespective of immigration status.

The federal personal

Responsibility and Work Opportunity Reconciliation Act (PRWORA) of 1996 greatly restricts the provision of many federal, state, and local publicly funded services to undocumented immigrants. Many public health and health care institutions have wrestled with the legal, administrative, and ethical conflicts generated by these limitations. The debate has been most visible in the state of Texas, where the legality of several public hospitals' provision of free primary and preventive health care to undocumented immigrants has been challenged.

Instead of serving their intended purpose of reducing illegal immigration and conserving public resources, PRWORA's restrictions on undocumented immigrants' access to publicly financed health services unduly burden health care providers and threaten the health of the community at large. These deleterious effects warrant the public health community's support of strategies to both repeal these restrictions and sustain the provision of health services irrespective of immigration status.

Intent and substance of PRWORA's restrictions

The enactment of PRWORA in 1996 went further than simply ending welfare as we knew it. The law also broke significant new ground in immigration policy by declaring that "current eligibility rules for public assistance and unenforceable financial support agreements have proved wholly incapable of assuring that individual aliens not burden the public benefits system" and that "it is a compelling government interest to remove the incentive for illegal immigration provided by the availability of public benefits."[1] To these ends, the law outlines standards in regard to legal and undocumented immigrants' eligibility for—and the provision of—services supported by the federal government and by state and local governments.

With respect to state and local public benefits, PRWORA declares that undocumented immigrants are ineligible for "any retirement, welfare, health, disability . . . or any other similar benefit for which payments or assistance are provided to an individual, household, or family eligibility unit by an agency of a State or local government or by appropriated funds of a State or local government."[1] Exceptions include "assistance for health care items and services that are necessary for the treatment of an emergency medical condition" and "public health assistance for immunizations with respect to immunizable diseases and for testing and treatment of symptoms of communicable diseases whether or not such symptoms are caused by a communicable disease."[1] PRWORA also allows provision of public benefits to undocumented immigrants if states enacted legislation after August 22, 1996, that "affirmatively provides for such eligibility" or if the US attorney general declares additional services exempt from the law's restrictions.[1]

Undocumented immigrants' health and access to services

The 300 000 to 500 000 undocumented immigrants that enter the United States each year arrive bearing a disproportionate burden of undiagnosed illness—including communicable diseases such as tuberculosis and HIV—and frequently lack basic preventive care and immunizations.[2-5] The adverse circumstances under which some undocumented immigrants enter the country, and the substandard conditions in which many live following their arrival, only exacerbate poor health.[6]

These health burdens are sustained and magnified by language barriers, lack of knowledge about the US health care system, and fear of detection by immigration authorities, all of which limit undocumented immigrants' ability to effectively access health services.[4,5,7] Undocumented immigrants are also frequently limited in their ability to access care by a lack of both health insurance and sufficient financial resources to pay for services.[5]

The consequences of undocumented immigrants' health burdens and barriers to accessing services extend beyond the individual to the entire community. The agricultural and food service settings in which many undocumented immigrants work, for example, can facilitate the spread of communicable diseases to other segments of the population.[6] Johns and Varkoutas also suggest that fear of detection has driven undocumented immigrants to pursue treatments through underground channels, which may have helped fuel the emergence of drug-resistant microbes.[8]

Responses to PRWORA's restrictions

For the most part, PRWORA's limitations on the provision of health services to undocumented immigrants have not been embraced by state and local officials. In light of the threats that undocumented immigrants' health conditions pose to communities, relatively few local jurisdictions have established policies explicitly limiting provision of health services based on immigration status.[9] Many publicly supported health care institutions in Texas, for example, have long provided free and discounted nonemergency care to all residents, even after the enactment of welfare reform legislation.[10] There are, however, a few notable exceptions to this trend, including institutions in San Diego, Albuquerque, and Fort Worth.[9,11]

In response to the ambiguity generated by this seemingly pervasive disconnection between policy and practice, administrators of the Harris County Hospital District, which includes the city of Houston and constitutes the third-busiest public health care system in the United States, sought guidance from Texas Attorney General John Cornyn in late 2000 to ascertain whether its proposed payment policy revisions (which would have permitted the district to provide free or discounted care to anyone who could show county residency and financial need) violated PRWORA and to determine the possible penalties for any such violations.[12] Attorney General Cornyn's subsequent opinion concluded that the welfare reform law prohibits the district from providing free or discounted nonemergency health care to undocumented immigrants, even if they reside within the district's boundaries, and that no state laws enacted since 1996 "expressly state the legislature's intent that undocumented aliens are to be eligible for certain public benefits."[13] With respect to potential penalties, the attorney general decided that, while PRWORA does not explicitly describe a penalty for providing public benefits to undocumented immigrants, "there may be sanctions to the district pursuant to conditions attached to federal funding" and that "there may also be legal consequences pursuant to state law for spending public funds for an unauthorized purpose."[13]

Cornyn's opinion has stirred an intense debate both in Texas and around the nation. Some of the state's local advocates and district attorneys have pressed for public inquiries into the activities of jurisdictions that choose to continue to provide free and discounted services; in Harris County, the local district attorney initiated a criminal investigation of the hospital district and its leadership.[14] Fearful of similar investigations in their own jurisdictions, some health care institutions in Nueces County, which includes Corpus Christi, and Montgomery County, just outside of Houston, have chosen to limit the services provided to undocumented individuals rather than leave their organizations and administrators exposed to prosecution.[9,10] Other parties that support hospitals' long-standing policies have obtained alternative legal interpretations of applicable state and federal laws that they claim justify the continued provision of discounted services to all residents irrespective of immigration status.[15]

While Harris County's district attorney has withdrawn his criminal investigation in an effort to achieve a workable compromise with health administrators, and calls for the initiation of similar inquiries around the state appear to have subsided, Attorney General Cornyn's opinion still stands to shape public health policy regarding undocumented immigrants not only in Texas but across the country.[16] Attorneys general and local prosecutors in other jurisdictions may draw on the opinion to initiate legal action against institutions that provide discounted services irrespective of immigration status. Should a court uphold Cornyn's opinion and related legal challenges, institutions that have not amended their policies to accommodate PRWORA's restrictions may face increased scrutiny.

Institutions in states such as California and New York, which have relatively large undocumented populations but so far appear to have been spared from legal inquiries, could conceivably be the next targets. Even if other jurisdictions' policies are not contested in court, the Cornyn opinion itself may have a chilling effect by discouraging undocumented immigrants from accessing health care as well as discouraging individual institutions from providing discounted services to undocumented populations.

How the restrictions jeopardize public health

The divergent reactions to Cornyn's opinion, the differing responses of health care providers, and the absence of definitive guidance from any level of government leave many publicly supported institutions in a state of legal and administrative uncertainty. The public health community should recognize, call attention to, and press for resolution of the threats posed to community health and welfare by this uncertainty and PRWORA's limitations on provision of health services.

First, these restrictions fail to consider the power and responsibility of state and local governments, and the institutions they fund, to protect the health, safety, and welfare of all who reside within the state's borders. While regulation of immigration has traditionally been a federal responsibility, Gostin notes that "part of the constitutional compact of our Union was that states would remain free to govern within the traditional sphere of health, safety, and morals."[17(p48)] Indeed, PRWORA's restrictions on the provision of health care infringe on states' "police power" and limit their ability to protect the health of their residents.[17,18]

Second, prohibiting the provision of discounted health care endangers access to services among undocumented immigrants' children, many of whom are born in the United States and are therefore eligible for publicly funded health care programs.[19] Findings of the Kaiser Commission on Medicaid and the Uninsured suggest that immigrants are often confused by state and federal eligibility restrictions and are intimidated by the threat of being discovered and deported.[20] As a result, even though PRWORA allows for provision of discounted immunizations and emergency services—and children born in the United States are eligible for government-funded health coverage—fear of immigration authorities or beliefs that their children do not qualify for services may prevent undocumented parents from seeking health care for their native-born children. A similar argument—that improving adults' access to services will improve children's access to care—has been offered as a rationale for expanding public health insurance coverage to parents of children enrolled in state Children's Health Insurance programs.[21]

Third, PRWORA's restrictions on the provision of health care services contradict the longstanding ethical obligations of clinicians by requiring providers to assume responsibilities traditionally reserved for federal immigration officials.[5,18] Ziv and Lo note that physicians who comply with mandates to deny services to undocumented immigrants "forgo the ethical ideal that patients' medical needs should be attended to without regard to their social, political, or citizenship status."[22(p1097)] In addition, while PRWORA does not place as great a burden on health professionals as Proposition 187, the ballot initiative that sought to deny many public services to undocumented immigrants and require clinicians to report undocumented individuals to the Immigration and Naturalization Service, a legislative order to deny services leaves the door open for further, more invasive intrusions on the confidentiality that facilitates trust between patients and providers.

Fourth, the administrative complexities generated by limits on the provision of services by publicly supported health care providers endanger access to care among legal residents. Guidelines issued by the US Department of Justice require that all patients be treated equally; therefore, all patients should be required to provide evidence of their immigration status.[9] Sorting through immigration documents for each patient, and turning away those who lack sufficient documentation but are unable to pay for the full cost of services, would increas e administrative costs and waiting times, reducing the efficiency of already overburdened safety-net institutions.[2]

Fifth, restricting access to preventive services while requiring institutions to continue to provide care for emergency conditions prevents administrators from putting public resources to their most cost-effective use. Laws such as the Emergency Medical Treatment and Labor Act require institutions to provide expensive acute health care to undocumented individuals when they present with emergency medical conditions.[6,23] In many cases, such as management of diabetes, asthma, or hypertension, preventive care can thwart the need for costly services to treat conditions that have progressed to emergency status.[24] Providing prenatal care to undocumented mothers has also been shown to be cost-effective.[25,26] Prohibiting the provision of these services prevents administrators from managing taxpayers' resources in the most cost-effective manner and may ultimately limit the health care safety net's ability to finance both public health and individual medical services.

Finally, limiting undocumented immigrants' access to health services weakens efforts to fight the spread of communicable diseases among the general population. While PRWORA's exemptions include the treatment of infectious diseases and their symptoms, conditions such as tuberculosis are not always easily detected as communicable diseases.[8] In addition, many cases of infectious disease are identified not when symptoms manifest themselves but when patients seek medical care for other unrelated conditions.[24] Consequently, identifying and treating communicable diseases in their earliest stages requires that undocumented immigrants be able to access services for all health conditions—not just those that have progressed to an emergency level or include symptoms of infectious disease—before others in the community are exposed.

Strategies for protecting access to health services

Given the significant threats posed by limits on undocumented immigrants' access to health services, the public health community should pursue a range of strategies to circumvent the barriers erected by PRWORA and avert the spread of legal challenges to other jurisdictions. The most obvious way in which institutions could unambiguously provide free or discounted primary and preventive health services to undocumented immigrants would be for states to "enact legislation which affirmatively provides for such eligibility."[1] The pursuit of state legislation, however, may fail to provide a sweeping and immediate solution to the problem, in that legislative action is subject to individual states' political climates, competing demands on lawmakers' attention, and the limited schedules of many legislatures.

PRWORA also allows publicly supported health care services to be exempted from eligibility restrictions under a determination by the US attorney general. Since the terrorist attacks on New York and Washington, however, there have been demands from the public to increase border security and heighten scrutiny of individuals illegally residing in the United States, and this situation almost certainly precludes the current US attorney general from advocating for the protection of additional public benefits for undocumented immigrants.

Federal legislation provides another opportunity for a solution. Representatives Sheila Jackson-Lee and Gene Green of Texas both introduced bills in the 107th Congress to amend PRWORA to include primary and preventive care among the list of services exempted from restriction. Should Congress fail to pass these or similar pieces of legislation, reauthorization of PRWORA could offer a sweeping resolution to the debate, and public health advocates should work to ensure that this issue is not overshadowed by other policy debates as lawmakers revisit welfare reform. In advocating for legislative solutions, public health advocates should, when feasible, seek untraditional alliances. Many business leaders, for example, have supported more generous immigration policies and could be effective allies.

If Congress chooses not to lift the restrictions on undocumented immigrants' access to services, health administrators should continue to work with law enforcement officials, particularly district attorneys in their respective communities, to reach agreements that permit institutions to sustain the provision of services critical to protecting the public's health, allocate resources to their most cost-effective uses, and avoid both criminal prosecutions of administrators and reductions in public funding. Hospital districts and public health institutions should also continue to provide free and discounted primary and preventive care services regardless of immigration status and allow the judicial system to determine what a reasonable outcome for this situation might be. Finally, public health leaders should be prepared to offer expert knowledge and file amicus curiae briefs on behalf of organizations and individuals who might face criminal prosecution or civil suits as a result of providing services to undocumented immigrants.

Conclusions

The public health community has an important role to play in advocating for a resolution of this debate that is based on sound public health and public management principles. Little to no evidence exists to suggest that public benefits, particularly health care services, lure undocumented immigrants to the United States. To the contrary, significant evidence does suggest that undocumented immigrants' use of public benefits is relatively low and that job opportunities and family issues are the primary factors motivating illegal immigration.[2,18,27,28] Furthermore, restricting undocumented immigrants' access to services unduly burdens health care institutions and threatens the health of entire communities. Consequently, public health advocates should work to ensure that policymakers seeking to reduce the number of undocumented immigrants in the United States focus their attention on strengthening border control and weakening the "pull factors" that actually drive illegal immigration, instead of endangering the public's health through misguided restrictions on provision of health services.

Acknowledgments

I wish to thank Peter Jacobson for his encouragement and comments throughout numerous revisions of this article.

References

1. Pub L No. 104-193, 110 Stat 2260.
2. *Hearings Before the U.S. House of Representatives Subcommittee on Immigration and Claims*, 104th Congress, 1st Sess (1995) (testimony of Michael Fix and Jeffrey S. Passel).
3. Illegal alien resident population. Available at: http://www.ins.usdoj.gov/graphics/aboutins/statistics/illegalalien/index. Accessed January 15, 2002.
4. Committee on Community Health Services, American Academy of Pediatrics. *Health Care for Children of Immigrant Families*. Chicago, Ill: American Academy of Pediatrics; 1997.
5. Loue S. Access to health care and the undocumented alien. *J Legal Med.* 1992;13:271–332.
6. Fallek S. Health care for illegal aliens: why it is a necessity. *Houston J Int Law.* 1997;19:951.
7. Berk M., Schur C. The effect of fear on access to care among undocumented immigrants. *J Immigrant Health.* 2001;3:151–156.
8. Johns K., Varkoutas C. The tuberculosis crisis: the deadly consequence of immigration policies and welfare reform. *J Contemp Health Law Policy.* 1998;15:101.
9. Center for Public Policy Priorities. The straight story: health care for uninsured undocumented immigrants in Texas. *Policy Page.* August 14, 2001:138.
10. Yardley J. Immigrants' medical care is focus of Texas dispute. *New York Times.* August 11, 2001:A18.
11. Jaklevic M. This side of the ethical border. *Modern Healthcare.* 2001;36:52–54.
12. Jaklevic M. Texas prosecutor probes free care. *Modern Healthcare.* 2002;37:20.
13. Office of the Attorney General of the State of Texas. Opinion No. JC-0394 (2001 Tex AG LEXIS 84).
14. Landa A. Illegal care? *Am Med News.* 2001;37:5.
15. Suval J. Paying the price. *Houston Press.* October 11, 2001; News and features.
16. Brewer S. DA drops investigation of immigrant health care. *Houston Chronicle* [online]. Available at http://www.HoustonChronicle.com. Accessed December 11, 2001.
17. Gostin L. O. *Public Health Law: Power, Duty, Restraint.* Los Angeles, Calif: University of California Press; 2000:48.
18. Fee A. Forbidding states from providing essential social services to illegal immigrants: the constitutionality of recent federal action. *Boston Public Interest Law J.* 1998;93.
19. Brenner E. The invisible children of illegal aliens. *New York Times.* March 28, 2001:A1.
20. Feld P., Power B. *Immigrants' Access to Health Care After Welfare Reform: Findings From Focus Groups in Four Cities.* Washington, DC: Kaiser Commission on Medicaid and the Uninsured; 2000.

21. Dubay L., Kenney G. *Covering Parents Through Medicaid and SCHIP: Potential Benefits to Low-Income Parents and Children*. Washington, DC: Kaiser Commission on Medicaid and the Uninsured; 2001.
22. Ziv T. A., Lo B. Denial of care to illegal immigrants—Proposition 187 in California. *N Engl J Med.* 1995;332:1095–1098.
23. Bilchik G. No easy answers. *Hospitals Health Networks.* 2001;5:58–60.
24. Brown E. Proposed immigrant care cuts threaten everyone. *Am Med News.* 1996;24:38.
25. Kuiper H., Richwald G. A., Rotblatt H., Asch S. The communicable disease impact of eliminating publicly funded prenatal care for undocumented immigrants. *Maternal Child Health J.* 1999;3:39–52.
26. Lu M. C., Lin Y. G., Prietto N. M., Garite T. J. Elimination of public funding of prenatal care for undocumented immigrants in California: a cost/benefit analysis. *Am J Obstet Gynecol.* 2000;182:233–239.
27. Berk M. L., Schur C. L., Chavez L. R., Frankel M. Health care use among undocumented Latino immigrants. *Health Aff.* 2000;4:51–63.
28. Rivera-Batiz F. Underground on American soil: undocumented workers and immigration policy. *J Int Aff.* 2000;2:485–501.

108

SLIPPING THROUGH THE NET

Social vulnerability in pandemic planning

Anna C. Mastroianni

Source: *Hastings Center Report*, 39:5 (2009), 11–12.

In the spring of 2009, a number of U.S. schools closed in response to government health directives designed to prevent the transmission of the contagious respiratory influenza virus known as H1N1. Thousands of children were asked to stay home and avoid congregating in groups. Public health authorities asked ill workers to stay home. As spring stretched into summer, camps sent symptomatic children home. The traditional public health containment strategy known as "social distancing" has rippled throughout affected communities. Parents have been forced to risk their jobs, take unpaid leave, or use limited sick leave to care for housebound children. Children who typically rely on school or camp meal programs have gone without. Local businesses have suffered when workers and shoppers stayed home. These experiences are now being repeated in the southern hemisphere as H1N1 moves south, but with the added burdens and complications that come with the more limited infrastructures and fewer resources of the developing world. The public health efforts to stem a flu outbreak have potentially serious social ramifications.

More importantly—and seemingly overlooked in pandemic planning for a virus such as H1N1—social context has major implications for the potential effectiveness of public health strategies to minimize morbidity and mortality and prevent the further spread of disease. For example, an undocumented restaurant worker receiving low wages and lacking job security and health benefits may have no real choice but to continue working through an illness, and may avoid seeking medical attention that he cannot afford and fears might lead to deportation. The worker's life situation makes it both impractical and inadvisable to respond to well-intentioned but unrealistic public health directives, putting both restaurant workers and diners at risk of infection. Policies that fail to take into account the realities of individuals' lives and the social contexts in which they live cannot hope to succeed. The

accomplishment of the public health goal of minimizing the effects of outbreaks may depend in significant part on social vulnerabilities that affect an
individual's or community's capacity to respond to public health directives.

Vulnerabilities and social contexts

Little attention has been given to the impact of social vulnerabilities on the
effectiveness of public health preparedness strategies, a shortcoming in both
policy-making and in how we think about the ethics of public health. How
should we incorporate thinking about social vulnerability into pandemic
planning? How should we account for social capacity to respond to directives
designed to prevent the spread of disease? Whose responsibility is it to address
those social barriers? Failure to account for social vulnerability may doom
a prevention effort and may lead to long-lasting distrust of the public health
system and of government generally in the affected population.

As in other areas of health policy, pandemic flu planning may acknowledge
vulnerability, but by using a categorical approach based on membership in an
identifiable population subgroup. For instance, policy guidelines and scholarly
work have referenced readily identifiable subgroups as more vulnerable in
determining priorities for distribution of scarce vaccines and antivirals. In
shortages of seasonal flu vaccine, those over sixty-five years of age typically
receive priority in vaccine distribution because of their vulnerability to severe
medical consequences. More recently, antivirals were recommended for treatment
of H1N1-infected pregnant women as a priority group. While this categorical
approach may be well meaning, the broad grouping of populations may mask
social vulnerabilities that require special attention, such as improved access
to health care and appropriately targeted directives.

Broadly defined categories of vulnerability tend both to exclude people
who belong in them and include people who do not. Groupings are necessary,
though, as public health policy-making must focus on the population level;
it cannot operate efficiently or effectively if it focuses on every individual at risk.
The difficulty is that policies risk failure if they cannot identify and address
individuals who cannot afford to practice social distancing—undocumented
workers, for in stance, and those who rely on community settings for their
livelihood or for their day-to-day existence (as in some developing world
settings). People with these characteristics cannot be adequately identified
with the classic social categories of gender, age, race, or ethnicity. Public
health policy needs to describe subgroups with sufficient specificity to account
for their particular needs and their ability and capacity to respond to public
health directives, but without creating so many groups as to become unworkable.

There is ample experience with this problem in other areas of health policy-
making, such as human subjects research, where some subpopulations have
been deemed more "vulnerable" than others. Florencia Luna argues eloquently
for a nuanced schema of *layers of vulnerability* rather than categorical

groups or subgroups.[1] She concludes that subpopulation status alone does not necessarily make an individual vulnerable, and that what matters is rather the context within which that status exists. Similarly, Ken Kipnis has argued for a taxonomy of vulnerability connected to appropriate policy responses.[2] Although Kipnis's approach was adopted in recommendations by the National Bioethics Advisory Commission, neither his nor Luna's approach has yet been reflected in policy-making. Nonetheless, they may be useful frameworks for a more nuanced understanding of how public health policy planning can address social context.

This is not to suggest that scholars in ethics and public health have completely ignored social context in challenging pandemic allocation priorities.[3] Similarly, public health practitioners are well aware that traditionally marginalized populations are far from homogeneous and that they may require specific approaches that respond to their identifiable social vulnerabilities.[4] The types of vulnerability, separately and in combination, call for specific and tailored responses as a matter of good public health planning and preparedness. In the case of flu, our current understanding is that concurrent health conditions and social vulnerability increase the likely severity and transmission. Pregnant women (and, implicitly, their developing fetuses) have been identified as a vulnerable subgroup in pandemic planning efforts, for example. Still, a more nuanced approach is possible: some pregnant women are more vulnerable than others—such as those suffering from chronic conditions that might exacerbate the effects of influenza exposure or those who have significant financial constraints on participating in prevention efforts, work in conditions (such as a day care center or hospital) where they are more likely to be exposed to the flu virus, or have caretaking responsibilities for other family members. The very same social vulnerabilities can thwart prevention efforts regardless of subgroup classification. These factors should worry anyone watching the H1N1 outbreak as it moves to the southern hemisphere—and potentially returns north in mutated and stronger form for the next flu season.

Drawing on community

Good public health practice and policy have a tradition of acknowledging social context. Prevention efforts have historically included the improvement of environmental and social conditions, such as by improving sanitation, providing clean drinking water, and promoting safe labor practices. The World Health Organization has long acknowledged the contribution of social conditions to health, defining health as a "state of complete physical, mental and *social* well-being and not merely the absence of disease or infirmity."[5]

Recent experiences with SARS and with Hurricane Katrina prove that public health responses will ultimately be carried out both in and by communities, and that community participation means more than action by the local health department. Communities know their social vulnerabilities better than anyone

216

else. Community-based prevention is something that public health workers know how to do, but they cannot act alone in a pandemic. Where sick children and workers are asked to stay home, employers need to be encouraged to develop telecommuting arrangements, guarantees of job security, and sufficiently flexible leave policies.[6] Schools may have to train students and teachers in proper hygiene practices, such as handwashing and etiquette for sneezing and coughing. Elected officials need to develop communication strategies for diverse media forms and for those not proficient in English. Social support networks need to be identified and strengthened to address the potentially stigmatizing effects of illness. If schools are closed, alternative sources for critical services rendered through the schools, such as breakfasts and lunches, need to be created. Shopping mall owners and schools may have to consult engineers about proper ventilation in public spaces. The list goes on; the upshot is that opportunities for stakeholder consultation and participation in pandemic planning should be encouraged.

Local public health departments know the makeup of their community in greater detail than is afforded by the categories of race, ethnicity, and income. But they need guidance, a roadmap of potential vulnerabilities and possible responses, so that an action plan can be developed and readily mobilized. With a better understanding of social vulnerabilities, pandemic planning policies will be more responsive to the real needs within communities and better able to stem the tide of the next public health crisis.

References

1. F. Luna, "Elucidating the Concept of Vulnerability: Layers Not Labels," *International Journal of Feminist Approaches to Bioethics* 2, no. 1 (2009): 121–39.
2. K. Kipnis, "Vulnerability in Research Subjects: A Bioethical Taxonomy," in *Ethical and Policy Issues in Research Involving Human Research Participants* (Bethesda, Md.: National Bioethics Advisory Commission, 2001), G-1–G-13.
3. N. Kass et al., "Ethics and Severe Pandemic Influenza: Maintaining Essential Functions through a Fair and Considered Response," *Biosecurity and Bioterrorism: Biodefense Strategy, Practice and Science* 6, no. 3 (2008): 227–36.
4. B. I. Truman et al., "Pandemic Influenza Preparedness and Response among Immigrants and Refugees," *American Journal of Public Health* 99 (May 21, 2009), electronic publication ahead of print, available at http://www.ajph.org/cgi/reprint/AJPH.2008.154054v1.
5. Preamble to the Constitution of the World Health Organization as adopted by the International Health Conference, New York, June 19–22, 1946; italics added.
6. Truman et al., "Pandemic Influenza Preparedness and Response."

Part 17

QUARANTINES AND CIVIL LIBERTIES

109

DETENTION AND THE EVOLVING THREAT OF TUBERCULOSIS

Evidence, ethics, and law

Richard Coker, Marianna Thomas,
Karen Lock and Robyn Martin

Source: *Journal of Law, Medicine & Ethics*, 35:4 (2007), 609–15.

Introduction

The issue of detention as a tuberculosis control measure has resurfaced following the prolonged detention of a patient with an extensively drug-resistant strain of tuberculosis in a prison cell in Arizona,[1] and the attempted detention in Italy and subsequent detention in Atlanta, Georgia of an American sufferer thought to have XDR-TB in May 2007.[2] These cases have reignited the debate over the evidence that supports detention policy in the control of tuberculosis, and its associated legal and ethical ramifications. This paper considers whether involuntary detention is justified where voluntary measures have failed or where a patient poses a danger, albeit uncertain, to the public, and discusses the need for strengthening evidence-based assessments of public health risk.

Globally, tuberculosis currently infects about a third of the world's population, with an estimated growth of one percent per year for the global incidence of active diseased.[3] This increase is driven in part by its association with Human Immunodeficiency Virus (HIV) and Acquired Immunodeficiency Syndrome (AIDS), both of which predispose their sufferers to tuberculosis through complex epidemiological and socio-economic interactions. Consequently, tuberculosis affects societies' most vulnerable and deprived populations. Of profound concern has been the recent rise in the prevalence of drug-resistant strains of the disease. The causes of this, like the interactions with HIV, are manifest and complex, but fundamentally iatrogenic in nature.

The emergence of an extensively drug-resistant form of tuberculosis (XDR-TB) was reported by the World Health Organization (WHO) in March 2006 following a worldwide survey that examined resistance to second-line drug therapies.[4] Multi-drug resistant tuberculosis (MDR-TB)[5] poses profound challenges, most notably because of the treatment costs and the prolonged duration of infectiousness. XDR-TB amplifies these concerns.

Drug resistance poses an enormous challenge to ongoing efforts to globally control TB, and raises concerns over a lethal global pandemic of increasingly drug-resistant forms of the disease. Although improved clinical care, strengthened health systems, and access to second line anti-tuberculosis drugs have improved cure rates for MDR-TB in recent years with reported survival rates of 60 percent, in the case of XDR-TB, the pattern is still very worrisome, especially amongst populations where HIV prevalence is high.[6] In a rural area of KwaZulu-Natal, for example, an alarming picture has emerged in relation to an outbreak of HIV-associated XDR-TB.[7] Forty-five percent of the 53 cases occurred in individuals who had not previously been treated for tuberculosis, suggesting active ongoing spread. All 44 individuals tested for HIV were co-infected, signifying substantial rapid progression to disease following infection. Rapid progression to death occurred in 98 percent of patients, with a median survival of only 16 days from the time of diagnosis.[8]

Responses to the emergence of XDR-TB

There has been an international response to the emergence of XDR-TB and the issues surrounding it in the context of tuberculosis control. The WHO restated its focus on preventative measures and updated its tuberculosis control strategy to account for XDR-TB, following a meeting of the Global Taskforce on XDR-TB in October 2006. In January 2007, guidance on involuntary detention in the context of human rights was issued in response to a paper by Singh et al., which highlighted the potential role for involuntary detention in the management of XDR-TB.[9] In this paper, involuntary detention was advocated as a last resort where voluntary measures had failed, and where the patient "wilfully" refused treatment and posed a danger to the public.[10] The South African Medical Research Council published a position statement taking a similar approach, in which the need for careful legal and ethical review was emphasized.[11]

Tuberculosis control measures within Europe

Legislation to support tuberculosis control varies across countries in Europe (see table).[12] Some countries, for example Switzerland, legislate for compulsory control measures such as examination, detention, and treatment, in addition to compulsory prevention measures such as screening and vaccination. In contrast, Spain has no compulsory measures for tuberculosis control. A recent review of public health legislation in 14 European states found that eight states sanction detention, either within the home or in an institution, for patients with tuberculosis.[13] Five of these states also sanction compulsory treatment for tuberculosis (Estonia, Czech Republic, Norway, Russia, and Switzerland). England, Germany, and Israel provide for compulsory detention but do not authorize compulsory treatment. The authority to detain is not limited to infectious cases, but may, in six countries, be sanctioned when patients refuse treatment. Whilst a court order is generally required to authorize detention, in Norway, however, physicians have the power to detain patients without an order. Norway also legislates for compulsory quarantine of individuals on the grounds of exposure to tuberculosis.[14]

Legislation for the detention of patients with tuberculosis in England and Wales is limited, under sections 37 and 38 of the Public Health Act 1984, to those with tuberculosis of the respiratory tract "in the infectious state." Built-in safeguards from the 1925 and 1936 Public Health Acts were removed in 1968, resulting in no current codified process of review and no limits to the duration of the detention or extension of the order; there is also no automatic right to legal representation.[15] As is the case in numerous states around the world, English legislation is undergoing a process of reform, partly in response to the revision of International Health Regulations. Like many states, English public health laws have been scrutinized and found wanting.[16]

Overarching the application of public health police powers in Europe are people's fundamental rights, which are enshrined in national law and contained in the European Convention for the Protection of Human Rights and Fundamental Freedoms (ECHR). The question of Convention rights in the context of the exercise of public health powers was raised in the 2005 case of *Enhorn v. Sweden*, in which an HIV positive man successfully challenged his detention by Swedish public health officials.[17] The means of transmission of HIV differ from those of tuberculosis, and it could be argued that the nature of transmitting tuberculosis through simply breathing justifies greater intrusion into private rights for the benefit of the public health. However, the European Court of Human Rights noted in *Enhorn* that there has been little case law on interpretation of the "infectious disease" exemptions in the European Convention, and took the opportunity to lay down some general principles governing those circumstances in which human rights might be infringed in pursuance of infectious disease control. Any exercise of a public health power which resulted in an infringement of the right to liberty contra Article 5 of the Convention, or an infringement of the right to private and family life contra Article 8, must satisfy the requirements that it is proportional to the public health threat, and that there is an "absence of arbitrariness" such that other less severe measures have been considered and found to be insufficient to safeguard the individual and the public. The institution where the detention is to take place must be appropriate to the nature of the disease and must provide opportunities for treatment as well as public health protection. It is also the case that Article 6 of the

Table Legal compulsory measures for selected European countries (ranked by number of control measures).

Country	Screening	Examination	Treatment	Detention	Vaccination	Isolation on the grounds of exposure	Exclusion from activities	Number of control measures
Spain	N	N	N	N	N	N	N	0
France	N	N	N	N	Y	N	Y	2
Germany	N	Y	N	Y	N	N	Y	2
Israel	N	N	N	Y	N	N	Y	2
Netherlands	Y	Y	N	N	N	N	N	2
Finland	Y	N	Y	N	N	N	Y	3
Poland	N	Y	Y	N	Y	N	Y	3
England	Y	Y	N	Y	N	N	Y	4
Estonia	N	Y	Y	Y	Y	N	N	4
Hungary	Y	N	Y	N	Y	N	Y	4
Switzerland	Y	Y	Y	Y	N	N	N	4
Czech	N	N	Y	Y	Y	N	Y	5
Norway	Y	Y	Y	Y	N	Y	Y	6
Russia	Y	Y	Y	Y	Y	N	Y	6

(Table modified from R. J. Coker, S. Mounier-Jack, and R. Martin, "Public Health Law and Tuberculosis Control in Europe," Public Health 121, no. 4 [2007]: 266–73.)

Convention, which protects the right to a fair trial, will invalidate a detention that fails to recognize opportunities for defense, review, and appeal. Although the higher risk of tuberculosis transmission may require proportionally greater restrictive measures than in the case of HIV, it is clear from the decision in *Enhorn* that statutory public health powers in many states of Rurope are vulnerable to challenge on human rights grounds. Although *Enhorn* was the first case to reach the courts, many detention practices in Europe would fail to stand up to scrutiny under the ECHR.[18]

A role for involuntary detention?

Jerome Singh et al.'s paper on the challenge posed by XDR-TB in South Africa stimulated afresh the debate about the use of detention to protect the public's health.[19] The debate originated a decade earlier when New York City, responding to an epidemic of drug-resistant tuberculosis in the early 1990s, passed laws that facilitated the detention of non-infectious individuals and shifted the burden of proof from an assessment of the risk posed to the public's health to an assessment of likely treatment compliance.[20] Thus, this novel approach did not distinguish between types of tuberculosis (for example, drug-sensitive diseases, MDR-TB, or indeed the as yet to be recognized XDR-TB), but on determinations of compliance and completion of treatment. Periods of detention for those with MDR-TB were longer than those with drug-sensitive disease, not because the threat posed to public health was greater (though it could be argued that this was the case) but because the treatment took much longer to complete. The current New York City law does not respond to differences in transmission dynamics or assessments of risk.

In relation to XDR-TB in South Africa, Singh et al. propose that under some circumstances, individuals might be isolated whilst awaiting susceptibility results. They advocate an initial voluntary isolation of patients with drug-resistant tuberculosis, separating those with multi-drug resistance from those with extensive drug resistance, and recommend coercive measures where voluntary isolation is declined, acknowledging that the duration of isolation may potentially be indefinite or until death in some cases of XDR-TB. The authors conclude: "Although such an approach might interfere with the patient's right to autonomy and will undoubtedly have human rights implications, such measures are reasonable and justifiable, and must be seen in a utilitarian perspective. Ultimately in such cases, the interests of public health must prevail over the rights of the individual."[21]

This statement raises a number of ethical issues. While considerable attention has been paid to the purpose and boundaries of human rights, the nature and scope of public health ethics have received less consideration. Human rights jurisprudence emerged from Western political philosophy, which prioritizes individual autonomy and the protection of individual physical, personal, and proprietary rights from interference by the state. Medical ethics, as distinct from public health ethics, have developed both temporally and substantively with human rights jurisprudence, resulting in principles of medical ethics also being underpinned by this central recognition of autonomy and private rights. For this reason, human rights and Western norms of medical ethics do not always sit comfortably in some cultures, such as Asian, African, or Islamic cultures, that prioritize the good of society or the community over the individual.

Public health practice, which has its roots not in medicine but in the work of early welfare reformers such as Edwin Chadwick, is premised on the philosophies of utilitarianism and social responsibility, or what we might now term communitarianism, rather than autonomy. Consideration of involuntary detention will thus require some reconciliation between the principles of human rights and autonomy on the one hand, and public benefit on the other. Such reconciliation is not an impossible task. John Stuart Mill's "Harm Principle" makes provision for the restriction of an individual's right to autonomy and self-determination in order to prevent harm to others and benefit liberty overall. This is a central tenet of the position taken by those advocating for the detention of individuals with tuberculosis who are perceived to pose a public health threat. In recognition of this principle, many human rights documents recognize that the public's health might justify some qualification of rights. Article 5(1) of the European Convention, for example, which is designed to protect liberty, allows for "the lawful detention of persons for the prevention of the spreading of infectious diseases." Similarly the Siracusa Principles, drawn up in 1984, contain a provision for departure from the 1966 International Covenant on Civil and Political Rights in situations of public emergency, including public health emergencies.[22] However, the scope and limits of the power to infringe upon the right to liberty in pursuance of infectious disease prevention and control need further clarification.

Public health and risk

An approach, which might enable the formulation of a body of public health ethics acceptable to human rights jurisprudence, is to introduce into the language of ethics and rights the notion of evidence-based assessment of risk. Singh and colleagues note in their argument for involuntary detention that detention "has met with some degree of success in the U.S., where it helped bring down TB infection rates in states such as New York in the 1990s." Yet this important assertion was unsubstantiated and no evidence was provided. Indeed, there appears to be very limited evidence to support a causal relationship between increased detention and reduction of TB incidence, a somewhat ironic position given the burden such interventions place on individuals in this age of evidence-based medicine.[23]

226

Public health regulation essentially constitutes an attempt to control risk by balancing the threat to the public's health against the limitations imposed on the individual by measures implemented to limit the overall risk. Inevitably, regulation constrains the rights of the individual in order to benefit the public interest and the greater good.[24] In the context of detention, it can be argued from a utilitarian perspective that if the utility gain to the greatest number exceeds the utility loss across society, then coercive measures are justifiable.[25] It follows that a risk assessment is necessary to determine this balance. This consideration of risk should inform determinations of whether involuntary detention should play a role in the control of tuberculosis, and objective evidence of the risks posed by tuberculosis is required to inform rational policymaking. The evidential standard supporting a policy of detention in tuberculosis control should surely be high in order to justify the infringement of human rights that detention entails.

Scientific investigation into tuberculosis greatly diminished during the 1970s, when the disease appeared to be effectively controlled and potentially eliminated. Much of the current knowledge regarding transmissibility is derived from studies of outbreaks and animal studies. Although the presence of the acid-fast bacilli in sputum is known to be highly predictive of infectiousness, drawing on advances in molecular analysis, we also know that smear-negative individuals can pose a risk, albeit substantially reduced.[26] Considerable uncertainty remains concerning the risk of transmission and the duration of this risk; thus, risk prediction is still an uncertain business. With the available evidence, we are not acting completely in the dark and may make inferences,[27] but if we wish to justify interventions on utilitarian grounds, we cannot continue to impose measures which infringe upon rights without rigorously pursuing further evidence to support utilitarian calculations of benefit.

In the context of uncertainly, policy decisions commonly rely on the perception of risk to the public health. This notion, if applied rationally, acknowledges both the probability and gravity of harm, while still considering personal, social, and cultural values. Even in the hands of "experts," interpretation of statistical data is subjective and liable to bias and error. This well-documented phenomenon becomes amplified by the incorrect use of statistical data in the determination of risk in other contexts. For example, in England, misinterpretation of statistics by a professor of paediatric medicine led to an overestimation of the risk of two cases of sudden infant death syndrome occurring in the same family, an error that led to a murder conviction for the infants' mother.[28]

A consensus is needed on what may be considered appropriate in balancing the common public health good with individual rights. There is insufficient evidence that a policy of detention is, in aggregate, beneficial to public health.[29] This does not mean, of course, that isolating an individual has no impact on transmission dynamics. Historically, isolation and quarantine *have* been effective in containing the spread of infectious disease and are among control measures recommended in the revised International Health Regulations. But coercive measures could impact positively or negatively on the behavior of those who are threatened with sanction, either by encouraging them to comply with treatment, or, in contrast with a public health perspective, by causing them to delay in seeking diagnosis and treatment.[30] While the impact on the individual might be readily determined, understanding the public health impact of these wider factors is more challenging.

A further consideration is the risk of stigmatization and discrimination.[31] The greatest burden of disease lies with socially disadvantaged groups: physical overcrowding, HIV, low income, and malnutrition all contribute to the susceptibility of the responsible organism. Tuberculosis stigmatizes,[32] and involuntary detention measures may serve to further stigmatize and marginalize the person, an issue potentially exacerbated if the place of detention is a prison rather than a health care setting.

Human rights and the Siracusa Principles

The Siracusa Principles offer a useful framework by which to examine whether coercive public health interventions are justified. The first of the principles is the notion of whether any proposed restriction on liberty is a legitimate objective of general concern. The objective of controlling tuberculosis and limiting drug resistance is undeniably both legitimate and in the public's interest. Is the restriction provided for and carried out in accordance with the law? Many democratic countries have legal structures in which coercive public health interventions are sanctioned. However, much of the public health legislation around the world was drafted before the development of contemporary medical responses to tuberculosis, notably the advent of effective anti-tuberculosis drugs, and before the development of contemporary human rights jurisprudence. Thus, it is often the case that public health legislation contains neither adequate legal safeguards to prevent inappropriate detention, nor adequate opportunities to defend, appeal, or review detention orders.

A second principle questions whether available alternatives that are less intrusive and restrictive have been tried. The weak evidence base noted above profoundly tests this notion of proportionality in regards to detention. Moreover, the evidence necessary to support other less restrictive interventions is also insufficient.[33]

Another principle addresses the arbitrary, unreasonable or discriminatory manner in which a sanction might be imposed. The detention of any group of tuberculosis patients may appear arbitrary without a fuller understanding of the risks.[34] More evidence is required in order to identify the individuals or groups to be targeted by these restrictions, and the optimum duration of detention. This is compounded by the fact that the prevalence of tuberculosis, particularly drug-resistant forms of tuberculosis, is not distributed evenly throughout society, resulting in detention measures that may in practice appear to be focused on particular ethnic groups or strata of society.[35]

Underpinning the Siracusa Principles is the explicit demand for evidence of public health benefit. A lack of evidence when attempting to justify an action is not a problem that is unique to communicable disease control. In other areas, however, notably in the context of environmental protection, the precautionary principle carries weight. But environmental protection does not test human rights in the same way as communicable diseases. Use of the precautionary principle to justify the detention of sufferers of disease has the potential to result in a significant invasion of individual rights. If we are to justify overriding human rights for the public good in the absence of evidence, we must do so within another framework of protection, protection against the abuse of power by the state. Such a framework must contain an acknowledgement of the duties incumbent not only upon individuals, but also upon public health agencies, and must address the manner in which society's most marginalized and vulnerable are treated. These are issues that have an implicit impact on an unwritten social contract between individuals and society.

Implicit in the Siracusa Principles is the little explored notion of how much burden or risk, if any, society is prepared to shoulder if basic individual rights and freedoms are to be protected at society's expense. In the absence of evidence, is coercion acceptable for the objective of public health protection? Social and cultural values determine where this balance is to be drawn.

While a utilitarian perspective, from which much debate draws, is dependent upon an evidence base that is yet to be established, Kantian or Rawlsian positions might justify interventions provided that societies accept that acting for the benefit of the public's health is right regardless of the outcomes. In societies where the determination of morally acceptable behavior is determined by a higher law, such as religious belief, it has been easier for states to impose interventions for the public good which result in a sacrifice of the individual. In some states, for example Malaysia, a state where English common law traditions are superimposed with Islamic law, there are statutory powers of compulsory vaccination and medical treatment. In secular societies however, where autonomy is prized, restrictions on rights that cannot be justified by rational argument will inevitably be controversial. In the U.K., for example, there are no powers of compulsory vaccination or treatment, and recent law reform proposals have rejected the introduction of such powers. History suggests that making vaccinations or treatments compulsory in the U.K. would be socially and politically unacceptable, unless they could be justified by scientific evidence and rational argument. A new consideration of the philosophy underpinning public health in the context of communicable diseases is needed before we can engage in a meaningful debate about the arguments for and against involuntary detention.

Conclusion

Controlling the spread of tuberculosis and preventing the development of drug resistance are legitimate public health objectives, but do not in themselves justify interventions which infringe upon human rights. Determination of the legitimacy of a coercive measure demands an analytical framework, and that framework should be underpinned by philosophical and scientific reasoning. Traditionally, in Western societies, public health interventions have been examined from a utilitarian perspective.[36] The Siracusa Principles and other interpretations of human rights, such as those by the European Court of Human Rights, draw upon utilitarianism to provide a coherent framework for analysis. But this framework is of limited value when considering the detention of individuals with tuberculosis because the evidence base is weak. In order to make consistent and coherent decisions in "hard cases," we need to develop an evidence base through research and to consider employing an alternative philosophy as the theoretical foundation of reflections on legitimacy. Otherwise, we will continue to muddle along, directed by "expert" opinion and political imperatives. If we remain wedded to the Siracusa Principles and their utilitarian justification, then the evidence base concerning tuberculosis must be strengthened to inform rational policy-making. In particular, information on the impact of the threat of detention on treatment compliance and the benefits gained from the detention of patients, particularly non-infectious patients, as well as its subsequent effects on the evolution of drug resistance, is vital. Such evidence should be provided by experimental work, formal theoretical risk analyses, and modelling. Legislation underpinning the detention of patients with tuberculosis must be reviewed in the light of advances in knowledge, and the requirements of due process must be clarified.

Public health requires the development of a coherent and discrete body of public health ethics. The involuntary detention of individuals with tuberculosis tests traditional medical ethical approaches that, broadly, are framed to govern the relationship between health care providers and patients, and which offer little in the way of guidance for the public health imperatives associated with communicable diseases. In particular, norms of public health ethics need to be grounded in well-developed social, political, and philosophical theory so as to provide a robust framework to support public health practice.

References

1. C. Kahn, "Man with Drug-Resistant TB Locked Up," *USA Today*, April 12, 2007.
2. L. Altman, "TB Patient Is Isolated After Taking Two Flights," *New York Times*, May 30, 2007.
3. World Health Organization, *Tuberculosis Facts*, 2007.

4. XDR-TB is defined as resistance to rifampicin and isoniazid, in addition to any fluoroquinolone, and to at least one of the three following injectable drugs used in anti-TB treatment: capreomycin, kanamycin, and amikacin. World Health Organization, "Extensively Drug-Resistant Tuberculosis (XDR-TB): Recommendations for Prevention and Control," *The Weekly Epidemiological Record* 81, no. 45 (2006): 430–32.

5. MDR-TB is defined as resistance to rifampicin and isoniazid with or without drug resistance to other anti-tuberculosis drugs.

6. R. J. Coker, "Review: Multidrug-Resistant Tuberculosis: Public Health Challenges," *Tropical Medicine and International Health* 9, no. 1 (2004): 25–40.

7. Centers for Disease Control, "Emergence of Mycobacterium Tuberculosis with Extensive Resistance to Second-Line Drugs – Worldwide, 2000–2004," *MMWR Morbidity and Mortality Weekly Report* 55, no. 11 (2006): 301–5; N. R. Gandhi, A. Moll, A. W. Sturm, R. Pawinski, T. Govender, U. Lalloo, K. Zeller, J. Andrews, and G. Friedland, "Extensively Drug-Resistant Tuberculosis as a Cause of Death in Patients Co-Infected with Tuberculosis and HIV in a Rural Area of South Africa," *The Lancet* 368, no. 9547 (2006): 1575–80.

8. *Id.* (Ghandi et al.)

9. J. A. Singh, R. Upshur, and N. Padayatchi, "XDR-TB in South Africa: No Time for Denial or Complacency," *PLoS Medicine* 41, no. 1 (2007): e50.

10. World Health Organization, *Report of the Meeting of the WHO Global Task Force on XDR-TB*, Geneva, 2006.

11. Position statement by the South African Medical Research Council, *Detention of Patients with Extensively Drug-Resistant Tuberculosis (XDR-TB)*, South African Medical Research Council, January 30, 2007.

12. R. J. Coker, S. Mounier-Jack, and R. Martin, "Public Health Law and Tuberculosis Control in Europe," *Public Health* 121, no. 4 (2007): 266–73.

13. *Id.*

14. *Id.*

15. R. J. Coker, "The Law, Human Rights, and the Detention of Individuals with Tuberculosis in England and Wales," *Journal of Public Health Medicine* 22, no. 3 (2000): 263–67.

16. R. Coker, "Communicable Disease Control and Contemporary Themes in Public Health Law," *Public Health* 120, Supplement (2006): 23–8, at discussion 28–9.

17. R. Martin, "The Exercise of Public Health Powers in Cases of Infectious Disease: Human Rights Implications," *Medical Law Review* 14, no. 1 (2006): 132–43.

18. R. Coker, "Civil Liberties and Public Good: Detention of Tuberculous Patients and the Public Health Act 1984," *Medical History* 45, no. 3 (2001): 341–58.

19. See Singh et al., *supra* note 9.

20. R. J. Coker, *From Chaos to Coercion: Detention and the Control of Tuberculosis* (New York: St. Martin's Press, 2000); L. O. Gostin, "Controlling the Resurgent Tuberculosis Epidemic: A 50-State Survey of TB Statutes and Proposals for Reform," *JAMA* 269, no. 2 (1993): 255–61; and L. O. Gostin, *Public Health Powers: The Imminence of Radical Change*, paper presented at the conference proceedings, New York City, December 4–5, 1992, at 268–90.

21. See Singh et al., *supra* note 9.

22. United Nations, Economic and Social Council, *Siracusa Principles on the Limitation and Derogation Provisions in the International Covenant on Civil and*

Political Rights, 1985; L. Gostin, *Public Health Law: Power, Duty, Restraint* (Berkeley/Los Angeles: University of California Press, 2000).

23. R. J. Coker, "Public Health Impact of Detention of Individuals with Tuberculosis: Systematic Literature Review," *Public Health* 117, no. 4 (2003): 281–87.

24. R. J. Coker, "The Law, Human Rights, and the Detention of Individuals with Tuberculosis in England and Wales," *Journal of Public Health Medicine* 22, no. 3 (2000): 263–67; see Gostin, *supra* note 22; G. Pinet, *Good Practice in Legislation and Regulations for TB control: An Indicator of Political Will*, World Health Organization, Geneva, May 2001.

25. R. Coker, "Just Coercion? Detention of Nonadherent Tuberculosis Patients," *Annals of the New York Academy of Sciences* 953 (2001): 216–23; R. Coker, "Tuberculosis, Non-Compliance and Detention for the Public Health," *Journal of Medical Ethics* 26, no. 3 (2000): 157–9.

26. K. A. Sepkowitz, "How Contagious Is Tuberculosis?" *Clinical Infectious Diseases* 23, no. 5 (1996): 954–62; M. A. Behr, S. A. Warren, H. Salamon, P. C. Hopewell, A. P. de Leon, C. L. Daley, and P. M. Small, "Transmission of Mycobacterium Tuberculosis from Patients Smear-Negative for Acid-Fast Bacilli," *The Lancet* 353, no. 9151 (1999): 444–49.

27. See Coker, *supra* note 20; Coker, *supra* note 23.

28. C. Heald, "What Future for Expert Witnesses?" BBC News Web site, July 13, 2005, *available at* <http://news.bbc.co.uk/1/hi/uk/4637687.stm> (last visited September 11, 2007).

29. See Coker, *supra* note 16; Coker, *supra* note 23.

30. S. Asch, B. Leake, R. Anderson, and L. Gelberg. "Why Do Symptomatic Patients Delay Obtaining Care for Tuberculosis?" *American Journal of Respiratory and Critical Care Medicine* 157 (1998): 1244–8; S. Asch, B. Leake, and L. Gelberg, "Does Fear of Immigration Authorities Deter Tuberculosis Patients from Seeking Care," *Western Journal of Medicine* 161, no. 4 (1994): 373–76; S. J. Heymann, R. Sell, and T. F. Brewer, "The Influence of Program Acceptability on the Effectiveness of Public Health Policy: A Study of Directly Observed Therapy for Tuberculosis," *American Journal of Public Health* 88, no. 33 (1998): 442–5.

31. G. Verma, R. E. Upshur, E. Rea, and S. R. Benatar, "Critical Reflections on Evidence, Ethics and Effectiveness in the Management of Tuberculosis: Public Health and Global Perspectives," *BMC Medical Ethics* 5, no. 2 (2004): E2.

32. S. Sontag, *Illness as Metaphor and AIDS and its Metaphors* (New York: Anchor Books, 1990).

33. See Coker, *supra* note 16; Coker, *supra* note 20; Coker, *supra* note 23.

34. R. Coker, "Tuberculosis, Non-Compliance and Detention for the Public Health," *Journal of Medical Ethics* 26, no. 3 (2000): 157–9.

35. M. R. Gasner, K. L. Maw, G. E. Feldman, P. I. Fujiwara, and T. R. Frieden, "The Use of Legal Action in New York City to Ensure Treatment of Tuberculosis," *New England Journal of Medicine* 340, no. 5 (1999): 359–66.

36. M. J. Roberts and M. R. Reich, "Ethical Analysis in Public Health," *The Lancet* 55, no. 359 (2002): 1055–9.

110

EVIDENCE AND EFFECTIVENESS IN DECISIONMAKING FOR QUARANTINE

Cécile M. Bensimon and Ross E. G. Upshur

Source: *American Journal of Public Health*, Supplement 1 97:S1 (2007), S44–S48.

When public health decisionmakers turned to quarantine during the recent severe acute respiratory syndrome (SARS) epidemic, difficult questions were raised about the legitimacy and acceptability of restrictive measures to attain public health goals. SARS also brought to light how scientific uncertainty can permeate public health decisionmaking, leading us to think about the relationship between the adequacy of evidence of the effectiveness of an intervention and its role in the justification of public health action.

In this article, we critically examine the role of evidence and effectiveness in decisionmaking for quarantine. It is our contention that the effectiveness of a public health intervention should not be defined exclusively in (absolute and objective) scientific terms but rather conceptualized relationally and normatively in public health decisionmaking.

In the aftermath of severe acute respiratory syndrome (SARS) and with an influenza pandemic on the horizon, the use of restrictive measures, such as quarantine and isolation, by public health authorities is back on the agenda of policymakers, ethicists, and health care providers in a way that has not been seen since the turn of the century. Then, systems of quarantine were quasi-institutions commonly erected at seaports as a means to control the infiltration of infectious diseases into local communities. Long before the notion of public health was formulated, both as a discipline and an institution, and even longer before the emphasis of security and protection embodied in the historic conception of the welfare state entered our political con-sciousness, the use of quarantine was a fundamental pillar of what were essentially public health measures. It is, thus, both one of the oldest tools of and a precedent to public health that in bygone years was viewed as a legitimate response to protect the public health and commercial inter-ests. For nearly half a century, however, when it appeared that infectious diseases were no longer a threat, quarantine became an antiquated inter-vention that was hardly ever considered an option, much less invoked on a large scale.

The society in which quarantine was invoked during SARS is fundamen-tally different than the world in which it was first conceived and enforced. Then, individuals had an obligation to respect restrictive measures. Today, they have the right not to. With the emergence of HIV/AIDS in the early 1980s, there was a renewed interest in quarantine that spurred an intense and often passionate debate about the use of restrictive measures for com-municable disease control in a liberal democratic society. But not long after the notion was (re)introduced, there was an almost unanimous consen-sus by advocates, practitioners, and scholars alike, that "the revival of [this] archaic doctrine"[1(p53)] was not, nor would ever be, a justifiable intervention for victims or carriers of HIV/AIDS. So when public health decisionmakers implemented a system of quarantine during the recent SARS epidemic, it raised difficult legal, political, ethical, moral, and philosophical questions about the legitimacy and acceptability of restrictive measures to attain pub-lic health goals.

The SARS epidemic also brought to light how scientific uncertainty can permeate public health decisionmaking, leading us to think about how to conceptualize the relationship between the adequacy of evidence of the effec-tiveness of an intervention and its role in the justification of public health action. Our objective then, is to critically examine the role of evidence and effectiveness in public health decisionmaking with respect to quarantine. It is our contention that the effectiveness of a public health intervention should not be defined exclusively in (absolute and objective) scientific terms but rather conceptualized relationally and normatively in public health decisionmaking.

In the following section, we will give a brief overview of the SARS out-break and the circumstances that lead to the implementation of quaran-tine. In the "Ethical Frameworks" section, we will look at how public health ethics frameworks inform an ethical analysis of quarantine, with a focus on the claim that the effectiveness of an intervention ought to be a guid-ing principle in public health decisionmaking. Following from a recent analysis of effectiveness by Richard Ashcroft, we will explore in the final section the role of effectiveness in public health decisionmaking and chal-lenge the dominant understanding of what effectiveness is in support of our view that public health decisionmaking is both normative and intersubjective.

Case description

When SARS emerged in February 2003, it quickly became clear that this was a new infectious disease "of international concern."[2(p14)] Although it is believed that the disease first emerged in southern China, it was first documented in Vietnam and later found to have spread mainly to Singapore, Taiwan, and Canada. (The spread of the disease on an international scale is astounding: "by March 12, 55 cases of SARS were recognized, mainly in hospitals in Hong Kong, Singapore and Hanoi. A month later, there were more than 3000 cases and 100 deaths in 20 countries worldwide. By May 8, 7000 cases, and by June 11, almost 8500 cases and more than 800 deaths, had been reported to the WHO from 29 countries."[3(p274)])

At the time that it was determined that it was infectious, little was known about SARS. It was within this context of inadequate evidence and incomplete knowledge that public health authorities deemed it appropriate to invoke the precautionary principle—a principle that seeks to implement preventive measures to respond to (real or perceived) risks in the face of uncertainty[4,5]—and turned to quarantine as a means to interrupt the spread of the disease. Every jurisdiction affected by SARS concluded that "the only possible measures against this outbreak were the centuries-old control measures used in epidemics before the age of antibiotics—isolation, contact-tracing and follow-up, quarantine, and travel restrictions."[3(p217)] As such, quarantine and isolation—indeed, one of the oldest tools of public health—were invoked on a scale unprecedented in several decades. (The terms *quarantine* and *isolation* are often used interchangeably although they actually point to different interventions. Quarantine is the isolation of persons with an infectious disease. Historically, quarantine referred to a 40-day period during which ships entering a port where infectious disease was prevalent were detained. Gostin provides succinct definitions of the 2 terms that show their different meanings. The modern definition of quarantine is "the restriction of activities of healthy persons who have been exposed to a communicable disease, during its period of communicability, to prevent transmission during the incubation period if infection should occur." In contrast, he continues, "isolation is the separation, for the period of communicability, of known infected persons in such places and under such conditions as to prevent or limit the transmission of the infectious agent."[6(p210)])

Perhaps the greatest challenge facing health care providers and public health decisionmakers at the onset of the SARS outbreak was that decisions on how to contain the spread of the disease had to be made against the backdrop of scientific and epidemiological uncertainty. Further exacerbating the uncertain nature of this new and seemingly virulent disease, most jurisdictions invoked quarantine, all the while debating whether it would prove to be an effective intervention. Upshur recounts such concerns, noting that "despite controversies over quarantine, there is no clear or agreed-on sense of what constitutes an effective quarantine."[7] Thus, invoking quarantine raised difficult questions about the justifiability of an intervention that may or may not be effective. In spite of this, public health authorities felt justified in invoking quarantine because it seemed, at the time, that it would be the only way to contain the spread of a disease of which very little was known.

But does quarantine not require cogent and legitimate justificatory power in view of the fact that it always represents a significant deprivation of liberty? (Gostin notes that isolation represents "the most serious form of deprivation of liberty that can be used against a competent and unwilling person"; it is not "complicated to decide whom to isolate, where to do so, or for how long."[8(p26)] The authors of the SARS study conducted for the US Centers for Disease Control and Prevention echoed this point, noting that isolation is "relatively straightforward scientifically, politically and socially [because] it makes sense to confine individuals who are ill with a communicable disease and limit their contacts."[9(p25)]) On what grounds, therefore, can public health authorities justify their decision to implement quarantine in spite of the absence of evidence of its effectiveness or the lack of consensus of what constitutes an effective quarantine? We will turn to recent scholarship on public health ethics to begin exploring this question.

Ethical frameworks in public health

The impetus to articulate an ethics for public health was the recognition that it presents distinct ethical considerations given its focus on population health (in contrast to clinical and research ethics' focus on individuals). An ethical framework for public health could also provide public health authorities with a common vocabulary for the analysis of decisions that come into conflict with the principle of respect for autonomy that is now ascendant in health care.

Upshur[10] proposes a public health ethics framework that identifies 4 principles—the harm principle, proportionality, reciprocity, and least restrictive measures—to guide public health intervention. In an article on the ethics of quarantine, he shows how the application of these 4 principles can provide the justification for the implementation of an autonomy-limiting strategy, such as quarantine.[7] Other public health scholars, such as Childress et al,[11] Callahan and Jennings,[12] Kass,[13] and Roberts and Reich,[14] have also contributed frameworks of analysis that give priority to distinct ethical considerations in public health. In doing so, they identify dilemmas that range "from maximizing utility to preventing harm to distributing benefits fairly [to] identifying program goals, determining effectiveness, minimizing burdens, proportionality, and procedural justice."[15(p236)] What is significant for the purpose of our analysis, however, is that these frameworks, almost unanimously, point to the importance of justifying public health intervention on the basis of its effectiveness. Kass succinctly summarizes this view: "Programs that are coercive," she argues, "should be implemented only in the face of clear public health need and good data demonstrating effectiveness."[16(p1780)]

Ethics and quarantine

In a similar vein, Barbera et al[17] examine the role of quarantine in the context of potential bioterrorist attacks to argue that large-scale quarantine should not be considered "a primary public health strategy in most imaginable circumstances,"[17(p2711)] because its effectiveness is questionable. Here they mean that there is no empirical evidence supporting the effectiveness of large-scale quarantine. That is, decisionmakers must consider whether the implementation of large-scale quarantine has a "reasonable scientific chance of substantially diminishing the spread of the disease,"[18(p2714)] with the caveat that there is no valid (public health or scientific) justification to order quarantine in an outbreak where there is low or no person-to-person transmission of the disease.

So although they allow that public health authorities ought to be able to consider the use of quarantine for other diseases and, thus, presumably, choose to invoke quarantine if it is deemed appropriate, they submit that authorities ought to seek or define "alternatives" to quarantine that "may have more scientific credibility" and that "may be more effective and more feasible."[17] Moreover, their conclusion that "with modern, in-depth understanding of specific diseases, [a] more specific and medically valid response [than quarantine] is appropriate than that used in the era of poor scientific understanding that established the practice of quarantine" suggests that quarantine is invalid as a modern public health intervention to achieve public health goals and is rendered irrelevant in the light of scientific advances.[17] Based on our interpretation of the article by Barbera et al,[17] we can, therefore, conclude that they argue that if there is no definitive evidence of the effectiveness of an intervention, then it is neither feasible nor justifiable.

In this logic, effectiveness of an intervention such as quarantine is a necessary condition for public health authorities to justifiably implement and enforce it. However, is it ever feasible to use restrictive measures if and when there is a lack of evidence of its effectiveness? Without definitive evidence, as was the case during the SARS experience, could public health authorities legitimately respond to an infectious disease outbreak in the logic of Barbera et al.[14]?

Evidence and effectiveness in decisionmaking

The uncertainty surrounding SARS created an epidemic of fear that spread with the disease and a sense of urgency to "discover" the "hard facts" about SARS. We expected medical and epidemiological experts to provide evidence-based truths about the disease and develop sophisticated measurements and risk calculations to resolve any, and all, uncertainty.[19] This is because it has perhaps become a given that the facts we gather to guide us in making decisions are grounded in the assumption that science determines the production of legitimate knowledge—the evidence—that directs the course and outcome of policy and decision processes and that scientific and technical experts are the only legitimate producers of knowledge.

This model of evidence-based decisionmaking is now ascendant in public health decisionmaking.[20,21] The linkage of evidence of effectiveness of an intervention to the justification for implementing it seems straightforward, almost a matter of common sense. For public health to restrict liberties, observes Callahan, it must provide "solidly based factual evidence,"[22(p21)] in other words, provide objective, scientific, hard facts to validate decisions that override autonomous decisionmaking. Indeed, the preference for scientifically measured evidence as a means to guide policy and interventions in public health underlies the logic of public health's basic science, epidemiology, which seeks to gather relevant contributors to disease, breaking these into quantifiable variables to map out the probabilities of risk. As Lupton argues, referring to Gifford's argument, the epidemiological conceptualization of risk "describes[s] relationships, which are objective, depersonalized, quantitative, and reduces the causality of disease to a single factor or combination of discrete factors whose effects may be traced in a cause-effect relationship similar to the biomedical model."[23(p84)] Risk is conveyed in statistical and abstract terms to render "propositions about general truths"[24(p132)]— truths, it is believed, that resolve uncertainties.

Yet, this conceptualization of evidence purports that epidemiological propositions are externally validated, paradoxically, outside of the social processes in which they occur. Findings about risk are regarded as objective statistical probabilities, as though it were, or could be, "a measured property."[25(p85)] Yet this obscures the contextual and (inter)subjective dimensions of public health science. Indeed, in epidemiological research, few question or even recognize the subjective nature of risk calculations; for example: How is risk defined? Whose judgement is to be considered in evaluating the acceptability of risk? Who should be involved in decisions about controlling risk? What constitutes adequate evidence used to measure risk?[19]

All of these questions point to the reality that evidence produced by epidemiological research, including clinical trials, cannot be divorced from the specific context from which they emerge—a context that is, we contend, inevitably historically limited. As Upshur[26] outlines, medical evidence has 7 essential characteristics that underpin the contingent nature of evidence. Viewed this way, conclusions about effective treatments or interventions can, thus, only ever be provisional. That is, something is believed to be true until there is better evidence available that will eventually lead to new truths.

Under these conditions, the following questions emerge: What constitutes sufficient proof to update beliefs in light of new evidence? Or, as Ashcroft puts it, "when should we regard a . . . proposition as proven?"[27(p132)] How do we establish that something is indeed effective, or ineffective, or no longer effective? In what sense are clinical and policy decisions about the effectiveness of a treatment or an intervention objective? These questions lie at the heart of public health decisionmaking yet remain largely unconsidered in both theory and practice.

Conceptualizing effectiveness

In his article, "What Is Clinical Effectiveness?"[28(p219–233)] Ashcroft paves a path for us to consider these questions about public health. He addresses the question of how effectiveness is established by challenging the notion that it is an objective assessment—that it is just an intrinsic property, "a physical property in its own right,"[29(p224)] attributed to treatments (or interventions or outcomes). He argues that effectiveness cannot be established meaningfully on the basis of objective measurements of the physical properties of treatments, but rather, it is established on the basis of what he calls "a family of properties" that include physical (intrinsic) properties and relational (intersubjective) properties. For something to be effective, it has to be a function of something else; in other words, it only makes sense in relation to that against which it is measured, analyzed, and compared, whether it is against objective end points, patient preferences, or societal or cultural commitments to constituent communities. In the sphere of clinical medicine, and by extension of public health, what is deemed to be effective is inextricably tied to, and largely the product of, understandings of ideas, interpretations of (community and patient) preferences, and cultural commitments. Effectiveness is, as Ashcroft[28] puts it, "effectiveness for some purpose," and, therefore, the multiple and complex considerations that accompany definitions of or conclusions about effectiveness are necessarily bound to claims of effectiveness and are often used to justify such claims.

Because public health action involves multiple communities, it seems reasonable to suggest that claims of effectiveness must necessarily seek and engage multiple perspectives. This would entail, or perhaps require, a reconceptualization or broadening of effectiveness that both recognizes and incorporates its relational and normative properties. That is, having evidence of the effectiveness of an intervention derived from a study, no matter how compelling it may be, neither resolves uncertainty nor sets a necessary course of action.[27,30] It certainly does not exhaust the concept of effectiveness.

By definition, then, effectiveness entails much more than empirical and scientific considerations but rather involves disparate perspectives that reflect the broader intellectual, institutional, and social context in which public health policies and interventions are made. Because, at the center of public health practice, are persons and practices, woven within the context of ideas and institutions that are the product of a complex social reality that is situated, historical, and intersubjective. It follows then that arguments about effectiveness cannot rest on what is simply one chosen perspective among many other legitimate interests and views.

Viewed this way, the evidence used in policy and decision processes is no longer understood exclusively as a scientific pursuit driven to measure effectiveness (or probabilities or risk) but is constitutively provisional and intersubjective and, therefore, can function normatively in decisionmaking only when it is inclusive in its definitions and consultative in its process. Evidence-based decisionmaking, although it can be extremely useful, is insufficient. Although it should be used to reflect on what constitutes a reasonable and well-justified decision, it cannot be understood or used as an outcome of decisionmaking rendered as an objective and absolute assessment of all relevant considerations. It ought to be understood and used as a process of reasoned or deliberated justification, one that takes into account a diversity of perspectives.

If the logic of our account of effectiveness is correct, then assessing effectiveness on either a priori grounds or by virtue of empirical evidence alone is insufficient. The decision whether quarantine is or can be effective depends as much on evidence from epidemiological studies as it does on explicitly identifying and addressing the preferences and cultural commitments of the affected and involved communities. It follows, then, that public health ought to engage our communities and prompt a dialogue on how best to confront communicable disease, as well as which restrictive measures are acceptable to our communities.

Further, by establishing that effectiveness has intersubjective dimensions, we necessarily need to reconceive the fact–value epistemological gap inherent in public health policymaking: fact, which relies on scientific reasoning; value, on normative ethical analysis (that is, to make decisions founded on particular conceptions of what is good, right, and effective). This way, public health decisions actually "carry with them varying levels of empirical certainty,"[31(p173)] often blurring the line between the fact–value distinction. The "effectiveness" of an intervention, therefore, cannot be the central criteria justifying interventions, if only because the dominant scientific and empirical notion of effectiveness in both theory and practice does not satisfy a claim to proof.

Conclusions

The decision to implement a system of quarantine cannot be justified or grounded in the notion of effectiveness simply determined in scientific terms. Uncertainty is never fully resolved, and as such, evidence-based decisionmaking ought to be used to reflect on what constitutes a reasonable and well-justified decision—not because it was scientifically measured or objectively assessed but because it can serve as a process of reasoned or deliberated justification, a process that would serve us well in making public health decisions and justifying the use of restrictive measures during public health emergencies.

The tendency to impart a fixed set of prescriptions and to reduce complex situations to technical problems resolvable by scientific expertise can be compelling in the face of so much uncertainty. Yet, in a democratic society, expertise cannot legitimately be limited and left to scientific experts. By validating other legitimate interests and perspectives in public health decisionmaking, we are simply acknowledging what is already a reality in how decisions are made, especially as they relate to quarantine. It is, therefore, incumbent on us to recognize and legitimize a broader notion of effectiveness—one that transcends the dominant conception that it derives from a set of proven and verifiable data to one that gives a voice to nonscientific, nontechnical perspectives, experiences, preferences, and cultural commitments. Such efforts are essential and not accidental.

Contributors

Ross Upshur originated the study (Ethical Challenges in the Preparedness and Response for SARS: An Interdisciplinary Research Study) from which this article originated. Cécile Bensimon led the writing of the article. Both authors conceptualized ideas and reviewed drafts of the article.

Acknowledgments

This project is part of a larger study, Ethical Challenges in the Preparedness and Response for SARS: An Interdisciplinary Research Study, which was funded by the Canadian Institutes of Health Research (grant SAR–67798). R. E. G. Upshur was financially supported by the Canadian Institutes of Health Research and by the Department of Family and Community Medicine of the University of Toronto.

The authors thank Iram Shaikh for her assistance in formatting the article.

Human participant protection

No human participants were involved in this study.

References

1. Parmet W. AIDS and quarantine: the revival of an archaic doctrine. *Hofstra Law Review*. 1986;14:53–90.

2. Plant A. J. SARS and public health: lessons for future epidemics. In: Koh T., Plant A. J., Hin Lee E., eds. *The New Global Threat: Severe Acute Respiratory Syndrome and Its Impact.* Singapore: World Scientific Publishing Co; 2003.

3. Koh T., Plant A. J., Hin Lee E. *The New Global Threat: Severe Acute Respiratory Syndrome and Its Impact.* Singapore: World Scientific Publishing Co; 2003.

4. Morris J. Defining the precautionary principle. In: *Rethinking Risk and the Precautionary Principle.* New York, NY: Butterworth-Heinemann; 2000:1–21.

5. Resnick D. B. Is the Precautionary Principle Unscientific. *Studies Hist Philos Biol Biomed Sci.* 2003;34:329–344.

6. Gostin L. O. *Public Health Law: Power, Duty, Restraint.* Berkeley, Calif: University of California Press; New York: Milbank Memorial Fund, 2000.

7. Upshur R. E. G. The Ethics of Quarantine. *Ethics Journal of the American Medical Association.* Available at: http://www.ama-assn.org/ama/pub/category/11535.html. Accessed January 2005.

8. Gostin L. O., Curran W. J. The limits of compulsion in controlling AIDS. In: *Hastings Center Report.* Garrison, NY: Hastings Center; 1986.

9. Rothstein M. A., Alcade M. G., Elster N. R., et al. *Quarantine and Isolation: Lessons learned from SARS.* Louisville, KY: Institute for Bioethics, Health Policy and Law, University of Louisville School of Medicine; 2003.

10. Upshur R. E. G. Principles for the justification of public health intervention. *Can J Pub Health.* 2002;93:101–103.

11. Childress J. F., Faden R. R., Gaare R. D., et al. Public health ethics: mapping the terrain. *J Law Med Ethics.* 2002;30:170–178.

12. Callahan D., Jennings B. Ethics and public health: forging a strong relationship. *Am J Public Health.* 2002;92:169–176.

13. Kass N. E. An ethics framework for public health. *Am J Public Health.* 2001;91:1776–1782.

14. Roberts M. J., Reich M. R. Ethical analysis in public health. *Lancet.* 2002;359:1055–1059.

15. Kass N. E. Public health ethics: from foundations and frameworks to justice and global public health. *J Law Med Ethics.* 2004:32:236.

16. Kass N. E. An ethics framework for public health. *Am J Public Health.* 2001;91:1780.

17. Barbera J., Macintyre A., Gostin L. et al. Large-scale quarantine following biological terrorism in the United States. *JAMA.* 2001;286:2711–2717.

18. Ibid, p. 2714.

19. Lupton D. Taming uncertainty: risk discourse and diagnostic testing. In: *The Imperative of Health: Public Health and the Regulated Body.* London, United Kingdom: Sage; 1995:77–105.

20. Rychetnik L., Hawe P., Waters E., Barratt A., Frommer M. A glossary for evidence based public health. *J Epidemiol Commun Health.* 2004;58:538–545.

21. Upshur R. E. G., Colak E. Evidence and argumentation. *Theor Med Bioeth.* 2003;24:283–299.

22. Beauchamp D., Steinbock B. *New Ethics for the Public's Health.* Oxford, United Kingdom: Oxford University Press; 1999:21.

23. Lupton, p. 84.

24. Ashcroft R. E. Current epistemological problems in evidence-based medicine. *J Med Ethics.* 2004;30:132.

25. Lupton D., p. 85.
26. Upshur R. E. G. Seven characteristics of medical evidence. *J Eval Clin Pract.* 2000;6:93–97.
27. Ashcroft R. E. p. 132.
28. Ashcroft R. E. What is clinical effectiveness? *Stud Hist Philos Biol Biomed Sci.* 2002;33:219–233.
29. Ibid, p. 224.
30. Upshur and Colak, Evidence and argumentation, 283–299.
31. Callahan D., Jennings B. Ethics and public health: forging a strong relationship. *Am J Public Health.* 2002;92:173.

111

LARGE-SCALE QUARANTINE FOLLOWING BIOLOGICAL TERRORISM IN THE UNITED STATES

Scientific examination, logistic and legal limits, and possible consequences

*Joseph Barbera, Anthony Macintyre, Larry Gostin,
Tom Inglesby, Tara O'Toole, Craig DeAtley,
Kevin Tonat and Marci Layton*

Source: *Journal of the American Medical Association*, 286:21 (2001), 2711–17.

Concern for potential bioterrorist attacks causing mass casualties has increased recently. Particular attention has been paid to scenarios in which a biological agent capable of person-to-person transmission, such as smallpox, is intentionally released among civilians. Multiple public health interventions are possible to effect disease containment in this context. One disease control measure that has been regularly proposed in various settings is the imposition of large-scale or geographic quarantine on the potentially exposed population. Although large-scale quarantine has not been implemented in recent US history, it has been used on a small scale in biological hoaxes, and it has been invoked in federally sponsored bioterrorism exercises. This article reviews the scientific principles that are relevant to the likely effectiveness of quarantine, the logistic barriers to its implementation, legal issues that a large-scale quarantine raises, and possible adverse consequences that might result from quarantine action. Imposition of large-scale quarantine—compulsory sequestration of groups of possibly exposed persons or human confinement within certain geographic areas to prevent spread of contagious disease—should not be considered a primary public health strategy in most imaginable circumstances. In the majority of contexts, other less extreme public health actions

244

are likely to be more effective and create fewer unintended adverse consequences than quarantine. Actions and areas for future research, policy development, and response planning efforts are provided.

During the past few years, the US government has grown increasingly concerned about the threat that biological terrorism poses to the civilian population.[1-3] A number of events have occurred that have raised awareness about the potential threat of bio-terrorism. These include the suspected attempt to disseminate anthrax by Aum Shinrikyo in Japan,[4] widespread occurrence of bioterrorist hoaxes,[5] and revelations about the bio-weapons programs in the former Soviet Union[6] and Iraq.[7] Most recently, the anthrax-related deaths, illnesses, and exposures in Florida and the New York City and Washington, DC, areas have generated even more concern.[8,9] It is now generally acknowledged that a large-scale bioterrorist attack is plausible and could conceivably generate large numbers of seriously ill exposed individuals, potentially overwhelming local or regional health care systems.[10-12] In the event of a large bioterrorist attack with a communicable disease, the potential for person-to-person transmission of the disease would create serious health care and emergency management problems at the local and federal levels.

Throughout history, medical and public health personnel have contended with epidemics and, in the process, evolved procedures to lessen morbidity and mortality. Historically, quarantine was a recognized public health tool used to manage some infectious disease outbreaks, from the plague epidemic in the 13th century to the influenza epidemics of the 20th century. During the past century in the United States, professional medical and public health familiarity with the practice of quarantine has faded. A review of the medical literature found no large-scale human quarantine implemented within US borders during the past 8 decades.[13] Despite this lack of modern operational experience, local, state, and federal incident managers commonly propose or have called for quarantine in the early or advanced stages of bio-terrorism exercises.[14] Management of some incidents that later proved to be hoaxes included the quarantine of large numbers of people for periods of hours while the purported biological weapon was analyzed.[4,15] A striking example of the inclination to resort to quarantine was demonstrated during a recent federally sponsored national terrorism exercise, TOPOFF 2000.[16,17] During the biological terrorism component of this drill, a national, large-scale geographic quarantine was imposed in response to a growing pneumonic plague epidemic caused by the intentional release of aerosolized *Yersinia pestis*, the bacteria that causes plague. An array of significant political, practical, and ethical problems became apparent when quarantine was imposed.

Given the rising concerns about the threat of bioterrorism and the concomitant renewed consideration of quarantine as a possible public health response to epidemics, it is important that the implications of quarantine in the modern context be carefully analyzed.

Quarantine vs isolation

One of the first challenges to address is the lack of a precise definition of *quarantine*. In the historical context, quarantine was defined as detention and enforced segregation of persons suspected to be carrying a contagious disease. Travelers or voyagers were sometimes subjected to quarantine before they were permitted to enter a country or town and mix with inhabitants. The term *quarantine* is derived from the Italian *quarante*, which refers to the 40-day sequestration imposed on arriving merchant ships during plague outbreaks of the 13th century.[18]

In the modern era, the meaning of the term *quarantine* has become less clear. The *Oxford English Dictionary* defines *quarantine* as "a period of isolation imposed on a person, animal or thing that might otherwise spread a contagious disease."[19] Unfortunately, during modern bioterrorism response exercises, this term has been used broadly and confusingly to include a variety of public health disease containment measures, including travel limitations, restrictions on public gatherings, and isolation of sick individuals to prevent disease spread. The authors believe it is most appropriate to use *quarantine* to refer to compulsory physical separation, including restriction of movement, of populations or groups of healthy people who have been potentially exposed to a contagious disease, or to efforts to segregate these persons within specified geographic areas. For clarity in this article, this action is termed *large-scale quarantine* to differentiate it from incidents of exposure by only a few persons. To avoid confusion, we do not use the terms *quarantine* and *isolation* interchangeably. We use the term *isolation* to denote the separation and confinement of individuals known or suspected (via signs, symptoms, or laboratory criteria) to be infected with a contagious disease to prevent them from transmitting disease to others.[20,21] It is operationally important that medical and public health emergency managers use accurate terminology.

Legislative framework for disease containment

The moral authority for human quarantine is historically based on the concept of the public health contract.[22] Under the public health contract, individuals agree to forgo certain rights and liberties, if necessary, to prevent a significant risk to other persons. Civil rights and liberties are subject to limitation because each person gains the benefits of living in a healthier and safer society.[23]

The statutory authority for the imposition of quarantine in the United States originated at a local level during the colonial period. Massachusetts established state quarantine powers in the first comprehensive state public health statute in 1797.[24(pp238–239),25] At approximately the same time (1796), a federal statute authorized the president to assist in state quarantines.[26] The act was later replaced by a federal inspection system for maritime quarantines.[27] Thereafter, the federal government became more active in regulating the practice of quarantine, and a 19th-century conflict between federal and state quarantine powers resulted. In the ensuing federalism debate, the states maintained that they had authority pursuant to police power.[28–30] The federal government maintained that its preeminent authority was derived from regulatory powers over interstate commerce. Today, states are primarily responsible for the exercise of public health powers. However, if the exercise of quarantine clearly would affect interstate commerce, the federal government may claim that its authority is supreme.[31,32] Following is a brief summary of which institutions or levels of government have statutory authority to apply quarantine in distinct contexts.

Local outbreaks in the United States

When an infectious disease is confined to a specific locale, the authority for quarantine usually rests with local or state public health officials. The authority is generally relinquished to the state when the event affects more than a single community or has the potential to spread across jurisdictional boundaries within the state. The individuality of each state authority has led to a widely divergent group of regulations providing for the use of quarantine.[33] Few local and state jurisdictions, however, have established specific policies and procedures to assist officials in deciding whether an individual event merits imposition of quarantine.[34]

Interstate and national outbreaks

The federal government has the authority to enact quarantine when presented with the risk of transmission of infectious disease across state lines.[35] Legislation stipulates that this is an executive decision to be made by the president. Once the decision has been made, the Centers for Disease Control and Prevention (CDC) is the federal agency authorized to manage federal quarantine actions.[36] The implementation apparatus for such an order could involve federal assets from other agencies, such as the Department of Defense or the Federal Emergency Management Agency, deploying in support of federal, state, or local authorities.[37] The federal government may also assert supremacy in managing specific intrastate incidents if so requested by that state's authorities or if it is believed that local efforts are inadequate.[35,38] Other legal venues for federal action may exist but have not been well delineated.[39]

Foreign outbreaks and US border control

For travelers seeking to enter the United States, the CDC has the authority to enact quarantine. At the turn of the 20th century, the Marine Hospital Service (forerunner to the modern US Public Health Service) established this federal power.[40] The authority was later delegated to the CDC's Division of Global Migration and Quarantine, currently consisting of 43 employees in the field and 30 at department headquarters in Atlanta, Ga.[41] In areas where Division of Global Migration and Quarantine personnel are not stationed, Immigration and Naturalization Service and US Customs Service personnel are trained to recognize travelers with potential illness of public health significance. While rarely used, detention of arriving individuals, including US citizens, is authorized to prevent the entry of specified communicable diseases into the United States. Using definitions delineated in this article, the detention of arriving passengers with visible signs of illness would be termed *isolation*.[42]

Currently, federal law authorizes cooperative efforts between the federal government and the states related to planning, training, and prevention of disease epidemics and other health emergencies.[43] Despite this, lines of authority between federal and state/local jurisdictions have not been sufficiently tested to ensure that all essential parties have clear understanding of the boundaries and interface between these potentially conflicting authorities. In a large-scale or rapidly evolving natural or deliberate biological incident, confusion and conflict in this public health authority may result. This issue was demonstrated in the TOPOFF exercise.[16,17]

Extensive reviews of the legal basis for quarantine actions have been published elsewhere and will not be reviewed in detail here.[21,44,45] Perhaps the most important understanding that can be extracted from these reviews is that though legal powers exist to quarantine in many contexts, the imposition of quarantine would likely be challenged in the courts using modern interpretations of civil liberties provided by the US Constitution. Additionally, courts have suggested that, in the event of a quarantine, detainees would have to be provided with reasonable amenities to reduce harm (eg, adequate shelter and medical care). Ultimately, extensive quarantines would likely cause the judicial system to become a slow and deliberate arbitrator between the conflicting ideals of public health and individual civil liberties. The CDC and many states are currently in the process of reexamining the legal authority for public health actions, including quarantine.[46,47]

Historical illustrations of adverse consequences of quarantine

United States history has demonstrated that quarantine actions themselves may cause harm. Large-scale quarantine today can be expected to create similar problems, perhaps to a greater degree. Three historical events in the

United States provide examples of the unintended consequences of quarantine implementation.

Increased risk of disease transmission in the quarantined population

One of the most controversial US quarantines was imposed by the New York City Port Authority in 1892 on ships traveling from Europe, where a cholera outbreak had occurred.[48] Cholera had been detected among immigrants, and the subsequent public health response included quarantining passengers aboard arriving vessels. Passengers of lower socioeconomic standing were clearly subjected to separate, more severe conditions than wealthy passengers. Authorities sequestered these impoverished immigrants below deck without sanitary provisions during the confinement. Cholera spread disproportionately among the poor on board the vessels and resulted in at least 58 deaths on one ship alone.[48]

Mistrust in government recommendations led to violence

The municipality of Muncie, Indiana, was confronted with an outbreak of smallpox in 1893.[49] Public health officials had great difficult convincing citizens that intrusive public health actions were necessary, in part because the diagnosis of smallpox was repeatedly challenged. Many infected citizens were isolated under home detention and their presumably uninfected family members were quarantined with them. Entire neighborhoods were quarantined by patrolling armed guards; violators were incarcerated. Mandatory vaccination was instituted. Violence broke out as some civilians resisted the public health impositions, and several public officials were shot. Public health officials ultimately concluded that their quarantine actions had been "an utter failure" as the public had repeatedly defied their quarantine efforts.[49]

Ethnic bias adversely altered public health decision making

A quarantine was instituted in the Chinese neighborhood of San Francisco, California, in 1900, after plague was diagnosed in several inhabitants.[50] The boundaries for the quarantine were arbitrarily established such that only Chinese households and businesses were included. This resulted in severe economic damage to the once-thriving Chinese business community. A federal court found the quarantine unconstitutional on grounds that it was unfair—health authorities acted with an "evil eye and an unequal hand."[51]

Key considerations in quarantine decisions

In most infectious disease outbreak scenarios, there are alternatives to large-scale quarantine that may be more medically defensible, more likely to effectively contain the spread of disease, less challenging to implement, and less likely to generate unintended adverse consequences. Decisions to invoke quarantine, therefore, should be made only after careful consideration of 3 major questions examined within the specific context of a particular outbreak: (1) Do public health and medical analyses warrant the imposition of large-scale quarantine? (2) Are the implementation and maintenance of large-scale quarantine feasible? and (3) Do the potential benefits of large-scale quarantine outweigh the possible adverse consequences?

1. Do public health and medical analyses warrant the imposition of large-scale quarantine?

Decision makers must consider whether large-scale quarantine implementation at the time of discovery of disease outbreak has a reasonable scientific chance of substantially diminishing the spread of disease. There is no valid public health or scientific justification for any type of quarantine in the setting of disease outbreaks with low or no person-to-person transmission, such as anthrax. Despite this, quarantine has been invoked in anthrax bioterrorism hoaxes in recent years.[4,15] Among the many diseases that are termed contagious (ie, capable of being spread by contact with sick persons), only a limited number could pose a serious risk of widespread person-to-person transmission. Of these contagious diseases with potential for widespread person-to-person transmission, only a limited number confer sufficient risk of serious illness or death to justify consideration of the sequestration of large groups or geographic areas. In addition to the agent characteristics, available treatment and prophylaxis options also create the context for the decision process. Public health responses must be accurately tailored to meet the specific risks and resource needs imposed by individual agents.

There are imaginable contexts in which a large-scale smallpox outbreak would generate reasonable considerations for quarantine. But even in the setting of a bioterrorist attack with smallpox, the long incubation period (10–17 days) almost ensures that some persons who were infected in the attack will have traveled great distances from the site of exposure before the disease is recognized or quarantine could be implemented. Subsequent issues with quarantine will remain problematic.

2. Are the implementation and maintenance of large-scale quarantine feasible?

If medical and public health principles lead to a judgment that quarantine is an effective and necessary action to stop the spread of a dangerous disease outbreak, the next set of issues that should be considered involves the logistics of actually establishing the large-scale quarantine. These issues are applicable to local, state, and federal decision makers.

250

Is there a plausible way to determine who should be quarantined?

Are there practically available criteria for defining and identifying a group or a geographic area that is at higher risk of transmitting a dangerous disease? As noted, depending on the disease-specific incubation period and due to the mobility of modern society, it is probable that a population exposed to a biological weapon will have dispersed well beyond any easily definable geographic boundaries before the infection becomes manifest and any disease containment measures can be initiated. Even within a specific locale, it will be initially impossible to clearly define persons who have been exposed and, therefore, at risk of spreading the disease. A quarantine of a neighborhood would potentially miss exposed individuals, but a large-scale quarantine of a municipality could include many with no significant risk of disease. Currently proposed or functional health surveillance systems have not yet demonstrated adequate proficiency in rapid disease distribution analysis.[52,53]

Are resources available to enforce the confinement?

The human and material resources that would be required to enforce the confinement of large groups of persons, perhaps against their will, would likely be substantial, even in a modest-sized quarantine action. The behavioral reaction of law enforcement or military personnel charged with enforcing quarantine should also be considered. It is possible that fear of personal exposure or public reaction to enforcement actions may compromise police willingness to enforce compliance.

Can the quarantined group be confined for the duration during which they could transmit the disease?

Quarantine will not be over quickly. The period during which confined persons could develop disease might be days or weeks, depending on the specific infectious agent. Development of illness among detainees could prolong the confinement of those remaining healthy. Resources and political resolve must be sufficient to sustain a quarantine of at least days, and probably weeks. Furthermore, the multiple needs of detainees must be addressed in a systematic and competent fashion. During previous events, the courts have required that those quarantined be detained in safe and hygienic locations.[44] Adequate food and other necessities must be provided. Competent medical care for those detained is an ethical and possibly constitutional requirement.[21] Transferring supplies across quarantine lines can be difficult, as can recruiting qualified medical personnel to enter quarantined areas. The shortage of trained medical persons to adequately care for quarantine detainees should be anticipated and was clearly demonstrated during the influenza epidemic of 1918.[13,54]

251

Given the presumption that biological terrorism would impose multiple competing demands for human and material resources within the affected region, decision makers must weigh the costs and benefits of devoting available assets to the maintenance of quarantine.

3. Do the potential benefits of large-scale quarantine outweigh the possible adverse consequences?

If valid public health and medical principles lead to a judgment that quarantine is an effective and necessary action to stop the spread of a dangerous disease outbreak, and it is established that a quarantine could logistically be put into place, the possible unintended adverse consequences of a quarantine action must then be carefully considered.

What are the health risks to those quarantined?

As noted herein, there are US historical examples in which persons with clear evidence of infection with a contagious disease have been quarantined together with persons with no evidence of infection.[48,49] It is now beyond dispute that such measures would be unethical today, but a recent event illustrates that this ethical principle might still be disregarded or misunderstood.[55] A passenger returning to the United States was noted to be ill and vomiting on an airline flight, and the passenger's consequent subconjunctival hemorrhages were initially mistaken to be a sign of a coagulopathic infection. On arrival at a major US airport, the plane was diverted and quarantined by airport authorities with all passengers on board, including the potential index case. They were released after an hour-long period of investigation, when public health authorities arrived and concluded that there was no dangerous contagion. Had this been an actual contagious disease, quarantined passengers may have been subjected to an increased risk by continued confinement on the parked aircraft with the ill person. At a minimum, passengers should have been allowed to disembark and remain in an area separate from the index case while this person was being evaluated.

What are the consequences if the public declines to obey quarantine orders?

It is not clear how those quarantined would react to being subjected to compulsory confinement. Civilian noncompliance with these public health efforts could compromise the action and even become violent. Historical quarantine incidents have generated organized civil disobedience and wholesale disregard for authority. Such conditions led to riots in Montreal, Quebec, during a smallpox epidemic in 1885.[24(pp285–286)] Some might lose confidence in government authorities and stop complying with other advised public health actions (eg, vaccination, antibiotic treatment) as well. The possibility also exists for development of civilian vigilantism to enforce quarantine, as occurred in New York City in 1892.[48] The rules of engagement that police are expected to follow in enforcing quarantine must be explicitly determined and communicated in advance. Protection of police personnel and their families against infection would be essential to police cooperation.

What are the consequences of restricting commerce and transportation to and from the quarantine area?

Halting commercial transactions and the movement of goods to and from quarantined areas will have significant economic effects that may be profound and long-term and reach well beyond the quarantine area. Much modern business practice relies on just-in-time supply chains. Shortages of food, fuel, medicines and medical supplies, essential personnel, and social services (sanitation) should be anticipated and provisions must be in place to deal with such issues. Postquarantine stigmatization of the geographic location and of the population quarantined should be anticipated.

Conclusions and recommendations

Public health disease containment measures must be based on scientific, disease-specific analysis

The essential first step in developing any disease containment strategy is to determine if the disease at issue is communicable. If not, then no consideration of quarantine should be pursued. If the disease of concern is contagious, then the specific mechanism of disease transmission must drive the disease containment strategy (eg, spread by cough at close distances or possibly over longer range, as has occurred in smallpox outbreaks; infrequent spread by cough at close distance, as in some plague outbreaks; or spread through person-to-person contact, as in Ebola outbreaks). Some progress in delineating disease containment strategies for bioterrorism-induced outbreaks has already occurred in the form of consensus public health and medical recommendations,[56–58] though more diseases must be addressed and public health actions examined. Political leaders in particular need to understand that a single strategy for limiting the spread of all contagious diseases is not appropriate and will not work. The political consequences of public health actions such as large-scale quarantine must also be carefully examined and understood. Modern US disaster response has consistently focused on assistance to those directly affected; in the case of bioterrorism, response will focus on both those potentially infected and those actually infected. With implementation of quarantine, the perception may be that those potentially and actually infected have instead been secondarily harmed by response actions.

In an outbreak of a contagious disease, disease containment may be more effectively achieved using methods that do not attempt to contain large groups of people. As noted, persons with clinical or laboratory evidence demonstrating infection with a contagious disease should be isolated, separate from those who do not have clinical or laboratory evidence of that contagious disease. Depending on the illness, this isolation may be primarily respiratory, body fluid, or skin contact isolation rather than full physical separation from all healthy people.

Additional, population-based public health intervention strategies should also be considered. Depending on the context, rapid vaccination or treatment programs, widespread use of disposable masks (with instructions), short-term voluntary home curfew, restrictions on assembly of groups (eg, schools, entertainment sites), or closure of mass public transportation (buses, airliners, trains, and subway systems) are disease containment steps that may have more scientific credibility and may be more likely to result in diminished disease spread, more practically achievable, and associated with less adverse consequences. For clarity, these alternative disease control measures should not be termed *quarantine* or *quarantine actions*.

Invest in new information tools and emergency management systems that would improve situational awareness during disease outbreaks

During large-scale contagious disease outbreaks, decision makers would be critically dependent on the availability of timely, accurate information about what is happening and what interventions are desirable and feasible. Emergency management and public health officials will need real-time case data and the analytic capacity to determine the epidemiological parameters of the outbreak to make the most appropriate disease containment decisions. Clinicians will seek information about the natural history and clinical management of the illness and ongoing analyses of the efficacy of treatment strategies. Rapid communication between the medical and public health communities may be especially important and in most locales is currently not conveyed by electronic means or through routine, well-exercised channels.

Provide incentives to foster specific public actions

Positive incentives may help to persuade the public to take actions that promote disease containment. The ready provision of adequate medical expertise, appropriate vaccines or antibiotics, or distribution of disposable face masks to the public in specific circumstances are examples of incentives that may positively influence population behavior to promote disease containment. Allowing family members to voluntarily place themselves at some defined, calculated risk of infection to care for their sick loved ones might encourage participation in a community's overall disease containment strategy. Assisting family members in these efforts by offering them some forms of protection against the disease could be a valuable aspect of an integrated disease containment strategy. For example, distribution of barrier personal protective equipment and education aimed at discouraging potentially dangerous burial rituals were successful interventions in controlling viral hemorrhagic fever in Africa.[59]

Devote resources to developing robust public communication strategy commensurate with the critical importance of this action

The development of strategies for communicating with the public throughout a disease outbreak is of paramount importance. Objectives of this strategy would include informing the public through multiple appropriate channels of the nature of the infectious disease and the scope of the outbreak, providing behavioral guidelines to help minimize spread of illness, and conveying details about how to get prompt access to effective treatment. Ideally, such messages would be conveyed by informed, widely recognized health experts such as the state health commissioner or US surgeon general. In a bioterrorist attack, the media's appetite for information will be limitless and health authorities must be prepared to provide accurate and useful information on a nearly continuous basis.[60] Advanced planning and preparation for such a media storm is essential. Once public credibility is lost, it will be difficult or impossible to recover. A well-informed public that perceives health officials as knowledgeable and reliable is more likely to voluntarily comply with actions recommended to diminish the spread of the disease. Effective information dissemination would work to suppress rumors and anxiety and enlist community support.

It is clear that public health strategies for the control of potential epidemics need to be carefully reevaluated. This process should ensure that civil rights and liberties are kept at the forefront of all discussions, as recently proposed by the congressionally created Gilmore Commission.[3] Further delineation of the authority to impose quarantine is required, and the political and psychological implications must be addressed. Given the complex multidisciplinary nature of this problem, further analysis of possible disease containment strategies would ideally include experts from the fields of medicine, public health, mental health, emergency management, law, ethics, and public communication. The process should specifically examine the various alternatives to quarantine that may be more effective and more feasible in addressing the containment of an infectious outbreak. Strict definition of terms such as *quarantine* must be maintained. With modern, in-depth understanding of specific diseases, more specific and medically valid response is appropriate than that used in the era of poor scientific understanding that established the practice of quarantine. The resulting work from this effort could provide a more comprehensive systems approach to disease containment in general.

Disclaimer

The opinions and findings in this article are those of the authors and should not be construed as official policies or positions of the US Public Health Service or the New York City Department of Health.

References

1. *Improving Local and State Agency Response to Terrorist Incidents Involving Biological Weapons: Interim Planning Guide.* Aberdeen, Md: US Army Soldier and Biological Chemical Command, Domestic Preparedness Office; August 1, 2000.
2. *Road Map for National Security: Imperative for Change: The Phase III Report of the United States Commission on National Security/21st Century.* Washington, DC: United States Commission on National Security/21st Century; January 31, 2001.
3. *Toward a National Strategy for Combating Terrorism. Second Annual Report to Congress of the Advisory Panel to Assess Domestic Response Capabilities for Terrorism Involving Weapons of Mass Destruction.* December 15, 2000. Available at: http://www.rand.org/nsrd/terrpanel/terror2.pdf. Accessed October 30, 2001.
4. Senate Government Affairs Permanent Subcommittee on Investigations. Global proliferation of weapons of mass destruction: a case study on the Aum Shinrikyo. October 31, 1995. Available at: http://www.fas.org/irp/congress/1995_rpt/aum/part05.htm. Accessed May 25, 2001.
5. Bioterrorism alleging use of anthrax and interim guidelines for management—United States, 1998. *MMWR Morb Mortal Wkly Rep.* 1999;48:69–74.
6. US General Accounting Office. *Biological Weapons: Effort to Reduce Former Soviet Threat Offers Benefits, Poses New Risks.* Washington, DC: US General Accounting Office; April 2000. GAO/NSIAD-00-138.
7. Zilinskas R. A. Iraq's biological weapons: the pastas future? *JAMA.* 1997;278:418–424.
8. Notice to readers: ongoing investigation of anthrax—Florida, October 2001. *MMWR Morb Mortal Wkly Rep.* 2001;50:877.
9. Centers for Disease Control and Prevention. CDC summary of confirmed cases of anthrax and background information. October 23, 2001. Available at: http://www.bt.cdc.gov/DocumentsApp/Anthrax/10232001pm/10232001pm.asp. Accessed October 24, 2001.
10. Carter A., Deutsch J., Zelicow P. Catastrophic terrorism. *Foreign Affairs.* 1998;77:80–95.
11. Office of Technology Assessment. *Proliferation of Weapons of Mass Destruction.* Washington, DC: Government Printing Office; 1993. OTA-ISC-559, 53–55.
12. Cilluffo F., Cardash S., Lederman G. *Combating Chemical, Biological, Radiological and Nuclear Terrorism: A Comprehensive Strategy.* Washington, DC: Center for Strategic and International Studies Homeland Defense Project; May 2001.

13. Gernhart G. A forgotten enemy: PHS's fight against the 1918 influenza pandemic. *Public Health Rep.* 1999;114:559–561.

14. Mayor's Office of Emergency Management, New York City. *Draft After Action Report for Operation RED-Ex Recognition, Evaluation, and Decision Making Exercise.* New York, NY: Mayor's Office of Emergency Management; May 2001.

15. Horowitz S. B'nai B'rith package contained common bacteria. *Washington Post.* April 29, 1997:B2.

16. *Top Officials (TOPOFF) 2000 Exercise Observation Report Volume 2: State of Colorado and Denver Metropolitan Area.* Washington, DC: Office for State and Local Domestic Preparedness Support, Office of Justice Programs, Dept of Justice, and Readiness Division, Preparedness Training, and Exercises Directorate, Federal Emergency Management Agency; December 2000.

17. Inglesby T. Lessons from TOPOFF. Presented at: Second National Symposium on Medical and Public Health Response to Bioterrorism; November 28, 2000; Washington, DC.

18. Cumming H. The United States quarantine system during the past 50 years. In: Ravenel M., ed. *A Half Century of Public Health.* New York, NY: American Public Health Association; 1921:118–132.

19. *Oxford English Dictionary.* 2nd ed. Oxford, England: Oxford University Press; 1989:983.

20. Jackson M., Lynch P. Isolation practices: a historical perspective. *Am J Infect Control.* 1985;13:21–31.

21. Gostin L. *Public Health Law: Power, Duty, Restraint.* New York, NY, and Berkeley, Calif: Milbank Memorial Fund and University of California Press; 2000.

22. Merritt D. The constitutional balance between health and liberty. *Hastings Cent Rep.* December 1986:2–10.

23. Gostin L. Public health, ethics, and human rights: a tribute to the late Jonathan Mann. *J Law Med Ethics.* 2001;29:121–130.

24. Hopkins D. *Princes and Peasants: Smallpox in History.* Chicago, Ill: University of Chicago Press; 1983.

25. Chapin C. State and municipal control of disease. In: Ravenel M., ed. *A Half Century of Public Health.* New York, NY: American Public Health Association; 1921:133–160.

26. Act of May 27, 1796, ch 31, 1 Stat 474 (repealed 1799).

27. Act of February 25, 1799, ch 12, 1 Stat 619.

28. Freund E. *The Police Power: Public Policy and Constitutional Rights.* New York, NY: Arno Press; 1904: 124–130.

29. Lee B. H. Limitations imposed by the federal constitution on the right of the states to enact quarantine laws. *Harvard Law Rev.* 1889;2:267, 270–282.

30. *Hennington v Georgia*, 163 US 299, 309 (1896).

31. *Gibbons v Ogden*, 22 US 1, 205–206 (1824).

32. *Compagnie Française de Navigation á Vapeur v Louisiana State Bd of Health*, 186 US 380, 388 (1902).

33. Gostin L. Controlling the resurgent tuberculosis epidemic: a 50-state survey of TB statutes and proposals for reform. *JAMA.* 1993;269:255–261.

34. Conright K. TOPOFF 2000: lessons learned from the Denver venue. Presented at: National Disaster Medical System Conference on Lifesaving Interventions; April 28, 2001; Dallas, Tex.
35. 42 USC §264a (2001).
36. 65 *Federal Register* 49906 (2000) (in reference to 21 CFR §1240).
37. United States Government Interagency Domestic Terrorism Concept of Operations Plan. January 2001. Available at: http://www.fas.org/irp/threat/conplan. html. Accessed May 4, 2001.
38. 65 *Federal Register* 49906 (2000) (amendment in reference to: Measures in the event of inadequate control, 42 USC §70.2).
39. Gostin L. Public health law in a new century, II: public health powers and limits. *JAMA.* 2000;283:2979–2984.
40. Knight W. The history of the US Public Health Service. 1999. Available at: http:// www.usphs.gov/html/history.html. Accessed November 4, 2001.
41. Centers for Disease Control and Prevention, Division of Global Migration and Quarantine. History of quarantine. Available at: http://www.cdc.gov/ncidod/dq/ history.htm. Accessed April 28, 2001.
42. Centers for Disease Control and Prevention. *Public Health Screening at US Ports of Entry: A Guide for Federal Inspectors.* Atlanta, Ga: National Center for Infectious Disease; March 2000. Available at: http://www.cdc.gov/ncidod/dq/ operations.htm. Accessed November 4, 2001.
43. 42 USC §243a (2001).
44. Gostin L. The future of public health law. *Am J Law Med.* 1990;16:1–32.
45. Parmet W. AIDS and quarantine: the revival of an archaic doctrine. *Hofstra Law Rev.* 1985;14:53–90.
46. Gostin L. Public health law reform. *Am J Public Health.* 2001;91:1365–1368.
47. Cole T. When a bioweapon strikes, who will be in charge? *JAMA.* 2000;284: 944–948.
48. Markel H. "Knocking out the cholera": cholera, class, and quarantines in New York City, 1892. *Bull Hist Med.* 1995;69:420–457.
49. Eidson W. Confusion, controversy, and quarantine: the Muncie smallpox epidemic of 1893. *Indiana Magazine of History.* 1990;LXXXVI:374–398.
50. Risse G. "A long pull, a strong pull, and all together": San Francisco and Bubonic Plague, 1907–1908. *Bull Hist Med.* 1992;66:260–286.
51. *Jew Ho v Williamson,* 103 F1024 (CCD Cal 1900).
52. Defense Advanced Research Projects Agency epidemiology software used during presidential inauguration [press release]. March 9, 2001. Available at: http://www.darpa.mil/body/newsitems/encompass_release.doc. Accessed November 4, 2001.
53. Centers for Disease Control and Prevention. Supporting public health surveillance through the National Electronic Disease Surveillance System (NEDSS). Available at: http://www.cdc.gov/nchs/otheract/phdsc/presenters/nedss.pdf. Accessed April 14, 2001.
54. Ross I. The influenza epidemic of 1918. *American History Illustrated.* 1968;3: 12–17.
55. Szanislo M. Plane quarantined due to passenger's illness. *Boston Herald.* October 25, 2000:2.

56. Inglesby T. V., Henderson D. A., Bartlett J. G., et al, for the Working Group on Civilian Biodefense. Anthrax as a biological weapon: medical and public health management. *JAMA*. 1999;281:1735–1745.

57. Henderson D. A., Inglesby T. V., Bartlett J. G., et al, for the Working Group on Civilian Biodefense. Smallpox as a biological weapon: medical and public health management. *JAMA*. 1999;281:2127–2137.

58. Inglesby T. V., Dennis D. T., Henderson D. A., et al, for the Working Group on Civilian Biodefense. Plague as a biological weapon: medical and public health management. *JAMA*. 2000;283:2281–2290.

59. Outbreak of Ebola hemorrhagic fever—Uganda, August 2000–January 2001. *MMWR Morb Mortal Wkly Rep*. 2001;50:73–77.

60. Ball-Rokeach S., Loges W. Ally or adversary? using media systems for public health. *Prehosp Dis Med*. 2000;15:62–69.

112

PUBLIC HEALTH SURVEILLANCE IN THE TWENTY-FIRST CENTURY

Achieving population health goals while protecting individuals' privacy and confidentiality

Michael A. Stoto

Source: *Georgetown Law Journal*, 96:2 (2008), 703–19.

Introduction

Surveillance, a core function of public health, is defined as "ongoing, systematic collection, analysis, and interpretation of health data essential to the planning, implementation, and evaluation of public health practice, closely integrated with the timely dissemination of these data to those who need to know."[1] In the context of a session that addresses how data and information can and should inform public health policy and practice, this discussion of surveillance calls attention to the disclosure and use of personal health information. In particular, public health surveillance programs require a careful balance between the development of statistical and epidemiological data and knowledge that are essential to achieving population health goals and the protection of individuals' privacy and confidentiality rights.

Public health surveillance, as it is usually defined, includes two very different activities. *Case surveillance* focuses on individuals, or sometimes small groups of individuals, and serves to identify those with certain diseases and takes action to stop disease spread beyond these identified individuals. Historically, case surveillance has been used for communicable diseases capable of causing great harm to the entire population if allowed to spread. The loss of privacy involved with this type of surveillance has been justified in terms of disease averted. In contrast, *statistical surveillance* uses populations to identify differentials and trends that can inform public health policymaking, including the allocation of resources. Individuals need not be identified for the surveillance to serve its purpose, so data can be gathered either anonymously or with promises of confidentiality, thus not violating privacy rights. Both surveillance approaches have roots going back centuries, but it was not until 1963 that Alexander Langmuir of the Communicable Disease Center (now the Centers for Disease Control and Prevention, or CDC) combined them in his classic definition of public health surveillance,[2] the basis for the CDC's definition quoted above.

Case surveillance and statistical surveillance have different goals and objectives, data sources, and methods. Over time, each approach has resolved the tradeoffs between population benefits and individuals' privacy and confidentiality rights in its own way. In recent years, however, new surveillance programs have been developed that combine, and sometimes confuse, the case and statistical approaches. Individual HIV case reporting, for instance, is advocated as a means of estimating the relative number of cases in different parts of the country in an effort to allocate federal resources.[3] In some parts of the country, individually identified hospital emergency room records are transmitted to health departments, which use them in statistical analyses to detect disease outbreaks and covert bioterrorist attacks.[4] Furthermore, individual case reports are increasingly utilized to monitor obesity, diabetes, and other non-communicable diseases.[5]

Novel approaches to disease surveillance that combine the objectives and approaches of case and statistical surveillance demand a reevaluation of the balance between preserving individuals' rights and the need for effective public health tools. To address these issues, this Essay begins by reviewing the history of public health surveillance to understand the tradeoffs that have been made in the past. The Essay then analyzes the three examples above to illustrate the issues involved and the new tradeoffs that must be addressed. Drawing on these analyses, the final Part proposes some considerations that can help public health find an appropriate balance between population benefits of surveillance and the protection of individuals' privacy and confidentiality rights.

I. History of public health surveillance[6]

The case surveillance approach is fundamental to public health as it uses the police power of the state to control communicable diseases. This approach was used in the Republic of Venice during the fourteenth century, for example, when authorities boarded ships to identify persons with symptoms of bubonic plague and prevent them from disembarking.[7] Similarly, in 1741, Rhode Island required tavern keepers to report patrons with contagious disease, including smallpox, yellow fever, and cholera, to local authorities.[8] A postcard reporting format was developed in Massachusetts in 1874, with the resulting information compiled into weekly reports.[9] In 1878, Congress authorized the forerunner of the United States Public Health Service to collect morbidity data for use in quarantine measures against "pestilential diseases" such as cholera, smallpox, plague, and yellow fever.[10] Compulsory reporting of infectious diseases began on a national basis in Italy in 1881, and in other European countries shortly afterwards.[11] At the global level, the World Health Organization (WHO) modified the International Health Regulations in 2005 to require that all countries notify the WHO of all events "which may constitute a public health emergency of international concern."[12] These regulations also require that countries have the core surveillance and response capacities needed to fulfill the international reporting requirements.[13]

All of these aforementioned surveillance programs focused on identifying individuals with infectious diseases and taking action amongst the identified individuals to control disease outbreaks. Smallpox, for example, was eradicated in the 1970s using a surveillance-based approach after earlier efforts to immunize nearly 100% of the population failed because of logistical difficulties.[14] The successful "ring strategy" that led to the success of the smallpox eradication campaign relied on intensive surveillance to identify cases, isolate all known cases, and immunize individuals who may have come in contact with cases.[15] Control strategies traditionally include monitoring, contact tracing, treatment, and quarantine[16]—indeed, before the development and widespread availability of antibiotics and vaccines in the twentieth century, this is most of what public health and medicine could do. Even after the advent of antibiotics, contact tracing helped to quell re-emerging tuberculosis (TB) in the United States in the 1990s and is still a common and effective public health tool.[17]

Although these days there are few cases of "pestilential diseases," the need for quick action to prevent the spread of infectious diseases remains. One of the main goals of surveillance for diseases such as TB and sexually transmitted diseases (STDs) is to identify infectious individuals before they infect others, thus preventing an exponentially growing epidemic. Case surveillance has received additional prominence with the increasing interest in emerging infections and, since the attacks of September 11, 2001, in bioterrorism.[18] Indeed, case surveillance was a critical tool in controlling SARS in 2003.[19]

However, despite its successes, case surveillance may be causing more harm than benefit in some cases. For instance, screening before and during pregnancy and after birth for phenylketonuria, sickle cell disease, neural tube defects, substance abuse, and HIV-infection has been especially problematic.[20] The screening methods may be reliable, but effective, acceptable, or affordable means of following up on identified cases are not widely available.[21] Especially when dealing with vulnerable populations, the stigma and discrimination often associated with being identified as having one of these conditions can overwhelm any potential benefit of the surveillance.[22] Furthermore, whether case finding can control disease outbreaks depends on the epidemiological dynamics of the condition—for example, whether cases are infectious before they become symptomatic, as with influenza, or afterwards, as with SARS—and the length of latency period.[23] For many diseases, case surveillance is simply not an effective strategy.

Over the course of the twentieth century, the primary cause of death shifted from infectious to chronic diseases; as a result the focus of surveillance shifted to populations rather than individuals.[24] Monitoring populations required statistical analysis of data from birth and death certificates, as well as health surveys based on scientifically chosen sample surveys, such as the National Health Interview Survey (NHIS)[25] and Behavioral Risk Factor Surveillance System (BRFSS).[26]

Registries are another source of data for statistical surveillance programs. The National Cancer Institute (NCI) Surveillance, Epidemiology, and End Results (SEER) system, which operates fifteen population-based cancer registries covering approximately 26% of the U.S. population, uses active surveillance methods to record all incident cases of cancer as well as their treatments and outcomes.[27] As a result, NCI is able to estimate cancer incidence and survival rates,[28] something that is not possible for most chronic diseases.

Surveillance of occupational morbidity and mortality—developed in concert with new regulations on workplace safety regulation—and injury surveillance became more common in the 1990s as public health turned its attention to intentional and unintentional violence.[29] A growing focus on health care quality in the early twenty-first century and attendant concerns about medical errors and iatrogenic injuries in recent years have led to intensified surveillance efforts, along with post-marketing surveillance for adverse effects of drugs and vaccines.[30]

II. New approaches to disease surveillance that demand a reevaluation of the balance between protecting individuals' rights and maintaining the effectiveness of disease control programs

When case-based surveillance was established as a public health function, the inherent loss of privacy was easily justified in terms of the benefits to those identified and, especially, the population at large. And for statistical approaches to surveillance, individuals' privacy was protected by releasing only aggregate numbers such as averages or proportions, as well as by suppressing small cells—that is, table entries representing fewer than five individuals.[31] Three recent examples, however, have combined both individual and statistical approaches, upsetting the careful balance between the usefulness of the statistical and epidemiological information and the importance of individuals' privacy and confidentiality rights. To understand the new tradeoffs that must be addressed, it is important to clarify the issues involved in these three examples.

A. HIV reporting: a case-based approach with a statistical purpose[32]

Although it is a communicable disease, AIDS cannot easily be controlled by reporting individuals with HIV infection to health departments. By the time the infection becomes apparent, years may have passed in which the individual has already infected many others. Rather, the primary reason for requiring HIV case reporting is statistical, specifically to prepare estimates of the prevalence of the condition to guide the allocation of federal resources.[33] This example raises two issues. The first issue is whether the loss of privacy involved in reporting someone who has HIV infection to public health authorities is justified by the public health benefits. The second issue is whether the statistical estimates derived from this surveillance system are accurate, and thus effective in achieving public health goals. If not, the justification for the loss of individual privacy is further undermined.

Since the beginning of the HIV/AIDS epidemic, surveillance efforts have been critical in determining the number and characteristics of individuals diagnosed with AIDS.[34] The current AIDS national surveillance system was implemented prior to the identification of HIV as the etiologic agent of AIDS and the development of an antibody test to determine HIV infection.[35] Each state requires that all patients diagnosed with AIDS be reported by name to their local, state, or territorial health department.[36] These reports are then forwarded (without names but with unique identifiers) to the CDC, where a national surveillance database is updated and analyzed, providing uniform data on trends and distribution of individuals diagnosed with AIDS.[37] Standard records for each case include information on age at diagnosis, sex, race and ethnicity, state of residence (and metropolitan area, if relevant), mode of exposure to HIV, month of AIDS diagnosis, date reported, and other information.[38] Statistical analysis of these surveillance data established, for instance, that HIV was transmitted sexually and through blood products and identified a series of risk factors (homosexual sex, multiple partners, intravenous drug use, and so on) that were useful in developing early prevention strategies.[39]

The AIDS surveillance system evolved over time by changing its case definition to reflect the growing clinical understanding of the disease and the availability of appropriate clinical diagnostic tests while maintaining its focus on AIDS rather than the underlying HIV infection.[40] The basic reporting responsibilities and procedures, however, remain unchanged. And until the development of potent antiretroviral therapies in the 1990s, AIDS case reporting, although imperfect, provided a relatively accurate picture of trends in HIV infection, especially relative prevalence of HIV in groups defined by geography, race and ethnicity, and primary mode of infection.[41] Estimates of HIV incidence and prevalence were made by statistical techniques such as calculating backward from reported AIDS cases according to well-established patterns of disease progression.[42] Since the 1990s, however, developments in therapy for HIV and AIDS have decoupled HIV infection and its progression to AIDS.[43] As a result, the timing of the progression from HIV infection to AIDS and from AIDS to death is increasingly difficult to predict, making

HIV incidence and prevalence estimates based on AIDS cases much less accurate, and AIDS case reports are no longer adequate to monitor trends in new HIV infections.[44]

HIV case surveillance—not to be confused with AIDS case surveillance —started in some states in the 1980s for contact tracing and to link people to care. This approach was not common at that time, however, since no effective treatment was available and also due to the difficulties with protecting the privacy and confidentiality of those with HIV. In response to concerns about the limitations of the current AIDS surveillance system in providing accurate information about trends in the HIV epidemic, CDC now recommends that all states and territories extend their AIDS surveillance activities to include case reporting of HIV infection.[45] As of February 2007, forty-seven states, the District of Columbia, and five U.S. dependent areas had implemented HIV case surveillance using the same confidential system for name-based case reporting currently used for AIDS cases.[46]

HIV case reporting is said to have a number of benefits relative to AIDS case reporting. In its official guidance on HIV surveillance, the CDC maintains that HIV case reporting will produce "a more realistic and useful estimate of the resources needed for patient care and services than does AIDS prevalence alone." Accounts of HIV case reporting in the popular press sometimes suggest that such a system will identify a larger number of infected individuals, and thus lead to greater federal funding for states who adopt such a system. The possibility that federal treatment funds might be allocated according to the number of individuals living with HIV rather than AIDS was brought to attention during Congressional debate about the Ryan White Care Act reauthorization in 2000, leading to great concern in areas such as San Francisco with "mature" epidemics[47]

Data from existing HIV case reporting systems, however, are incomplete in several important ways. In contrast to the AIDS case reporting system, which is relatively complete, the HIV reporting system collects data only from persons who choose to be tested and who do so at a non-anonymous testing site (i.e., where the HIV test result is linked with identifying information, including patient and provider names). Thus, HIV case reporting data exclude individuals who are infected but have not been tested as well as those who utilize anonymous testing sites or home collection test kits. Because of this selectivity, HIV case reporting by name is unrepresentative of the larger population of infected persons. Further, because reported HIV cases could represent infections that are anywhere from a few weeks to a few years old, the data would reflect the time that individuals chose to be tested rather than when the individual became infected. As a result, HIV case reporting data provide only partial information about HIV prevalence, rather than information about HIV incidence, that is, new HIV infections.[48]

In its report *No Time To Lose*, the Institute of Medicine

> concluded that a new surveillance system focused on HIV incidence
> is needed in order to more effectively guide HIV prevention plan-
> ning, resource allocation, and evaluation decisions at the national,
> state, and local levels. To the extent possible, the system would
> provide estimates at the state and local level and for the population
> groups at highest risk for HIV infection.[49]

In particular, the Institute recommended that CDC

> create a surveillance system that can provide national population-
> based estimates of HIV incidence. The recommended surveillance
> system would estimate new HIV infections using blinded [blood
> samples collected for other purposes from] well-characterized sentinel
> populations (e.g., drug users in treatment, people attending sexually
> transmitted disease clinics and tuberculosis clinics, clinics serving
> women of reproductive age), surveys that characterize the populations
> served by those sites, and advanced testing technologies that are able
> to identify recent HIV infections.[50]

In conclusion, the value of the additional information that reporting individually identified HIV cases might provide either for the individual or in terms of more accurate statistical data or funding allocations is less than some would anticipate. In this context, the loss of privacy and confidentiality in reporting individual HIV cases to health departments may not be justified.

B. Syndromic surveillance: collecting individual-level data to detect disease outbreaks[51]

Heightened awareness of the risks of bioterrorism since the September 11th attacks, coupled with a growing concern about naturally emerging and re-emerging diseases such as West Nile, SARS, and pandemic influenza, have led public health policymakers to realize the need for early warning systems. The sooner health officials know about an attack or a natural disease outbreak, for instance, the sooner that they can treat those who have already been exposed to the pathogen to minimize the health consequences, vaccinate some or all of the population to prevent further infection, and identify and isolate cases to prevent further transmission.[52] Responding to this need, many health departments have developed "syndromic surveillance" systems, in which individually identified hospital emergency room records are analyzed statistically to detect possible disease outbreaks and covert bioterrorist attacks.[53]

Syndromic surveillance, however, requires public health agencies to acquire large amounts of routine, individually identified health data before there is any indication of a disease outbreak. If an outbreak were known to be occurring there would be no argument about the need for these data, but most of the time, of course, there is no outbreak. The problem is that the legal structures that balance public health requirements with the protection of privacy and confidentiality do not contemplate surveillance systems that can be justified only in retrospect, that is, if they detect an outbreak. To understand the trade-offs, it is important to consider both the likely efficacy of syndromic surveillance and the privacy and confidentiality risks involved.

Traditional public health surveillance programs monitor disease using pre-specified case definitions and employ manual data collection, human decision making, and manual data entry.[54] In contrast, current electronic surveillance systems employ sophisticated information technology and statistical methods to gather and process large amounts of data and display the information for decision makers in a timely way. For instance, syndromic surveillance systems assume that during an attack or a disease outbreak, people will first develop symptoms, then stay home from work or school, attempt to self-treat with over-the-counter (OTC) products, and eventually see a physician with nonspecific symptoms, all days before they are formally diagnosed and reported to the health department.[55] To identify such behaviors, syndromic surveillance systems regularly monitor existing data for sudden changes or anomalies that might signal a disease outbreak.[56] Syndromic surveillance systems have been developed to include data on school and work absenteeism, sales of OTC products, calls to nurse hotlines, and counts of hospital emergency room (ER) admissions or reports from primary physicians for certain symptoms or complaints.[57]

The possibility "of earlier detection and more rapid response to a bioterrorist event has tremendous intuitive appeal,"[58] but there are practical concerns about the use of these systems in state and local public health practice. In statistical terms there is a relatively narrow window between what can be detected in the first few days and what is obvious.[59] As a result, the statistical value of syndromic surveillance for detecting bioterrorist attacks has not yet been demonstrated.[60] In addition, syndromic surveillance's success "depends on local health departments' ability to respond effectively."[61]

When a syndromic surveillance system sounds an alarm, health departments typically wait a day or two to see if the number of cases continues to remain high or if a similar signal is found in other data sources. Doing so, of course, reduces both the timeliness and sensitivity of the original system. If the health department decides that an epidemiological investigation is warranted, it may begin by identifying those who are ill and talking to their physicians. If this does not resolve the matter, additional tests must be ordered and clinical specimens gathered for laboratory analysis. Health departments might also choose to initiate active surveillance by contacting physicians to see if they have seen similar cases.[62]

267

Arthur Reingold provocatively noted the challenges confronting syndromic surveillance: characterizing the types of bioterrorist events that it is likely to detect, determining whether it can help identify the population at risk in a more timely way during a bioterrorist event, determining the appropriate response to apparent increases in illnesses signaled by syndromic surveillance, and ultimately demonstrating that it can reduce morbidity and/or mortality following a bioterrorist event.[63] Reingold also questioned whether syndromic surveillance will produce useful information about naturally occurring diseases and the importance of identifying the circumstances under which it is likely to strengthen local and state public health departments.[64]

Moreover, since the development and implementation of syndromic surveillance systems began in recent years, success in gaining access to personal health data has been mixed. Varying interpretations of the Health Insurance Portability and Accountability Act (HIPAA) Privacy Rule[65] are at the heart of the problem. Although some argue that the Privacy Rule permits data owners to disclose protected health information to public health authorities,[66] covered entities[67] cite the rule in refusing to provide data to researchers and health departments.[68] In addition to HIPAA, a variety of federal, state, and local public health laws enable, restrict, and otherwise influence the ability to share data for public health surveillance purposes.[69] Concerns about protecting proprietary data also influence data sharing for public health purposes.

While the HIPAA Privacy Rule may allow covered entities to provide data to public health authorities, it does not require them to do so.[70] As a result, covered entities may feel exposed to liability in lawsuits: because the release is not mandatory, arguably the entity has a choice about releasing the data. Such concerns reflect an apparent misunderstanding of the distinction between HIPAA and disease reporting laws. HIPAA does not provide for disease reporting mandates—such mandates have their basis in state public health laws. Rather, HIPAA privacy rules include exemptions that allow for disease-reporting under state public laws,[71] and these laws typically mandate reporting not only of specific diseases but also of clusters of disease or unusual health events that may indicate a public health threat.[72]

The crux of the problem is that syndromic surveillance requires the collection of large amounts of data before there is any indication of a disease outbreak. Indeed, the purpose of gathering the data is to identify when such an outbreak may be occurring. Routine data of this sort are generally not covered by existing public health reporting laws, which focus on specific diseases.[73] One solution to this ethical and legal dilemma may be found in distinguishing between the need for statistical and individual-level information. In practice, health departments would gather only aggregate data—which is anonymous—for statistical detection of possible events. In addition, an informatics system would allow public health agencies to go back to identified source records if and when evidence of a possible event emerges. At the point when there is evidence of an emerging event of concern, reporting personal information would be justified under existing public health reporting laws. In addition to resolving the legal dilemma, this approach would help to control the costs of false positives in syndromic surveillance, since initial investigations could be performed electronically rather than by sending teams out to the field. While this would require more sophisticated information technology than current public health reporting systems typically possess, it provides a way to balance public health needs and individual rights to privacy and confidentiality.

C. Screening for diabetes and obesity: case reporting applied to non-communicable diseases

Although the focus of public health surveillance was originally on infectious diseases, population-level chronic disease surveillance has a long history. The analysis of vital statistics by cause of death was pioneered in the nineteenth century by William Farr in England and Lemuel Shattuck in the United States.[74] And as indicated above, population-based surveys such as the National Health Interview Survey (NHIS) and the Behavioral Risk Factor Surveillance System (BRFSS) and registries such as the NCI's SEER system for cancer surveillance are long established. This sort of surveillance system provides statistical data for the entire population as well as groups defined by demography, socioeconomic status, geography, and other factors.[75]

Recent developments in chronic disease surveillance, however, have focused on individuals rather than populations. Rather than identifying trends and differentials between increasingly fine-grained populations, screening efforts seek to identify individuals with undetected chronic diseases such as diabetes.[76] The anonymity and confidentiality traditionally used in the collection of statistical data on chronic diseases is no longer possible, raising questions about whether the benefits to the individuals concerned and to public health generally—which depend on the reliability of the screening programs and the interventions that follow—justify the loss of their privacy.

New York City's health commissioner Thomas Frieden, for instance, wrote that "[l]ocal health departments do a good job of monitoring and controlling conditions," such as infectious diseases, "that killed people 100 years ago," but have not kept pace with the epidemiologic transition to the non-communicable diseases which are now responsible for 80% of deaths in the United States.[77] One way to address non-communicable diseases, as Frieden notes, is to establish disease registries such as those already in place for tuberculosis and cancer.[78] Registries can both improve management of patients and track the effectiveness of community-based interventions.[79] New York has also conducted telephone surveys gathering information at the local level about diagnosed diabetes, self-reported obesity and other risk factors, as well as a health and nutrition examination survey to gather actual physical and laboratory measurements.[80]

In December 2005, the New York City Board of Health adopted a diabetes surveillance program that includes mandatory reporting of glycosylated hemoglobin to a registry established by the city's Department of Health and Mental Hygiene.[81] Laboratories are required to report glycosylated hemoglobin levels, a measure of the degree to which an individual's diabetes is under control, along with the identity of the patient and the physician who ordered the test.[82] The resulting information "will be used to map the epidemiology of diabetes and to monitor the epidemic."[83] The registry is also intended to help improve the treatment of individual cases by providing physicians with lists of patients with poor glycemic control, treatment recommendations, and suggestions about advising patients regarding diabetes management.[84] In the future, patients may receive a letter directly from the health department if their glycosylated hemoglobin value is above a level to be determined.[85] Patients will be allowed to opt out, but their data will remain as part of the registry.[86]

Although "the endeavor has aroused concern about patients' privacy and . . . the role of health departments," Dr. Frieden responds that the surveillance program aims "to respond to an epidemic of a chronic disease with the type of surveillance and other tools that health departments routinely use to prevent and control communicable diseases."[87] Three other potential problems suggested by the HIV surveillance example discussed above have apparently not been addressed. First, the registry will only contain information on those who have been tested, and will contain no information on individuals with undiagnosed diabetes. Second, undoubtedly some of those who are tested will not have a regular source of health care, so the link to the physician who ordered the test will be meaningless. Finally, it seems likely that the registry will contain duplicative reports on the same individuals, perhaps linked to different physicians or using different patient identifiers.

Other programs attempt to identify individuals with an elevated risk of developing such diseases, such as obese and overweight children. For instance, as a result of a state law passed in 2003 ("Act 1220"), public schools in Arkansas measure students' body mass index (BMI), and on this basis send annual confidential reports to parents of children who are obese or at risk of obesity.[88] Act 1220 also mandates improved access to healthier foods in schools and the creation of local committees to promote physical activity and nutrition.[89]

The rationale for such programs is that early detection of disease and interventions to change behavioral risk factors can prevent severe consequences later in life. The ethical question is whether the health benefits of this screening—to the individual and to society—justify the violation of privacy and confidentiality. The magnitude of the health benefits depends on the efficacy of early detection and intervention. Although well established in theory, empirical evidence about the efficacy of programs that track individuals with diabetes, obesity, and other risk factors is lacking in practice. For instance, an evaluation three years after the Arkansas program began found that the major policy changes at the district and school levels regarding food availability and physical activity, as well as the BMI measurement and reporting process, have been accepted by schools, parents, and children.[90] There is little evidence so far, however, about changes in diet and activity patterns at home, or obesity levels.[91]

Conclusion

A basic principle of public health is to employ the least restrictive option that achieves population health goals. From this perspective, surveillance programs must strike a balance between the potential population benefits of the statistical and epidemiological data and knowledge, on the one hand, and protecting individuals' privacy and confidentiality rights on the other. The examples discussed here suggest four considerations that can help find an appropriate balance.

First, policy makers must evaluate whether the proposed public health intervention is likely to achieve its public health goals. If not, the challenges to privacy and confidentiality need not be addressed. As illustrated in the examples above, public health interventions are sometimes not as effective as promised.

Second, policy makers should clearly determine the public health need for individual rather than aggregate statistical data, and opt for the latter if it serves public health needs. The HIV case reporting examples indicate, for instance, that individual-level data may not be needed for public health purposes. HIV case reports do not, as the analysis shows, actually provide more accurate data on HIV incidence and prevalence than existing alternatives.[92]

Third, policy makers should consider intermediate solutions. Individual-level syndromic surveillance data are not needed until aggregate data suggest a disease outbreak may be underway. Developing the information technology to gather aggregate data and then link back to the records that generated an alert when necessary would be preferable. With respect to diabetes and its risk factors, it may be more effective to identify the population groups that are highly affected and target risk reduction and treatment strategies at them, rather than at individuals. Identifying schools with a high proportion of overweight children and enhancing their physical education programs and altering their food availability may be more effective and less stigmatizing in the long run than notifying the parents of children who are overweight.

Fourth, policy makers should clarify the circumstances under which population goals may override protection of individuals' privacy and confidentiality rights. Although no single factor is ever definitive, the following should be considered:

The extent to which the disease in question is transmissible from person to person. This consideration would argue in favor of surveillance for HIV infection and syndromic surveillance for bioterrorism or pandemic influenza, but not for obesity or diabetes screening.

Availability of reliable screening methods. One of the problems with identifying overweight children is that, while obesity is certainly a risk factor for diabetes later in life, it is not clear that childhood obesity is a good predictor of adult diabetes risk.

The extent to which identification and reporting of cases benefits those with the condition. A minimum requirement here is the availability of an effective treatment. The development of new and effective HIV medications in the 1990s, for instance, altered the balance of benefits and risks associated with HIV testing. It is less clear that reporting individuals with HIV infection to the local health department actually leads to better access to needed care.[93] With respect to diabetes and obesity, losing weight does reduce the risk of diabetes, but does identifying obese children lead them to lose weight and maintain the loss long enough to significantly reduce the risk of diabetes?

The extent to which identification and reporting of cases is effective in controlling the outbreak in the population. Epidemiological dynamics—whether cases are infectious before or after they become symptomatic, the length of a pathogen's latency period and similar factors—are important. Case surveillance was able to help control the SARS outbreak in Toronto and Asia in 2003 because those infected developed symptoms before they were contagious.[94] The opposite is true of influenza—people may infect others a day or two before they develop symptoms themselves—making case surveillance less effective.[95] Obesity is clearly not contagious in the usual sense, but a population dynamic is possible: if fitness becomes the norm, individuals may lose weight because obesity is socially unacceptable.

Vulnerability of the affected population. Stigmatization and discrimination against those identified through a screening program can be worse when those identified are part of a vulnerable population, and this should be considered when considering a surveillance program that identifies individuals. For example, one could ask whether, if statistics reveal that a disproportionate number of obese children are African American or Hispanic, these groups are harmed.

Ultimately, surveillance is a double-edged sword. The information from surveillance programs is critically needed to inform and guide public health policy and manage public health programs. However, all surveillance data derive from individuals' personal health information, meaning that their privacy and confidentiality are at risk. Therefore, before a surveillance program is initiated, a careful, case-by-case analysis balancing the benefits of the information for public health purposes and the rights of the individuals who are the subjects of the data is needed.

Notes

1 Stephen B. Thacker & Ruth L. Berkelman, *Public Health Surveillance in the United States*, 10 Epidemiologic Revs. 164, 164 (1988) (quoting Ctrs. for Disease Control, Comprehensive Plan for Epidemiologic Surveillance ii (1986)).

2 *See* Alexander D. Langmuir, *The Surveillance of Communicable Diseases of National Importance*, 268 NEW ENG. J. MED. 182, 182–83 (1963).

3 *See* INST. OF MED., MEASURING WHAT MATTERS: ALLOCATION, PLANNING, AND QUALITY ASSESSMENT FOR THE RYAN WHITE CARE ACT 12 (2004) (recommending use of either code- or name-based individual case reporting to "improve consistency, quality, and comparability in HIV case reporting for [Ryan White CARE Act] allocation purposes").

4 *See* Kenneth D. Mandl et al., *Implementing Syndromic Surveillance: A Practical Guide Informed by the Early Experience*, 11 J. AM. MED. INFORMATICS ASS'N 141, 143–44 (2004) ("Real-time data streams from . . . emergency department encounters have been established successfully in a number of regions."); Michael A. Stoto, *Syndromic Surveillance*, ISSUES SCI. & TECH., Spring 2005, at 50 ("This theory [of syndromic surveillance] was turned into a reality when some health departments . . . began to monitor hospital ER admissions and other data streams.").

5 *See, e.g.*, UNIV. OF ARK. FOR MED. SCI. FAY W. BOOZMAN COLL. OF PUB. HEALTH, YEAR THREE EVALUATION: ARKANSAS ACT OF 2003 TO COMBAT CHILDHOOD OBESITY 27 (2006) (describing Arkansas legislation mandating in-school obesity screening); Thomas R. Frieden, *Asleep at the Switch: Local Public Health and Chronic Disease*, 94 AM. J. PUB. HEALTH 2059, 2059 (2004) (describing New York City's diabetes surveillance program).

6 Much of this Part appeared in substantially similar form in MICHAEL A. STOTO, PUBLIC HEALTH SURVEILLANCE: A HISTORICAL REVIEW WITH A FOCUS ON HIV/ADDS 2–6 (2003), *available at* http://www.rand.org/pubs/drafts/2005/DRU3074.pdf.

7 *See* Stephen B. Thacker, *Historical Development, in* PRINCIPLES AND PRACTICE OF PUBLIC HEALTH SURVEILLANCE 1, 3 (Steven M. Teutsch & R. Elliott Churchill eds., 2d ed. 2000).

8 *See id.* at 4.

9 *See id.*

10 *See id.* at 3.

11 *See id.*

12 WORLD HEALTH ORG. [WHO], *Revision of the International Health Regulations, in* FIFTY-EIGHTH WORLD HEALTH ASSEMBLY RESOLUTIONS AND DECISIONS 14, 17 (2005), *available at* http://www.who.int/gb/ebwha/pdf_files/WHA58/WHA58_3-en.pdf.

13 *See id.* at 16, 47–49.

14 *See, e.g.*, IAN GLYNN & JENIFER GLYNN, THE LIFE AND DEATH OF SMALLPOX 200–01 (2004) (crediting the successful eradication of smallpox to the combination of vaccination and "surveillance-containment," also known as "ring strategy").

15 *See id.* at 201.

16 *See* Thacker, *supra* note 7.

17 *See* INST. OF MED., ENDING NEGLECT: THE ELIMINATION OF TUBERCULOSIS IN THE UNITED STATES 3 (2000) (discussing the resurgence of tuberculosis in the late 1980s and early 1990s, and claiming that "[t]he highest priority is the identification and treatment of infected contacts of individuals with . . . tuberculosis"); INST. OF MED., MICROBIAL THREATS TO HEALTH: EMERGENCE, DETECTION, AND RESPONSE 159–70 (Mark S. Smolinski et al. eds., 2003) (advocating the continued use and development of surveillance strategies in order to combat future outbreaks).

18 *See* Mandl et al., *supra* note 4, at 142.

19 *See* David L. Heymann & Guénaël Rodier, *Global Surveillance, National Surveillance, and SARS*, 10 EMERGING INFECTIOUS DISEASES 173, 174 (2004) (describing the case surveillance measures taken by the WHO Global Influenza Surveillance

Network and the Global Outbreak Alert and Response Network in Southeast Asia and Canada that led to the identification of SARS and subsequent recommendations for national and international response).

20 *See* REDUCING THE ODDS: PREVENTING PERINATAL TRANSMISSION OF HIV IN THE UNITED STATES 25–35 (Michael A. Stoto, Donna A. Almario & Marie C. McCormick eds., 1999).

21 *See id.*

22 *See id.* at 34–35.

23 *See* Christophe Fraser et al., *Factors That Make an Infectious Disease Outbreak Controllable*, 101 PROC. NAT'L ACAD. SCI. 6146, 6146 (2004).

24 *See* STOTO, *supra* note 6, at 5–6.

25 For more information, see National Health Interview Survey, http://www.cdc.gov/nchs/nhis.htm (last visited Aug. 23, 2007).

26 For more information, see BRFSS: Turning Information into Health, http://www.cdc.gov/brfss (last visited Aug. 23, 2007).

27 *See* National Cancer Institute, SEER: Surveillance, Epidemiology, and End Results Program 2, 7, http://seer.cancer.gov/about/SEER_brochure.pdf (last visited Oct. 13, 2007).

28 *See id.* at 7.

29 *See, e.g.*, INST. OF MED., REDUCING THE BURDEN OF INJURY: ADVANCING PREVENTION AND TREATMENT 23, 64–71 (Richard J. Bonnie et al. eds., 1999) (identifying injury as an important public health problem and outlining the major injury surveillance systems).

30 *See* INST. OF MED., THE FUTURE OF DRUG SAFETY: PROMOTING AND PROTECTING THE HEALTH OF THE PUBLIC 114–15 (Alina Baciu et al. eds., 2007) (recommending that the FDA "develop and implement active surveillance of specific drugs and diseases as needed"); INST. OF MED., TO ERR IS HUMAN: BUILDING A SAFER HEALTH SYSTEM 9 (Linda T. Kohn et al. eds., 2000) (focusing on human error in medical care and recommending, among other things, "[a] nationwide mandatory reporting system that provides for the collection of standardized information"). *See generally* INST. OF MED., CROSSING THE QUALITY CHASM: A NEW HEALTH SYSTEM FOR THE 21ST CENTURY (2001) (focusing on failures of the American health care system and outlining recommended changes).

31 *See* Michael A. Stoto, *Statistical Issues in Interactive Web-based Public Health Data Dissemination Systems* 21, 32–33 (RAND Health, Working Paper No. WR-106, 2003), *available at* http://www.rand.org/pubs/working_papers/2005/RAND_WR106.pdf.

32 Much of this Part originally appeared in STOTO, *supra* note 6, at 21–25.

33 *See* INST. OF MED., *supra* note 3, at 12.

34 *See* Lawrence O. Gostin, John W. Ward & A. Cornelius Baker, *National HIV Case Reporting for the United States: A Defining Moment in the History of the Epidemic*, 337 NEW ENG. J. MED. 1162, 1162 (1997).

35 *See id.* at 1162–63 (examining the history of HIV/AIDS surveillance).

36 *See id.* at 1163.

37 *Id.*

38 *Id.*

39 *See* INST. OF MED., *supra* note 3, at 1.

40 *See* Ctrs. for Disease Control and Prevention, *Guidelines for National Human Immunodeficiency Virus Case Surveillance, Including Monitoring for Human Immunodeficiency Virus Infection and Acquired Immunodeficiency Syndrome*, 48 MORBIDITY & MORTALITY WKLY. REP., Dec. 10, 1999, at 1–2 [hereinafter CDC, *Guidelines*].

41 *See id.*
42 *See* RON BROOKMEYER & MITCHELL H. GAIL, AIDS EPIDEMIOLOGY: A QUANTITATIVE APPROACH (1994).
43 *See* CDC, *Guidelines, supra* note 40, at 1–2.
44 *See id.*
45 *See* CDC, *Guidelines, supra* note 40, at 3.
46 *See* CDC, HIV Infection Reporting, *available at* http://www.cdc.gov/hiv/topics/surveillance/reporting.htm.
47 *See* INST. OF MED., *supra* note 3, at 8–9.
48 INST. OF MED., NO TIME TO LOSE: GETTING MORE FROM HIV PREVENTION 17–18 (Monica S. Ruiz et al. eds., 2001); *see also* Mira John et al., *New Approaches to HIV Surveillance: Means and Ends: A Summary Report of the Law, Policy and Ethics Conference on HIV Surveillance* 2–3 (CIRA Working paper, Vol. II, Issue 2, 1998), *available at* http://cira.med.yale.edu/law_policy_ethics/newapproaches.doc.
49 INST. OF MED., *supra* note 48, at 21.
50 *Id.* at 22.
51 Much of this section appears in substantially similar form in Michael A. Stoto, *Syndromic Surveillance in Public Health Practice, in* INFECTIOUS DISEASE SURVEILLANCE AND DETECTION 63 (2007). Reprinted with permission from the National Academies Press, Copyright 2007, National Academy of Sciences.
52 *See* James W. Buehler et al., *Syndromic Surveillance and Bioterrorism-Related Epidemics,* 9 EMERGING INFECTIOUS DISEASES 1197, 1197–98 (2003).
53 *Id.*
54 *See supra* Part I.
55 *See* Mandl et al., *supra* note 4, at 143.
56 *See id.* at 142–43.
57 *See* Stoto, *supra* note 4, at 49–50.
58 *Id.* at 51.
59 *Id.* at 54.
60 *See id.*
61 *Id.* at 51.
62 *Id.*
63 *See* Arthur Reingold, *If Syndromic Surveillance Is the Answer, What Is the Question?,* 1 BIOSECURITY & BIOTERRORISM: BIODEFENSE STRATEGY, PRAC., & SCI. 77, 78–81 (2003).
64 *See id.*
65 *See* Standards for Privacy of Individually Identifiable Health Information, 45 C.F.R. §§ 160, 164 (2005); *see also* Health Insurance Portability and Accountability Act of 1996, Pub. L. No. 104-191, 110 Stat. 1936 (codified as amended in scattered sections of 26 U.S.C., 29 U.S.C., 42 U.S.C.).
66 *See* 45 C.F.R. § 164.512(b) (2005) (permitting disclosure of protected health information to public health authorities for certain purposes, such as controlling disease and reporting child abuse or neglect); *see also* Marie C. Pollio, *The Inadequacy of HIPAA's Privacy Rule: The Plain Language Notice of Privacy Practices and Patient Understanding,* 60 N.Y.U. ANN. SURV. AM. L. 579, 591 (2004) (asserting that the Privacy Rule requires no authorization for uses and disclosures required by law or made as part of public health activities).
67 Covered entities include health care plans, health care providers, and health care clearinghouses. 45 C.F.R. § 160.102(2005).
68 *See* ASS'N OF ST. & TERRITORIAL HEALTH OFFICIALS, THE IMPACT OF THE HIPAA PRIVACY RULE ON SYNDROMIC SURVEILLANCE 3 (2004), *available at* http://biotech.

law.lsu.edu/cdc/astho/29724_ASTHO.pdf; Daniel Drociuk, J. Gibson & J. Hodge, Jr., *Health Information Privacy and Syndromic Surveillance Systems*, 53 Morbidity and Mortality Wkly. Rep. (Supp.) 221, 221–25 (2004), http://www.cdc.gov/mmwr/ preview/mmwrhtml/su5301a40.htm.

69 *See* Ass'n of St. & Territorial Health Officials, *supra* note 68, at 3.

70 See 45 C.F.R. § 164.512(b) (2005).

71 *Id.*

72 *See, e.g.,* Ariz. Rev. Stat. Ann. § 36-785 (2007); 20 Ill. Comp. Stat. 2305/2.1 (2007); Iowa Code § 135.145 (2007).

73 *See, e.g.,* Ariz. Rev. Stat. Ann § 36-785 (2007); 20 Ill. Comp. Stat. 2305/2.1 (2007); Iowa Code § 135.145 (2007).

74 *See* Thacker, *supra* note 7, at 4.

75 *See supra* notes 29–30 and accompanying text.

76 *See* Stoto, *supra* note 6, at 5.

77 Frieden, *supra* note 5, at 2059.

78 *See id.*

79 *See id.*

80 *See id.*

81 *See* Robert Steinbrook, *Facing the New Diabetes Epidemic—Mandatory Reporting of Glycosylated Hemoglobin Values in New York City*, 354 New Eng. J. Med. 545, 545 (2006).

82 *See id.* at 546.

83 *Id.* at 546.

84 *See* Lawrence O. Gostin, *Law as a Tool To Facilitate Healthier Lifestyles and Prevent Obesity*, 297 JAMA 87, 88 (2007).

85 *See* Steinbrook, *supra* note 81, at 547.

86 *See* Gostin, *supra* note 84, at 88; Steinbrook, *supra* note 81, at 547.

87 Steinbrook, *supra* note 81, at 545.

88 *See* Ark. Code Ann. §§ 20-7-134 to -135 (2007).

89 *See id.* § 20-7-135.

90 Univ. of Ark. for Med. Sci., Fay W. Boozman Coll. of Pub. Health, *supra* note 5, at 27.

91 *See id.* at 28.

92 *See* Inst. of Med., *supra* note 54, at 19–21 ("[A] system of population-based HIV incidence estimation will provide the most accurate and timely data for these objectives.").

93 *See id.* at 18 ("[C]ontact with a health department after testing HIV-infected was not associated with receipt of timelier care.").

94 *See* Fraser et al., *supra* note 23, at 6146.

95 *Id.* at 6150.

113

PRIVACY, DEMOCRACY AND THE POLITICS OF DISEASE SURVEILLANCE[1]

Amy L. Fairchild, Ronald Bayer and James Colgrove

Source: *Public Health Ethics*, 1:1 (2008), 30–8.

Surveillance is a cornerstone of public health. It permits us to recognize disease outbreaks, to track the incidence and prevalence of threats to public health, and to monitor the effectiveness of our interventions. But surveillance also challenges our understandings of the significance and role of privacy in a liberal democracy. In this paper we trace the century-long history of public health surveillance in the United States situating that history in the context of the broad social, political, and ideological forces that have shaped our conceptions of privacy. Although we focus here on the United States, the debates over privacy that unfolded in the 1960s were repeated in many European nations. The themes we explore here, then, provide a framework for examining the relationship between privacy and public health in other contexts.

The discovery that cases of paralytic polio in 1955 were caused by a single manufacturer of Salk vaccine, the linkage of toxic shock syndrome to tampons in 1979, the identification of the sentinel cases of AIDS on the East and West coasts in the early 1980s, the recognition of West Nile, SARS and Avian flu at the turn of the twenty-first century—all were the result of surveillance systems, through which alert and troubled physicians could communicate with public health officials, enabling identification of an emerging pattern. In each instance, it was such vigilance that permitted the recognition of new threats and the initiation of measures that could limit the human toll.

Surveillance serves as the eyes of public health. Our focus, in this paper, is on the ongoing, name-based reporting of cases of disease to state and local health departments, which is intended to serve as the basis for program planning, implementation and evaluation (Foege *et al.*, 1976; Thacker and Berkelman, 1988). It has provided the foundation for planning, intervention and disease prevention and has been critical of epidemiological research into patterns of morbidity and mortality for a wide variety of diseases and conditions. Registries have been essential for tracking individuals and their conditions over time. Over the course of the twentieth century, public health officials have reiterated the importance of surveillance, arguing that without the name and location of diseased individuals they worked 'in the darkness of ignorance' and might 'as well hunt birds by shooting into every green bush' (Trask, 1915, 2; Biggs, 1907; Trask, 1911; Johnson, 1918; Parnall, 1918). It was the prospect of what surveillance might offer that raised hopes—for the delivery of services, for life-saving knowledge and for protection of individuals and communities. Hermann Biggs, a titanic figure in the history of public health who was perhaps the most important late nineteenth and early twentieth century architect and philosopher of public health surveillance, made it clear that names of the diseased were never collected 'in order to keep clerks or adding machines busy' (Biggs, 1913, 150). Toward the end of the twentieth century, Surgeon General David Satcher would state the value of surveillance as plainly as had Biggs: 'In public health, we can't do anything without surveillance . . . that's where public health begins' (Porter and O'Hara, 2001, B9).

Yet surveillance has also served to trigger the imposition of public health control measures, such as contact tracing, mandatory treatment and quarantine. The threat of such intervention and long-term monitoring has provoked alarm and rendered surveillance suspect for those concerned about the unwarranted exercise of State authority and intrusions on privacy in the name of public health.

Privacy evokes worlds of intimacy. Alan Westin, who had assumed a central role in asserting the significance of privacy in the second half of the 20th century, believed that privacy met a psychological need, not only for exercising autonomy but also for enjoying opportunities for emotional release and self-reflection (Westin, 1967). To protect such vital needs, privacy required a 'sanctuary', a means of 'prohibiting other persons from seeing, hearing, and knowing' (Bostwick, 1976, 1456). Charles Fried, who served as Solicitor General under President Ronald Reagan, wrote of privacy that it was as necessary to 'relations of the most fundamental sort as oxygen is for combustion' (Tribe, 1988, 1302). Privacy thus represented a precious good valued in and of itself.

Disease reporting always involves trade-offs among competing social, ethical and legal interests and values. Whether these tensions become manifest is a matter of historical contingency. If the routinization of surveillance has tended to mask these fundamental conflicts, moments of controversy have illuminated them. Although this paper focuses on the history and ethics of surveillance in the United States, the themes provide a framework for examining the relationship between privacy and public health in other contexts.

Privacy goes public

It was in the 1960s in the shadow of the legacy of McCarthyism that concerns about the status of privacy in America began to mount. Fueling these concerns were technological developments that were laying the groundwork for the transformation of the social organization and control of the most intimate information about individuals. The allure of computerization and the promise of efficiencies that might be achieved through the centralization of vast networks of data were most dramatically illustrated by a 1966 proposal to create a National Data Center, which would have brought together vast amounts of federal information regarding population, housing, wages, jobs, education, health and taxes into a single database. The national outcry it provoked was of sufficient magnitude to scuttle that project, though other aggregation efforts would continue (Hanus and Reylea, 1976). In response to mounting concerns about such data collection, Supreme Court Justice William O. Douglas, who had emerged as privacy's tribune, would declare that 'We are rapidly entering the age of no privacy, where everyone is open to surveillance at all times; where there are no secrets from government.' More ominously, he continued, citizen dossiers were now 'being put on computers so that by pressing one button all the miserable, the sick, the suspect, the unpopular, the offbeat people of the nation can be instantly identified' (*Osborne v. U.S., Lewis v. U.S., Hoffa v. U.S.*, 1966).

It was the potential threat of such abuse that, beginning in 1965, sparked Congressional debates about what personal information to protect and how best to protect it (Regan, 1995). The 92nd and 93rd Congresses witnessed the introduction of nearly 300 bills focused on access to, and dissemination of, personal data (Hanus and Reylea, 1976). And so began a complex process of seeking to set the boundaries on the seemingly relentless impulse to acquire, store and make use of personal data in an effort to limit the threat of the 'dossier society'.

Whatever the effort to determine such limits across a range of policy domains, public health disease reporting continued to enjoy a privileged status, shielded from scrutiny by assumptions about its traditions. Professional codes of medical ethics and their strong precedents for protecting intimate health information provided adequate sanctuary from the broader assault on privacy (Packard, 1964; Westin, 1967). Even the harshest critiques of modern life and computerization assumed that a well-honed, time-tested system of normative constraints provided sufficient protection for privacy in the medical and public health arenas.

That public health seemed to respond to the growing sensitivity about matters of privacy contributed to the sense that the self-governing norms of doctors and public health officials provided sufficient protection. For example, by the mid-1960s, health departments had brought to an end the convention of routinely providing newspapers the names and addresses of individuals diagnosed with dangerous contagious diseases.

Another factor that shielded public health from mounting concerns about the menace of the computer was that health departments were decidedly lagging behind the technological curve. Indeed, in 1962, National Institutes of Health (NIH) and PHS officials called for 'fully exploit[ing]' the potential of computers, particularly when it came to registries of chronic diseases, including tuberculosis and cancer. Health officials continued to manage registry data by filing cards by hand, with the assistance of clerks, or punch card systems. For sizeable registries, matching data, eliminating duplicates and abstracting and summarizing data was a daunting task. 'These problems', federal health officials concluded, 'have contributed to the limited research use of registries to date', allowing for little more than tracking the grossest changes in incidence over time (Phillips *et al.*, 1962, 503–4).

But the increasing scrutiny of the extent of data collection and the adequacy of individual privacy protections ultimately posed challenges to the 'ancient and predominantly honorable traditions' of medical record-keeping. In 1973, the Secretary of the Department of Health, Education, and Welfare's (DHEW) Advisory Committee on Automated Personal Data Systems noted that it was 'not prepared for the discovery that', even when intended only for reporting or research, identifiable health 'data are often totally vulnerable to disclosure' (Department of Health, Education, and Welfare, 1973). Building on the growing imperative to protect the subjects of research that the DHEW committee did not recommend that the subjects who were 'asked to provide data for statistical reporting and research' give their consent. Nor did it suggest independent oversight of this process analogous to either an institutional review board (IRB) or judicial body. Instead the committee insisted that individuals be aware that collection efforts were taking place. Additionally, it sought to protect those records from disclosure as part of its proposed Code of Fair Information Practices (Department of Health, Education, and Welfare, 1973).

Just as the scandal of Tuskegee fueled a searching investigation of research practices, the Watergate revelations animated Congressional debate about how to address the misuse of personal information (Regan, 1995). The resultant 1974 Privacy Act declared, 'Congress finds that the right of privacy is a personal and fundamental right protected by the Constitution of the United States' (Tribe, 1988, 1311). Yet it merely codified the 1973 Department of Health, Education, and Welfare's Code of Fair Information Practices, which had stipulated that there must be 'no personal data record-keeping systems whose very existence is secret', made transparency in record-keeping involving 'personally identifiable' data a requirement, gave individuals access to their records and limited secondary disclosures of data (Regan, 1995, 76; Hanus and Reylea, 1976). The act left public health surveillance untouched. Further, the act noted that agencies may 'take any appropriate action otherwise prohibited' if 'the public health or public safety may be adversely affected or significantly threatened' (Privacy Act of 1974).

Given the Privacy Act's focus on the appropriate uses of data already in hand, it is remarkable that the study commission's mandate posed challenges to conventional assumptions that surrounded disease surveillance activities. At last, concerns about privacy pierced the shield that had protected such efforts from challenge. Drawing on growing calls to limit or perhaps prohibit altogether data acquisition in the absence of a compelling State interest (Michigan Law Review, 1975), the study commissioners were skeptical about the necessity for the reporting of the names of people with diseases. Noting that over half of the states provided no statutory confidentiality protections—indeed, one allowed for the possibility of 'public inspection' and another gave 'citizens the right to examine public records' of disease—the commission called for new privacy regulations. But the commission went further: such reform 'would still not preclude the possibility that subsequent contact by agents of authorities to whom the information is properly reported will startle or embarrass an individual unnecessarily, particularly if the individual is not aware that a report was made.' In a radical departure, it recommended that when any kind of reporting occurred 'pursuant to a statute', public health included, 'the *individual* [be] notified of each such disclosure' (Assistant Secretary for Planning and Evaluation and Secretary of the US Department of Health and Human Services, 1977). [Emphasis added.] While the proposals would have no immediate impact on the practice of surveillance, they were a reflection of the changes in American cultural and political life that had set the stage for the articulation of a constitutional right to privacy that in turn would arm those who were troubled by the failure to subject public health surveillance to careful scrutiny.

From *Griswold v. Connecticut* in 1965, in which the United States Supreme Court upheld the right of physicians to prescribe birth control to married couples on the grounds of privacy, to *Roe v. Wade* and *Doe v. Bolton* in 1973, in which the Court subsequently upheld the right of a woman to make decisions about terminating her pregnancy, America charted a new course on privacy. In commenting on the robust notion of privacy that emerged, a leading Constitutional scholar, Lawrence Tribe, wrote, such rights were derived from both the explicit and implicit provisions of US Constitution and Bill of Rights, involving protection of individuals against the state. He concludes that, 'Wherever located, they have inspired among the most moving appeals to be found in the judicial lexicon' (Tribe, 1988, 1308–9).

The judicial embrace of an invigorated conception of privacy and the emergence of the patients' rights movement would ultimately set the stage for a constitutional challenge to surveillance by public health departments in the 1977 case of *Whalen v. Roe*. In 1972, New York State modified its public health law, requiring the state department of health to keep a computerized record of the names and addresses of anyone prescribed drugs considered to carry a high potential for abuse but also acceptable medical uses. These included opium and its derivatives, methadone, amphetamines and methaqualone, which were used to treat conditions like epilepsy, narcolepsy, hyperkinesias, migraine headaches and schizo-affective disorders. The purpose of the computerized surveillance file—which built on earlier efforts to monitor people who had become addicted to opiates in the course of medical treatment—was to enable health officials to conduct systematic queries of the database so that they could identify individuals obtaining prescriptions from multiple doctors or receiving more than a 30-day prescription per month. They also sought to identify doctors who over- or misprescribed potentially addictive drugs.

Although *Whalen* involved the reporting of prescriptions, not illness, it had a direct bearing on disease notification. Although *physicians* had unsuccessfully challenged public health authority to conduct surveillance decades earlier, for the first time since surveillance had become a centerpiece of public health activity, *individuals* who were the subjects of reporting relied upon the claims of privacy to resist the authority of the State to collect their names.

In 1972 New York State created a computerized surveillance file—which built on earlier efforts to monitor people who had become addicted to opiates in the course of medical treatment—to enable health officials to conduct systematic queries of the database so that they could identify individuals obtaining prescriptions from multiple doctors or receiving more than a 30-day prescription per month. They also sought to identify doctors who over- or misprescribed potentially addictive drugs. Some 41 health department employees had access to the newly centralized files and were authorized to look into cases of potential abuse. Records were to be kept for 5 years in a secure system before being destroyed. Security measures included a locked wire fence and alarm system for the room receiving state copies of the prescriptions by mail. Computer tapes were kept in a locked cabinet and run on a computer that was inaccessible from other terminals (*Roe v. Ingraham*, 1975). Unauthorized disclosure of personal identities carried fines of up to $2000 or 1 year in prison (*Whalen v. Roe*, 1977). Two cases were investigated within the first 20 months of the act (*Roe v. Ingraham*, 1975).

Despite the new course it had charted on privacy in the arena of reproductive rights, in 1977, the US Supreme Court unanimously held that the law was 'manifestly the product of an orderly and rational legislative decision' and that the State's interests in policing drug abuse 'would support a decision to experiment with new techniques for control.' It was up to the legislature to determine whether this endeavor amounted to 'the foolish expenditure of funds to acquire a mountain of useless information' (*Whalen v. Roe*, 1977).

Further, it ruled that because the state did, in fact, safeguard confidentiality and limit access, privacy was not invaded or abridged. In short, the computer storage of records did not of itself represent a violation of privacy. While 'broad dissemination' of intimate personal information would constitute an invasion of privacy, even this, Justice Brennan added in his concurring opinion, could be justified by 'compelling state interests'. The court, however, found no evidence that the law would not be properly administered or enforced. Although it was possible that the record might be subpoenaed and made part of a court record, the court concluded that this remote possibility 'is surely not a sufficient reason for invalidating the entire patient-identification program' (*Whalen v. Roe*, 1977).

The decision rejected the notion that a single chink in the armor of privacy would threaten the clinical relationship. The statute did not, therefore, represent state interference in medical decision-making. While patients might refuse needed medications based on concerns about potential disclosures, the law neither deprived patients of access to needed medications nor prohibited physicians from prescribing them. Indeed, the court noted that the state had processed 100,000 prescriptions per month without inciting any other patient objections. Disclosure of private patient information not only to the state health agencies, but to doctors, hospital personnel and insurance companies might be 'unpleasant', but it was 'an essential part of modern medical practice' even when such 'disclosure may reflect unfavorably on the character of the patient'. And then, critically, the court gave its imprimatur to surveillance more generally, citing venereal disease, child abuse, deadly weapons injuries and fetal death reports, including abortion records, as 'familiar examples' of legitimate public health reporting (*Whalen v. Roe*, 1977).

In ruling in favor of New York State, however, the Court did express sympathy for those who had raised concerns about privacy: 'We are not unaware of the threat . . . implicit in the accumulation of vast amounts of personal information in computerized data banks or other massive government files', wrote Justice Stevens for the court. In a concurring opinion, Justice Brennan affirmed that 'most troubling' in this case was the issue of computer storage. While a new technology did not invalidate otherwise legitimate data collection and storage, he argued, 'The central storage and easy accessibility of computerized data vastly increase the potential for abuse of that information, and I am not prepared to say that future developments will not demonstrate the necessity of some curb on such technology.' In this particular instance, however, such a curb was not necessary because of the state's 'carefully designed program' of 'numerous safeguards' (Brennan, 1977).

Thus, in the first—and still the only—public health surveillance case considered by the US Supreme Court, the tribunal turned back a challenge to the constitutionality of such efforts. But the politics of surveillance would not so easily be resolved. In the last decades of the twentieth century, the potential subjects of surveillance moved beyond the status of plaintiffs to become active participants in the process of policy making, empowered by a new democratic ethos, which was given by the women's rights, gay rights, consumer rights movements and environmental movements. The stage was set for a new kind of popular participation in public health discussions.

The extraordinary two-decade battle that erupted over AIDS exemplified the new political landscape. In the 1990s, gay men and other AIDS advocates resisted efforts to make name-based reporting of HIV a requirement, because of fears of how public health registries could be used to foster discrimination in employment, housing and insurance. Moreover, some feared the possibility that such lists could be used as a prelude to the imposition of isolation or quarantine.

Concomitantly, parents of children with disabilities successfully changed the terms of birth defects surveillance in Minnesota, requiring the state to allow unwilling parents to opt out of reporting. The history of immunization registries likewise underscores the complex forces called into play as efforts were made to extend surveillance from the monitoring of disease or disability to the enforcement of health. Mirroring early concerns about clinical authority, advocates of child health confronted opponents who were concerned about interference with parental autonomy in matters affecting their families. Within the past 2 years, patient advocates within the American Diabetes Association forced New York City health officials to place limits on an initiative to track cases of diabetes.

But just as often, patients with serious illnesses have pushed for better tracking of their conditions when the consequences of notification have been viewed as beneficial. In those cases, the subjects of surveillance have been willing to compromise their own privacy for the sake of some other good. Labor advocates thus supported occupational disease reporting because it would represent a first step to State protections from hazardous worksite conditions. For progressive era public health labor reformer Alice Hamilton, the State was not an 'invading hostile power'. She asserted, 'what is the federal government? It is ourselves—ourselves organized' (Viseltear, 1973, 991). Similarly, cancer activists regarded disease registries as crucial to the much needed research that could lead to more effective prevention and treatment. Thus, the terms of trade have been affected by persistent patterns of social inequality in America. The needs and preferences, when they could be given a voice, were often different for the relatively privileged and those made vulnerable by race or class. Minorities often had to trade privacy for basic health care services. But it was not always social inequality that was determinative. Those for whom access to health services was not a problem traded privacy for advancements in research, which could lead to more sophisticated or effective therapies.

The invocation of the claims of privacy by powerful entities could be the subject of dispute by the less powerful. Labor and its allies, for example, saw the efforts of large employers to thwart surveillance by the National Institute of Occupational Safety and Health as nothing other than a subterfuge, an effort to shield records that would make clear how workers were endangered.

But the articulation of an exacting standard of privacy did not always reflect such interests. When citizens in Illinois and New York sought data from the states' cancer registries as part of their grassroots efforts to understand the environmental risks posed to their communities, health officials demurred, asserting that their legal duty to protect privacy required that they prohibit access to deidentified data when there was even a remote risk of disclosure. The impulse was not to withhold information from the public, but it represented a conception of an obligation to protect private information for a competing public good.

HIPAA: privacy and the public health 'carve-out'

It was when the US sought to chart a new course on the protection of medical privacy that the multiple contextual, social and ideological forces that drove some groups to ardently defend privacy and others to champion surveillance came together. In 1993, as President Bill Clinton proposed a massive transformation of the health care system in order to provide universal coverage, privacy advocates expressed consternation about how medical records could be protected as the management of health care became increasingly centralized. In the wake of the defeat of Clinton's proposals, a broad bipartisan coalition in Washington retained its commitment to the matter of health privacy. The Health Insurance Portability and Accountability Act of 1996 (HIPAA) that resulted was part of a broader effort at administrative simplification for computer-based communication for the health care and insurance industries. Once again, the promise of computers was viewed as requiring protections against the threat that they could pose.

The passage of HIPAA set the stage for a complex political process that would extend over 6 years as the Congress struggled with the act's mandate to craft a medical privacy statute. The act called upon the Secretary of Health and Human Services to provide the Congress with recommendations regarding what such legislation should entail. If the Congress failed to pass a privacy law within 3 years, the secretary would be charged with issuing federal privacy regulations.

Despite the enormous significance of the passage of HIPAA and the vast array of issues that the act placed on the congressional agenda, it was unambiguous about the nearly sacrosanct status of public health surveillance. The salience of privacy and the urgency of moving to protect patients against intrusions that threatened the confidentiality of their medical communications could not undermine state requirements that physicians, laboratories and health care institutions report by name those affected by notifiable conditions. And so a public health 'carve-out'—all the more striking given the contemporaneous conflicts over other kinds of surveillance—was central to Secretary Donna Shalala's guidance to Congress as it began to consider privacy legislation: consent would not be sought for acquiring personally identifiable information or sharing such data within and among state and local health departments. Those recommendations mirrored the explicit intent of Congress: 'Nothing in this part', declared HIPAA, 'shall be construed to invalidate or limit the authority, power or procedures established under any law proving for the reporting of disease or injury, child abuse, birth or death, public health surveillance or public health investigation or intervention' (Health Insurance Portability and Accountability Act of 1996, 1178b).

The text of the Shalala's proposals incorporated sweeping language about the importance of both privacy for democratic life and surveillance for the protection of the welfare of society. Citing President Clinton's concerns— 'technology should not be used to break down the wall of privacy and autonomy; free citizens are guaranteed in a free society'—the secretary deplored the prevailing legal structure that 'did not effectively control information about individuals' health'. At the same time she termed public health surveillance 'the single most important tool for identifying infectious disease that are emerging, [or] are causing serious public health problems. . . .' (Confidentiality of Individually-Identifiable Health Information, 1997).

For advocates of privacy who had long labored for national standards to protect medical records from inspection by law-enforcement officials, researchers who had not secured informed consent, or marketers who sought to troll medical records for potential customers, the political opportunity opened by the passage of HIPAA was one that had to be seized. In testimony before a congressional committee the Health Privacy Project's Janlori Goldman, a stalwart of the medical privacy movement, declared:

> Over the course of a person's lifetime the record of one's life collected through . . . largely unregulated networks can make real the 'womb to tomb dossier' . . . If people continue to lose control over the ability to choose when, what and to whom to divulge personal sensitive information they will be unwilling to step forward and fully participate in society, fearing unwanted disclosure, judgments, discrimination, surveillance stigma and loss of jobs, credit, housing and family. . . . A new framework is needed that intertwines the values of protecting patient privacy and fostering health care initiatives.

Hoary assumptions about a tension between privacy and public welfare had to be abandoned, Goldman claimed. Securing privacy was not antithetical to good research, good health care and public health. Rather, privacy served as the foundation for such goods. What subverted privacy would subvert such goods (Goldman, 1998).

In the ultimately fruitless effort of the Congress to craft a privacy legislation in the 3 year period specified in HIPAA, a plethora of bills were drafted. In all but two the public health carve-out remained virtually intact.

With the failure of Congress to meet its own deadline for the passage of privacy legislation, Secretary of Health and Human Services, Donna Shalala, issued comprehensive guidelines in 2000 for public comment. More than 50,000 responses were received. Strikingly, the regulations covering public health surveillance drew relatively little hostile attention. Even those organizations that might have been expected to use the occasion of the formal comment period to underscore concerns about how public health surveillance compromised the right to privacy chose not to do so. In fact, when the American Civil Liberties Union raised objection to a proposed provision that would have permitted the release of health records to government health data systems involved in policy, planning and management functions, it did so by pointing without challenge to the public health carve-out (Weich and Weiss, 2000). A strategic decision had been made that the HIPPAA privacy regulations were not the context within which to wage a battle over public health surveillance.

If civil liberties organizations elected not to make the extension of HIPAA to public health surveillance a priority, advocacy organizations for people with particular illnesses struck a different posture and sought to vigorously defend the traditions of public health reporting. In so doing they revealed that, however important the protection of privacy was, it was not always preeminent. As the American Cancer Society underscored the importance of cancer registries, it warned about dire consequences if potential subjects of name-based case reporting were able to opt out (Dominique, 2000). The March of Dimes, originally focused on the prevention of polio and more recently committed to confronting birth defects, noted that while 'deidentified' information might be appropriate for some public health functions, the failure to collect names in birth defects registries would subvert the critically important ability to undertake necessary follow-up investigations. 'While the individual has an interest in maintaining the privacy of his or her health information', said the organization, 'Public health authorities have an interest in the overall health and well being of the entire population' (Weiss, 2000).

The final privacy regulations were published on March 27, 2002 after 6 years of contention. Despite lingering concerns about gaps in the new protective regime, many privacy advocates saw the moment as a milestone. A year earlier in testimony before a Congressional subcommittee Janlori Goldman said, 'Americans should be proud of what Congress set in motion with HIPAA and with the thoughtful and deliberate way in which [the Department of Health and Human Service] carried out its Congressional mandate' (Goldman, 2001).

An enduring tension

However cherished, privacy is not, at the beginning of the twenty-first century an absolute value—nor has it ever been. It is 'constantly forced into accommodation with other important individual or societal values', as one commentator observed (Flaherty, 1972, 21). Nowhere is this clearer than in the context of disease surveillance.

Public health evokes deep concerns about protection from naturally occurring and socially created threats to well-being and even survival. From the last decades of the nineteenth century, when systematic disease notification was described as the 'eyes' of public health, to the last decades of the twentieth century, when the image of 'radar' was used to describe the role of disease reporting, public health officials and other proponents of surveillance underscored the necessity of limiting privacy in the name of the common good. When challenged by doctors or by patients, public health officials argued that the claims of the individual had to yield to the needs of the collective and that protecting communal health, safety and security was preeminent. They offered assurances that disease registries were not public records, open to general examination, and, indeed, pressed for laws to shield the identities of those reported. On occasion they were compelled to compromise, agreeing to receive coded reports in lieu of names, as in the case of venereal diseases for much of the twentieth century and HIV at its end. Sometimes they compromised the principle of universal reporting by granting individuals the opportunity to remain beyond the scope of a particular registry. This was true both for immunization and birth defects registries, where staunch opponents in some US states were able to convince legislators that surveillance opened the door to either unacceptable government interference with parental autonomy or, particularly in the case of congenital defects, inappropriate stigmatization of both children and parents.

The capacity to give voice to claims for privacy or State protection determined the occurrence, scope and outcome of clashes over surveillance. Concerns about government and corporate threats to personal information emerged at the very movement that a host of social movements had begun to challenge medical paternalism. Indicative of this broad transformation was adoption of the Code of Fair Information Practices in 1973 and passage of the Privacy Act the following year. For the first time, individuals had the right to know when personal information was included in government files. This right, in turn, created the prospect for a broadened public role in determining what records were created, how they were used, and what methods were employed to protect them from unwarranted disclosure.

It was not only the efforts of those with disease that served to define the new era. Organizations such as the March of Dimes and the American Cancer Society became forceful institutional advocates for surveillance efforts. Those who were seized by concerns about invasions of privacy or overly intrusive government also joined the fray. They could be hostile to the social welfare functions of the State or committed to civil liberties as vital to a democratic order. Although antagonists on one level, libertarians at opposite ends of the political spectrum might come together around the politics of surveillance. A range of diverse groups have consistently pushed back against disease surveillance: the American Civil Liberties Union; antivaccination activists; libertarian organizations committed to thwarting a protective role for government; and grass-roots religious groups expressed concern that birth defects surveillance was a prelude to abortion.

As they faced the recurrence of old debates or fundamentally new challenges posed by surveillance, privacy advocates have argued that good public health and the protection of privacy need not be seen as in tension. Indeed, proponents of privacy in the latter part of the twentieth century have invoked instrumental claims when warning of the consequences of intrusions on what they viewed as sacrosanct domains. They have sought to demonstrate that limits on the confidentiality of the doctor–patient relationship would subvert not only clinical care but also the public's health. In the context of anxieties about how national security considerations could narrow the purchase of privacy, Janlori Goldman wrote, 'the codification of vague promises that power will not be abused and good judgment will be employed ignore the historical lesson that during a crisis, privacy and civil liberties are given little weight in the balancing of competing law enforcement, national security, and commercial interests. Preserving public health and protecting privacy can—and must—go hand in hand' (Goldman, 2005, 526–27). But alarm extends beyond the issue of national defense. Goldman has worried, too, about efforts to draw clinical medicine and public health into a closer relationship. While arguing for the most stringent protections of surveillance data, she, like other privacy advocates, has asserted that it is essential to address the question of whether an effective public health always requires the use of personally identifiable reports. There is no necessary trade-off, in this view, between a robust commitment to privacy and good public health practice.

The history of disease reporting over the course of the past century brings us to a very different conclusion. We believe that it is clear that there is an enduring tension between privacy and public health surveillance (Ingelfinger and Drazen, 2004; McKenna, et al., 2004). This tension is sometimes expressed in bitter controversies. On other occasions, those who believe that their needs require greater surveillance have themselves decided to trade some degree of privacy.

Enduring tension, however, does not necessarily produce either inevitable or unending conflict. Just as the emergence of disputes is historically contingent, so too is the arrival of their conclusions. On occasion, debates about disease notification have come to an end because one side has triumphed over the other. In other instances compromise has, at least temporarily, removed the source of contention. Finally, conflicts have come to an end when opponents' interests have shifted to what they considered other more urgent matters such as access to treatment. Thus, for example, the bitterly contested issue of HIV name reporting in the US largely came to a close when advocates recognized that it was critical for securing funding for AIDS programs (Ornstein, 2006). But the end of conflict does not foreclose the possibility of renewed debate. Even apparently settled matters involving surveillance may be subject to challenge.

But, however controversies have been settled, it is nonetheless clear that they have always involved a tradeoff between privacy and public health action. In the end, we believe that it is not possible to resolve the conflict between privacy and greater public health surveillance, nor do we think it desirable to do so. The vitality of democratic communities necessitates an ongoing effort to negotiate and renegotiate the boundaries between privacy— society's 'limiting principle' (Tribe, 1988)—and public health—which, at its best, has sought to expand the role of government as a guardian against disease and suffering.

Note

1 The authors are with Daniel Wolfe, the authors of Searching Eyes: Privacy, the State, and Disease Surveillance in America (University of California Press, 2007).

References

Assistant Secretary for Planning and Evaluation and Secretary of the U.S. Department of Health and Human Services. (1977). *Personal Privacy in an Information Society: The Report of the Privacy Protection Study Commission*, Chapter 7, Record-Keeping in the Medical-Care Relationship. http://aspe.hhs.gov/datacncl/1977privacy/c7.htm, accessed December 2, 2004.

Biggs, H. (1907). Compulsory Notification and Registration of Tuberculosis. Address before the National Association for the Study and Prevention of Tuberculosis. *Transactions of the National Tuberculosis Association*, **3**, 39–56.

Biggs, H. (1913). Venereal Diseases in New York. *Monthly Bulletin of the Department of Health of the City of New York*, **3** (6), 141–154.

Bostwick, G. L. (1976). Comment: A Taxonomy of Privacy: Repose, Sanctuary, and Intimate Decision. *California Law Review*, **64**, 1447–1483.

Brennan. (1977). concurring opinion, *Whalen v. Roe*, 429 U.S. 589; 97 S. Ct. 869; 51 L. Ed. 2d 64.

Confidentiality of Individually-Identifiable Health Information. (1997). Recommendations of the Secretary of Health and Human Services, pursuant to section 264 of the Health Insurance Portability and Accountability Act of 1996. Submitted to The Committee on Labor and Human Resources and the Committee on Finance of the Senate and the Committee on Commerce and the Committee on Ways and Means of the House of Representatives. September 11, http://aspe.hhs.gov/admnsimp/pvcrec0.htm, accessed December 2, 2004.

Department of Health, Education, and Welfare. (1973). Records, Computers and the Rights of Citizens: Report of the Secretary's Advisory Committee on Automated Personal Data Systems. http://aspe.os.dhhs.gov/datacncl/1973privacy/c3.htm, accessed December 2, 2004.

Dominique, H. (2000). Comments on Notice of Proposed Rulemaking: Standards for Privacy of Individually Identifiable Health Information, Use, and Disclosures for Public Health Activities, Comment #18087, February 17.

Flaherty, D. H. (1972). *Privacy in Colonial New England*. Charlottesville, VA: University Press of Virginia.

Foege, W. H., Hogan, R. C., and Newton, L. H. (1976). Surveillance Projects for Selected Diseases. *International Journal of Epidemiology*, **5** (1), 29–37.

Goldman, J. (1998). Testimony before the House Committee on Ways and Means, March 24. http://www.healthprivacy.org/usr_doc/33816%2Epdf, accessed April 18, 2006.

Goldman, J. (2001). *Assessing HIPAA: How Federal Medical Record Privacy Regulations Can Be Improved*. Testimony before the House Committee on Energy and Commerce, Subcommittee on Health, March 22. http://energycommerce.house.gov/reparchives/107/hearings/03222001Hearing134/Goldman182.htm, accessed April 18, 2006.

Goldman, J. (2005). Balancing in a Crisis? Bioterrorism, Public Health and Privacy. *Journal of Health Law*, **38** (3), 481–527.

Hanus, J. J., and Reylea, H. C. (1976). A Policy Assessment of the Privacy Act of 1974. *American University Law Review*, **25** (3), 555–593.

Health Insurance Portability and Accountability Act of 1996. (1996). Public Law 104–91.

Ingelfinger, J. R., and Drazen, J. M. (2004). Registry Research and Medical Privacy. *New England Journal of Medicine*, **350** (14), 1452–3.

Johnson, P. (1918). Social Hygiene and the War. *Social Hygiene*, **4**, 91–137.

McKenna, M. T., Wingo, P. and Gibson, J. J. (2004). Letter to the editor. *New England Journal of Medicine*, **351** (6), 613.

Michigan Law Review. (1975). Project: Government Information and the Rights of Citizens. *Michigan Law Review*, 73 (6–7), 971–1340.

Ornstein, C. (2006). California May Start Tracking HIV Patients by Name. *Los Angeles Times*, 18 January, B3.

Osborne v. U.S., Lewis v. U.S., Hoffa v. U.S. 385 U.S. 323, 87 S. Ct. 439 (1966).

Packard, V. (1964). *The Naked Society*. New York: David McKay.

Parnall, C. (1918). An Outline of the Present Scope of Public Health Administration in Cities. *Journal of the Michigan State Medical Society*, **17**, 393–96.

Phillips, W. Jr, Gorwitz, K., and Bahn, A. K. (1962). Electronic Maintenance of Case Registers. *Public Health Reports*, **77** (6), 503–510.

Porter, R. and O'Hara, J. (2001). Better Health Through Better Data. *San Diego Union-Tribune*, June 22, B9.

Privacy Act. (1974). 5 U.S.C. § 552A, section p, no. 3., www.usdoj.gov/oip/privstat.htm, accessed December 2, 2004.

Regan, P. M. (1995). *Legislating Privacy: Technology, Social Values, and Public Policy*. Chapel Hill, NC and London: University of North Carolina Press.

Roe v. Ingraham. (1975). 403 F. Supp. 931.

Thacker, S. B. and Berkelman, R. L., Public Health Surveillance in the United States. *Epidemiologic Reviews*, **10**, 164–90.

Trask, J. W. (1911). A Digest of the Laws and Regulations of the Various States Relating to the Reporting of Cases of Sickness. *Public Health Bulletin*, **45**, 5–10.

Trask, J. W. (1915). Vital Statistics: A Discussion of What They Are and Their Uses in Public Health Administration. *Public Health Reports*, **30**, Supplement 2.

Tribe, L. (1988). *American Constitutional Law*, 2nd ed. Mineola, NY: Foundation Press.

Viseltear, A. J. (1973). Emergence of the Medical Care Section of the American Public Health Association, 1926–1948. *American Journal of Public Health*, **63** (11), 986–1007.

Weich, R. and Weiss, C. (2000). Comments of the American Civil Liberties Union on the Proposed Rule of the U.S. Department of Health and Human Services regarding Standards for Privacy of Individually Identifiable Health Information. February 17.

Weiss, M. (2000). Comments on Notice of Proposed Rulemaking: Standards for Privacy of Individually Identifiable Health Information, Use, and Disclosures for Public Health Activities, Comment #17685, February 17.

Westin, A. (1967). *Privacy and Freedom*. New York: Antheneum.

Whalen v. Roe. (1977). 429 U.S. 589; 97 S. Ct. 869; 51 L. Ed. 2d 64.

114

THROUGH THE QUARANTINE LOOKING GLASS

Drug-resistant tuberculosis and public health governance, law, and ethics

David P. Fidler, Lawrence O. Gostin and Howard Market

Source: *Journal of Law, Medicine & Ethics* (Winter, 2007), 616–28.

Introduction

Dramatic events involving dangerous microbes often focus attention on isolation and quarantine as policy instruments. The incident in May–June 2007 involving Andrew Speaker and drug-resistant tuberculosis (TB) joins other communicable disease crises that have forced contemplation or actual application of quarantine powers. Implementation of quarantine powers, which encompasses authority for both isolation and quarantine actions, is important not only for the handling of a specific event but also because the use of such authority provides a window on broader issues of public health and the legal rules, ethical principles, and governance systems that support it. Debates about quarantine powers reflect political and social attitudes about public health that often tell us more about this policy endeavor than acts of isolation and quarantine themselves.

This article uses the Speaker incident to explore how isolation and quarantine authority provides a lens through which to assess public health commitments, competencies, and capabilities. We describe the Speaker incident itself, which played out in national and global media in revealing and disturbing ways. Much of the controversy focused on the application of federal quarantine powers, so the incident connects to the larger political, governance, and legal issues quarantine authority raises. We analyze quarantine powers by reflecting on some historical manifestations and by exploring the current stale of isolation and quarantine authority in public health law and ethics in the United States. The article's final section looks beyond the question of quarantine powers in the United States to consider global implications of the Speaker case, including the challenges of addressing the growing problem of drug-resistant TB.

The Andrew Speaker incident: background and overview

Background to the Speaker incident: rise of concern about drug-resistant TB

For many in the United States, Andrew Speaker's odyssey represented their first exposure to multi-drug resistant TB (MDR-TB) and extensively drug-resistant TB (XDR-TB) and the potential need for public health officials to exercise quarantine powers to address these threats. While TB is treatable with the first-line drugs isoniazid and rifampicin, MDR-TB is resistant to them.[1] XDR-TB is also resistant to isoniazid and rifampicin, to any fluoroquinolone, and to at least one of the three injectable second-line drugs: amikacin, kanamycin, and capreomycin.[2]

Speaker's situation did not, however, arise in a vacuum. Public health awareness about the growing MDR-TB and XDR-TB problems was rising in 2006, as evidenced by the issuance of a global alert about XDR-TB by the World Health Organization (WHO).[3] This alert came after analysis of new surveillance data that indicated XDR-TB was a widespread and growing problem around the world, but particularly in Eastern Europe, South Africa, and Asia.[4] The data on XDR-TB's prevalence, and the lack of treatment options, raised the question whether public health authorities needed to consider compulsory measures, including isolation, to contain its spread and impact on population health.[5] This issue was significant enough for the WHO to issue, in January 2007, guidance on human rights and involuntary detention as an XDR-TB control strategy.[6] Thus, even before Speaker became a household name, public health officials were worried about MDR-TB and XDR-TB and were, in connection with XDR-TB, anticipating the possible need to exercise quarantine powers against infected persons.

Overview of the Speaker incident[7]

In the same month, January 2007, in which the WHO issued guidance on involuntary detention and XDR-TB, Andrew Speaker underwent a chest X-ray and CT scan, which revealed an abnormality in his lungs. His sputum smear tested, however, negative for TB. In March 2007, Speaker had a diagnostic bronchoscopy, tested positive for TB, and was prescribed a standard regimen of first-line anti-TB drugs. The positive TB result was confirmed in April, and the Georgia Public Health Laboratory (GPHL) began testing Speaker's TB isolate for susceptibility. On April 25, Speaker reported to the Fulton County TB Clinic and advised it of his plans for traveling overseas in May, and the clinic asked for the susceptibility testing to be expedited. The next day the GPHL began susceptibility testing, and the U.S. Centers for Disease Control and Prevention (CDC) received samples for susceptibility testing on April 27.

Between April 30 and May 9, susceptibility testing at the GPHL indicated that Speaker had MDR-TB. On May 10, Speaker, his family, private physician, and the Fulton County Health Department (FCHD) met to discuss his MDR-TB infection. At this meeting, Speaker was told not to undertake his international travel, scheduled to start on May 14. Also on May 10, the FCHD began to review legal options for restricting a patient infected with untreated MDR-TB, and, on May 10–11, the Georgia Department of Public Health (GDPH) and the CDC discussed options for restricting the travel of a person harboring untreated MDR-TB. On May 11–12, the FCHD attempted to hand-deliver a written advisory to Speaker concerning his MDT-TB infection but could not locate him.

Unbeknownst to any public health official, Speaker had, on May 11, advanced his departure date from May 14 to May 12, and he departed Atlanta for Europe on May 12. On May 18, the GPDH notified the CDC that Speaker had traveled internationally, and the CDC began the effort to locate him in Europe. CDC tests of samples from Speaker indicated on May 22 that he had XDR-TB, and, on the same, day, U.S. Customs and Border Protection initiated a nation-wide border alert for Speaker based on information provided by the CDC.

The CDC tracked Speaker down in Rome on May 22 (May 23 in Rome), informed him of the XDR-TB diagnosis, and told him not to travel on commercial aircraft because he posed a significant threat to other people. Speaker indicated to the CDC he would stay in Rome while the CDC explored options for managing his infection and transporting him back to the United States. However, Speaker instead flew to Prague, Czech Republic on the morning of May 24, and then flew from Prague to Montreal later that day. On May 24, unable to locate Speaker, the CDC requested that the U.S. Transportation Security Administration issue an order to prevent Speaker from boarding any U.S. bound flight, and the CDC notified the Italian Ministry of Health. Also on May 24 (May 25 in Europe), the U.S. Department of Health and Human Services (DHHS) notified the WHO that Speaker's situation may constitute a public health emergency of international concern under the International Health Regulations (2005).

On May 25, Speaker re-entered the United States from Canada by automobile, and, despite being aware of the border alert, the border guard allowed Speaker into the United States. The CDC located Speaker by cell phone in New York State, ascertained Speaker's location, and ordered him to drive to Bellevue Hospital in New York City for clinical evaluation and federally mandated isolation. Upon arrival at Bellevue Hospital, the CDC served him a provisional federal quarantine order – the first such federal order since

1963. Speaker was isolated in a secure ward, where he underwent clinical evaluation to ascertain the status of his infection. After interviewing Speaker, the CDC began the process of contact tracing passengers on flights taken by Speaker, which required the cooperation of international, federal, state, and local health authorities.

While under the federal isolation order, Speaker elected to return to Atlanta on May 28, after which time his story began to appear in the media. Undisputed facts about his case, and diverging positions aired in the media, gained attention, and generated controversy about what had happened, what had gone wrong, and who was to blame. Through his own resources, Speaker was transferred on May 31 from Atlanta to the National Jewish Medical Center (NJMC) in Denver for treatment of his XDR-TB. The CDC rescinded the federal isolation order on June 2 when the Denver County Health Department placed Speaker under its isolation order.

Controversy about Speaker's case continued after his transfer to Denver because his statements did not mirror the facts presented in the CDC briefings. These divergent positions were aired in hearings Congress held on June 6, at which CDC Director Dr. Julie Gerberding and Speaker (via telephone) testified. Controversy about the Speaker incident flared again when the NJMC and CDC announced on July 3, after the results of further tests, that Speaker did not have XDR-TB but MDR-TB. This announcement gave Speaker the opportunity to continue his criticism of the CDC. It also required the CDC to explain why the new diagnosis would not have changed actions vis-à-vis Speaker because of the danger untreated MDR-TB poses to public health, especially with respect to long-distance air travel.

Media attention was drawn back to the case when tort litigation against Speaker was initiated in Montreal in mid-July by passengers who traveled with him from Prague to Montreal. Speaker had surgery at the end of July 2007 to remove a portion of a lung infected with the MDR-TB, and, after the surgery, he was declared non-contagious and released from the NJMC on July 26, after which he flew home to Atlanta.

Quarantine in history: more than a medical matter

Recitation of key facts in the Speaker case does not, however, capture the emotions, controversies, and accusations it generated. The believed presence of XDR-TB, the scope of the international travel, the behavior and claims of the infected individual, the reactions of public health authorities, the failure of border control mechanisms, and the utilization of federal quarantine powers combined to heighten the significance of this incident for every level of public health policy and practice.

For many, the exercise of federal quarantine powers was the development that brought all the elements of the episode into focus and generated questions for individuals, public health officials, and governments. Although the application of federal public health authority does not exhaust the complexities of Speaker's case, the use of federal quarantine power became this incident's gravitational pull in terms of attention and controversy. The exercise of such authority became important not only in its own right but also because it highlighted issues confronting public health that deserve greater attention. The exercise of quarantine power in the Speaker case became a looking glass for examining public health law, ethics, and governance in the early 21st century.

The idea that involuntary detention for public health purposes reflects political and social phenomena beyond breaking the chain of pathogen transmission is, of course, not new. One common response to epidemics, across time and national boundaries, has been the use of individual and group control measures.[8] If we look at isolation and quarantine actions as part of the progression of an epidemic, we can detect impulses that often help shape it. These include the following: (1) avoiding the ill, or those perceived to be ill, particularly if the disease is thought to be contagious; (2) negotiations over how experts and the community at large understand the disease, especially in terms of cause, prevention, and amelioration; (3) the complex political, economic, and social battles that guide or obstruct a community's efforts to respond to the epidemic; and (4) the extent to which ethnicity and perceptions about a social group associated with a disease frame the responses that shape control measures aimed at individuals or communities.

Many societies have responded to visitations of contagious diseases by avoiding and isolating the ill. The Old Testament records involuntary detention and social distancing and their corresponding sanitary procedures,[9] including the use of the ram's horn or shofar, traditionally sounded during the Jewish High Holidays, to signal a case of diphtheria or other contagious disease in the community. In ancient Greece, the writings of Thucydides (c. 460–c. 400 B.C.) and Hippocrates (c. 460–c. 370 B.C.) demonstrated that Greek societies attempted to avoid contact with the contagious.[10] The Roman authority on medicine, Galen of Pergamon, warned that specific diseases made it "dangerous to associate with those afflicted."[11] In A.D. 549, the Byzantine emperor Justinian enacted one of the first laws requiring restraint and isolation of travelers from regions where the plague was known to be raging. Similar forms of detention for plague directed against sailors and foreign travelers were also practiced in seventh-century China and other parts of Asia and Europe during the Middle Ages. Not surprisingly, these quarantine actions recognized the relationship between epidemic disease transmission and human movement and migration.[12]

The word *quarantine* originates from the Italian words *quarantenara* and *quaranta giorni*, which referred to the 40-day period during which Venice isolated ships before their goods, crew, and passengers could disembark during the plague-ridden days of the 14th and 15th centuries. In about 1374, Venice enacted its 40-day quarantine regulation, and, in 1403, the municipality established the first maritime quarantine station, or lazaretto, on the island of Santa Maria di Nazareth. From medieval times on, shutting the gates of a city or port to those suspected of being ill, and isolating sick people within, represented the best, and often the only, means for stemming an epidemic.

The growth of international commerce and travel during the Renaissance and the subsequent three centuries contributed to the spread of infectious diseases around the globe. To prevent the entry of contagion, sanitary cordons (literally a ring of armed soldiers guarding against entry of diseased persons) and quarantines were used in France, Britain, Austria, German, Russia, and other European and Asian nations from the 14th through 19th centuries.[13] By the mid-1800s, in response to devastating cholera and plague epidemics imported into Europe from Turkey and Egypt, and the economic burdens created by different national quarantine systems, European nations with the strongest commercial or colonial interests began to engage in international cooperation.[14] These efforts included attempts to harmonize quarantine policies, a process aided by the emergence of the germ theory of disease in the late 19th century.[15] Commencing in 1851, these International Sanitary Conferences continued well into the 20th century,[16] generated the first uses of international law for public health purposes, and led to the creation of the first international health organizations.[17]

The history of quarantine, including attempts to harmonize its application, demonstrates that quarantine has had different meanings to different peoples. The interdependence of the medical understanding of contagious diseases and social control measures seems intuitive, but past epidemics suggest a more complex interaction of medical knowledge and the actual practices of disease control, revealing in the application of isolation and quarantine a complex mixture of scientific, political, economic, and social factors. This mixture reveals much about the way a society constructs its responses to infectious diseases and thus makes isolation and quarantine measures a reflection of a community's make-up and evolution.

During the first half of the 19th century in the United States, for example, the notion that a microbe might cause an epidemic was not widely accepted by medical experts or the public. Anti-contagionists held that changes in the atmosphere and environmental sources of filth (e.g., human and animal waste) caused diseases. Under this view, the "cure" was cleaning up the environment. The anti-contagionist perspective conveniently supported the opposition of merchants and traders to the burdens national quarantine systems imposed on commerce. Similarly, some countries favoring the theory of contagion and the practice of quarantine worried about the growth of the economic and political power of nations, such as Great Britain, seeking to pare back the impact of national quarantine policies on their international economic activities.

Medical and economic dogma and political interests were not, however, always anti-quarantine. Scientific doctrine and economic attitudes proved more flexible in practice than in theory. Isolation and quarantine measures were often mounted by governments that did not subscribe to the germ theory of disease and that supported trade expansion. Epidemics of yellow fever in the United States during the late 18th and early 19th centuries – a period of devout anti-contagionism among medical professionals – often inspired some quarantine regulations.

When studying the history of social control measures as responses to epidemics in the United States over the past two centuries, a strong leitmotif is the use of such measures as a medical rationale to isolate and stigmatize groups reviled for other reasons. David Musto asserts that isolation and quarantine actions constitute more than the mere "marking off or creation of a boundary to ward off a feared biological contaminant lest it penetrate a healthy population" because one cannot consider quarantine as merely disease control without minimizing the "deeper emotional and broadly aggressive character" of a policy that separates persons from the community.[18] The blame, stigma, and ostracism associated with isolation and quarantine are especially real for diseases linked to the poor, aliens, or the disenfranchised: "When an epidemic illness hits hardest at the lowest social classes or other fringe groups, it provides that grain of sand on which the pearl of moralism can form."[19]

Quarantine governance and public health law and ethics

The manner in which quarantine powers have been intertwined with religious, political, economic, and social practices, interests, values, and prejudices makes quarantine authority an important governance topic. Isolation and quarantine involve the compulsory application of public authority to individuals or groups and, thus, these acts create tensions between protecting population health and respecting individual autonomy and dignity. These tensions stimulate the heightened interest isolation and quarantine trigger, as seen in Speaker's case. Principles in public health law and ethics shape the governance task of managing those tensions, and these principles provide insight into how societies organize and perceive the use of the power to implement isolation and quarantine measures.

Isolation and quarantine distinguished and defined

From a governance perspective, delineation of the different facets of a government's quarantine powers is important legally and ethically. These powers encompass the authority to detain persons involuntarily for public health purposes. Although isolation and quarantine are often used interchangeably, they are not the same. Quarantine involves the restriction of the movement of persons who have been exposed, or potentially exposed, to infectious disease, during the period of communicability, to prevent transmission of infection during the incubation period.[20] Quarantine seeks to prevent the spread of dangerous, highly contagious pathogens, such as smallpox, plague, and Ebola fever, particularly if medical countermeasures are ineffective or unavailable.

Isolation involves separating, for the period of communicability, *known* infected persons from the community so as to prevent or limit the transmission of the infectious agent.[21] Modern science and medicine can usually detect whether a person has an infectious condition. Accordingly, isolation often is the action taken rather than quarantine, and this outcome is particularly true for TB. Isolation is, where possible, linked to treatment, including directly observed therapy (DOT) for TB, which the detaining authority offers to, or imposes on, persons subject to isolation orders.[22]

Jurisdictional complexities involving isolation and quarantine actions

Public health authorities possess a variety of powers to restrict the autonomy or liberty of persons who pose a public health threat because they are infected with, or have been exposed to, dangerous, contagious pathogens. These authorities can direct individuals to discontinue risk behaviors (e.g., "cease and desist" orders), compel them to submit to physical examination or treatment, and detain them using public health or criminal justice powers.[23]

Legal authority to exercise these powers in the United States can be found at local, state, and federal levels. These jurisdictional levels generate federalism questions: what level of government may apply which rules in what situations? Answers to these questions depend on the origin and extent of the public health threat. Local and state laws apply if the threat is confined to a city, county, or state. If the threat is imported from a foreign country, or if the pathogen is being transmitted across state lines, then federal law applies.

When it comes to the exercise of isolation and quarantine powers, reality tends to be messier than the conceptual realm. Public health officials need clear lines of authority in emergency situations, often the moments when isolation and quarantine measures might be required. Unfortunately, confusion about which level of government should take the lead often occurs, thus revealing the ability of quarantine powers to spotlight difficulties federalism poses for public health. The Speaker case illustrates the complexities federalism presents because the episode involved local, state, and federal authorities in the effort to try to ensure that Speaker did not pose a public health threat.

State authority for isolation and quarantine

State governments derive isolation and quarantine authority within their borders from the police power,[24] and all states have such powers, although actual laws vary significantly. In many cases, disparate legal regimes pose no problem for the exercise of quarantine powers, but lack of uniformity can adversely affect coordination between local, state, and federal officials. Typically, public health detention powers are found in laws that address sexually transmitted diseases,[25] TB,[26] and other communicable diseases.[27] When a novel disease emerges, states sometimes find they lack legal power to act, as occurred with severe acute respiratory syndrome (SARS), because their laws have not expressly authorized action for the emerging threat.[28] This problem has highlighted how many state laws on isolation and quarantine are antiquated scientifically and in their protection of civil liberties.[29] The need to consider the exercise of quarantine powers more seriously has exposed aspects of the relationship between law and public health, particularly its neglect.

Recent threats have, however, forced state governments to review their quarantine powers. President Bush stressed, for example, the need for states to analyze their isolation and quarantine laws as a homeland security priority.[30] The review process has included nearly 40 states adopting, in whole or in part, the Model State Emergency Health Powers Act (Model Act), which was drafted after the anthrax attacks in 2001 in order to provide states with a tool with which to assess their legal preparedness for public health emergencies. A controversial aspect of the Model Act centered on its compulsory powers provisions, which revealed the power of isolation and quarantine measures to concentrate political and legal attention on public health challenges. The importance of the legal review and reform processes has been underscored since 2001 through events such as the SARS outbreak and legal preparedness activities related to pandemic influenza. The imposition of an isolation order on Speaker has again stimulated states to scrutinize their isolation and quarantine laws.

Federal authority for isolation and quarantine

Questions about isolation and quarantine measures also reveal substantive and procedural problems in federal law. The federal government's isolation and quarantine authorities are contained in the Public Health Service Act,[31] which grants the Secretary of DHHS authority to make and enforce regulations to prevent the introduction, transmission, or interstate spread of communicable diseases into or within the United States and to apprehend, detain, or conditionally release individuals infected with "quarantinable diseases" specified by executive order.[32] The president has, to date, identified cholera, diphtheria, infectious TB, plague, smallpox, yellow fever, viral hemorrhagic fevers (e.g., Lassa, Marburg, Ebola, Crimean-Congo, South American), SARS, and pandemic influenza as quarantinable diseases under federal law.[33] The federal government can enforce isolation and quarantine measures by criminal sanctions or judicial injunction.[34]

The Speaker case exposed problems with federal isolation and quarantine authorities. For example, federal powers apply to a specific list of diseases, thus depriving the federal government of flexibility when responding to novel threats. The listing approach requires the president, for each new threat, to make the disease quarantinable through executive order, which is what transpired when SARS and fears of pandemic influenza emerged. Federal law also fails to authorize the federal government to use a range of measures, including individual screening, contact tracing, and DOT, all of which may be useful in dealing with disease threats, including MDR-TB and XDR-TB. Finally, federal law does not include appropriate due process protections because it does not give individuals subject to isolation or quarantine orders a right to a fair hearing. The Constitution requires an impartial hearing for persons under civil confinement or detention,[35] including those infected with TB.[36] Current federal quarantine authority is, therefore, arguably unconstitutional.

Constitutional and judicial review of isolation and quarantine actions

The Constitution does not mention isolation or quarantine. However, in discussing imports and exports, it recognizes the right of states to execute inspection laws, which are incident to the exercise of quarantine powers.[37] In 1824, Chief Justice Marshall suggested that states have authority to quarantine under their police powers.[38] Since Marshall's time, courts have upheld the exercise of compulsory detention powers for public health purposes.[39] This jurisprudence reveals deference by the courts, which usually regarded isolation or quarantine actions as presumptively valid. Judicial activity in U.S. public health has primarily been driven by challenges mounted against the exercise of quarantine powers during epidemics, notably TB.[40]

In these cases, the judiciary asserted some control over isolation and quarantine measures. Following the "rule of reasonableness" established in *Jacobson v. Massachusetts*, courts insisted that use of quarantine powers be justified by "public necessity," and that states may not act "arbitrarily" or "unreasonably."[41] Courts have also set four limits on isolation and quarantine authority:

1. The subject must be actually infectious or have been exposed to infectious disease Health authorities must demonstrate that individuals are infected or were exposed to disease and, thus, pose a public health risk.[42] Courts have been reluctant to stigmatize citizens in the absence of reasonable proof.[43] Thus, isolation of persons with TB must demonstrate that they are infectious, or would be infectious if they stopped taking their medication.

2. Safe and habitable conditions Courts periodically insisted on safe and healthful environments for those subject to isolation or quarantine because public health powers are designed to promote well-being, and not to punish.[44] The Supreme Court held, for example, that civilly committed mental patients have a right to "conditions of reasonable care and safety," "freedom from bodily restraint," and "adequate food, shelter, clothing and medical care."[45]

This requirement is germane to the case of Robert Daniels, an XDR-TB patient who has been compulsorily isolated in the "jail" section of a hospital in Maricopa County, Arizona. The American Civil Liberties Union filed suit arguing that Maricopa County denied Daniels constitutionally required habitable conditions because he is regularly stripped searched, not allowed to exercise or go outside, and denied basic amenities such as regular visits and access to a telephone.[46] While this lawsuit was pending, Maricopa County transferred Daniels to NJMC, where Speaker was being treated.

3. Justice and non-discrimination A federal court struck down one of the most invidious measures in public health history in *Jew Ho v. Williamson.*[47] At the turn of the 20th century, public health officials quarantined an entire district of San Francisco, ostensibly to contain an epidemic of bubonic plague, but the quarantine operated exclusively against the Chinese community. The federal court held the quarantine unconstitutional because health authorities acted with an "evil eye and an unequal hand."[48] *Jew Ho* forms part of the leitmotif noted earlier – that governments are sometimes tempted to use their quarantine powers as an instrument of prejudice against vulnerable individuals or populations.[49] This theme informed controversies that arose during MDR-TB outbreaks in the 1990s when New York and other cities targeted the mentally ill, drug addicts, and homeless persons for DOT, while affluent groups were spared.[50]

The Supreme Court has described civil commitment as a "massive curtailment of liberty."[51] Although civil commitment cases often concern the mentally ill, the principles these cases enunciate also apply to isolation and quarantine measures. As one court explained in the context of TB, "[I]nvoluntary commitment for having communicable tuberculosis impinges on the right to liberty, full and complete liberty, no less than involuntary commitment for being mentally ill."[52] Some courts have required actual danger to the public as a condition of civil confinement in both mental health[53] and infectious disease[54] contexts. For example, in the case of *In re City of New York v. Doe*, the court required clear and convincing evidence of the person's inability to complete a course of TB medication before permitting compulsory restraint.[55]

Given the strict standard of review, courts could require the government to demonstrate that there are no less restrictive alternatives to achieve the public health objective.[56] The government might have to offer, for example, DOT as a less restrictive alternative to isolation. However, the government does not have to go to extreme, or unduly expensive, means to avoid confinement[57] because the judiciary is not likely to require the state to provide economic incentives and benefits to induce compliance. In the TB context, New York City health officials argued that they could not be required "to exhaust a pre-set, rigid hierarchy of alternatives that would ostensibly encourage voluntary compliance . . . regardless of the potentially adverse consequences to the public health."[58]

4. Procedural due process Persons subject to detention are entitled to procedural due process. As the Supreme Court recognized, "[T]here can be no doubt that involuntary commitment to a mental hospital, like involuntary confinement of an individual for any reason, is a deprivation of liberty which the State cannot accomplish without due process of law."[59] The procedures required depend on the nature and duration of the restraint.[60] Certainly, the government must provide elaborate due process for long-term, non-emergency, detention.[61] Noting that "civil commitment for any purpose constitutes a significant deprivation of liberty,"[62] and that commitment "can engender adverse social consequences," the Supreme Court has held that, in a civil commitment hearing, the government has the burden of proof by "clear and convincing evidence."[63]

In *Greene v. Edwards*, the West Virginia Supreme Court held that persons with infectious TB are entitled to similar procedural protections as persons with mental illness facing civil commitment.[64] These safeguards include the right to counsel, a hearing, and an appeal. The invasion of liberty occasioned by detention, the implications of erroneously finding a person dangerous to the public's health, and the value of procedures in determining complex facts justify rigorous procedural protections.

The limits courts have placed on government use of isolation and quarantine reflect not only the threat posed by pathogenic microbes but also the rule of law. Whether and how isolation and quarantine are applied reveals aspects of politics, economics, and cultures in many societies. The relationship of quarantine powers to the rule of law is similarly instructive about governance strategies to balance individual rights and the public good. Jurisprudence on isolation and quarantine reveals a way of thinking about how political power should be, at each step, subject to legal rules and procedures.

Revising federal law: the proposed new federal quarantine regulations

Having effective public health powers operating within the rule of law encourages constant re-evaluation of legal rules and procedures, and the exercise of quarantine powers provides a powerful way to stimulate interest in such re-assessment. In keeping with this dynamic, and recognizing the problems with existing federal quarantine powers, the DHHS proposed new regulations in 2005,[65] which provide another opportunity to evaluate how quarantine powers can protect public health within the rule of law.

1. Scope of federal power The Public Health Service Act authorizes the "apprehension, detention, or conditional release" of individuals for diseases listed by executive order. The proposed regulations would broaden the scope of federal power because they define "ill person" to include the conditions linked with quarantinable diseases, such as fever, rash, persistent cough, or diarrhea. This approach embodies an important shift that allows the federal government to adapt and respond more rapidly to novel threats. This empowerment has the corresponding effect, under the rule of law, of heightening scrutiny of how the federal government exercises such broader powers.

2. Due process   The proposed regulations empower federal public health officers to quarantine ill passengers provisionally for up to three business days. Thereafter, officers can order full quarantine on grounds of a reasonable belief that a person or group is in the qualifying stage of a quarantinable disease. The length of quarantine may not exceed the period of incubation and communicability, which can range from weeks to months, as in the case of XDR-TB. During quarantine, officers can offer individuals prophylaxis or treatment, but a refusal can result in continued deprivation of liberty.

Under the revised regulations, the federal government does not intend to provide individuals with hearings during provisional quarantine, but individuals can request an administrative hearing to contest a full isolation or quarantine order. Interestingly, the federal government offered Speaker the right to a hearing in connection with its isolation order, a right not found in the federal quarantine regulations (FQR) that applied to Speaker. It appears as if the federal government sought guidance on the right to a hearing from the proposed revisions to the FQR, which suggests recognition of the constitutionally suspect lack of due process in the existing regulations.

The administrative process in the proposed FQR includes a hearing that comports with elements of due process: notice, hearing before a public official, and right of communication with counsel. Still, deficiencies remain: (1) individuals must request a hearing, which may delay or prevent independent review for those who do not understand or take the initiative; (2) the proceedings can be informal, even permitting hearings based exclusively on written documents; and (3) the hearing officer may be a federal public health employee who makes a recommendation to the CDC Director. The European Court of Human Rights found a similar scheme in violation of Article 5 of the European Convention on Human Rights, which requires a hearing by a "court."[66]

As of this writing, the federal government has not adopted the proposed revisions to the FQR. The public health community supported many proposed revisions, but critics worried about invasions of liberty, privacy, and property that the revised regulations would arguably produce. Due process experts disliked the lack of any hearing for provisional isolation or quarantine and the failure to provide more robust due process for those subject to full isolation or quarantine orders. Privacy advocates worried that the proposed regulations would undermine the protection of an individual's personal and health information. The travel industry criticized the costs the proposed rules would impose on it to collect, protect, and transmit passenger information.

The Speaker case has re-focused attention on the unadopted revision of the FQR and may, thus, contribute to new efforts by the federal government to update this fundamental set of federal public health laws. Whether the Speaker incident proves a powerful catalyst for such a significant change remains to be seen.

The ethics of involuntary detention of persons with infectious TB

Civil libertarians draw attention to the substantial personal interests affected by isolation and quarantine actions. Individuals subjected to confinement lose their liberty, suffer invasions of individual rights (including loss of privacy), face stigma because their community is aware of the infectious danger they pose, may have their bodily integrity compromised because of compulsory treatment, and endure socio-economic burdens such as the loss of income during their detention, and possibly thereafter. These issues are important individual interests, and state and federal governments should do all they can to mitigate these harms, as well as ensure that they exercise quarantine powers in accordance with the rule of law.

From an ethical perspective, the fact that detention is a drastic measure does not mean that isolation and quarantine are inappropriate. Persons with infectious, or potentially infectious, TB pose a risk to the public. TB can be spread by airborne droplets among persons congregated in confined spaces for extended durations, including long-haul travel in a bus, metro, train, or plane, as well as in group settings such as mental institutions, hospitals, nursing homes, and homeless shelters. Consequently, detention may be ethically justifiable, and provided that it is necessary, it is used as a last resort and applied in keeping with notions of human dignity and natural justice.

Speaker's case is an example of an ethically appropriate exercise of isolation powers. He had infectious TB. Whether his infectious TB was XDR-TB, as previously thought, or MDR-TB, as eventually diagnosed, does not change the ethical (or the epidemiological) analysis. Public health authorities first attempted less restrictive measures, such as treatment combined with "no travel" instructions, but twice Speaker did not comply and put the health of others at risk. Further, the federal government offered Speaker the opportunity to exercise his right to a hearing, a right guaranteed by the Constitution if not the existing FQR. In each location of isolation, Speaker has been detained in highly therapeutic, humane facilities. Disagreements about the "facts" of his case[67] do not change these conditions of ethical confinement: a dangerous infectious condition, less drastic alternatives attempted, procedural due process offered, and humane conditions of isolation.

In the ethical realm, Speaker's behavior raises another facet of the dynamics of isolation and quarantine in modern societies – the responsibility of individuals in the increasingly challenging and dangerous world of public health governance. Isolations of infectious TB patients typically, if not universally, involve failure of the patients to heed instructions concerning treatment or interacting with other persons.[68] Government officials do not today blow the ram's horn to warn of contagious disease in the community, but warnings about appropriate individual behavior are given in ways that trigger ethical, if not legal, responsibilities of citizens to do no harm to others.

Beyond quarantine: global dimensions of the Speaker incident and drug-resistant tuberculosis

Although the exercise of quarantine powers made the Speaker incident a window on public health ethics, law, and governance, the incident involved other features that deserve mention. In particular, the Speaker case was international in scope and implications, which draws attention to the global dimensions of this incident and the problem of drug-resistant TB. This section considers global facets of the Speaker case.

The global dimensions of U.S. public health law

The Speaker case highlighted issues in U.S. public health law related to the international aspects of his travels. Speaker's plans to travel to Europe after being diagnosed with MDR-TB raised the issue about which governmental body can prevent a U.S. citizen from leaving the United States. Local, state, and federal public health officials conferred about ways to prevent Speaker's international travel, but he had already left the country. While local and state powers are still relevant, the international context of foreign travel suggests that the relevant constitutional level of government to prevent persons with dangerous, contagious pathogens from traveling internationally from the United States is the federal government. Federal law presently does not contain provisions relating to preventing disease exportation; rather, the focus is on preventing or addressing disease importation.[69] Existing statutory law and the proposed revisions to the FQR do not address the need to empower the federal government to prevent persons who pose a public health risk from traveling outside the country.

A second international issue centered on the federal government's attempts to convince Speaker to report to Italian public health authorities after the CDC made the XDR-TB diagnosis. Did the federal government have the legal authority to enforce quarantine powers on U.S. nationals present in the territory of other nations? Generally, the federal government cannot enforce federal law outside the United States unless Congress intended for the law in question to have such extraterritorial effect,[70] and no such intent can be located in federal public health law. In fact, Congress prescribed that the FQR shall be applicable only to individuals coming into a state or possession of the United States from a foreign country or possession.[71]

The U.S. border guard's failure to detain Speaker upon his re-entry into the United States, despite the border guard knowing of the CDC's health alert, has generated concerns about the inability of U.S. border control systems to handle public health threats. These concerns existed prior to the Speaker incident, as illustrated by an Institute of Medicine study on the system of quarantine stations at U.S. ports of entry.[72] The study argued that this system "no longer protect[s] the US population against microbial threats of public health significance that originate abroad."[73] Improving public health capabilities at U.S. borders requires improved leadership, laws and regulations, infrastructure, training, interagency collaboration, and funding. How Speaker's re-entry into the United States was handled indicates both some progress (e.g., the CDC health alert reached the border control personnel in time to detain Speaker) and continuing problems (e.g., Speaker was allowed into the country without compliance with the health alert) that require more political commitment and financial resources from Congress.

Drug-resistant tuberculosis and the new International Health Regulations

The World Health Assembly adopted the revised International Health Regulations in May 2005 (IHR 2005),[74] and the Speaker incident intersected with this new international agreement immediately before the IHR 2005 entered into force on June 15, 2007. The IHR 2005 appeared in three ways in the Speaker case. First, the federal isolation order against Speaker connected to ongoing debate about whether compulsory measures may increasingly be needed to contain the global spread of XDR-TB. The IHR 2005 acknowledges that isolation and quarantine may be required, but the regulations oblige States Parties to implement compulsory measures consistently with scientific, public health, and human rights principles. In that regard, the WHO has issued guidance on involuntary detention for XDR-TB control in light of human rights norms.[75]

Second, although the IHR 2005 was not yet in force, the United States formally notified the WHO that the Speaker situation may constitute a public health emergency of international concern (PHEIC) pursuant to the IHR 2005.[76] This action connected to debates within the WHO about whether XDR-TB cases could trigger the IHR 2005's notification obligations by being disease events that might constitute a PHEIC. Prior to the Speaker incident, a WHO task force asserted that XDR-TB is not a PHEIC because notification of such an emergency is "only intended for outbreaks of acute disease, rather than the 'acute-on-chronic' situation of . . . XDR-TB."[77] Alarm about the XDR-TB problem suggests that this pathogen is dangerous and is of global concern, perhaps creating the need for State Parties to the IHR 2005 to follow the U.S. lead in viewing this pathogen within the scope of the surveillance obligations of the regulations.

Third, CDC Director Julie Gerberding drew attention to the IHR 2005 in comments to the press about the Speaker episode. Gerberding stated that the IHR 2005 contained "wonderful statements of principles" but do not provide "operational details of things like who should pay to move a patient, or who should care for a patient."[78] She also stated, "I think a central question that we will be grappling with is, whose patient is it?"[79]

These comments about the IHR 2005 require scrutiny. The IHR 2005 was never designed to answer the kinds of questions Gerberding raised. In addition, the application of general principles of international law answers these questions. Under the principle of sovereignty, the country in which a patient is physically located has primary responsibility for public health activities and persons within its territory and jurisdiction. Under the principle of non-intervention in the domestic affairs of states, the home country of a patient has no right to intervene in the sovereign affairs of the host country concerning public health.

These principles mean that, in Speaker's case, Italy had primary responsibility for public health vis-à-vis Speaker when he was physically present in Italy, and that the United States could ask, but not legally require, that Italy undertake certain actions regarding Speaker. Absent a specific treaty obligation, Italy was under no duty to transport Speaker back to the United States or pay for such transport. If the United States wanted to transport him home, then the United States would be responsible for the costs of such transport. Under international law, no confusion existed about whose patient Speaker was while he was in Italy, or what country had to pay to transport him home.

Easy legal answers do not, of course, produce funds and capabilities to transport a U.S. citizen thought to be infected with XDR-TB back to the United States, particularly when federal agencies had no plans or resources to execute such an action. Whether and how to generate such funds and capabilities are, however, national policy questions not issues of international law or lacunae in the IHR 2005.

The global problem of drug-resistant tuberculosis

In many ways, Speaker is an atypical victim of infection by drug-resistant TB. As the statistics about XDR-TB suggest, the typical XDR-TB patient is not white, affluent, highly educated, well traveled, and media savvy. The change in Speaker's diagnosis from XDR-TB to MDR-TB does not lessen the problems both forms of drug-resistant TB present to population health, particularly those in transition and developing countries with high rates of HIV/AIDS and weak to non-existent public health systems. The "looking glass" quarantine powers provide for examining public health law, governance, and ethics generates much less guidance when contemplating how to respond to the global march of drug-resistant TB. The task list for altering this trajectory is formidable: improve surveillance for drug-resistant TB; craft better non-pharmacological interventions that protect population health and respect individual rights; develop more accurate diagnostic technologies to improve the ability to distinguish MDR-TB from TB and XDR-TB from MDR-TB; control the synergy between HIV/AIDS and TB more effectively; invent new antibiotic treatments; and build health infrastructure capacity to handle these tasks. How these tasks will be accomplished is something on which neither the Speaker case nor the quarantine looking glass provides much insight.

Conclusion

In all likelihood, the Speaker episode will enter the annals of public health history as a case involving an incredible set of facts and sequence of events, as well as deeper implications for public health and the governance systems, legal rules, and ethical principles that support this policy endeavor. This article focused on how the use of federal quarantine power against Speaker connects to, and helps illustrate, the ways in which isolation and quarantine reveal features about the place of public health in the politics, economics, cultures, and governance philosophies of societies.

The Speaker case teaches valuable lessons about challenges public health governance confronts from the individual to the global level, especially in the context of a pathogen increasingly resistant to the tools of modern medicine. Speaker's odyssey focused attention on the threat XDR-TB and MDR-TB present, but heightened awareness is not a policy response. An episode at the end of July 2007 involving two persons infected with drug-resistant TB who ignored instructions from Taiwanese authorities not to travel and flew from Taiwan to China anyway[80] is a reminder that the individual, national, and international governance challenges that Speaker's case highlighted have not disappeared as his story fades from the front pages.

Speaker's case also provides lessons on the importance of public health law on isolation and quarantine because, like the threats of bioterrorism and pandemic influenza, this case forced another round of scrutiny of state, federal, and international legal rules that relate to compulsory measures. This case emphasizes the need for the federal government to finalize its proposed revision of the FQR in such a way that the new regulations provide a stronger basis for federal action in the future. The trajectory of drug resistance in TB will, in all likelihood, confront public health officials with the need to consider compulsory measures for individuals infected with highly dangerous and contagious pathogens. Public health principles and the rule of law encourage the crafting of the best possible legal framework before more threats emerge.

Finally, Speaker's case illustrates the limits of public health law and the importance of ethical obligations in communicable disease contexts permeated with danger, uncertainty, and fear. Public health's reliance on voluntary compliance with treatment and travel instructions involving TB patients depends on such patients understanding the public health consequences of their behavior. The likelihood of increased cases of drug-resistant TB only heightens the individual's ethical role in public health governance.

With respect to public health governance, law, and ethics, what the quarantine looking glass reveals has changed over time. Through this looking glass, we see how societies cope with transformations in scientific understandings of pathogenic threats and political commitments to individual rights. But these changes, and the historical distance between the first Venetian lazerello and Speaker's isolation, do not diminish what we can learn from the focus quarantine powers bring to bear on our political, social, and personal understandings of population and individual health.

References

1. Centers for Disease Control and Prevention, "Tuberculosis: General Information, July 2007," *available at* <http://www.cdc.gov/tb/pubs/tbfactsheets/tb.htm> (last visited September 19, 2007); Centers for Disease Control, "Multi-Drug Resistant Tuberculosis (MDR-TB), July 2007," *available at* <http://www.cdc.gov/tb/pubs/tbfactsheets/mdrtb.htm> (last visited September 19, 2007).
2. Centers for Disease Control and Prevention, "Extensively Drug-Resistant Tuberculosis (XDR-TB), July 2007," *available at* <http://www.cdc.gov/tb/pubs/tbfactsheets/xdrtb.htm> (last visited September 19, 2007).
3. World Health Organization, "XDR-TB Update 2006: Message from the WHO Director of Stop TB, Dr. Mario Raviglione," *available at* <http://www.who.int/tb/xdr/dir_stb_message_25sep06/en/index.html> (last visited September 19, 2007).
4. World Health Organization, "Emergence of XDR-TB," *available at* <http://www.who.int/mediacentre/news/notes/2006/np23/en/index.html> (last visited September 19, 2007).
5. See, e.g., J. A. Singh, R. Upshur, and N. Padayatchi, "XDR-TB in South Africa: No Time for Denial or Complacency," *PLoS Medicine* 4, no. 1 (2007): e50, *available at* <http://www.pubmedcentral.nih.gov/articlerender.fcgi?artid=1779818> (last visited September 19, 2007).
6. World Health Organization, "WHO Guidance on Human Rights and Involuntary Detention for XDR-TB Control, Jan. 24, 2007," *available at* <http://www.who.int/tb/xdr/involuntary_treatment/en/index.html> (last visited August 14, 2007) [hereinafter cited as WHO].
7. This description of the Speaker case is taken from a number of sources, including the Centers for Disease Control and Prevention, "Interim Timeline: Actions to Protect Public Health – Investigation of U.S. Traveler with XDR TB," *available at* <http://www.cdc.gov/tb/XDRTB/timeline.htm> (last visited August 14, 2007) and J. L. Gerberding, Director, Centers for Disease Control and Prevention, *Recent Case of Extensively Drug Resistant TB: CDC's Public Health Response,*

Testimony before the Committee on Appropriations Subcommittee on Labor, Health and Human Services, and Education, U.S. Senate, June 6, 2007, *available at* <http://www.cdc.gov/washington/testimony/6-06-07_XDR_TB_testimony.html> (last visited September 19, 2007).

8. See, e.g., C. F. Mullet, "A Century of English Quarantine, 1709–1825," *Bulletin of the History of Medicine* 23, no. 6 (1949): 527–45; G. Rosen, *A History of Public Health* (New York: MD Publications, 1958); O. P. Schepin and W. V. Yermakov, eds., *International Quarantine* (Madison, CT: International Universities Press, 1991): at 125–58; C.-E. Winslow, *The Conquest of Epidemic Disease: A Chapter in the History of Ideas* (New York: Hafner, 1967).

9. F. H. Garrison, *A History of Medicine*, 4th ed. (Philadelphia: W. B. Saunders, 1928): at 60. There are many doctrines for avoiding contagion in the Five Books of Moses. For a useful description, see *id.*, at 67–70; Winslow, *supra* note 8, at 79–82; E. Lieber, "Skin Diseases: Contagion and Sin in the Old Testament," *International Journal of Dermatology* 33, no. 8 (1994): 593–95.

10. Hippocrates, *Nature of Man* (chap. 9), in G. E. R. Lloyd, ed., *Hippocratic Writings* (London: Penguin, 1978): at 266; Thucydides, *The Peloponnesian Wars* (New York: Penguin, 1978). Analysis of the concept of infection as understood by the ancient Greeks is offered by O. Temkin, "An Historical Analysis of the Concept of Infection," in O. Temkin, *The Double Face of Janus and Other Essays in the History of Medicine* (Baltimore: Johns Hopkins University Press, 1977): at 456–71.

11. See Winslow, *supra* note 8, at 74.

12. W. W. Ford, "A Brief History of Quarantine," *Johns Hopkins Hospital Bulletin* 25 (1914): 80–86; W. H. McNeill, *Plagues and Peoples* (Garden City, NY: Doubleday/Anchor, 1976): at 124–35.

13. G. E. Rothenberg, "The Austrian Sanitary Cordon and the Control of the Bubonic Plague: 1710–1871," *Journal of the History of Medicine and Allied Sciences* 28, no. 1 (1973): 15–23.

14. N. Howard-Jones, "Origins of International Health Work," *British Medical Journal* (May 6, 1950): 1032–37.

15. D. P. Fidler, *International Law and Infectious Diseases* (Oxford: Clarendon Press, 1999): at 35–42.

16. See Schepin and Yermakov, *supra* note 8, at 9–27; Rothenberg, *supra* note 13; N. Howard-Jones, "The Scientific Background of the International Sanitary Conferences, 1851–1938," *WHO Chronicle* 28 (1974): 229–47, 369–84, 414–26, 455–70, 495–508.

17. See Fidler, *supra* note 15, at 21–57.

18. D. F. Musto, "Quarantine and the Problem of AIDS," *Milbank Quarterly* 64, Supplement 1 (1986): 97–117, at 98.

19. *Id.*, at 106.

20. D. L. Heymann, ed., *Control of Communicable Diseases Manual*, 18th ed. (Washington, D.C.: American Public Health Association, 2004): at 621.

21. *Id.*, at 617–19.

22. R. Coker, "Just Coercion? Detention of Nonadherent Tuberculosis Patients," *Annals of the New York Academy of Science* 953b, no. 1 (2001): 216–23.

23. L. O. Gostin, *Public Health Law: Power, Duty, Restraint*, 2nd ed. (New York/Berkeley: Milbank Memorial Fund and University of California Press, forthcoming 2008).

24. *Gibbons v. Ogden*, 22 U.S. 1, 25 (1824); *Hennington v. Georgia*, 163 U.S. 299 (1896).

25. National Conference of State Legislatures, *Sexually Transmitted Diseases: A Policymaker's Guide and Summary of State Laws* (Denver: National Conference of State Legislators, 1998): at 85–91.

26. H. Markel, *When Germs Travel: Six Major Epidemics That Have Invaded American Since 1900 and the Fears They Unleashed* (New York: Pantheon Books, 2005): at 13–46; L. O. Gostin, "Controlling the Resurgent Tuberculosis Epidemic: A Fifty State Survey of Tuberculosis Statutes and Proposals for Reform," *JAMA* 269, no. 2 (1993): 256–61.

27. L. O. Gostin, S. Burris, and Z. Lazzarini, "The Law and the Public's Health: A Study of Infectious Disease Law in the United States," *Columbia Law Review* 99, no. 1 (1999): 59–118.

28. National Conference of State Legislatures, "Overview of State Public Health Preparedness," January 28, 2002, *available at* <http://www.ncsl.org/programs/press/ 2002/snapshot.htm#quarantine> (last visited September 19, 2007).

29. D. S. Reich, "Modernizing Local Responses to Public Health Emergencies: Bioterrorism, Epidemics, and the Model State Emergency Health Powers Act," *Journal of Contemporary Health Law and Policy* 19, no. 2 (2003): 379–414.

30. White House, *National Strategy for Homeland Security*, July 2002, *available at* <http://www.whitehouse.gov/homeland/book/nat_strat_hls.pdf> (last visited September 19, 2007).

31. 42 U.S.C. §§ 264–272 (2005).

32. 42 U.S.C. § 264 (2005).

33. Executive Order no. 13,295, *Revised List of Quarantinable Communicable Diseases*, April 4, 2003, *available at* <http://www.cdc.gov/ncidod/sars/executiveorder040403.htm> (last visited September 19, 2007); Executive Order: Amendment to Executive Order no. 13,295, *Relating to Certain Influenza Viruses and Quarantinable Communicable Diseases*, April 1, 2005, *available at* <http://www.whitehouse.gov/news/releases/2005/04/20050401-6.html> (last visited September 19, 2007).

34. 42 U.S.C. §271 (2005); 28 U.S.C §1331 (2005).

35. *O'Connor v. Donaldson*, 422 U.S. 563, 580 (1975).

36. *Greene v. Edwards*, 263 S.E.2d 661 (W. Va.1980).

37. U.S. Constitution, art. I, § 10, cl. 2. See *Brown v. Maryland*, 25 U.S. (12 Wheat.) 419 (1827); W. Cowles, 'State Quarantine Laws and the Federal Constitution," *American Law Review* 25, no. 1 (1891): 45–53.

38. See *Gibbons, supra* note 24, at 205.

39. D. J. Merritt, "The Constitutional Balance Between Health and Liberty," *Hastings Center Report* 16, no. 6 (1986): S2–S10; D. J. Merritt, "Communicable Disease and Constitutional Law: Controlling AIDS," *New York University Law Review* 61, no. 5 (1986): 739–99.

40. See *Greene, supra* note 36 (requiring the same due process for TB detention as for civil commitment for mental illness); *In re Halko*, 54 Cal. Rptr. 661 (Cal. Ct. App. 1966) (upholding detention for TB); *Jones v. Czapkay*, 6 Cal. Rptr. 182 (Cal. Ct. App. 1960) (refusing to find county health officials liable for secondary case of TB after initial case left quarantine); *White v. Seattle Local Union No. 81*, 337 P.2d 289 (Wash. 1959) (holding that union did not wrongfully remove officer who was confined for TB).

41. *Jacobson v. Massachusetts*, 197 U.S. 11 (1905).

42. *Smith v. Emery*, 42 N.Y. Supp. 258, 260 (1896) ("The mere possibility that persons may have been exposed to disease is not sufficient. . . . They must have been exposed to it, and the conditions actually exist for a communication of the contagion."); *Arkansas v. Snow*, 324 S.W.2d 532 (Ark. 1959) (holding that commitment for TB treatment requires a finding that the patient is a danger to the public health).

43. See, e.g., *State v. Snow*, 324 S.W.2d 532, 533 (Ark.1959) (officials have to provide evidence of active TB to justify involuntary commitment).

44. *Kirk v. Wyman*, 65 S.E. 387, 391 (S.C. 1909) ("even temporary isolation in [a pesthouse] would be a serious affliction"). *Souvannarath v. Hadden*, 116 Cal. Rptr. 2d 7 (Cal. Ct. App. 2002) (upholding state law forbidding detainment of noncompliant MDR-TB patient in a jail); *Benton v. Reid*, 231 F.2d 780 (D.C. Cir. 1956) (persons with infectious disease are not criminals and should not be detained in jails); but see *Ex parte Martin*, 188 P.2d 287 (Cal. 1948) (upholding quarantine in county jail despite the fact that it was overcrowded and had been condemned).

45. *Youngberg v. Romeo*, 457 U.S. 307, 315, 319, 324 (1982). See also *City of Milwaukee v. Ruby Washington*, Supreme Court of Wisconsin, 2007 WI 104, July 17, 2007, *available at* <http://www.wicourts.gov/sc/opinion/DisplayDocument.html?content=html&seqNo=29744> (last visited September 19, 2007) (holding that Wisconsin law authorizes "confinement to a jail . . . provided the jail is a place where proper care and treatment will be provided and the spread of disease will be prevented").

46. A. Kairi, 'ACLU Brings Suit Against Arizona for Quarantine of Tuberculosis Patient: Robert Daniels Reportedly Strip Searched Regularly and Denied Visits with Family," June 1, 2007, *available at* <http://www.associatedcontent.com/article/265889/aclu_brings_suit_against_arizona_for.html> (last visited September 19, 2007).

47. *Jew Ho v. Williamson*, 103 F.10 (C.C.N.D. Cal. 1900).

48. *Id.*, at 24.

49. D. Markovits, "Quarantines and Distributive Justice," *Journal of Law, Medicine & Ethics* 33, no. 2 (2005): 323–44.

50. N. N. Dubler, R. Bayer, and S. Landeshan et al., *The Tuberculosis Revival: Individual Rights and Societal Obligations in a Time of AIDS* (New York: United Hospital Fund, 1992).

51. *Vitek v. Jones*, 445 U.S. 480, 491 (1980).

52. See *Greene, supra* note 36, at 663.

53. See, e.g., *Suzuki v. Yen*, 617 F.2d 173, 178 (9th Cir. 1980).

54. See *Souvannarath, supra* note 44, at 11–12 (discussing California statute that requires a finding that a TB patient is both a danger to the public health and substantially unlikely to complete treatment before the patient can be confined for treatment); *In re Halko, supra* note 40, at 661 (holding that isolation of person with TB does not deprive a person of due process if the health officer has reasonable grounds to believe he is dangerous).

55. *In re City of New York v. Doe*, 614 N.Y.S.2d 8, 9 (App. Div. 1994). Sec also *City of York v. Antoinette R.*, 630 N.Y.S.2d 1008 (N.Y. Sup. Ct. 1995) (upholding detention for TB treatment upon clear and convincing evidence that less restrictive means would not result in successful treatment).

56. *Id.* (*In re City of New York*), at 8; *City of Milwaukee, supra* note 45. The most developed expression of the right to less restrictive alternatives is in mental health cases. See, e.g., *Lessard v. Schmidt*, 349 F. Supp. 1078 (E.D. Wis. 1972).

57. See *City of Milwaukee, supra* note 45 (holding that it was appropriate for the courts to consider cost when determining the place of confinement); L. O. Gostin, "The Resurgent Tuberculosis Epidemic in the Era of AIDS: Reflections on Public Health, Law, and Society," *Maryland Law Review* 54, no. 1 (1995): 1–131.

58. Response to Public Comments Concerning Proposed Amendments to Section 11.47 of the Health Code 7, March 2, 1993.

59. See *O'Connor, supra* note 35, at 580 (Chief Justice Berger, concurring).

60. *Washington v. Harper*, 494 U.S. 210 (1990).

61. See, e.g., *In re Ballay*, 482 F. 2d 648, 563–66 (D.C. Cir. 1973).

62. *Addington v. Texas*, 441 U.S. 418. 426 (1979).

63. *Id.*, at 425.

64. See *Greene, supra* note 36, at 661.

65. Department of Health and Human Services, Control of Communicable Diseases (Proposed Rule), 42 CFR Parts 70 and 71 (November 30, 2005).

66. "Case of *X v. United Kingdom*: Confinement of Persons of Unsound Mind in the United Kingdom," in V. Berger, ed., *Case Law of the European Court of Human Rights, Volume I: 1960–1987* (Dublin: Round Hall Press, 1989): at 167.

67. See, e.g., J. Schwartz, "Tangle of Conflicting Accounts in TB Patient's Odyssey," *New York Times*, June 2, 2007, at A1.

68. See, e.g., *City of Milwaukee, supra* note 45 (affirming the compulsory isolation of TB patient who failed to follow treatment instructions).

69. 42 U.S.C. §264 (2005).

70. *Equal Employment Opportunity Commission v. Arabian American Oil Co.*, 499 U.S. 244 (1991).

71. 42 U.S.C. §264 (2005).

72. Committee on Measures to Enhance the Effectiveness of the CDC Quarantine Station Expansion Plan for U.S. Ports of Entry, *Quarantine Stations at Ports of Entry: Protecting the Public's Health* (Washington, D.C.: National Academies Press, 2006).

73. *Id.*, at 2.

74. World Health Organization, *Revision of the International Health Regulations, 58th World Health Assembly*, May 23, 2005, *available at* <http://www.who.int/gb/ebwha/pdf_files/WHA58/WHA58_3-en.pdf> (last visited September 19, 2007).

75. See WHO, *supra* note 6.

76. See Gerberding, *supra* note 7, at 9.

77. World Health Organization, *Global Task Force on XDR-TB, Update: February 2007*, at 5, *available at* <http://www.who.int/tb/xdr/globaltaskforce_update_feb07.pdf> (last visited September 19, 2007).

78. Quoted in Schwartz, *supra* note 67, at A1.

79. Quoted in *id.*

80. Associated Press, "Report: Chinese Officials Locate Taiwan Tuberculosis Patients Who Traveled to China," *China Post*, July 28, 2007, *available at* <http://www.chinapost.com.tw/news/2007/07/28/116356/Report:-Chinese.htm> (last visited September 19, 2007).

115

KEEPING THE ILL OUT

Immigration issues in Asia concerning the exclusion of infectious diseases

*Andreas Schloenhardt**

Source: *Hong Kong Law Journal*, 35:2 (2005), 445–80.

The topic of this paper is the prohibition of entry of persons with infectious diseases in the countries of East and Southeast Asia. The paper examines legislative and regulatory mechanisms in Asia to bar would-be immigrants from entry if it is found or suspected that they carry infectious diseases such as tuberculosis, cholera, HIV, and certain other diseases. Further, the paper outlines the characteristics and transmission of these diseases, recent outbreaks, as well as international health regulations that address the issues of entry prohibitions and quarantine. The paper concludes by arguing that immigration restrictions are rarely, if ever, successful in preventing and suppressing the spread of infectious diseases; it proposes international cooperation and behavioural change as more appropriate tools to contain such diseases.

Introduction and background

The recent appearance and re-emergence of diseases[1] such as Creutzfeldt-Jakob, Severe Acute Respiratory Syndrome (SARS), Marburg disease, and the Avian Influenza have put infectious diseases not only on the front-pages of newspapers and back on public health agendas; it has also resulted in sometimes draconian border control measures and has generated a broader debate on the nexus between infectious diseases and national security. It has stimulated a reconsideration of laws and policies regarding border control and quarantine. The SARS crisis in Hong Kong and other Asian cities, the current concern about the impact of bird-flu in Vietnam, and the continuing exclusion of HIV/AIDS infected persons from countries such as Singapore demonstrate the close link between infectious disease and economic consideration which impact directly and indirectly on security and stability in the Asia Pacific region.

The nexus between infectious diseases and security, and the exclusion of persons considered "diseased", however, are nothing new. Isolation and quarantine measures have been documented since the Middle Ages and the Renaissance and have continued well throughout the 20th century and into the new millennium. Some 750 years ago, Italy's growing trade across the Mediterranean exposed the country to new diseases brought in by rodents, other animals and cargo, as well as humans. In 1374, the cities of Milan and Mantua introduced controls and bans on overland trade and, in Milan, those who arrived sick or had any contact with infectious diseases were isolated. In the coastal town of Ragusa ships were isolated and maritime commerce quarantined.[2] The Spanish discovery of the New World in 1492 brought new diseases to the Americas where reportedly tens of thousands died as a result of exposure to smallpox and other diseases formerly unknown to American natives.[3] Pandemics of cholera have moved with global trade around the world for the past two centuries.[4]

More recently, new diseases have emerged and spread around the globe. HIV/AIDS was first discovered in the United States and is now among the main causes of premature death in southern Africa, parts of Asia and increasingly in the South Pacific. SARS first emerged in Guangzhou in Southern China and within weeks was communicated throughout East Asia and to Canada. The Avian Influenza currently causes a new crisis in parts of Southeast Asia. Elsewhere, old diseases re-emerged in new areas; the outbreak of Ebola in the former Zaire, Marburg disease in Angola, the Hanta virus pulmonary syndrome (HPS) in the United States.

The main factors behind the emergence of new and re-emergence of old infectious diseases include, *inter alia*, microbial adaptation and change, complacency by governments and the public, environmental degradation, human demographics and related behavioural changes, and globalisation.[5] "International trade rules", says Scott Burris, "contribute directly to two major sets of factors commonly identified in analyses of disease emergence and persistence: 1) economic dislocation, poor sanitation, and poverty in 'source' countries; and 2) the movement of pathogens through trade routes."[6] With increasing global trade and travel, infectious disease can move around the world within days and lead to often catastrophic consequences, often caused by hysteria, paranoia and overreaction rather than by the disease itself.

Not surprisingly, countries continue to attempt to contain diseases by quarantine measures and by excluding those from entry who are regarded as risks to public health. The detention and exclusion of infected persons has a direct impact on bilateral and multilateral relations, on the economies of sending and destination countries, and potentially on national and regional security. Thus, infectious diseases have an impact on international relations, but international relations also impact on the nature and spread of infectious diseases.

In the decision to bar infectious diseases from entry, careful consideration needs to be given to a variety of questions such as: what diseases to exclude and whether to follow national standards or international health regulations? Whether to just test all would-be immigrants or whether also to exclude, and/or detain and quarantine them? Who to exclude: all immigrants or only those seeking permanent settlement? What weight should be given to factors such as public health and economic cost considerations? What message does exclusion send to the public at large?

This paper examines these questions, focusing specifically on immigration restrictions in East and Southeast Asia. The prime concern will be on legislative and regulatory measures that bar the entry of infected persons in Brunei Darussalam, Cambodia, PR China and its Special Administrative Regions (SAR) Hong Kong and Macau, Japan, Republic of Korea (South Korea), Lao PDR, Malaysia, Papua New Guinea, Philippines, Singapore, Taiwan,[7] Thailand and Vietnam. Not examined here are the public health systems and the administrative and enforcement arrangements in these jurisdictions. Further, the main focus will be on exclusion clauses, not on testing requirements. The paper will analyse the existing normative framework in these countries with reference to the diseases that are excluded and in light of international health standards. The paper concludes by developing a range of practical recommendations to prevent, contain and suppress the cross-border spread of infectious diseases more effectively.

The legislative framework

Immigration law

Countries have a range of legislative tools to prevent the arrival of unwanted foreigners. Visa requirements, for example, enable countries to select immigrants well before they arrive at the border. Exclusion clauses and other prohibitions render those people ineligible for immigration that are unwanted for a variety reasons.[8] For example, individual persons or certain groups of immigrants are regarded as undesirable foreigners if their presence in the territory can potentially cause danger, threats or expenses to the economy, public health, morale or security of the host jurisdiction. In order to prevent the entry of these immigrants, the immigration laws of the countries and territories of the Asia Pacific region contain exclusion clauses that bar certain persons from being admitted to the country prior to arrival.

Economic considerations, for instance, lead receiving jurisdictions to bar those persons from immigration who have insufficient means to support themselves and their dependants during their stay in the territory.[9] Most jurisdictions in the region prohibit people from entering if they are likely "to become a public charge", to place demands on social security systems, or if they are "vagrants, paupers and beggars".[10] Thailand and the Philippines also bar those persons from entry who seek unskilled or other low-level employment.[11] Moreover, illiterate and "incompetent" persons are prohibited

318

immigrants in the Philippines.[12] Brunei and Taiwan exclude those from immigration who show no willingness or no ability to leave the country or territory again in the future.[13]

Second, some jurisdictions in the region perceive the presence of certain individuals or groups of persons as dangerous or otherwise undesirable for reasons of public morality. Malaysia, the Philippines, Singapore and Thailand, for instance, prohibit prostitutes from entering,[14] as well as those who procure or live off the earnings of another person's prostitution.[15] Moreover, the Philippines explicitly bar "persons who practice polygamy" from admission into the country.[16]

Third, jurisdictions prohibit the entry of persons whose presence in the territory can potentially pose a threat to political stability and national security. For this reason, all countries and territories in the region bar persons from entering who have been convicted of (and sentenced for) a crime[17] or who are involved in criminal organisations.[18] Moreover, persons, such as terrorists, who are suspected of threatening or overthrowing the government or the political and administrative institutions of the receiving territory, are not allowed to enter.[19] This prohibition also extends to persons who are suspected of being affiliated with groups that promote these intentions.[20] Persons who are considered potential threats to public safety beyond these categories can be excluded under general clauses that allow prohibition for the protection of national security and sovereignty.[21]

Fourth, some jurisdictions bar the entry of a variety of other people. This includes, for example, people who have previously been removed from that country.[22] In most jurisdictions, prohibitions also extend to the family and dependants of prohibited immigrants.[23] Moreover, unaccompanied and orphan children are barred from entering the Philippines.[24]

Finally, jurisdictions exclude those persons who pose a danger to the receiving country for reasons of public health. Persons who suffer contagious, "loathsome", infectious or otherwise dangerous diseases are barred from entering the territory.[25] Also, the mentally ill, "idiots" and other "insane persons" are not allowed to enter most territories in the region.[26] Those countries that require medical examinations prior to admission into the territory also prohibit the entry of persons who have failed to undergo the examination and those who have not been vaccinated against certain diseases.[27]

For persons who do not fall into any of these categories, but who are viewed as *persona non grata*, the law of all countries and territories in the region provides special discretionary powers for the Minister or Director of Immigration to prohibit their entry.[28]

Prohibited immigrants are barred from entering the territory and are denied visas, unless the Minister or Director of Immigration makes individual exemptions. If persons classified as prohibited immigrants are found in the territory, or if their status changes after arrival so that they become prohibited immigrants, the laws of all countries and territories in the Asia Pacific region provide that they be detained and removed as soon as practicable. In some circumstances, such persons also face criminal charges.[29]

Prohibiting persons from entering a country is an expression of national sovereignty over immigration. There is no doubt that it is important to control the movement of people for reasons of national security, public health and economic stability. It is legitimate that the exclusion clauses discriminate against persons whose presence in the country poses threats to economic and political life, to certain individuals or to society as a whole. But the prohibition clauses can also bar people who may be in desperate need of protection and asylum.

Infectious diseases

The various immigration laws authorising the exclusion of certain foreigners generally do not specify what infectious diseases warrant exclusion or, in other words, what types of diseases are to be kept out. Only the immigration laws of PR China and Singapore specify that persons infected with HIV/AIDS (Singapore),[30] or "leprosy, AIDS, venereal diseases, contagious tuberculosis" (PR China)[31] are prohibited from entry. The Philippine Immigration Act 1940 makes specific mention of epilepsy.[32]

Elsewhere, the immigration laws simply state that persons suffering from "infectious",[33] "contagious",[34] "epidemic",[35] or "loathsome"[36] diseases are prohibited from entry into that jurisdiction, but these laws do not further specify which particular diseases are excluded. This specification is left to supplementary immigration regulations[37] or to relevant health laws.[38] In some cases the diseases are not specified at all and specification is left to the discretion of Ministers or other senior health officials.[39]

In Hong Kong, for example, the Quarantine and Prevention of Disease Ordinance[40] and its subsidiary legislation, the Prevention of the Spread of Infectious Diseases Regulations ('PSIDR'),[41] provide the legal basis for the prevention and control of infectious diseases in the Hong Kong SAR. The Ordinance is primarily concerned with the prevention of the transmission of an infectious disease into and from the Hong Kong SAR. In contrast to other Asian countries Hong Kong does, however, not exclude any diseases per se in its *Immigration Ordinance*. To illustrate the working of this system, on 27 March 2003, the Director of Health[42] ordered an amendment to the First Schedule of the Ordinance, under the Quarantine and Prevention of Disease Ordinance (Amendment of First Schedule) Order 2003,[43] adding SARS to the list of infectious diseases, thus empowering the Director of Health under the relevant provisions of Chapter 141 and its subsidiary legislation to legislate on SARS.[44]

Under provisions of the Quarantine and Prevention of Disease Ordinance, health officials can board an aircraft, vessel,[45] or train[46] for the purposes of detecting an infectious disease. Masters of any vessel or aircraft are required to declare the presence of an infectious disease on board.[47] Moreover, the

Quarantine and Prevention of Disease Ordinance grants statutory powers to health officials to conduct medical examinations of any passenger for the purposes of detecting an infectious disease,[48] and to quarantine any infected person wishing to land in Hong Kong until such time as the disease is no longer contagious.[49] Hong Kong also has a specific provision in the *Prevention of Infectious Diseases Regulations* (reg 27) empowering a health officer to prohibit a person with SARS from leaving Hong Kong.

Excluded diseases

Although there have been major improvements in sanitary conditions in the industrialised parts of the world and often revolutionary developments in medical science and the treatment of infectious diseases, there has been remarkably little change in the quarantine and prohibition measures instituted by countries to prevent the spread of disease across borders. In contrast, in recent years the list of excluded diseases has grown with the addition of, for example, HIV/AIDS and SARS.

The last century has witnessed unprecedented levels of medical research into the causes and contributory circumstances of infectious diseases. It has seen the development of new treatment, antibiotics, and immunisations against diseases such as diphtheria, hepatitis, influenza, measles, mumps, polio, rubella, and tetanus, and in 1977 the World Health Organization (WHO) confirmed the eradication of smallpox. Hygienic conditions have improved dramatically accompanied by the increased use of refrigeration and improved quality of drinking water. As a result, life expectancies in all industrialised countries have almost doubled since the late 19th century.[50]

This development, however, has not been matched in developing nations where sanitary conditions for a majority of people remain poor and are often worsened by growing urbanisation and the uncontrolled growth of urban slums which do not have access to fresh drinking water, electricity and proper sewage. Access to basic medical treatment remains limited in many countries of Africa, Asia, Latin America and the South Pacific. Even where proper treatment and medication is available, it is often too expensive for those in most dire need. The monopoly and patents over many drugs held by pharmaceutical companies in developed nations further increases the price for drugs.

Unsurprisingly, developing nations are most vulnerable to new diseases such as HIV/AIDS for which no or only very expensive treatment exists. Old diseases also continue to re-emerge with unprecedented consequences.

In 1997, Allyn Taylor reported:

"For example, case reports of tuberculosis have increased twenty-eight percent since the mid-1980s, and the disease remains the world's leading cause of death from a single infectious agent; recent estimates suggest that approximately ninety million new cases of tuberculosis will occur globally during this decade. Also in this decade, a cholera epidemic swept through Latin America after that region had been cholera-free for many years. In addition, dengue hemorrhagic fever stormed Latin America, causing outbreaks in Cuba, Brazil, Venezuela, and Costa Rica. Diphtheria has appeared in Russia, anthrax has appeared in the Caribbean, and bubonic plague has appeared in India. In Africa, infectious diseases are increasing in scale and frequency. Cholera and meningitis are increasingly common, and there have been recent outbreaks of epidemic yellow fever in Kenya, Rift Valley fever virus in Egypt, and Lassa fever in West Africa. In Southeast Asia, cases of communicable disease have increased in the last decade, including high numbers of polio, neonatal tetanus, leprosy, tuberculosis, and diarrhoeal disease cases."[51]

The following part of this paper will take a closer look at those diseases that are commonly excluded under the immigration laws in Asian countries. These include tuberculosis, cholera, plague, diphtheria and Ebola. Further, the exclusion of HIV/AIDS infected persons will be examined, and close consideration will be given to new diseases such as SARS and the avian bird flu.

Tuberculosis

TB – as tuberculosis is often referred to – is a highly contagious, airborne bacillus that thrives on oxygen. While some of the pathology of TB is not fully understood, the bacteria survives within the human's immune cells which otherwise destroy bacteria and viruses. The bacteria's primary host is the human body and infection spreads through direct person-to-person contact through talking, coughing or spitting and inhalation by the uninfected persons.

Given the ease with which tuberculosis spreads, it has been estimated that one-third of the world's population is infected with TB. However, only eight to ten million develop active disease and, according to WHO data, two million die each year. Most of these cases occur in sub-Saharan Africa and Southeast Asia, with smaller yet significant rates reported in Eastern Europe. Disease rates are especially high if TB coincides with HIV/AIDS infection.[52]

In most developing nations, tuberculosis has largely been eradicated, though there has been some resurgence of new drug-resistant strains of tuberculosis and some higher infection rates among HIV/AIDS patients. Moreover, immigration of infected persons appears to be the main cause of tuberculosis in industrialised nations, contributing disproportionately to the resurgence of TB.

A report published in the United States in late 2000 estimated that:

"In 1998, immigrants accounted for nearly 42 percent of the 18,361 tuberculosis cases nationwide, although they represented just over 10 percent of the total population. Health officials said that TB rates in specific groups of immigrants reflect the occurrence of tuber-culosis in their home countries. The disease is particularly endemic in Latin America, Asia, and Africa. . . . Studies of TB in immigrants have indicated that most patients are infected in their home countries, but develop the active form of the disease once they are in the United States. . . . Nationally, the immigrant groups with the highest number of TB cases are Mexicans, Filipinos, Vietnamese, Indians, Chinese, Haitians, and Koreans."[53]

Tuberculosis is perhaps the most common disease which results in exclu-sion of the infected person from admission to a foreign country. As the disease can spread by casual contact, has often fatal consequences and is more common in some parts of the world than in others, it is not surprising that many, if not most countries prohibit the entry of persons suspected of carrying the disease. In some nations, access is only denied to persons with active tuberculosis.

Cholera

Cholera is an acute bacterial diarrhoeal disease which may result in a life threatening dehydration which must be treated urgently. In untreated cases, death may occur in a few hours and the case fatality rate may exceed 50 per cent.

Cholera can be transmitted by contaminated water, ingestion of con-taminated food or water, or by fish or shellfish obtained from contaminated water. The cholera organism can survive for long periods in water or ice. Airborne transmission or transmission by casual contact is not possible; however, severely ill patients are usually isolated.[54]

In 2003, WHO received reports from 45 different countries of 111,575 cases of cholera with 1,894 deaths. 96 per cent of these cases were reported in Africa. In the Asia Pacific region, only PR China, and Hong Kong (229 cases), Japan (16), and Singapore (1) notified cases of cholera to WHO.[55]

Endemic cholera occurs in parts of Africa, Asia and Central Europe. A pandemic cholera that began in Asia in 1961, spread to Africa in 1970 and to South America twenty years later. It was first identified in Peru in 1991 where during that year 300,000 persons were infected and 3,000 people died of cholera. Peru immediately notified the World Health Organization of the outbreak, as is required by the International Health Regulations. Conse-quently, many other countries moved to restrict trade and travel to and from Peru resulting in estimated losses of US$700 million by the Peruvian economy.[56] Most recently, cholera outbreaks have been reported in Senegal, where 54 people died in a single week in April 2005.[57] In industrialised countries, Cholera usually occurs in imported cases from returned travellers.

Cholera vaccine is available. The disease can best be avoided by not con-suming food and liquids which may potentially be contaminated with cholera bacteria. Also contact with the vomitus and faeces of an infected person especially during the illness and for several days after symptoms of illness cease should be avoided. Thus, common sense and proper personal care may be the better ways to contain the disease than entry prohibition and quarantine measures which continue to be applied by some countries.[58]

Plague

The plague – or black death as it has often been referred to – is an infection caused by an organism usually carried by rodents. It is transmitted to humans by flea bite or ingestion of the faeces of fleas. It can also be transmitted from human to human when a plague patient develops pneumonia and spreads infected droplets by coughing; plague epidemics usually start this way.[59]

The most recent major outbreak of plague was reported in parts of India in 1994; though India only confirmed the outbreak and reported it to the WHO long after the media reported the first occurrences of the disease. Thousands of people fled from the outbreak area thus causing a further spread of the disease to other parts of India. Other countries responded to the outbreak by closing airports to planes arriving from India and banning trade and travel to and from India. The panic in some places went so far that overseas Indian workers were released and returned to India, even though some had not lived there for many years. It has been estimated that the "embargoes" imposed on India in the aftermath of the 1994 outbreak of pneumonic plague caused losses of US$ 1.7 billion to the Indian economy.[60]

Many of the border control and quarantine measures adopted by countries in response to the plague epidemic in India in 1994 were unwarranted and, at times, in violation of international standards. It is thus unsurprising that in light of the danger of huge economic losses, countries are often reluctant to report the outbreak of infectious diseases. However, as the plague can be spread so easily and has very high fatality rates, it is not surprising that many countries prohibit the entry of and quarantine persons suspected of carrying the disease.

Diphtheria

Diphtheria is an acute bacterial disease of the tonsils, pharynx, larynx, nose and occasionally other mucous membranes, skin, conjunctivae, and genitalia. It is carried by humans only and is transmitted by droplet spread through contact with a patient or carrier, or articles soiled with discharges from infected lesions. Case fatality rate is 5–10 per cent for non-cutaneous diphtheria and higher if there is a delay in diagnosis and treatment with antitoxin.[61]

Since the introduction of widespread immunisation, diphtheria has become very uncommon; thus few countries continue to list the diseases as an excluded disease, although quarantine and isolation remain widespread. Diphtheria is preventable by vaccination and is well-controlled in most countries. The most recent significant outbreak occurred in Russia and other former Soviet republics in the 1990s. The epidemic reached its peak in 1996. By that time there had been 140,000 cases with 4,000 deaths.[62]

Ebola

Ebola hemorrhagic fever is a viral disease transmitted to humans from infected animals and animal materials, though – as with many aspects of this disease – the ways of transmission are not fully understood. Within a week of infection, rashes, often containing blood, appear all over the human body, causing the patient to bleed from both the mouth and the rectum. Mortality rates of Ebola are as high as 90 percent though it is said that patients usually die from shock rather than blood loss.[63]

Outbreaks of Ebola fever have largely been restricted to some parts of Africa. In particular, a 1995 epidemic of the diseases in the then Zaire (now the DR Congo) made worldwide headlines, causing 245 deaths.[64] WHO estimates that since the discovery of the virus in 1976 "approximately 1850 [cases] with more than 1200 deaths have been documented".[65]

There is, to date, no known cure for the disease. Patients are usually isolated to decrease the risk of transmission. Some countries have introduced measures to exclude would-be immigrants from entry if they are suspected of carrying the Ebola disease. These measures appear to be of little use for a disease which develops so rapidly and for which the exact mode of transmission is not yet known.[66] Ebola is also not a reportable disease under the International Health Regulations.

Marburg disease

Closely related to Ebola is the Marburg haemorrhagic fever, a rare yet highly fatal virus. Marburg disease is characterised by high fever and significant bleeding, rapid deterioration and death of the patients resulting from blood loss or, as in the case of Ebola, from shock. The mortality rate is estimated to be between 83 and 90 percent.

Transmission of Marburg disease is rather difficult in that it requires extremely close contact with an infected person, usually with that person's blood or other body fluids. Airborne transmission and transmission by casual contact do not seem to be possible. Some outbreaks have been linked to animals, especially monkeys, but more recent research appears to confirm that animals die of Marburg too rapidly to be viable reservoirs of the virus. Its semblance to other diseases make detection of the Marburg disease particularly difficult.[67]

Marburg first came to the attention of health authorities following outbreaks in the late 1960s in Southern Africa from where it was imported into the Balkans and Germany. The disease again made headlines in 2005 when Angola reported 266 cases of Marburg haemorrhagic fever of which 244 cases were fatal (as on 20 April 2005); this is the largest and deadliest known outbreak of the disease.[68]

National health authorities and the WHO consider the risk of international spread of Marburg disease very low. Transmission requires close contact with the patient and evidence suggests transmission can only occur after the onset of symptoms.[69] Marburg fever is not a reportable disease under the *IHR*. Some countries have legislation to deny entry to persons suspected of carrying the disease though given the rapid deterioration of patients it is highly unlikely that infected persons can spread the disease by travel.

Severe Acute Respiratory Syndrome (SARS)

The disease now known as SARS or "Severe Acute Respiratory Syndrome" was the first new significant infectious disease to emerge in the 21st century. SARS was a formerly unknown syndrome and was given its first case definition by the WHO on 15 March 2003.[70] According to the clinical case definition by the WHO, the virus begins with a fever of over 38 degrees Celsius and is followed by the development of one or more symptoms of lower respiratory tract illness such as cough and breathing difficulties after a period of two to seven days.[71] Some cases have also reported the presence of diarrhoea.[72]

The incubation period of the disease has been found to be between two and seven days.[73] Nevertheless, periods of 10 days have been reported in some cases,[74] leading to the inference that an infected person could theoretically be a carrier of the virus for up to 10 days while not presenting any symptoms. Therefore, it becomes considerably more difficult to detect and contain the spread of the virus. However, reports suggest that the virus is not contagious until the patient becomes symptomatic.[75]

Moreover, in contrast to other respiratory illnesses, SARS has been found to be most infectious after 10 days of its initial transmission.[76] At that stage, and for reasons yet unknown, patients either subsequently recover, or, in contrast, undergo rapid decline "to severe respiratory illness, often requiring ventilatory support".[77] It has been estimated that approximately 10 to 20 percent of SARS patients require ventilation support.[78]

The virus originally occurred in animals, probably the masked palm civet cat, in southern China in 2002 and later jumped to humans.[79] The transmission of SARS is believed to occur when one person comes within close contact of an infected person, resulting in "exposure to infected respiratory droplets expelled during coughing or sneezing", or "following contact with body fluids during certain medical interventions".[80] The virus is also believed to survive in human excrement (which has been attributed to the community outbreak within the Hong Kong SAR through faulty drainage and sewage systems, infecting some 300 residents living within the same housing estate in late March 2003).[81]

The mortality rate for SARS varies significantly depending, in particular, on the age of the infected person; it has been reported to be directly proportional to the age of the patient and is further exacerbated in patients suffering an "underlying chronic disease".[82] In Hong Kong, the mortality rate during the 2003 SARS outbreak was reportedly 17.1 percent, considerably higher than the corresponding figure of 7 per cent in other parts of China.[83] Based on data received from affected countries, the average global mortality rate of the disease according to the WHO is approximately 11 per cent.[84]

The first human infections with SARS occurred in Guangdong Province in China in November 2002, though the Chinese Government initially tried to suppress information about the outbreak.[85] On 12 March 2003, the Hong Kong Government officially notified WHO of "an outbreak of respiratory illness among health care workers."[86] That same day, a "global alert" on SARS was issued by WHO.[87] The SARS outbreak in Hong Kong was the largest recorded outside of mainland China spanning a period of over three months, with a total of 1,755 reported cases,[88] and claiming 299 deaths in Hong Kong alone.[89] According to the WHO, by 7 August 2003, a total of 8,422 SARS cases had been reported in 30 countries with 916 deaths. Of the probable cases, 5,327 (or 63 percent) were in China, 1,755 (21 percent) in the Hong Kong SAR and 665 (8 percent) in Taiwan.[90] The 2003 Outbreak affected every sector of the Hong Kong community, extending beyond the health sector, to the territory's economy and employment, resulting in significant social disruption.[91] It is estimated that globally the SARS led to economic losses of US$10 billion.[92]

SARS was first "imported" into Hong Kong on 21 February 2003 by an infected physician who had treated atypical pneumonia patients in Guangdong Province, PR China.[93] The doctor stayed in a city hotel and subsequently infected at least 16 guests and other foreign visitors on the same floor.[94] As a result, the virus was carried along international air travel routes as hotel guests returned home. In the following days, outbreaks were reported in hospitals in Hong Kong, Vietnam, Singapore, and Canada.[95]

Travel advisories were issued by the WHO to countries with "recent local transmission"[96] when it was found that infected persons and close contacts of infected persons were continuing to travel, thereby transmitting the disease to other passengers and bringing it to their travel destinations. On 2 April 2003, the WHO issued a travel advisory suggesting that travellers defer "all but essential travel"[97] to Hong Kong. It was not until 23 June 2003,[98] 20 days (twice the disease's maximum incubation period) after the last reported case on 2 June, that Hong Kong was finally removed from the WHO's list of "areas with recent local transmission", thereby bringing the 2003 SARS outbreak in Hong Kong to a close.[99] The global outbreak was to continue until the last travel advisory imposed on Beijing was removed by the WHO on 24 June 2003, followed by the removal of Taiwan from the WHO's list of areas with recent local transmission on 5 July 2003,[100] deeming all "human chain[s] of transmission" to be effectively broken.[101]

On 16 April 2003, the WHO officially announced the "causative agent" of the virus to be a coronavirus that had, as yet, never been detected in humans.[102]

To date, no effective vaccine or cure has been found.[103] The treatment administered to patients during the 2003 outbreak included a variety of antibiotics to presumptively treat known bacterial agents of atypical pneumonia. Steroids, ribavirin, and other antimicrobials have also been known to be administered, often in combination.[104] However, it is yet unknown which treatment is the most effective.[105] Equally, it remains unclear whether restrictions on people movement, quarantine, and the exclusion of SARS-patients from immigration is necessary and warranted.[106]

Avian influenza (bird flu)

A disease that has made it to the front pages of newspapers in 2004/2005 is the avian influenza or bird flu which is an infectious disease of birds. While epidemics of the disease have occurred for many decades, recent cases in Southeast Asia and in particular transmission of the disease to humans resulting in death have caused new concern about this disease.

For a long time it was thought that the avian influenza virus would not infect animals other than birds or pigs. Following an epidemic in Hong Kong in 1997, the first infections of humans were documented. The virus caused severe respiratory disease in 18 persons, of whom six died. Research into the causes and circumstances of these cases found that close contact with live infected poultry was the source of human infection. Consequently, within three days an estimated 1.5 million birds were destroyed in Hong Kong thus reducing the risk of further infections. Others report that more than 200 million birds and poultry have died and have been culled in Southeast Asia between late 2003 and 2004. However, the disease continues to haunt other parts of Southeast Asia, especially Vietnam and, most recently, Cambodia and Indonesia. During the outbreaks in 2004 alone, 43 cases of human infections were reported with 31 reported deaths.[107]

The most common measure to prevent the spread of the disease has been the mass destruction of poultry population in infected areas to halt further spread of epidemics and reduce opportunities for human exposure to the virus. Vaccinations against influenza, too, may reduce the risk of infection, as does the wearing of protective clothing, but there is, to date, no reliable vaccine for the avian bird flu. However, little research has been undertaken into the transmission of disease to humans. There is, as yet, no evidence that bird flu can spread from humans to humans, thus calls for the exclusion of infected persons from immigration carry little argument.

HIV/AIDS

Perhaps the most controversial addition to the list of infectious diseases that provides ground for the exclusion of foreigners is HIV/AIDS. The debate has been particularly heated in the United States where, in 1987,[108] first AIDS and then HIV infection was added to the list of "dangerous, contagious diseases" which bar foreigners from entry into the US.[109]

The disease was first discovered in 1981 when investigators in New York and Los Angeles noted unusually frequent occurrence of Kaposi's sarcoma and pneumocystic carinii among sexually active gay men. In 1983–1984, researchers isolated a virus from patients with AIDS. The Centres for Disease Control (CDC) in the United States named the disorder Acquired Immune Deficiency Syndrome (AIDS) in recognition of its transmission to previously healthy individuals.[110]

The WHO and the United Nations estimate that at the end of 2004, between 35.9 and 44.3 million people are living with HIV globally, approximately 1.3 million in Southeast Asia (not including India). Fourteen thousand new infections occur daily, mostly (approximately 95 per cent) in developing nations.[111]

In essence, AIDS is caused by an infection with what has come to be known as the Human Immunodeficiency Virus (HIV). The HI-virus enters and attacks the white blood cells, more specifically a subpopulation of the white blood cells knows as the "helper cells". These helper cells are responsible for initiating the human body's response to typical viral attacks. Once HIV enters the cells, it starts replicating itself. The host cells are eventually irrevocably damaged or destroyed, leaving the body unprotected against a wide range of disease-causing microbes, thereby increasing the probability of acquiring infections typically associated with AIDS. As HIV breaks down the immune system, it opens the door to other opportunistic infections which would ordinarily be repelled by the body's white blood cells. Because of the damage caused to the body's immune system by HIV, even everyday infections can result in serious illness or death. AIDS is the last stage of the HIV infection, during which the immune system has been substantially weakened and is unable to fight off even the most basic infections. About half the people with HIV will develop AIDS within approximately 10 years, but the time between infection with HIV and the onset of AIDS can vary greatly. The severity of the HIV-related illness or illnesses will differ from person to person, according to many factors, including the overall health of the individual.[112]

HIV is a disease which can only be spread through contact with and/or transmission of blood, breast milk, semen or vaginal fluids. It can also be transmitted prenatally. Casual or airborne transmission is not possible; HIV/ AIDS cannot be spread by casual contact with an infected person, neither through saliva, sweat or tears, and cannot be carried by insects. Before HIV can be transmitted, there must be exposure to the living virus, entry of the virus into the host, and successful replication within the host. Fears that other, thus far undiscovered, methods of transmitting HIV may exist are not supported by scientific evidence.[113]

Despite the limited ways in which the disease can spread and although the transmission between humans is only possible through close, intimate contact or by sharing intravenous instruments such as needles, to combat the "AIDS epidemic" some countries introduced quarantine and restrictions on international travel in the 1980s and 1990s. Entry prohibitions for persons infected with HIV/AIDS remain intact in Brunei, Singapore and also the United States. Similarly, in China "any foreigner suffering from AIDS" is prohibited from entering the country.[114] Vietnam restricts the entry of HIV-positive foreigners to prevent "economic and social losses".[115] In the Philippines, too, foreigners seeking to stay for six months or more must be AIDS-free.[116] Thailand, in contrast, initially prohibited the entry of foreigners infected with AIDS in 1985[117] but repealed this prohibition in 1992.[118]

A study of national AIDS policies published in 1996 found that:

> "[t]he reasons why nations set up immigration policies that bar entry of HIV-infected persons are diverse – a desire to do something to contain infection, the presence of strong nationalistic tendencies, limited concern regarding individual rights, and monetary worries about straining national health care resources."[119]

In support of the restrictive policies, L. J. Nelson III wrote as recently as 1997:

> "The policy favouring free movement of peoples may have to bow to the necessities of controlling the further spread of the disease. . . . Under certain circumstances, increasing barriers to international travel may be an appropriate means of dealing with the AIDS epidemic. . . . Since its primary modes of transmission are sexual contact and the use of contaminated needles by intravenous drug abusers, there may be some justification for some limited restrictions on international travel to combat it. . . . Restrictions on persons seeking to travel to and from countries where HIV infection is especially common might assist in controlling the further spread of the disease."[120]

There has been strong criticism of the exclusion of HIV/AIDS infected persons. Many have argued that this policy has no public health purpose and does not assist in containing the disease. Research centres have repeatedly recommended that HIV/AIDS be removed from lists that warrant exclusion from immigration.[121] The WHO, too, rejects policies of screening and excluding immigrants for HIV/AIDS:

> "1 No screening program of international travellers can prevent the introduction and spread of HIV infection;
> 2 HIV screening programs for international travellers would, at best, and at great cost, retard only briefly the dissemination of HIV both globally and with respect to any particular country;
> 3 HIV screening of international travellers would divert scarce resources away from educational programs, protection of the blood

supply, and other measures intended to prevent parental and perinatal transmission. This diversion would be difficult to justify because of the epidemiological, legal, economic, political, cultural, and ethical factors militating against adoption of such a policy."[122]

It has been held that the policy of exclusion creates a false sense of fear regarding the threat that the disease poses and, in return, generates a false sense of security if infected persons are kept out. The exclusion is seen by many as discriminatory, especially against gays and foreigners, and an infringement of human rights.[123]

International Health Regulations

The International Health Regulations are the main international instrument to prevent and control the spread of infectious diseases across borders. The origins of international cooperation of that kind go back to the mid 19th century when epidemic diseases spread with great speed across Europe as a result of improved transportation across the continent. European countries then attempted to combat the spread of cholera, plague and yellow fever. A first International Sanitary Conference met in Paris, France in 1851 to address the European cholera epidemics.[124]

The objectives of the early international efforts to prevent and suppress the spread of infectious diseases were as much an attempt to contain the diseases as to ensure minimum interference with cross-border trade and travel. The conflict between quarantine measures on the one hand and economic and commercial demands on the other has been an essential feature of international law and diplomacy in this field for the past 150 years. At the same time, there has always been a recognition that attempts to control diseases by the imposition of rigid border measures is largely illusory.[125]

In 1874, at the Fourth International Sanitary Conference, first proposals were made to create a permanent international health organisation.[126] Further conventional initiatives followed in the 1890s and early 1900s. The International Sanitary Convention was adopted in 1892. A specific Convention addressing the plague followed in 1897. In 1903, a new International Sanitary Convention came into being, replacing the earlier agreements.[127]

The aftermath of World War II saw the creation of the United Nations which brought with it the establishment of the World Health Organization (WHO) as the UN's chief health agency. WHO was created at the International Health Conference in New York from 19 June to 22 July 1946 as the first of the post-war international organisations to be established as a specialised agency under Article 57 of the Charter of the United Nations.[128]

The purpose of the World Health Organization, as stated in its Constitution,[129] is the "attainment by all peoples of the highest possible level of health".[130] To that end, WHO seeks to "stimulate and advance work to eradicate epidemic and endemic diseases."[131] Beginning in 1947, the organisation established a system of global epidemiological information and still publishes a weekly report containing global data on infectious diseases.

The World Health Assembly (WHA) was designed as the WHO's key policy making body; its decisions are binding upon all WHO Member States unless an individual Member submits a reservation which has been accepted by the WHA.[132] Articles 19–22 of the WHO Constitution authorise the organisation to draft conventions, agreements and regulations inter alia on "sanitary and quarantine requirements and other procedures designed to prevent the international spread of disease" to be adopted by the WHA. On 25 July 1951 at the Fourth World Health Assembly, the WHA adopted a new set of International Sanitary Regulations[133] which, in 1969, were renamed International Health Regulations (IHR).[134]

The essential aim of the IHR is "to ensure the maximum security against the international spread of diseases with the minimum interference with world traffic". The IHR provide a set of (maximum) measures that Member States may impose to restrict international traffic and travel to contain the spread of epidemic diseases. The IHR initially applied to six diseases: cholera, plague, relapsing fever, smallpox, typhus, and yellow fever – largely the same diseases that were considered one hundred years earlier. The IHR were slightly modified for cholera in 1973. In 1981, smallpox was excluded from the list in view of its global eradication. The IHR currently only apply to three epidemic diseases: cholera, plague, and yellow fever.[135]

Signatories to the IHR have numerous obligations under the treaty in order to prevent, suppress and report the outbreak of cholera, plague, typhus and yellow fever. With respect to these diseases, the Regulations create legally binding obligations in three key areas: first, State Parties have an obligation to notify WHO about any outbreak of cholera, plague and yellow fever within their territories and provide details about the area and type of outbreak, the number of persons affected, and any prophylactic measures taken. Second, the Regulations provide a range of minimum as well as maximum border control and quarantine measures to contain the spread of the diseases. Thus the Regulations seek to ensure that Signatories adopt adequate but not excessive measures to contain any outbreak within their borders and protect themselves from the spread of outbreaks elsewhere. Third, the IHR contain a range of other guidelines for the implementation of domestic measures, including procedures with respect to the international transport of goods, cargoes, luggage, mail, and the means of transport.[136]

There is a question whether the IHR apply to disease beyond the three "quarantinable diseases" explicitly mentioned in the Regulations. Since their implementation, there has been some debate whether the IHR also apply to diseases not specifically named. In 1957, the WHA decided that the then International Sanitary Regulations applied to diseases not explicitly mentioned in the text.[137] There appears to be consensus now that "[t]he regulations arguably establish maximum measures restrictive of international traffic that Member Nations may take with respect to the spread of other epidemic diseases."[138] Thus, the IHR are relevant to infectious diseases not explicitly listed in the regulations in that they establish a maximum threshold for quarantine and border control measures.

In theory, individual Member States can also seek for other diseases to be added to the list under the IHR. This would require a formal submission of a proposal to that effect by that State to the WHA. This discussion has largely arisen in the context of HIV/AIDS related restrictions, though it has been found "unlikely that the World Health Assembly would allow such restrictions upon the free movement because they would be wasteful, ineffective, and contrary to the dictates of the WHO Global [AIDS] Strategy".[139] There is no information on proposals to add other infectious diseases.

Since their creation some 50 years ago, the International Health Regulations have repeatedly been criticised for failing to contain the spread of diseases successfully. While some have described the IHR as unnecessarily intrusive on international trade and travel, others have held that the Regulations do not go far enough and, in particular, offer too much leniency to non-cooperative countries. Fidler argues that the IHR "have largely been considered a failure in their main objectives of maximising the protection against the spread of infectious diseases and minimising interference with world traffic".[140]

There has been some criticism about the emphasis of the IHR on border control measures generally, and that they overstate the usefulness of border control measures in the prevention of infectious diseases. It has been suggested that quarantine, exclusion and detention measures do little to contain the spread of diseases and that they can never completely prevent the importation and exportation of diseases.

Some have criticised the IHR for failing to address new emerging and re-emerging diseases such as HIV/AIDS, Hantavirus pulmonary syndrome, haemorrhagic fever, diphtheria, and tuberculosis, among others.[141] In fact, the diseases currently within the ambit of the IHR are largely the same as those that were discussed at the first international conferences 150 years ago.[142]

Equally significant are concerns about compliance by Signatories and enforcement of the International Health Regulations. The cholera outbreak in Latin America and the plague outbreak in India in the 1990s have demonstrated that countries often have little incentive to comply with the IHR obligations, that they fail to notify the WHO about new outbteaks, that they often impose excessive restrictions on cross-border trade and travel, and that no international agency has the authority to ensure that State Parties meet their IHR obligations.[143]

States have repeatedly failed to notify the WHO in the hope that the outbreak of infectious diseases will go unnoticed and in fear of embargoes and exclusions imposed by neighbouring countries and the international community. On other occasions, countries have adopted measures that exceed the maximum threshold established by the IHR, often with severe socio-economic consequences for their neighbours. The World Health Organization, however, remains powerless over non-compliance by its Members. Since its creation, a criticism has been expressed to the effect that WHO "may advise, assist, coordinate and recommend, but it is not enabled to legislate or execute".[144]

Following the cholera epidemic in Latin America, the plague in India and the Ebola crises in the DR Congo (the then Zaire) in the mid 1990s, the World Health Assembly commenced a process of comprehensive review of the International Health Regulations, specifically with a view that:

1   The current role and function of the IHR should be revised and expanded. The current practice of reporting only three specific diseases should be replaced by reporting to the WHO defined syndromes representing diseases of international importance.
2   The IHR should be expanded to include a description of inappropriate interventions and should provide clear indications as to why these actions are not required.
3   A handbook explaining the requirements of the revised IHR should accompany the new Regulations.
4   The revised IHR should be integrated into all surveillance and control activities at global, regional, and national levels.[145]

It has also been recommended that the IHR should be expanded beyond the three diseases now subject to the Regulations to address the increasing importance of emerging diseases. Some have recommended the inclusion of specific diseases, such as AIDS and SARS,[146] while others have suggested expanding the regulations to "all health threats of international importance".[147]

After drafting several revisions, it is anticipated that the WHA will adopt a modified set of Regulations in 2005; however, radical changes cannot be expected.[148]

The way forward

History has shown that one of the most immediate responses to new and re-emerging infectious diseases are closures of national borders, the introduction of quarantine and control measures, the issuing of travel advisories, and other measures aimed at "keeping the ill out". However, there is, to date, very limited, if any, evidence to support the perception that immigration control and the exclusion of "diseased" foreigners contribute much to the containment of infectious diseases and the protection of public health. In contrast, these restrictions have had detrimental effects on national economies, global trade, travel and tourism.[149] These measures, in addition, have too often been abused as a tool to discriminate against minorities and infringe upon human rights, especially in the context of HIV/AIDS.

The entry-prohibitions for persons suspected of carrying infectious diseases and other quarantine and control measures were created at a time when global trade and travel were starting to emerge at low pace, especially by ship. These measures, however, are ill-configured for an era in which millions of people cross borders on a daily basis and in which air-travel allows easy access to most cities around the world within less than 24 hours. The volume of international trade and travel is still increasing, especially within and among the countries of East and Southeast Asia. International organisations and many experts recognise that efforts to slow – let alone stop – the spread of infectious diseases at international borders are illusory and that national efforts to control epidemics are thwarted by the availability and growth of global trade and travel.[150]

Given the very limited effect of immigration restrictions on the spread of infectious diseases, the question must be asked whether such measures are at all warranted and should be continued. As early as 1919, at the session of the Permanent Committee of the [Health] Office, Professor Roco Santoliquido, President of the Permanent Committee, suggested:

> "[t]he concept of quarantine should be abandoned and instead by strengthening and development of national health services and the creation of an improved attitude to national health on the part of the general public, the international transmission of disease would be circumscribed and prevented."[151]

The risks of infectious diseases do not stem from the nationality and ethnicity of a person. They come from poor sanitary conditions in many countries of the world, limited or no access to clean water and food, the lack of medication, vaccinations and health care, and from human conduct, especially sexual behaviour. Thus, as Scott Burris put it, "reducing the threat of infectious disease will require changes in everything from food preparation practices, through sexual behaviour, to the way physicians and patients make decisions about using antibiotics."[152]

Any strategy to prevent and suppress the spread of infectious diseases must balance the sovereignty and security interests of the nation state against the rights of individuals. A comprehensive response to the perceived threat of infectious diseases must combine achievable long-term goals, which offer real solutions to the public health, political, demographic, and socioeconomic dimensions of the problem, with short-term measures that address the immediate needs.

The remaining parts of this paper offer a range of proposals for mechanisms that, in combination, seek to provide a comprehensive approach for the way forward in the control of infectious diseases. These proposals must not be seen as purely normative and regulatory principles; they are intended to serve as a general framework for future law reform and policy change, providing a set of best practice guidelines.

Protection of public health

The main objective of any strategy to prevent, control and contain the spread of infectious diseases must be the protection of public health and the well-being and safety of individuals. Political and economic considerations must not jeopardise the health of persons or compromise public health systems.

It has to be recognised though that the exclusion of infected persons does not contribute to the protection of public health, especially if the disease cannot be spread by casual contact. There is, too date, no medical or scientific data to support claims that the exclusion of diseases that cannot be spread casually will protect public health.[153]

There is, however, some evidence suggesting that these measures have a negative impact on public health: first, they create a false sense of security and a mistaken belief that people are safe simply because "the ill" are kept out. This point has been made in particular in the context of SARS and HIV/AIDS.[154] Second, it has been held that prohibitive immigration regulations may contribute to persons trying to immigrate clandestinely for fear of being rejected at the border or simply to avoid lengthy control procedures. If infected persons "go underground" they are even further removed from access to preventative and public health care and thus may contribute to the spread of infectious diseases.[155] The laws that bar certain individuals and groups of persons from entering are factors that contribute to clandestine and otherwise illegal immigration. The exclusion and prohibition clauses may discourage some people from migrating to a particular destination,[156] but they do not take away the incentives for migration. This is particularly the case in circumstances where people are desperate to flee unemployment, poverty or persecution and where migrant smugglers offer ways to circumvent entry restrictions.[157]

Germs and viruses do not know nor recognise international borders. Thus, border control and quarantine measures can rarely, if ever, prevent the spread of infectious diseases. Instead, to protect public health, priority should be given to improving domestic public health systems. "Prevention of infectious diseases requires detection, reduction, and elimination at the sources of these diseases, which in turn requires improvements in basic health services and conditions for all peoples."[158] Intrusive powers should be the very last resort to contain diseases and exclusion and quarantine measures should be limited to infectious disease where transmission may occur airborne or through random casual contact with infected persons.

Discrimination and human rights

As mentioned earlier, a major concern in the use and application of restrictive immigration measures is the potential for discrimination and the issue of human rights. The early attempts by European countries to restrict access by persons suspected of carrying diseases and persons arriving from selected countries were often seen as discriminatory measures against persons from Africa and Asia.[159] Similar observations have been made about contemporary measures excluding persons suspected of carrying infectious diseases such as tuberculosis and haemorrhagic fevers which mostly occur in developing nations.[160] In the context of HIV/AIDS it has been held that the exclusion policies are directly aimed at gays, lesbians, persons from Southern Africa, other developing nations, and "people of colour".[161] This point is best manifested in the US policy which prohibited the entry and ordered the detention of refugees from Haiti suspected of being infected with HIV/AIDS.[162]

Exemptions from the observance of human rights cannot be justified simply by claiming that they are required for public health reasons. In light of the fact that no convincing and compelling rationale has yet been found in support of the exclusions of many diseases, the resulting discrimination is generally not justifiable. The very limited and largely unproven benefits of exclusion clauses usually outweigh the humanitarian costs. As Lawrence Gostin put it, countries must not "use infectious disease control as a pretext for discrimination by targeting individuals based on their nationality, race, religion, or other status."[163]

At the same time, it needs to be recognised that – depending on the type of disease and its transmission – some infectious diseases affect some parts of the population more than others. To avoid discrimination and infringements of human rights, consultation with representatives of the communities most at risk is central to any strategy to contain diseases and is an expression of inclusion and solidarity.[164]

It has to be recognised that women are often at particular risk of infection and that discrimination against women on health grounds is widespread. In many countries, women have limited, if any, access to medication, vaccinations and health care. Regarding sexually transmitted diseases, including HIV/AIDS, the subordination of women means that they are often unable to negotiate safe-sex practices and thus cannot avoid infections with diseases carried by their sexual partners. It is therefore necessary to improve public health care for women and girls and work towards environments in which women can independently be informed and responsibly decide on matters relating to their health and sexuality.[165]

A further point which appears to be inseparable from any debate about migration is the floodgate argument and the fear that any relaxation or abolition of exclusion clauses will instantaneously lead to unlimited influxes of diseased persons from abroad. These fears, however, have no substance and no statistical support. They ignore the realities and push and pull factors of contemporary migration. They fail to consider that many if not most persons suffering from infectious diseases live in developing countries and have neither the means nor the motivation to migrate abroad in large numbers. It must be stated clearly that advocating a more relaxed attitude towards immigration control only means that a person who otherwise qualifies for admission under the immigration law of the destination country could not be denied admission solely on account of his or her (suspected) infection.[166]

Financial considerations

Financial considerations are often used as a justification to exclude persons who are suspected of carrying infectious diseases. Many countries argue that admission of persons who carry such diseases would impose a significant burden on public health systems, especially if the disease warrants lengthy medical treatment, medication, and if the infected persons have many more years to live. Not surprisingly, this argument is particularly prominent among those who defend the exclusion of HIV/AIDS patients[167] but it has equally been used by Governments restricting the entry of persons with other infectious diseases.

There can, of course, be no doubt that the treatment of many of the diseases discussed here is expensive. What is, however, questionable is the arbitrary line that is drawn between certain diseases and the inconsistency with which the financial argument is used. This is particularly obvious considering that the most common diseases, including long-term illnesses and heart conditions, are not excluded from entry even though the costs of their treatment significantly exceeds those required for the treatment of HIV/AIDS and other diseases. Peter Bart's article, published in 1998, states:

> "In reality, no study has been done to show that HIV-infected immigrants are any more likely to wind up on the public dole than other aliens, particularly those suffering from other costly diseases. Still, hundreds of thousands of immigrants are allowed into the United States each year, many of whom may suffer from other terminal diseases, such as heart disease, kidney failure, and cancer, any of which could place at least as great a burden on the [health care system of the receiving country]."[168]

Economic impacts

Perhaps more legitimate are concerns about the economic impact that exclusion clauses and other travel restrictions may have on national economies and global commerce. The recent experiences of SARS and the avian bird flu have shown that the measures that followed the outbreak of these diseases have severely restricted trade and travel within and among the affected countries and were felt around the world.

Since the early sanitary agreements of the 19th century and the creation of the World Health Organization, the international agreements have acknowledged that border and health control measures interfere with trade and travel and, as such, also impact on administrative and political relationships.[169] As a result countries are at times reluctant to publicly confess and notify international organisations about the outbreak of infectious diseases for fear they may face embargoes and isolation.

As the example of India's handling of the plague in 1994 has shown, many countries consider health as a barrier to trade. However, economic considerations must stand behind the protection of public health and human life generally. Countries must, at all times, cooperate with international organisations, notify them about outbreaks, and inform their populations adequately at the earliest possible time. However, countries must exercise great caution when implementing restrictive and often punitive control measures.

International cooperation

This paper has repeatedly stressed that international cooperation is at the heart of any strategy to contain infectious diseases and that it is perhaps the only way to prevent and suppress these diseases effectively. Countries often have limited, if any, power to control infectious diseases locally and prevent their spread elsewhere. Many nations have set too low standards for public health and the prevention of disease; others maintain overly harsh restrictions needlessly affecting travel, trade, and individual freedom.[170]

The challenges posed by globalisation and infectious diseases are transnational in nature; the solutions therefore need to be collaborative and multilateral. "The distinction between national and international health policy has become irrelevant."[171]

Regrettably, too many countries have too often been reluctant to adopt adequate and proportionate measures to prevent the spread of infectious diseases and have failed in notifying and cooperating with other nations and international organisations. Countries fear economic and political consequences and worry about their prestige and public opinion if they openly confess to the outbreak of infectious diseases. There is some perception in some countries that "they could get away with it" and contain epidemics simply by covering them up.[172] These attempts have, however, largely been unsuccessful and have unnecessarily put public health and human life at risk.

The challenge of international cooperation, according to David Fidler, is "vertical" and "horizontal": "The vertical challenge is to incorporate and deepen the commitment of each state to infectious disease control within its own territory. The horizontal challenge is to harmonise the commitment to fighting infectious diseases in states throughout the world."[173] In relation to the Asian region, Myonsei Sohn suggested that:

"[t]he establishment of a comprehensive public health law network could help to influence each nation in Asia to comply with global governance of public health infrastructures which would help maintain the health of Asia's population, and in turn, the health of the international community."[174]

Development and aid

The emergence and re-emergence of infectious diseases is not spread evenly around the world. The achievements of the industrialised nations in the prevention and control of infectious diseases during the 20th century has not yet been matched by the developing countries. Especially, countries in sub-Saharan Africa and in parts of Asia are disproportionately affected by diseases such as Ebola, Marburg, tuberculosis, cholera, plague and HIV/AIDS. Research released in 2004 found that parasitic and infectious diseases account for 1.2 per cent of disease-related mortality in industrialised nations but for 43 per cent in developing nations.[175] The situation is further complicated by the fact that the monopoly on new drugs, vaccinations and the like is usually held by pharmaceutical companies in industrialised nations which can make effective preventive medication inaccessible to poor countries.[176]

Developing nations have limited, if any resources and capacities to prevent the outbreak and spread of infectious diseases. These nations require substantial financial and technical assistance to improve their health systems and sanitary conditions, and the costs will have to be borne by industrialised nations.[177] The provision of inexpensive medication, and of sterile medical and surgical equipment, too, plays an important role in preventing infectious diseases.[178]

Behavioural change and education

One of the most immediate, inexpensive, yet most efficient ways to prevent the spread of infectious disease is a change in human behaviour. Individual behaviour has a direct impact on transmission with and exposure to diseases. The notion that the threat of diseases comes solely from the outside and can be avoided through rigid exclusion laws is illusory as long as too many people engage in risky behaviour and expose themselves to infectious diseases, often unnecessarily. This problem is worsened by community groups and religious leaders who advocate unsafe sexual practices by discouraging the use of condoms.[179]

Responsible and careful behaviour significantly reduces the chances of becoming infected with many diseases. Such behaviour should be encouraged by all levels of government and society through information, education and counselling.[180]

This issue is best illustrated in the context of HIV/AIDS, where it has been proven that adoption of responsible behaviour does significantly reduce the risk of infections. The proper and consistent use of safe sexual practices, condoms, and sterile needles largely eliminates the risk of acquiring or transmitting the virus.[181] Equally, a reduction in the number of sexual partners, too, has proven health benefits; however, contemporary society has on the one hand adopted more relaxed attitudes towards long-term monogamous relationships and on the other hand it continues to prevent some parts of society from forming such relationships.[182]

A final important point in preventing and suppressing infectious disease is education. Efforts to inform the public about how infectious diseases are transmitted and how people can best prevent an infection have a direct impact on the spread of diseases. Equally, secrecy, censorship and restrictions on information concerning infectious diseases severely hinder any effective response. One of the most valuable means of infection control is also the least intrusive and least expensive: health education to promote safer behaviours and better sanitary practices (such as hand washing, disinfection, masks, ventilation, and avoidance of contacts) can be highly effective in reducing the risks of infectious diseases.[183]

Conclusion

The lack of comprehensive and profound knowledge on many aspects of infectious diseases, their transmission, prevention and treatment, is perhaps the main obstacle in combating this phenomenon more effectively. One of the most immediate responses to the emergence and re-emergence of infectious diseases must be scientific research and the collection of data and information on the causes of outbreaks, the role played by national governments and health agencies, international organisations and the legal frameworks that exist at domestic and multilateral levels, and the results need to be woven into a more coherent strategy as part of future policy change and law reform.

Notes

* The author wishes to thank Mr Angus Graham for his excellent support and research assistance.

1 These diseases are sometimes referred to as "emerging infectious diseases" which are defined as "diseases of infectious origin whose incidence in humans has increased within the past two decades or threatens to increase in the near future"; see Scott Burris, "Law as a Structural Factor in the Spread of Communicable Disease" (1999) 36 *Houston Law Review* 1755, 1759–1760.

2 David P. Fuller, "Microbialpolitik: Infectious Diseases and International Relations" (1998) 14 *American University Int'l l Law Review* 1, 8.

3 Mary E. Wilson, "Travel and the Emergence of Infectious Diseases" (1995) 1 *Emerging Infectious Diseases* 39, 39; Fidler (n 2 above), p 17.

4 Burris (n 1 above), p 1762.

5 David P. Fidler *et al*, "Emerging and Reemerging Infectious Diseases: Challenges for International, National, and State Law" (1997) 31 *Int'l Lawyer* 773, 775.

6 Burris (n 1 above), pp 1774–1775.

7 In this study "PR China" refers to the Chinese mainland, the People's Republic of China. "Taiwan" refers to the Republic of China or Chinese Taipei. Since the revolution in 1949 both Chinas claim to be the "official" China. Internationally, the PR China is widely recognised as the official China. The Government of the PR China considers Taiwan a so-called "renegade province".

8 *See* generally Jend Vedsted-Hansen, "Non-admission policies and the right to protection: refugees' choice versus states' exclusion?", in Frances Nicholson and Patrick Tworney (eds), *Refugee Rights and Realities, Evolving International Concepts and Regimes* (Cambridge University Press, 1999), pp 269–270.

9 Section 8(2)(a) Immigration Act 1958 (Brunei); s 8(3)(a) Immigration Act 1959/1963 (Malaysia); Section 8(1)(a) Migration Act 1978 (PNG); s 29(a)(5) Immigration Act 1940 (Philippines); s 8 (3)(c) Immigration Act 1959 (Singapore); art 17(9) Immigration Law (Taiwan); s 12(2) and (9) Immigration Act 1979 (Thailand).

10 Section 8(2)(g) Immigration Act 1956 (Brunei); s 8(3)(g) Immigration Act 1959/1963 (Malaysia); Section 29(a)(4) Immigration Act 1940 (Philippines); s 8(3)(g) Immigration Act 1959 (Singapore).

11 Section 29(a)(14) Immigration Act 1940 (Philippines); s 12(3) Immigration Act 1979 (Thailand).

12 Section 29(a)(9) Immigration Act 1940 (Philippines).

13 Section 8(2) Immigration Act 1958 (Btunei); art 17(1) Immigration Law (Taiwan).

14 Section 8(2)(e) Immigration Act 1956 (Brunei); s 8(3)(e) Immigration Act 1959/1963 (Malaysia); s 29(a)(4) Immigration Act 1940 (Philippines); s 8(3)(e) Immigration Act 1959 (Singapore); s 12(8) Immigration Act 1979 (Thailand).

15 Section 8(2)(e), (f) Immigration Act 1956 (Brunei); s 8(3)(f) Immigration Act 1959/1963 (Malaysia); s 29(a)(4) Immigration Act 1940 (Philippines); s 8(3)(f) Immigration Act 1959 (Singapore); s 12(8) Immigration Act 1979 (Thailand).

16 Section 29(a)(7) Immigration Act 1940 (Philippines).

17 Section 8(2)(d) Immigration Act 1956 (Brunei); s 8(3)(d) Immigration Act 1959/1963 (Malaysia); s 29(a)(3) Immigration Act 1940 (Philippines); s 8(3)(d) Immigration Act 1959 (Singapore); art 17(7) Immigration Law (Taiwan); s 12(6) Immigration Act 1979 (Thailand).

18 Article 17(a) Immigration Act 1992 (Indonesia).

19 Section 8(2)(i) Immigration Act 1956 (Brunei); art 17(b) Immigration Act 1992 (Indonesia); s 8(3)(i) Immigration Act 1959/1963 (Malaysia); s 29(8)(a) Immigration Act 1940 (Philippines); s 8(3)(i) Immigration Act 1959 (Singapore).

20 Section 8(2)(j) Immigration Act 1956 (Brunei); s 8(3)(j) Immigration Act 1959/1963 (Malaysia); s 8(3)(j) Immigration Act 1959 (Singapore).

21 Article 9 Law on Immigration 1994 (Cambodia); art 12, Law on Control of the Entry and Exit of Aliens 1986 (PRC); art 17(c) Immigration Act 1992 (Indonesia); s 9(1)(a) Immigration Act 1959/1963 (Malaysia); s 12 Immigration Act 1940 (Philippines); ss 8(3)(a) and 9 Immigration Act 1959 (Singapore); art 17(13) Immigration Law (Taiwan); s 12(7) Immigration Act 1979 (Thailand); Article 6(4) Ordinance on Entry, Exit, Residence and Travel of Foreigners 1992 (Vietnam).

22 Section 8(2)(l) Immigration Act 1956 (Brunei); art 17(e) Immigration Act 1992 (Indonesia); s 8 (3)(k) Immigration Act 1959/1963 (Malaysia); ss 29(a)(15) and (16) Immigration Act 1940 (Philippines); s 8(3)(l) Immigration Act 1959 (Singapore); art 17(11) Immigration Law (Taiwan); s 12(11) Immigration Act 1979 (Thailand).

23 Section 8(2) Immigration Act 1958 (Brunei); s 8(3)(n) Immigration Act 1959/1963 (Malaysia); s 29(a)(10) Immigration Act 1940 (Philippines); s 8(3)(n) Immigtation Act 1959 (Singapore).

24 Section 29(a)(14) Immigration Act 1940 (Philippines).
25 Section 8(2)(c)(ii) Immigration Act 1956 (Brunei); s 8(3)(b) Immigration Act 1959/1963 (Malaysia); s 8(1)(b)(ii) Migration Act 1978 (PNG); s 29(a)(2) Immigration Act 1940 (Philippines); s 8(3)(b) Immigration Act 1959 (Singapore); art 17(8) Immigration Law (Taiwan); s 12(4) Immigration Act 1979 (Thailand); art 6(3) Ordinance on Entry, Exit, Residence and Travel of Foreigners 1992 (Vietnam).
26 Section 8(2)(b) Immigration Act 1956 (Brunei); s 8(3)(b) Immigration Act 1959/1963 (Malaysia); s 8(7)(b)(i) Migration Act 1978 (PNG); s 29(a)(1) Immigration Act 1940 (Philippines); s 8(3)(b) Immigration Act 1959 (Singapore); art 17(8) Immigration Law (Taiwan); s 12(4) Immigration Act 1979 (Thailand).
27 Section 8(2)(c)(i) Immigration Act 1956 (Brunei); s 8(3)(c) Immigration Act 1959/1963 (Malaysia); s 8(1)(c) Migration Act 1978 (PNG); s 8(3)(c) Immigration Act 1959 (Singapore); s 12(5) Immigration Act 1979 (Thailand).
28 Section 8(2)(k) Immigration Act 1956 (Brunei); s 8(3)(k) Immigration Act 1959/1963 (Malaysia); s 8(3)(k) Immigration Act 1959 (Singapore); s 12(10) Immigration Act 1979 (Thailand).
29 The entry of prohibited immigrants in an offence under s 20 Immigration Act 1958 (Brunei); art 29 Law on Control of the Entry and Exit of Aliens 1986 (PRC); s 8(5) Immigration Act 1959/1963 (Malaysia); s 16(1)(a) Migration Act 1978 (PNG); s 8(5) Immigration Act 1959 (Singapore).
30 Section 8(3)(ba) Immigration Act 1959 (Singapore): "The following persons are members of the prohibited classes: . . . any person suffering from Acquired Immune Deficiency Syndrome or infected with the Human Immunodeficiency Virus."
31 Article 7(4) Rules Governing the Implementation of the Law of the PRC on the Entry and Exit of Aliens 1986: "Aliens coming under the following categories shall not be allowed to enter China: . . . (4) An Alien suffering from mental disorder, leprosy, AIDS, venereal diseases, contagious diseases and other infectious diseases."
32 Section 29(a)(2) Immigration Act 1940 (Philippines).
33 Section 8(2)(b)(ii) Immigration Act 1956 (Brunei); art 7(4) Rules Governing the Implementation of the Law of the PRC on the Entry and Exit of Aliens 1986; s 8(3)(b) Immigration Act 1959/1963 (Malaysia); s 8(3)(b) Immigration Act 1959 (Singapore).
34 Section 8(2)(b)(ii) Immigration Act 1956 (Brunei); s 8(3)(b) Immigration Act 1959/1963 (Malaysia); s 29(a)(2) Immigration Act 1940 (Philippines) "dangerous and contagious"; s 8(3)(b) Immigration Act 1959 (Singapore); art 17(8) Immigration Law (Taiwan).
35 Article 11(1)(1) Immigration Control Act 1992 (Republic of Korea); art 6(3) Ordinance on Entry, Exit, Residence and Travel of Foreigners 1992 (Vietnam).
36 Section 29(a)(2) Immigration Act 1940 (Philippines).
37 Ministerial Regulations under s 12(4) Immigration Act 1979 (Thailand).
38 Quarantine and Prevention of Disease Act 1934 (Brunei); Law on the Prevention and Treatment of Communicable Diseases (PRC); Communicable Disease Prevention Act 2000 (Republic of Korea); Prevention and Control of Infectious Diseases Act 1988 (Malaysia); Quarantine Regulations 1956 (PNG); Infectious Diseases Act (Singapore); Communicable Disease Control Act 1944 (Taiwan); Communicable Diseases Act 1980 (2523) (Thailand).
39 Ministerial Regulations under s 12(4) Immigration Act 1979 (Thailand).
40 Cap 141, LHK [hereinafter QPDO]. The drafting of the QPDO "was based on the principles stipulated in the International Health Regulations (the 'IHR') . . .". See SARS Expert Committee, Hong Kong SAR, *Public Health Legislation on Infectious Diseases Control in Hong Kong* (Hong Kong: Department of Health: 2003) at 1 [*Public Health Legislation*]. *See also*, David P. Fidler, "'SARS: Political Pathology of the First Post-Westphalian Pathogen" (2003) 31 *Journal of Law,*

Medicine & Ethics 485, 487; J. Speakman *et al*, "Quarantine in Severe Acute Respiratory Syndrome (SARS) and Other Emerging Infectious Diseases" (2003) 31 *Journal of Law, Medicine & Ethics* 63, 64.

41 Prevention of the Spread of Infectious Diseases Regulations, Cap 141B LHK [hereinafter PSIDR].

42 The Director of Health is attributed the responsibility "for the enactment of a total of 23 public health legislations," including the *QPDO*: SARS Expert Committee, Hong Kong SAR, *Briefing Paper For SARS Expert Committee On Prevention and Control of Communicable Diseases in Hong Kong* (Hong Kong: Department of Health: 2003) at 5.

43 L.N. 79 of 2003.

44 Prior to SARS being added to the list, there were 27 infectious diseases listed in the First Schedule. These were: Acute Poliomyelitis, Amoebic Dysentery, Bacillary Dysentery, Chickenpox, Cholera, Dengue Fever, Diphtheria, Food Poisoning, Legionnaires' Disease, Leprosy, Malaria, Measles, Meningococcal Infections, Mumps, Paratyphoid Fever, Plague, Rabies, Relapsing Fever, Rubella, Scarlet Fever, Tetanus, Tuberculosis, Typhoid Fever, Typhus, Viral Hepatitis, Whooping Cough, and Yellow Fever. Severe Acute Respiratory Syndrome became the 28th infectious disease to be listed on the First Schedule to the QPDO.

45 QPDO, s 22(1): "Any vessel or aircraft arriving in Hong Kong may be visited by a health officer, who may exercise all or any of the powers vested in him by section 31, and shall deal with the vessel or aircraft in the manner prescribed by or under this Ordinance."

46 QPDO, s 29(1): "The guard of any train on which a case of any quarantinable disease is present shall on arrival at the first station report the facts to the station master, who shall telephone or telegraph them to a health officer."; s 29(2): "The station master shall detain the carriage in which the sick person is and all other occupants thereof for examination by a health officer, and shall detach the carriage from the rest of the train and keep it at the station until the examination has been made, or send the carriage to another station at which the examination can be more expeditiously carried out and from which the sick person and other persons may be more easily conveyed to a hospital or place of isolation"; s 29(3): "Any person suffering or suspected to be suffering from any such disease shall be removed to a hospital or place of isolation and remain there until discharged by the officer in charge thereof."

47 QPDO, s 28(2): "The master of any vessel or aircraft shall report to a health officer any case of infectious disease which he knows to exist, or to have existed during the voyage, on his vessel or aircraft."

48 QPDO, s 31: "On the arrival of any vessel at the quarantine anchorage, a health officer shall go on board and put to the master and surgeon, if any, or to any other person on board such questions as he deems necessary in order to ascertain the state of health of persons on board, the sanitary condition of the ship and cargo and the sanitary conditions of the port of departure or of intermediate ports touched at, and may require the presence for inspection and examination of all persons on board, and may inspect every part of the ship and demand to see the journal or log book and all the ship's papers."

49 QPDO, s 37: "Whenever a health officer shall so require, all passengers on board any vessel which is infected or suspected vessel with respect to any quarantinable disease or so many as he may direct shall be taken to a quarantine station and there kept and attended to for such a time as he may deem proper before allowing them to return on board the vessel or to be transferred to any other vessel or to land in Hong Kong. The period of detention shall in no case be

greater than is permitted by this Ordinance or any regulation made thereunder"; s 38: "A health officer may detain in a quarantine station, until such time as the disease is no longer communicable to others, any person desirous of landing in Hong Kong who on arrival is found to be suffering from an infectious disease."

50 Allyn L. Taylor, "Controlling the Global Spread of Diseases: Toward a Reinforced Role for the International Health Regulations" (1997) 33 *Houston Law Review* 1327, 1332.

51 *Ibid.*, pp 1333–35 [footnotes omitted].

52 *See* generally, B. K. Mandal *et al, Infectious Diseases* (Blackwell, 6th ed, 2004) 187–188.

53 Susan Sachs, "More screening of immigrants for tuberculosis sought" (31 Dec 2000) 28(1/2) *Migration World Magazine.*

54 Mandel *et al* (n 52 above), pp 126–127.

55 WHO, "Cholera, 2003" (2005) 79(31) *Weekly epidemiological record* 281, 283.

56 Fidler *et al* (n 5 above), p 778; David P. Fidler, "Mission Impossible? International Law and Infectious Diseases" (1996) 10 *Temple Int'l and Comparative Law Journal* 493, 498.

57 WHO, "Cholera, Senegal" (2005) 80 *Weekly Epidemiological Record* 134.

58 Mandel *et al* (n 52 above), p 127; WHO, "Plague" (2005) 80 *Weekly Epidemiological Record* 138–140.

59 Mandel *et al* (n 52 above), p 110.

60 Fidler *et al* (n 5 above), p 778; Fidler (n 56 above), p 498; Taylor (n 50 above), p 1348.

61 Mandel *et al* (n 52 above), pp 33–35.

62 Burris (n 1 above), p 1765.

63 *See* further, Mandal *et al* (n 52 above), pp 228–230; WHO, "Ebola haemorrhagic fever – Fact Sheet" (2005) 79(49) *Weekly Epidemiological record* 435–439.

64 Fidler *et al* (n 5 above), p 778.

65 WHO, "Ebola haemorrhagic fever – Fact Sheet" (2005) 79(49) *Weekly Epidemiological record* 435, 438.

66 WHO, "Ebola haemorrhagic fever – Fact Sheet" (2005) 79(49) *Weekly Epidemiological record* 435, 435–436.

67 Mandel *et al* (n 52 above), p 229; WHO, "Marburg haemorrhagic fever – Fact Sheet" (2005) 80 *Weekly Epidemiological Record* 135–138.

68 For recent reports see, for example, Sharon LaFraneier & Denise Grady, "Fear slows virus fight in Angola" (18 April 2005) *International Herald Tribune* (Bangkok ed) 5; WHO, "Marburg, haemorrhagic fever, Angola" (2005) 80 *Weekly Epidemiological Record* 134–135.

69 WHO (n 67 above), p 136.

70 WHO, *World Health Report 2003: Shaping the Future* (WHO, 2003) 73–74.

71 WHO (n 75 below); SARS Expert Committee, Hong Kong SAR, *SARS in Hong Kong: From Experience to Action* (Hong Kong Department of Health, 2003) 5; US Department of Health and Human Services (n 72 below).

72 Approximately 10–20% report the presence of diarrhoea: US Department of Health and Human Services, *Severe Acute Respiratory Syndrome (SARS)* (US Department of Health and Human Services, 2004) 18, online: Centres for Disease Control and Prevention www.cdc.gov/ncidod/sars/factsheet.htm.

73 WHO (n 74 below); WHO (n 75 below).

74 WHO, *Preliminary Clinical Description of Severe Acute Respiratory Syndrome* (WHO, 2003) online: WHO www.who.int/csr/sars/clinical/en.

75 WHO, *Alert, Verification and Public Health Management of SARS in the Post-Outbreak Period* (WHO, 2003) online: WHO www.who.int/csr/sars/postoutbreak/en.

76 WHO, *Severe Acute Respiratory Syndrome (SARS)*, WHO, 113th Sess., Annex, Agenda Item 8.3, WHO Doc EB113/33 (2003) 2.

77 *Ibid.*

78 WHO (n 74 above)

79 Alfred DeMaria Jr, "The Globalization of Infectious Diseases: Questions Posed by the Behavioural, Social, Economic and Environmental Context of Emerging Infections" (2004) 11 *New England Journal of Int'l and Comparative Law* 37, 48.

80 WHO, *World Health Report 2003: Shaping the Future* (WHO, 2003) 74. *Cf* Mandal *et al* (n 52 above), p 63.

81 The community outbreak occurred in the Amoy Gardens Housing Estate: WHO (n 80 above), p 74.

82 WHO (n 76 above), p 2.

83 Sarah J. Marshall, "World Health Organization, Expert Committee Finds Little Fault in Hong Kong's Response to SARS" (2003) 83(11) *Bulletin World Health Organization* 848 at 848.

84 WHO (n 80 above), p 74; Christopher-Paul Milne, "Racing the Globalisation of Infectious Diseases" (2004) 11 *New England Journal Int'l & Comparative Law* 1, 6. This figure is subject to further variation depending on the age of the patient. The mortality rate for a 24-year-old patient is 1% and 50% for patients 65 years of age and above: Abu S. M. Abdullah *et al*, "Lessons From the Severe Acute Respiratory Syndrome Outbreak in Hong Kong" (2003) 9(9) *Emerging Infectious Diseases* 1042, 1043.

85 Fidler (n 40 above), p 491; Jacques de Lisle, "Atypical Pneumonia and Ambivalent Law and Politics: SARS and the Response to SARS in China" (2004) 77 *Temple Law Review* 193, 206.

86 *Severe Acute Respiratory Syndrome (SARS)*, WHO, 54th Sess., Annex, Agenda Item 14, WHO Doc. WPR/RC54/8 (2004) 3.

87 Hong Kong Special Administrative Region, SARS Expert Committee, *Public Health Control Measures* (Hong Kong Department of Health, 2003) 4.

88 This figure includes 386 hospital staff and medical interns who were infected: Hong Kong SAR, Health, Welfare and Food Bureau, *SARS Bulletin* (23 June 2003) (Hong Kong Health, Welfare and Food Bureau, 2003) 1.

89 Marshall (n 83 above), p 848. Note: the figure given by the SARS Expert Committee is 300 deaths: SARS Expert Committee, Hong Kong SAR, *SARS in Hong Kong: From Experience to Action* (Hong Kong Department of Health, 2003) 6.

90 WHO (n 80 above), p 75. For more statistics, *see* W. K. Lam *et al*, "Overview on SARS in Asia and the World" (2004) 8 *Respirology* 2, 2; Lawrence O. Gostin *et al*, "Ethical and Legal Challenges Posed by Severe Acute Respiratory Syndrome" (2003) 290 *Journal of the American Medical Association* 3229, 3229; SARS Expert Committee, Hong Kong SAR, *SARS in Hong Kong: From Experience to Action* (Hong Kong Department of Health, 2003) 5.

91 Social effects of the 2003 Outbreak in the Hong Kong SAR include the closure of schools from 29 March 2003 until the resumption of classes "in phases" during April and May 2003: SARS Expert Committee (n 87 above), p 7. Household contacts of SARS patients were placed under home confinement and quarantine, travel warnings issued by the WHO had enormous detrimental effects on the travel industry, while patients and ethnic groups experienced prejudice and discrimination during the period. Furthermore, the psychological impact on health care workers and families of SARS patients was incalculable: WHO, *Severe Acute Respiratory Syndrome (SARS): Status of the Outbreak and Lessons for the Immediate Future* (WHO, 2003) 2.

92 Milne (n 84 above), p 6.

93 WHO, *Severe Acute Respiratory Syndrome (SARS): Status of the Outbreak and Lessons for the Immediate Future* (WHO, 2003) 1.

94 WHO (n 80 above), pp 74–75.

95 WHO, (n 93 above), p 1.

96 WHO Press Release, "SARS – Hong Kong Removed From List of Areas With Local Transmission" (23 June 2003), online: WHO www.wpro.who.int/sars/docs/pressreleases/pr_23062003_.asp.

97 WHO, "Update 17 – Travel Advice – Hong Kong Special Administrative Region of China, and Guangdong Province, China" (2 April 2003), online: WHO www.who.int/csr/sars/archive/2003_04_02/en.

98 WHO, "Update 86 – Hong Kong Removed From List of Areas with Local Transmission" (23 June 2003), online: WHO www.who.int/csr/don/2003_06_23/en.

99 Since the Hong Kong SAR was declared SARS-free by the WHO on 2 June 2003, there has been no new reported case of SARS in Hong Kong: "Hong Kong Steps Up Measures After China's SARS Case Confirmed" *Asian Economic News* (12 January 2004), online: Asian Economic News www.findarticles.com/p/articles/mi_m0WDP/is_2004_Jan_12/ai_112093272.

100 WHO (n 80 above), p 78.

101 WHO (n 75 above).

102 WHO, "Severe Acute Respiratory Syndrome (SARS) – Multi-Country Outbreak – Update 31: Coronavirus Never Before Seen in Humans is the Cause of SARS" (16 April 2003), online: WHO www.who.int/csr/don/2003_04_16/en/. The coronavirus in humans was later found in "almost identical" form in the masked palm civet cat and raccoon dog, considered a delicacy in Mainland China. However, the role played by such "domesticated game animals" in the transmission of the disease is inconclusive: WHO (n 80 above).

103 WHO (n 80 above), p 78.

104 WHO (n 74 above). Treatment during the 2003 Outbreak also included the administration of "corticosteroids, antiviral therapy, [and] Chinese medicine": SARS Expert Committee, Hong Kong SAR, *SARS in Hong Kong: From Experience to Action* (Hong Kong Department of Health, 2003) 14.

105 WHO (n 74 above).

106 Mandel *et al* (n 52 above), p 63.

107 DeMaria Jr (n 79 above), p 52; Lawrence O. Gostin, "Pandemic Influenza: Public Health Preparedness for the Next Global Health Emergency" (2004) *Journal of Law, Medicine and Ethics* 565, 566; WHO, "Avian influenza, Cambodia" (2005) 80 *Weekly Epidemiological Record* 133 at 133–134.

108 *Supplemental Appropriations Act* 1987, Pub L No 100–171, 518, 101 Stat 391, 475 (known as the *Helms Amendment*).

109 *Immigration and Nationality Act* § 1182(a)(6). The term "dangerous contagious disease" under the *Immigration and Nationality Act* 1952 included a list of eight diseases: chancroid, gonorrhoea, granuloma inguinale, HIV, infectious leprosy, lymphogranuloma venereum, infectious stage syphilis, and active tuberculosis. The provision was substituted (now termed "communicable disease of public health significance") by the *Immigration Act* 1990, Pub L No 101–649, 601, 104 Stat 4978, 5067. *See* further Christine N. Cimini, "The United States Policy on HIV Infected Aliens: Is Exclusion an Effective Solution?" (1991–1992) 7 *Connecticut J Int'l Law* 367 at 368–376; Juan P. Osuna, "The Exclusion from the United States of Aliens infected with the AIDS Virus: Recent Developments and Prospects for the Future" (1993) 16(1) *Houston Journal Int'l Law* 1 at 5–39.

110 Leonard J. Nelson III, "Current Developments: International Travel Restrictions and the AIDS Epidemic" (1997) 81 *American Journal of International Law* 230, 232–233.

111 Milne (n 84 above), p 4.

112 Peter A. Bart, "Lambskin Borders: An Argument for the Abolition of the United States Exclusion of HIV–Positive Immigrants" (1998) 12 *Georgetown Immigration Law Journal* 323, 324–325; Cimini (n 109 above), p 377; Mandal *et al* (n 52 above), pp 169–171; Milne (n 84 above), p 4; *cf* Fernando Chang-Muy, "HIV/AIDS and International Travel: International Organisations, Regional Governments, and the United States Respond" (1990–1991) 23 *NYU Journal Int'l Law & Politics* 1047, 1047.

113 Bart (n 112 above), p 343; *see* further Mandal *et al* (n 52 above), pp 169–170.

114 Sarah N. Qureshi, "Global Ostracism of HIV-Positive Aliens: International Restrictions Barring HIV-Positive Aliens" (1995) 19 *Maryland Journal of Int'l Law and Trade* 81, 93 with reference to 43 *International Digest of Health Legislation* 33 (1992).

115 *Ibid.*, p 94 with reference to (1993) 44 *International Digest of Health Legislation* 43.

116 *Ibid.*, p 95.

117 Ministerial Regulations No 11 (1986) under *Immigration Act* 1979 (Thailand).

118 Oureshi (n 114 above), p 87.

119 Peri H. Alkas & Wayne X. Shandera, "HIV and AIDS in Africa: African Policies in Response to AIDS in relation to Various National Legal Traditions" (1996) 17 *Journal of Legal Medicine* 527, 541.

120 Nelson (n 110 above), p 235.

121 Bart (n 112 above), p 344; Cimini (n 109 above), p 375.

122 Cited in Bart (n 112 above), p 349.

123 Osuna (n 109 above), p 14; *cf* Nelson (n 110 above), p 231.

124 Gostin (n 127 below), p 413; Nelson (n 110 above), pp 233–234.

125 Fidler *et al* (n 5 above), p 16; Taylor (n 50 above), p 1340.

126 Fidler *et al* (n 5 above), p 24.

127 Lawrence O. Gostin, "World Health Law: Toward a New Conception of Global Health Governance for the 21st Century" (2005) 5 *Yale Journal of Health Policy, Law & Ethics* 413, 414. For a complete list of international agreements *see* Fidler (n 134 below), pp 22–23 and 24–26.

128 Frank Gutteridge, "The World Health Organization: Its Scope and Achievements" (1963) 37(1) *Temple Law Quarterly* 1, 2.

129 14 UNTS 185, hereinafter WHO Constitution.

130 Article 1 WHO Constitution.

131 Article 2 WHO Constitution.

132 Article 3 WHO Constitution. *Cf* Nelson (n 110 above), p 234.

133 175 UNTS 216.

134 David P. Fidler, *International Law and Infectious Diseases* (Clarendon, 1999) 59–61.

135 Gostin (n 127 above), p 415.

136 Fidler (n 56 above), p 495.

137 WHO, *Fourth Report of the Committee on International Quarantine*, 10th WHA, 4th Session, Official Records No 79 (1957) Annex 1, at 495 cited in Chang-Muy (n 112 above), p 1049.

138 Nelson (n 110 above), p 234.

139 Chang-Muy (n 112 above), p 104 with reference to WHO, *Global Strategy for the Prevention and Control of AIDS*, UN Doc A/43/341 (1988) 5.

140 Fidler (n 2 above), p 26.

141 Taylor (n 50 above), pp 1346–1347.

142 Fidler (n 40 above), pp 487–488.

143 Fidler (n 134 above), pp 68–70; Fidler (n 56 above), pp 495, 499; Fidler *et al* (n 5 above), p 778; Taylor (n 50 above), pp 1329–1330.

144 Gutteridge (n 128 above), pp 6–7.
145 Fidler *et al* (n 5 above), p 779; Taylor (n 50 above), p 1352; Fidler (n 134 above), pp 71–79.
146 Milne (n 84 above), p 34; *cf* Fidler (n 40 above), p 488.
147 Gostin (n 107 above), p 568; Taylor (n 50 above), p 1351.
148 Gostin (n 127 above), pp 415–416.
149 Gostin (n 107 above), pp 569–570.
150 Fidler *et al* (n 5 above), p 783; Taylor (n 50 above), p 1347.
151 Gutteridge (n 128 above), p 2.
152 Burris (n 1 above), p 1780.
153 On HIV/AIDS *see* Bart (n 112 above), p 343.
154 On SARS *see* Elim Chan & Andreas Schloenhardt, "The 2003 SARS Outbreak in Hong Kong: A Review of Legislative and Border Control Measures" (2004) *Singapore Journal of Legal Studies* 484 at 505–506. On HIV/AIDS *see* Bart (n 112 above), p 343; Nelson (n 110 above), p 235.
155 Bart (n 112 above), p 343; Cimini (n 109 above), p 380.
156 Xinghuo Pang *et al*, "Evaluation of Control Measures Implemented in the Severe Acute Respiratory Syndrome Outbreak in Beijing, 2003" (2003) 290 *Journal of the American Medical Association* 3215 at 3220.
157 Andreas Schloenhardt, "Immigration and Refugee Law in the Asia Pacific Region" (2002) 32(3) *Hong Kong Law Journal* 519 at 529–530.
158 Taylor (n 50 above), p 1361.
159 *See* further "To Protect Europe from 'Asiatic' Diseases" in Fidler (n 134 above), pp 28–35.
160 Gostin (n 127 above), p 419.
161 Chang Muy (n 112 above), p 1058.
162 *See* further Elizabeth McCormack, "HIV-infected Haitian Refugees: An Argument against Exclusion" (1993) 7 *Georgetown Immigration Law Journal* 149–171.
163 Gostin (n 107 above), p 570.
164 Gostin (n 107 above), p 571. *Cf* Cimini (n 109 above), p 377.
165 Burris (n 1 above), p 1776.
166 Bart (n 112 above), p 356; Cimini (n 109 above), p 384.
167 Cimini (n 109 above), p 384.
168 Bart (n 112 above), pp 354–355.
169 Gostin (n 107 above), p 571; Nelson (n 110 above), p 234.
170 Fidler (n 56 above), p 496; Gostin (n 127 above), pp 417–418; Taylor (n 50 above), p 1337.
171 Fidler *et al* (n 5 above), p 776.
172 See the points raised by Gostin (n 107 above), p 571.
173 Fidler (n 2 above), p 15.
174 Myongsei Sohn *et al*, "Globalization, Public Health, and International Law" (2004) 32 *Journal of Law, Medicine and Ethics* 87 at 87.
175 Milne (n 84 above), p 18.
176 Burris (n 1 above), p 1774.
177 Fidler (n 40 above), p 501.
178 Nelson (n 110 above), p 235.
179 Bart (n 112 above), p 348; Burris (n 1 above), p 1764.
180 Cimini (n 109 above), pp 380, 384.
181 Bart (n 112 above), p 350.
182 Burris (n 1 above), p 1779.
183 Osuna (n 100 above), p 21; Gostin (n 107 above), p 569.

116

PRELUDE TO THE PLAGUE

Public health and politics at America's
Pacific gateway, 1899

Robert Barde

Source: *Journal of the History of Medicine*, 58 (2003), 153–86.

Abstract

San Francisco played a crucial role in the formulation of American
immigration policy vis-à-vis Asia in the late nineteenth and
early twentieth centuries. During this period, it was often
difficult to differentiate political struggles over the exclusion of
Asians from other conflicts. This article examines one such
arena: an acrimonious, well-documented argument in 1899 between
Federal and various State and local authorities over the arrival
of a Japanese passenger liner that may—or may not—have
been carrying bubonic plague. Six months later, the plague
unquestionably arrived, resulting in the well-known San Francisco
plague epidemic of 1900 in which more than 110 people died.
Reviewing the 1899 prelude, the public attitudes of the various
health authorities, and the way the press reported health issues,
collectively give some sense of that historical space where the
regulation of public health, politics, and the immigration industry
intersected and were fiercely contested.

Bubonic plague descended on San Francisco in the year 1900. Representing
the first confirmed cases of bubonic plague in the United States, this epidemic
took more than 100 lives. The San Francisco plague outbreak was widely
reported at the time in the local and national newspapers and public health
journals; over the years, historians and legal scholars have written extensively
about this event.[1] The present article seeks not to add to that already volu-
minous literature, but to focus on a related event in the preceding year—one

350

that was, in retrospect, a harbinger of the public health and political battles to come.

On 27 June 1899, the Japanese passenger liner *Nippon Maru* arrived in San Francisco following her third crossing of the Pacific. The previous year's maiden voyage had been received in the United States with much fanfare as a signal of a coming golden age of trade across the Pacific. This particular journey, however, would bring her only notoriety and controversy. The *Nippon Maru*, the loveliest ship ever to steam through the Golden Gate, was to become a carrier of death and, perhaps, the plague itself.

This description of the *Nippon Maru* incident incorporates not only the movements of the ship and its passengers and crew, but also a number of related contextual factors: the state of knowledge about the etiology of the plague; evolving federal control of immigration and public health matters vis-à-vis state and local authorities; local political factions and disputes; the roles of the popular and medical press; and the divergent attitudes of whites toward either Japanese or Chinese communities. The historical space under consideration is where the immigration industry and the regulators of public health intersected with fierce partisan political contests, where important intermediaries in this struggle were the daily newspapers and medical journals that provided the public with information—or, more than occasionally, misinformation—that helped form public opinion. Previous authors have asserted that this process was driven by anti-Chinese nativism and/or the desire of health authorities at various levels to increase the powers of their particular office by exercising greater control over the public's health.[2] Although agreeing that these motivations existed, I argue that local political battles, factional in-fighting, and medical uncertainty predominated, both in the *Nippon Maru* incident and in the more serious events that followed.

Just as the *Nippon Maru*'s maiden voyage betokened Japan's expanding contacts with the world, so, too, was the United States increasing its presence in Asia. Troops moved back and forth to the Philippines and Hawaii; and American businessmen and missionaries went prospecting for wider contacts with China and Japan. Goods of all sorts were increasingly moving in both directions. Asian passengers, too, were crossing the ocean in ships of all descriptions. Among the new dangers that might accompany such intercourse was the heightened possibility of diseases reaching the American mainland via Asia.

To ward off such invaders, Americans depended on preemptive inspection abroad, and inspection at the U.S. port. The National Quarantine Act of 1893 granted the President the power (among other things) to post officers of the Marine Hospital Service to U.S. consulates in foreign ports. Every vessel leaving for the United States was to have its cargo and passengers inspected, and the "consular bill of health" presented to the Collector of Customs on arrival in the United States. The second bulwark was the inspection and, when deemed appropriate, disinfection and quarantine at the port of arrival. The Quarantine Station on Angel Island, operated by the U.S. Marine Hospital Service (the direct ancestor of the U.S. Public Health Service), came to play that role for San Francisco after opening in 1891.[3]

Conventional (white American) wisdom of the day was that Asia and its living conditions were perhaps even *more* conducive to cholera, smallpox, plague, yellow fever, and other diseases than was Europe. At the heart of the "Disease Early Warning System" in the Pacific were Sanitary Inspectors attached to U.S. consulates in Yokohama, Manila, and Honolulu. They reported regularly on local health conditions, especially those that might affect ships and people traveling to the U.S. mainland. Inspectors would also report on how well the local health establishment handled the predeparture inspection and disinfection of ships bound for the United States. Health authorities on the American mainland would pay special attention to any vessel arriving from a port where, say, plague had broken out or where the isolation and disinfection processes were known to be inadequate.

Dr. Stuart Eldridge, the American Sanitary Inspector in Yokohama, crisply stated the case in his report of October 1899:

> The position of Yokohama renders it, in some sense, the sanitary gateway of the Far East. Through this port passes all the travel from China, that center of infection, where epidemics rage with little or no effort made for their control, where plague and cholera seem to have become endemic and small pox, ever present. . . . Through it or from it go, too, all the Japanese passengers for United States ports in numbers already large and steadily increasing. . . . Precautions of the most stringent character on the part of the United States seem fully warranted. It was, undoubtedly, a knowledge of these facts that induced you in 1894 to appoint a representative of the Bureau at this point.[4]

Charged with minimizing the possibility of disease aboard any ship bound for the United States, the Sanitary Inspectors had little in the way of resources. Without disinfecting facilities or boarding vessels of their own, they had to cajole and bully local authorities into acting according to American standards when it came to inspecting and disinfecting ships bound for the United States. Passengers from the Japanese interior were inoculated and quarantined if coming from a known area of infection, then inspected, and their passport or ticket stamped before being allowed to board a ship headed directly for an American port. Ships originating in Yokohama were inspected by the resident *American* Sanitary Inspector and, if passed, given the consular bill of health needed for entry into the United States. Sanitary Inspector Eldridge noted that the same was true for ships originating in China or the Philippines. "Should any sickness of suspicious nature exist on board at arrival at Yokohama, (the Sanitary Inspector will) immediately visit the vessel, *irrespective of the fact that she has successfully passed the Japanese inspector of quarantine* [emphasis added], afterwards acting according to the circumstances."[5]

The American government was not alone in this obsession with trans-Pacific hygiene. Well before annexation, the government of independent Hawaii also maintained "sanitary inspectors and stationed them in Hongkong, Amoy, Nagasaki, Kobe, and Yokohama."[6] They feared infection from Chinese and Japanese laborers coming to work on the plantations, and upon arrival all Asian laborers were subjected to "from fourteen to twenty-one days' detention at the quarantine station on Mauliola Island, where their clothing and baggage is disinfected."[7]

High on the list of dreaded invaders was bubonic plague—a product of the bacillus now generally called *Yersenia pestis*. This old enemy had resurfaced in China in the nineteenth century. In 1894, bubonic plague appeared in Canton and Hong Kong, spreading to India (1896), Egypt, and South Africa, and even to continental Europe. By 1907, the annual death toll in India alone would exceed one million people.[8]

In 1896, Surgeon General Wyman was so worried at reports of the bubonic plague outbreak in China that he sent his most brilliant young scientist, Dr. Milton J. Rosenau, to head the Quarantine Station on Angel Island. Two months later, the Surgeon General ordered quarantine stations on the Pacific Coast to disinfect the baggage of all Chinese entering the United States. Even "several hundred bags of mail from the Orient were opened, each letter punctured, spread out, and fumigated."[9]

Up to 1899, the mainland United States had been spared, with no cases of bubonic plague having been documented with absolute certainty.[10] But, in an age aware of the process of "globalization" (if not the word itself), the spread of bubonic plague in other parts of the world was ominous. For a city such as San Francisco, open as it was to international intercourse of all sorts, the threat was very, very real.

This particular outbreak in Asia came when conventional wisdom about the plague and other diseases, and how to fight them, was in a state of flux. New theories were being developed, leading to deep differences within the medical profession. Just when the *Nippon Maru* was arriving with its controversial—and perhaps deadly—cargo, San Francisco's newspapers carried news of startling "discoveries" and miraculous new "cures." Such scientific advances promised to be the "silver bullets" that would fight diseases that were mass killers: smallpox, cholera, yellow fever, anthrax, diphtheria, and bubonic plague. That some of the "advances" were given substantial credence, even within the medical community, indicates how precarious knowledge was of diseases such as bubonic plague and how to combat them.

On 7 July, The *Examiner* ran a story that "London Doctor Discovers the Germ of Cancer" and that a "Serum Which Will Cure the Disease Expected Soon." Dr. Lambert Lack "discovered that the disease invariably began with an injury of a particular character to what is known as the basement membrane of the mucous membrane and its allied structures. . . . Having arrived at this important truth, he set to work to produce cancer in the lower animals, and succeeded. To produce a disease at will is the first step toward finding a cure for it. . . . Hence it is reasonable to expect that in a short time Dr. Lack will be in a position to give to the world a serum for the cure of cancer."

The London Pathological Society endorsed Dr. Lack's conclusions, as did a few physicians in San Francisco. The San Francisco *Examiner* quoted Dr. Winslow Anderson, editor and owner of the *Pacific Medical Journal*, who thought that "as we now have serum for small pox, for diphtheria, for pneumonia, for typhoid fever . . . it does not seem improbable to me that a serum or anti-toxine should be discovered [for] cancerous growths." Some within the San Francisco medical community were more skeptical. Dr. R. Beverly Cole was "not prepared to believe that the cancer germ has been found. Honest physicians, stimulated by inducements to research, rush into print before the facts justify the act. . . . Even Pasteur's discovery has not yet proven of utility. It is not practical. Not one cure of rabies is on record."[11]

Some, like Dr. W. P. Burke, eschewed mere skepticism. Dr. Burke told the *Examiner* that he did "not believe in the germ theory of disease of any kind, cancer included. . . . It is needless to say that I do not believe that any 'serum' of any kind will be found to destroy the 'germs' after they will have entered the body. The cure is to raise up the standard of tissue to a degree of health to prevent the further inroad of the so-called germ."[12]

With so much dubious information being given the public about the causes and cures of diseases in general, it would be surprising if public debate about bubonic plague was not similarly racked by ignorance and disagreement.

This was a decade during which a new set of theories was being developed in Europe and Asia, based on the work of disciples of Louis Pasteur and Robert Koch. In 1894, Alexandre Yersin and Shibasuburo Kitasato independently identified the plague bacillus. Four years later, Paul Simond published work hypothesizing that the rat flea was the key mechanism for transmitting the plague to humans. Time, and the work of other scientists, bore out Simond's explanation, but in the short run it was hotly disputed—in the popular press and in such California-based medical journals as the *Occidental Medical Times* and the *Pacific Medical Journal*.[13] Only in 1908 did the Commission for the Investigation of Plague in India firmly and finally establish that bubonic plague is a flea-borne disease carried by the rat flea and transmitted by its bite.

Until then, the most that public health authorities had to go on was a vague belief that plague and rats were somehow connected. An editorial in the *Pacific Medical Journal* early in 1900 summed up the existing thinking:

> Bubonic plague [has] always been closely identified with filth and pollution. The plague is a contagious disease [and] is probably not infectious, that is, it cannot be carried by the air and gain entrance

into the human economy through breath. Rats and mice . . . may spread the disease to an alarming extent by contaminating food, etc. More dangerous that these, however, are probably mosquitos, flies, fleas, and pediculi, as they not only come in actual contact with the human body, but also puncture the skin, or make abrasions on their new host, inoculating the individual with the plague poison. Infected cargoes, clothing, food, etc, may of course inoculate whole communities in the manner indicated.[14]

Four years later, W. J. Simpson—perhaps the world's most experienced public health officer when it came to plague—wrote that "The agency by which plague is transmitted from the rat to man is unfortunately still a matter of conjecture. . . . The theory of Simonds [that transmission is through the bite of the rat flea] is a fascinating theory, but it still requires much more evidence in its support than exists at present."[15]

A general presumption among non-Asians was that the plague was very much an Asian—and, especially, a Chinese—affliction. According to the *Examiner*, "The plague, black death, or bubonic fever seems to develop in long-accumulated filth in the densely populated Chinese districts. The Mongolians [i.e., the Chinese] die of it by thousands."[16] Such views were a blend of anti-Chinese racial hostility and medical theories that relied on a slavish devotion to the relatively recent discovery that pathogenic organisms— "germs"—were responsible for a great many diseases.

"Medical scapegoating" of resident Chinese had a long, inglorious history on the West Coast. Blame for just about any public health failure, from smallpox to cholera to syphilis, was laid to that "degraded race"—a process that on the East Coast saw such labels successively pinned on the Irish, then the Italians and, later, the East European Jews.[17] Writing thirty years before the great 1906 catastrophe, one of San Francisco's physicians observed: "The Chinese were the focus of Caucasian animosities, and they were made responsible for mishaps in general. A destructive earthquake would probably be charged to their account."[18] The major bacteriological discoveries of the 1880s, identifying the organisms that caused typhoid fever, tuberculosis, cholera, diphtheria, and tetanus changed only the language of the scapegoating, not the target.

The discovery of the plague bacillus made it seem all the more likely that bubonic plague was a contagious disease, transmitted like cholera or yellow fever. If the plague "germs" got into dust or into the excretions or exhalations of people infected with the disease, a popular perception was that a healthy person could get the plague "by inhaling the dust from infected houses, or by drinking infected liquids or eating infected foods."[19]

Such was the setting for the *Nippon Maru's* fateful third trip to San Francisco. According to Sanitary Inspector Eldridge, "this voyage of the *Nippon Maru* appears to have been a particularly unfortunate one." The *Nippon Maru* had set out from Hong Kong on 20 May, scheduled to call in Nagasaki, Yokohama, and Honolulu, but by the time the ship arrived in San Francisco, she was more than two weeks late.

Trouble surfaced on 26 May, when a teenage Chinese passenger (a "coolie," according to the *Examiner*) died less than an hour after the ship's surgeon had seen him in apparent good health. According to friends, the victim had a history of heart problems, and according to the ship's surgeon, all the glands appeared normal. But the Japanese medical officers in Nagasaki performed their own examination of the glands under a microscope. Their conclusion: bubonic plague.

Perhaps the Japanese were a bit hasty. Perhaps they should have been alert to the difficulties of identifying the plague bacillus; visual identification, even under a microscope, was not foolproof. The best method of making sure that something that *looked* like a plague bacillus really *was* a plague bacillus was to inject it into several laboratory animals. If the animals developed plague symptoms and died, that would have been conclusive proof. But such inoculations took about a week to play out, and few travelers or ship owners were willing to wait that long.

The *Nippon Maru*'s passengers went into the Nagasaki quarantine station, there to have their bodies bathed; their clothing, bedding, and baggage disinfected by steam; and the ship itself given a thorough washing with strong carbolic acid. "The Japanese sent us up for fumigation," reported passenger J. A. Welch, a veterinary surgeon. "The women put on old kimonos and the men attired themselves in their oldest clothes. After fumigation, we threw the old things away."[20] A week later, the ship was allowed to continue on to Hawaii. Although news of the quarantining had been sent ahead to San Francisco, where it was received and publicized on 18 June, Sanitary Inspector Eldridge thought the need for quarantine was a trifle overblown and unnecessary.

His views were contradicted by what happened next. Three days short of Honolulu, death again visited the *Nippon Maru* when one of the Chinese steerage passengers died in twenty-two hours, accompanied by "convulsions, suppression of urine, and symptoms of pulmonic congestion." Dr. Deas, the ship's surgeon, decided not to have the body buried at sea, but kept it for examination in port. The microscopic examination by Dr. Alvarez, the bacteriologist of the Hawaiian government, showed "considerable numbers of a short bacillus, rounded at both ends, and like the bacillus of bubonic plague." That was enough for Dr. D. A. Carmichael, Sanitary Inspector and Surgeon at Honolulu's Marine Hospital Service.[21] He dashed off a letter to his colleague at the Quarantine Station on Angel Island and to the Surgeon General, alerting them to the strong possibility of plague aboard the *Nippon Maru*. Absent any telegraphic connection to the mainland, his warning had to be carried by the *Rio de Janeiro*, leaving for the coast that very afternoon.[22]

In Honolulu, the local agent of the Japanese Toyo Kisen Kaisha (TKK) line, which owned the *Nippon Maru*, pleaded with the Honolulu Board of Health to let the ship's passengers and freight land. Sanitary Inspector

Carmichael recommended that the vessel be held and disinfected. Repeatedly, the Honolulu Board rejected both proposals. None of the passengers bound for the mainland were permitted to debark; nor was any of the freight destined for Honolulu allowed in. TKK managed to charter the recently refitted *City of Columbia* at $350 per day as a quarantine ship. The seven Honolulu-bound cabin class passengers were transferred to the *City of Columbia*, while the 244 Asians in steerage were taken to the Mauliola Island quarantine station; all would be held the seven days required by Hawaiian law. Only at 1:30 pm on 22 June, after four days of strict quarantine and after transferring those Honolulu cabin passengers to their shipboard quarantine, did the *Nippon Maru*, still with all of her 2,500 tons of freight, continue her sad journey to San Francisco.

Still aboard in the "Asiatic steerage" was a 29-year-old Japanese woman, originally bound for Honolulu. She had been ill—suspiciously so—and the Honolulu port physician had refused to let her land, on "account of the precarious condition the removal would only hasten the fatal termination."[23] During the onward voyage to San Francisco, her condition worsened, "and the signs of the plague became more manifest day by day. She died on 25 June, and her body was at once thrown over the side."[24]

It was later reported that conditions on board the *Nippon Maru* were deteriorating, to the point "that almost all the cabin passengers were in a state of panic." Apparently, the captain was able to enlist three physicians among the cabin passengers to aid the ship's surgeon in disinfecting the steerage compartments, a recommendation of the Honolulu port physician. It is unclear whether the steerage passengers themselves assisted in this, or whether anyone questioned why the first- and second-class cabins were not also disinfected.[25]

While the *Nippon Maru* was en route to San Francisco, inspections by culture and by inoculation were performed in Honolulu on the body of the dead Chinese passenger. Confirming earlier suspicions, Dr. Alvarez denounced the culprit as being the bacillus of bubonic plague. On 26 June, the *Examiner* printed the news, based on "special correspondence" from Honolulu dated 18 June. Word that the plague might be coming had reached the mainland, where it joined a highly combustible mix of local politics, a fractured medical community, and a condescending suspicion of just about anything arriving from Asia.

San Francisco's popular press was fiercely partisan, something to bear in mind when reading excerpts from the local newspapers. William Randolph Hearst's *Examiner* supported Mayor Phelan and the Democrats (at least for the moment).[26] The *Chronicle* and *Call*, however, were staunchly Republican, although frequently siding with reformers against Republican bosses. The local medical press was no less prone to taking *a priori* positions based on political affiliation. Under Winslow Anderson, the *Pacific Medical Journal* would steadfastly support pronouncements on the public's health made by

Republican governors to whom he owed his position on the State Board of Health. Both the state medical society and its official organ, the *Occidental Medical Times*, were bitter rivals of Anderson's enterprises and not directly beholden to any political party.[27]

The daily newspapers threw down the gauntlet early: no sooner had the *Examiner* printed its warning of the *Nippon Maru*'s deadly cargo than its rivals belittled any possibility of the plague coming through the Golden Gate. "No Danger Here From the Plague; It Cannot Possibly Enter" said the *Call* on the 27 June, quoting Health Officer William Lawlor:

> The disease will not get a foothold here, it cannot. . . . To make the disease epidemic there must be the same conditions existing as obtain in Asiatic countries. The people here do not live together like pigs, and they know how to take care of themselves. In the countries where the plague flourishes the domestic animals occupy the house with the people. There is no idea of ever cleaning the floor, and when an appearance of cleanliness is desired all the people do is to put a new layer of matting on the floor. They have no idea of sanitary precautions and they foster the plague by the very way in which they live. If the quarantine regulations are properly enforced at this port there can be no danger of any case of the plague getting in here. With the quarantine at Honolulu in addition to the local precautions, the entrance of the plague is impossible."[28]

San Franciscans may have been psychologically unprepared to confront the possible arrival of plague. There was a presumption that the climate was favorable to good health in general and an obstacle to plague in particular. The new City Bacteriologist, Barbat, expressed a widespread sentiment that "This is a good, bracing, healthful climate, and plague germs would have here a comparatively hard time of it."[29] Statistics quoted in the *Pacific Medical Journal* showed San Francisco to have a mortality rate comparable to large cities such as New York, Washington, Baltimore, and Boston, and predicted that street and sewer improvements would soon lower San Francisco's rate by a third.[30] For the year preceding the *Nippon Maru's* arrival, the annual report by the City's Board of Health made no mention of plague; tuberculosis, heart disease, and pneumonia were listed as the principal causes of death.[31]

Health Officer Lawlor was but one of several claimants to the mantle of health protector of the city, and they fought fiercely to protect their domains. When the *Nippon Maru* arrived on 27 June, representatives of the major aspirants to the throne were either new or inexpert in the politics of health. The prospect of plague coming to the city's very doorstep soon thrust them into a maelstrom of public controversy.

On one hand was the new San Francisco Board of Health. By California law, "the Board of Health of the City and County of San Francisco consists of the Mayor of the city and county and four physicians in good standing, residing in the City and County of San Francisco, *appointed by the Governor* [emphasis added]."[32] *State* elections had just enabled Republicans to gain control of the *city's* Board of Health when Henry Gage, a conservative Republican, was elected Governor. On 13 June, the new Board—Democratic mayor James Phelan, plus Gage's Republican appointees—took office and set about replacing its officers and employees, all of whom served "at its pleasure" and all of whom had been allies of Mayor Phelan.[33]

Phelan had first run in 1896 on a "reform" platform, part of a "good government" campaign to bring accountability to San Francisco politics and to curb the power of political bosses in the City. The cornerstone of Phelan's strategic plan was a new Charter for the city of San Francisco. Two key provisions would give the mayor power to appoint municipal officials in policy-making positions, while expanding the number of positions covered by the civil service provisions, thus placing such positions beyond the bosses' reach. Fiercely opposed by the antireform elements in both parties, the Charter had been approved by voters in 1898 but would not go into effect until 1900.[34]

Thus, when the new State-appointed Board of Health took office, the party patronage and blatant nepotism driving the appointments stood in marked contrast to the new processes that had been approved by the city for its own government. Control of the Board of Health's 240-odd positions was not a trivial matter for local politicians, nor was several thousand dollars in "inspection fees" that the Quarantine Office could be expected to generate.[35] Dr. O'Brien was out as Health Officer ("the executive officer of the Health Department," at the then princely salary of $3,000 per year), and Dr. W M. Lawlor was in; Lawlor's place as physician at San Quentin prison was taken by Dr. Casey, a nephew of Prison Director Hayes. The new Bacteriologist to the Board would be Dr. W. F. Barbat, brother to new Board member Dr. J. H. Barbat.[36] The *Examiner*, undoubtedly hoping to embarrass the Republicans, prominently listed every position and person affected by the patronage turnover, from Assistant City Physician to Assistant Police Surgeon on down to Messenger and Janitor, attributing each and every appointment to the machinations of "Colonel" Dan Burns, the Republican political boss.

The Board also appointed its own Quarantine Officer, "who shall be a physician in good standing." Governor Gage, via his new Board of Health, had seen to it that Dr. J. E. Cohn was appointed as the State Quarantine Officer in San Francisco, to replace Dr. William P. Chalmers effective 1 July. Sections 3013–3021 of the State's Health Code specified how the San Francisco quarantine officer should go about preserving the Golden State from foreign infection; Chalmers reported having inspected 568 vessels in 1898, generating $3,700 in "fees" (another resource that made the office attractive.) Although Chalmers' relations with the local Board of Health had been amicable and more or less collegial, his dealings with the Federal health authorities were not. Over the coming weeks, both Chalmers and Cohn would frequently complain that the Federals ignored them to the point of disrespect and that their position carried so little power relative to the Federal quarantine doctors on Angel Island.

The State of California thought it should have some say in matters of public health. In its *Report* for that year, the State Board of Health bemoaned *its* lack of control over health threats to its foremost city:

> It would appear that the State of California has no jurisdiction over her seaports so far as quarantine regulations are concerned. The United States Marine Hospital Service has assumed exclusive control, and neither the State nor any local health authorities are considered in dealing with vital questions which arise concerning the public health. In our judgment, this state of affairs should not be allowed to continue. . . . [S]hould an infectious or contagious disease enter this State through its waterways, some one acting for the State could be held responsible, which cannot now be justly done.[37]

The key Federal player on the scene was no ordinary bureaucrat or physician. Dr. Joseph J. Kinyoun was Director of the Quarantine Station on Angel Island, and his qualifications far outstripped those of the medical men on the Board of Health: medical studies at St. Louis Medical College, M. D. from Bellevue Hospital Medical College (1882), further studies at Johns Hopkins, and Ph.D. (1896) from Georgetown University. The *Examiner* touted him (correctly) as having studied with Yersin and with Roux at the Pasteur Institute, with Koch in Berlin, and with other plague experts across Europe. He had joined the Marine Hospital Service in 1886 and the following year established a one-room laboratory on Staten Island, N.Y., that performed pioneering work on cholera. The "Kinyoun-Francis" sterilizer was a disinfecting apparatus widely used among quarantine stations. His Hygienic Laboratory later evolved into the National Institutes of Health, and Kinyoun served as its director until early 1899.

On 30 April 1899, less than two months before the *Nippon Maru* arrived, he was ordered to take command of the San Francisco Quarantine Station.[38] For the Director of the Hygienic Laboratory, this was not necessarily a promotion. It seems that the methodical, but plodding, Kinyoun had fallen from the Surgeon General's favor, to be replaced by the rising star, Rosenau. On the mechanisms that spread bubonic plague, Kinyoun was more knowledgeable than most members of the medical profession of his day—but his knowledge was limited. Unfortunately, his knowledge of the political side of public health was even more limited and lacked the deft, diplomatic touch that Rosenau had shown. Future events would also show that Kinyoun despised the Chinese as "crafty, deceitful, and hopelessly contemptuous of science."[39]

He arrived on 11 June, greeted by "fogs and cold wind [and] . . . a severe earthquake shock which occurred the night after we arrived in 'Frisco.' " His "impressions of San Francisco were not the pleasantest, because everything seemed so much at variance with that which we left in Washington," impressions perhaps reinforced by being obliged to spend nearly a week in San Francisco before being allowed into his quarters on Angel Island. The Island's remoteness produced in Kinyoun a social, as well as physical, estrangement from San Francisco that would color his entire tour of duty there.[40]

Kinyoun inherited a rather ungainly situation. His predecessor (at one remove) at Angel Island, Rosenau, had had his share of troubles with Cohn's predecessor as State Quarantine Officer, Dr. W. P. Chalmers. Rosenau's reports of his travails with Chalmers are a veritable *opéra bouffe*. Chalmers formally complained that the proper discharge of his responsibilities had been prevented by Rosenau, who replied charging malfeasance, negligence, corruption, and obstruction, from matters as serious as allowing suspect ships to enter uninspected to quarrels over whether or not incoming mail would be fumigated.[41] Rosenau had summed up the situation in 1897: "Our relations to the local board of health has been one of opposition on their part to the establishment of the bay inspection service. . . . The local quarantine officer insists that the superior authority in all matters relative to the quarantine of this port was vested in his office."[42]

An 1878 Quarantine Act provided for Federal public health authorities to take over the quarantine process if and when state authorities failed to do so. This resolved none of the questions of overlapping jurisdictions. The National Quarantine Act of 15 February 1893 also came up short. The 1893 Act followed the New York epidemics of 1892 and was, in effect, a compromise between those who wanted to use "diseased immigrants" as a pretext for restricting *all* immigration and those who favored separating public health issues from the debate over restricting immigration.[43] The Act did call for a set of national quarantine regulations and a uniform way of inspecting incoming people and goods for diseases, but these were to be administered by the Marine Hospital Service *in cooperation* with local and state boards of health. How such cooperation was to be achieved was never spelled out and was rarely achieved without much initial friction.

Nor were Californians of one mind on this issue. In the three years preceding the *Nippon Maru*'s arrival, Washington received conflicting demands for action on quarantine procedures in San Francisco. In January 1897, the mayor and the Board of Health of San Francisco signed a joint letter supporting Chalmers' complaints and protesting "against the Federal quarantine officer in boarding vessels [and] granting free pratique in absence of and without cooperation of State quarantine officer." This, after having requested that "the pratique of the national quarantine officer shall be necessary . . . in addition to any requirements of the laws of the State of California." What seems to have been at issue was not whether ships getting clearance (the granting of 'pratique') from the Federal quarantine officers was *necessary*, but whether or not it was *sufficient*. Commercial interests in California were of the opinion that sufficient it was, and the Chamber of Commerce, the State legislature, and Senator Perkins and Representatives Hilborn and Loud wrote letters to the Secretary of the Treasury demanding that the quarantine function be placed exclusively in the hands of the national quarantine authorities." The Chamber of Commerce went so far as to promise help in defending shipowners who refused to pay the State quarantine duties (there was no charge for Federal services) as a way of "contesting this vexatious and unjust annoyance."[44]

In mid-1899, it was *still* unclear which laws—state or Federal—would be obeyed and who would enforce them. Hawaii, for example, called for a quarantine of seven days, because scientists were beginning to believe that bubonic plague would show up within seven days in laboratory animals into which suspect bacilli had been deliberately inserted. However, the standard American (Federal) quarantine period for bubonic plague was the same as for cholera—fourteen days. Such seeds of potential discord were planted in almost every state, especially in California.

When the *Nippon Maru* finally entered San Francisco early on the morning of Tuesday, 27 June, she carried 61 cabin class passengers, plus 32 Japanese and 106 Chinese passengers in steerage.[45] There was another, most unwelcome passenger, indicated by the bright yellow flag flying ominously from her mast, one recognized everywhere as "the dread symbol of violent disease."[46]

Chauncey St. John, the Deputy Surveyor of the Port, took no chances. His Customs men would normally have been among the first to board a ship, usually as soon as she reached Meiggs Wharf. With the yellow flag flying over the *Nippon Maru*, however, he thought it best not to risk putting his inspectors aboard. His superior, the Collector of Customs, accepted St. John's proposal to have a launch keep a tight patrol of the suspect ship day and night.[47]

Kinyoun did visit the ship—several times, in fact. He questioned Ship's Surgeon Deas and Captain Allen to verify the recent medical events on board. Kinyoun quickly decided what would be the fate of the *Nippon Maru* and her cargo, directing the ship to Angel Island, where all passengers and crew were to be transferred to the Quarantine Station and held "in antiseptic imprisonment" (as the *Chronicle* put it) for the required fourteen days. The ship and her cargo would then be taken "to the fumigating hulk [the *Omaha*] off San Quentin, where disinfectants will be forced into every nook and cranny."[48] After the ship had been cleansed of possible contaminants, Kinyoun allowed that she could be taken by a temporary crew to her berth at the Pacific Mail's docks and unloaded.

In accordance with Kinyoun's orders, the *Nippon Maru* continued not to the docks of San Francisco, but to a spot about a mile and a half to the leeward side of the Quarantine Station on Angel Island, there to drop anchor.

That evening, all of the cabin class passengers were transferred to the Quarantine Station. The following morning, the steerage passengers and most of the crew landed at the Station. Kinyoun then ordered a thorough search of the ship, one that turned up nine stowaways. All were Japanese who had boarded at Yokohama and "had been hidden and provided with food by the Japanese firemen of the steamer. They had found sleeping quarters in the coal bunkers, and until the ship was searched by Dr. Kinyoun's order their presence was unknown to the Maru's officers."[49]

No sooner had Kinyoun made his decisions known than a very fierce, very public controversy erupted. A coterie of cabin passengers, certain that there was no plague aboard their ship, sent telegrams to the Secretary of the Treasury and to the San Francisco Chamber of Commerce, denying the existence of plague and protesting that the stay in quarantine would delay their travels. Front-page exposure was given these protests by the *Bulletin*, especially as the signers included some rather socially prominent personalities. Added to the inconvenience and delay suffered by all passengers, the quarantine-disinfection process ruined a good many personal possessions:

> The passengers, cabin and steerage alike, will be compelled to submit their belongings to the same heroic course of treatment as did the sailors and soldiers on the [troop] transports *Grant* and *Sheridan*. The appearance of the fumigated clothes of these unfortunates is still fresh in the memory of San Franciscans. Their garments were shrunken and shriveled, their shoes in most cases completely ruined and all the silks and other Japanese souvenirs brought home for friends in this country, spoiled beyond reparation. Among the Maru's passengers are a number of British tourists to whom the destruction of their English made garments will be quite a serious matter.[50]

Before Kinyoun made his decisions public, the local authorities seemed to think that they would have some say in safeguarding their city. Dr. J. H. Barbat (the Board of Health member, not W. F. Barbat, his bacteriologist brother) was prominently quoted in the *Chronicle*, staking out the locals' administrative turf:

> We shall not permit the *Nippon Maru* to dock until we are thoroughly convinced that there is no danger of the plague being introduced into this city. This is a grave matter and we shall exercise every precaution. Dr. Cohn, (State) Quarantine Officer, has already been aboard the vessel and made an examination. There will be no conflict between this Board and the Federal authorities regarding this matter.[51]

However, Kinyoun's decision to treat the ship's *passengers* differently from the ship itself met with howls of protest from the San Francisco Board of Health. Never mind that just days before they had dismissed as impossible the prospect of plague coming to the city by the bay. If there were some—any—possibility of the plague gaining a foothold, then every conceivable precaution must be taken. Why was the physical vessel not subject to the same extended quarantine as its passengers? How could local health authorities be certain that the Federals had done a thorough job of fumigation and disinfection?

The debate changed on Wednesday afternoon, when two fishermen caught something rather unexpected off Fort Point (what would today be the south end of the Golden Gate Bridge): two lifeless Asian bodies, held upright in life preservers marked with the words *Nippon Maru.*

The bodies were those of Japanese stowaways. Fearful that if discovered they would be sent back to Japan, they conspired with the crew to be lowered over the side in the wee hours of Wednesday morning. Even though the lights of Tiburon seemed close, the *Nippon Maru* was still several miles from the Marin mainland. The stowaways never made it, drowning in the rough waters of Raccoon Strait.

The bodies were bought to the landing at the foot of Baker Street, and

> ... the Coroner was notified by telephone and the wagon from the Morgue was hurried to the scene. ... Coroner Hill decided that an inquest was not only unnecessary but incompatible with public safety ... and the bodies with their effects were cremated last evening. Prior to the cremation of the bodies Dr. Zabala [the autopsy surgeon] and Coroner Hill extracted the glands of the two men to have a bacteriological examination made for bubonic bacilli, and those of one man were found greatly enlarged—a symptom of plague. The glands were delivered to the bacteriological expert of the City Health Department, and on his report Dr. Lawlor will formulate his plan of action after the steamer, crew and passengers are released from the Federal quarantine.[52]

Coroner Hill was certain that, although the Japanese had died by drowning, they had also been afflicted with plague. For his part, the city's Health Officer was sorely vexed that the two Japanese had evaded the (Federal!) quarantine. Dr. Lawlor vented his ire to the *Examiner*:

> I anticipated difficulty with the Federal quarantine officials from the beginning. The same trouble has been experienced in New Orleans, New York and other seaports, where all kinds of diseases were permitted to spread from infected ships through the laxity or inefficiency of the Federal quarantine authorities. ... Goodness knows how many Japs have succeeded in getting ashore alive.[53]

An escalating war of words between Kinyoun and the local health authorities was amplified by headlines in the *Examiner*. At the top of its front page on Friday, 30 June, the *Examiner* shrieked that "San Francisco Is Endangered By The Federal Quarantine Officer" (Figure 1). W. F. Barbat, the bacteriologist of the Board of Health, revealed that the drowned men had swollen glands and that his microscopic examination showed the presence of bacilli that *looked* like those of bubonic plague. However, his office was not set up for inoculating laboratory animals, and the only facilty that belonged to the PHS was on Angel Island. Barbat claimed that conducting such a definitive test or transporting his slides was simply too great a danger to the public's health. Kinyoun openly scoffed at such provincial

SAN FRANCISCO IS ENDANGERED BY THE FEDERAL
QUARANTINE OFFICER.,
INFECTED NIPPON MARU SENT TO THE MAIL DOCK

Police Captain Spillane, Under Orders From the Board of Health, Will Station a Guard This Morning to Prevent the Landing of Freight or Passengers.

DR. WILLIAM F. BARBAT'S MICROSCOPIC EXAMINATION OF THE GLANDS

Figure 1 Headline from the San Fancisco *Examiner*, 30 June 1899. Text following caption: "Under a magnifying power of 1,200 diameters, the bacilli found in the glands taken from the dead bodies of the Japanese who escaped from the Nippon Maru closely resembled the bacilli of bubonic plague, but the final tests were not completed yesterday."

incompetence. "I think," he said to the *Chronicle*, "that there are must be two kinds of bubonic plague: the real thing, and State Quarantine bubonic plague."[54]

In another action that roused the ire of the locals, Kinyoun refused to let the State Quarantine officer (Dr. Chalmers) come aboard the *Nippon Maru* for an inspection. Chalmers had been the object of Rosenau's contempt, and now Rosenau's successor was telling him that he, the State Quarantine Officer, could not board a plague ship unless he, too, went into quarantine. Such Federal arrogance! The Board will hear of this!

But what most incited local criticism was Kinyoun's decision to release the *Nippon Maru*—just the ship, not the passengers—from its quarantine off Angel Island. As promised, Kinyoun had seen to it that the ship was thoroughly fumigated and disinfected. Although he continued to hold the passengers on Angel Island for the promised fourteen days, on 29 June he "granted the vessel pratique . . . as it had complied with all the regulations prescribed by the Secretary of the Treasury relative to the disinfection of vessels. . . . I have done my duty, and have nothing to do with what the San Francisco Board of Health may then consider necessary."[55]

At this, the Board of Health decided to assert its authority. At a public meeting, the Board voted to invoke Section 31114 of the Political Code of California, making it an offense punishable by a fine of $100 to $1,000 and arrest, should anyone land passengers from any vessel without the permission of the *State* Quarantine Officer. The Board also refused a request from Surgeon Gassaway at the Marine Hospital for Kinyoun to have access to the cultures from the glands of the dead Japanese. Only an opportunity to inspect the photographic slides was offered him.[56]

Just after daybreak, a temporary crew took the *Nippon Maru* to her berth at the Pacific Mail's docks (Figure 2). No one from the *Nippon Maru* was allowed to go ashore. Captain Spillaine of the San Francisco police vowed that to enforce the order "if necessary, the police will be armed with rifles." The police allowed neither freight nor persons to be unloaded. Only on food for the crew would the police relent: provisions were placed halfway up the gangplank, with one crewman allowed to come halfway down to fetch them.

Eight hours later, State Quarantine Officer Chalmers appeared. He sent a note to Captain Roberts, ordering him to move the *Nippon Maru* "into the stream"—that is, to take her out into the Bay. Roberts declined, saying that he had no authority to move the ship. Very well, said Chalmers, if you cannot or will not move the ship, we will remove the gangplank and you will *stay* on the ship! "I go out of office at midnight, and my duty ceases then. Of course, the Japanese company is the loser for its obstinacy. . . . If it chooses to keep up its present form the Board can prevent the landing of any freight or of the crew until the company comes to terms."[57] June 30 was his last day in office; perhaps he meant to go out in triumph.

Figure 2 "Nippon Maru at the Pacific Mail docks, San Francisco, c. 1899." (From the Bancroft Library, University of California, Berkeley, reprinted with permission.)

That same day a report from bacteriologist Barbat convinced the public—or, at least, the *Examiner*—that the plague had arrived in the person of the two drowned Japanese, and that more of it could come ashore from the *Nippon Maru*. By now the *Examiner* was fully on the side of the local health authorities, and its front-page headlines on 1 July were unequivocal: "Dr. Barbat Positive That Bacilli Are Those of the Bubonic Plague." Furthermore, thundered the *Examiner*, "the ship will be moved if every policeman in the city has to haul on the tow line."

Over the next few days, the *Examiner* included in its coverage numerous suggestions that "the quarantine was not as strict under Federal methods as it might be." People were in contact with those in quarantine who should not have been, and were later reported walking the streets of San Francisco or Belvedere (on the Marin side of the Golden Gate). It was alleged that even Kinyoun and his colleagues at the Quarantine Station were not personally complying with strict quarantine. Hearst's *Examiner* had changed its attitude to one of hostility toward Kinyoun and the prerogatives of the Federal quarantine station—perhaps as just another opportunity to make money from making the news, but more likely because Kinyoun's views coincided with those of the *Examiner*'s competitor. The *Chronicle*, meanwhile, more perceptively saw this brouhaha as a "Renewal of the Old Fight Over Who Shall Quarantine the City."

Agent W. B. Curtis, acting for the *Nippon Maru*'s owners, was in a quandary as to which quarantine authorities his company should obey. "This has been a fight between two branches of government, and we have had to stand the brunt of it. This [TKK's San Francisco route] is a new enterprise, and it seems as though, not satisfied with big port charges, everything else must conspire to crush it. . . . It is merely political claptrap, an effort to make political capital, and we are the sufferers."[58] Although certain that with time he could win some sort of judicial reprieve, any further delay would have been risky—perhaps another week of losses of $400 per day plus dock charges, not to mention all the negative publicity focused on the fledgling passenger line.

On 1 July, the TKK agreed to having the ship towed to the south quarantine grounds near Mission Rock and fumigated a second time. Captain Anderson of the Pacific Mail arranged for the tug Sea King to tow the *Nippon Maru* stern first into the Bay. As the *Nippon Maru* was being towed from her berth, the chief steward for the Pacific Mail is reported to have said, "Now I hope 'The *Examiner*' is satisfied. 'The *Examiner*' had more to do with this than anyone else."[59]

The new quarantine officer, Dr. Cohn—on his first official day of duty—promptly took a launch out to the *Nippon Maru*, accompanied by Health Officer Lawlor and four health inspectors. Cohn and Lawlor oversaw the preparation of

> chemical solutions which destroy every form of infectious bacilli, and the sprays and gases were soon forced into every crevice where a germ might be lodged. The disinfectants used were formaldehyde, formaline, corrosive sublimate, black oxide of manganese, and sulphuric acid. The cabins were sealed up and the gas was injected through the keyholes until the rooms were filled. To disinfect the cargo covers of the hatches were raised sufficiently to permit the insertion of the nozzles through which the gas is pumped . . . Other men were engaged in washing every inch of exposed surface with a strong solution of corrosive sublimate. Forty chlorine lamps were lighted and the fumes soon permeated the whole ship.[60]

Cohn and Lawlor were less successful in asserting their authority vis-à-vis the passengers. They went over to Angel Island, intending to inspect the passengers in detention there, but this was Kinyoun's domain and he allowed neither Cohn nor Lawlor ashore. Kinyoun reported merely that everyone was in good health, that there had been no signs of plague, and that he would continue to share the passengers' confinement for the full fourteen days.

The following day, 2 July, the *Nippon Maru* was released from her quarantine by the State. At noon, Dr. Cohn officially raised the quarantine and the anchor was hoisted.[61]

On 11 July, Kinyoun lowered the yellow flag and raised the federal quarantine. Two hours and $200 in duties later, the cabin passengers were cleared by Customs, then cleared by Immigration and told that they would leave the following day. The steerage passengers were informed that their effects would take another two days to go through. The sternwheeler *Caroline* left the Jackson Street wharf at 6 o'clock the next morning, 12 July, to bring the cabin passengers back from Angel Island. All were in a festive mood. Even Kinyoun, who handed each person a Certificate of Health, was praised for his handling of the situation and absolved of responsibility for the cramped conditions.

A cloud briefly darkened the proceedings: State Quarantine Officer Cohn, aboard his tug the *Governor Perkins*, "shot out from the wharves with the yellow flag flying. Her whistle signaled the *Caroline* to stop, and Dr. Cohn was seen making preparations to go aboard. The passengers began to shiver."[62] But Cohn did not propose subjecting the *Nippon Maru*'s passengers to double jeopardy. "He merely wanted to see the bill of health. He saw it and stamped his approval on it," sending the *Caroline* on her way.[63]

Afterward

The travail of the *Nippon Maru*'s passengers was over, but the conditions creating such a tempest would fester for months to come, until a true crisis forced a resolution of sorts. The disagreements over jurisdiction and the suspicions of political motives continued to smolder, not always in the background. The embers were fanned by the press acting as surrogates for either the Federals and the locally out-of-power elite (*Chronicle/Call*) or the currently in-power San Francisco authorities (*Examiner*).

Health Officer Lawlor continued to flail the Federals for laxity in maintaining a *cordon sanitaire* around Angel Island. He claimed that, owing to a discrepancy between Immigration's head count of the *Nippon Maru* passengers and that of the State quarantine officer, five or six people remained unaccounted for. On 21 July, he told the *Examiner* (in a story *not* reported in the rival *Chronicle*) that he was investigating whether more than two of the Japanese stowaways had escaped from the *Nippon Maru*. "If there has been a bunch of these Japanese stowaways turned loose in the city I want to know about it." Lawlor continued his war against the Federals by other means. On 29 July, "official notice was given . . . by the Board of Health to a large number of owners and agents of property occupied by Chinese to take steps immediately to place their buildings in a proper sanitary condition, or suffer the penalty of arrest and prosecution." Although surely an aftereffect of the plague scare, this particular order seemed to focus on inappropriate indoor plumbing—mandating cast iron sanitary pipes rather than ones of sheet iron and proper connections to the sewer system. The *Examiner* observed that, "for some reason that has not yet been fathomed, the Chinese have an aversion to metal sinks. . . . Oriental tenants have frequently torn out the [metal] kind approved by law and substituted wooden sinks at their own expense."[64]

It is curious that local attention centered exclusively on the Chinese community. After all, it was a *Japanese* ship that (possibly) brought the plague, and *Japanese* stowaways who were widely presumed to have been infected with the disease. Less than a year later, Chinatown and its inhabitants would be vilified as the center of infection and quarantined. Why did the *Nippon Maru* incident engender no such "medical scapegoating" of the Japanese?

In large part, this can be explained by the small number of Japanese living in California compared with Chinese, and their living overwhelmingly in rural areas, rather than concentrated in San Francisco. There were but 1,147 Japanese in California in 1890, and only 10,151 a decade later. In 1900, San Francisco's Chinese population stood at about 14,000, and Japanese at only 1,800. Less threatening to white Americans in their numbers, the Japanese and their representatives in the United States also "were willing to do almost anything . . . to get differential treatment" for their overseas subjects.[65] This meant going to great lengths to separate themselves from the Chinese in the American public's estimation. In 1900, Californians' anti-Asian energy was focused on extending the Chinese Exclusion Act, and the Japanese successfully avoided having the Act applied to them. Only later would Phelan and others successfully exploit fear of Japan's growing military successes (especially after the Russo-Japanese War) and the increasing number of Japanese arrivals in California to rouse popular support for excluding the Japanese.

One of the more important outcomes of the *Nippon Maru* incident was the credence it would give to future business claims that admitting the presence of plague would result in great losses to those who depended on the movement of people and goods. Exhibit A, of course, was the TKK, which certainly sustained a blow to its corporate bottom line. First, there was the condition of the ship itself:

> At present the steamer is not a fit place in which to live, for the stench of the disinfectant is so intense that in some of the cabins it is stifling. What of the bedding and blankets was left aboard I soaked with the liquid and cannot be used before passing through the laundry. The upholstering is impregnated with the stuff, and on the return trip will furnish a constant reminder of the bubonic plague scare, which not only startled San Francisco, but caused a fight between the State and Federal authorities that has not ended yet.[66]

Then there was the matter of the *Nippon Maru*'s cargo. Seventy tons of cargo destined for Honolulu was still in the hold and would have to be delivered on the return journey. Chinese merchants in San Francisco had a big consignment of fireworks on board, and it was unlikely that they would be delivered in time for the Fourth of July. All the overland freight would be more than two weeks late. With the ship's return sailing to Asia also delayed, much of what would have been her return cargo was diverted to other lines. Each of these items clanked into the TKK's loss column.

The current passengers were being handsomely fed while on Angel Island— at TKK's expense. Further, the *Nippon Maru* would have few passengers on her return journey. Many people who had intended taking passage had cancelled their trips or changed to another vessel. And no wonder—who would travel on the "plague ship"?

Of further concern was the *Nippon Maru*'s crew. The ship was scheduled to leave on 8 July, and with some luck the repairs and reloading could be accomplished in time. But would there be a crew to sail her? If Cohn insisted on requarantining the passengers and crew, just as he had refumigated the ship, it would be a rather long while before the crew was back aboard. As it happened, Cohn did not insist and Kinyoun let the crew out on 9 July, after only twelve days in quarantine and two days before the passengers. Captain Allen was also given charge of the remaining stowaways for transport back to Japan.

More consequential was the disruption of the port of San Francisco. It became a chaotic place indeed, as the *Nippon Maru* had monopolized the Pacific Mail's docking facilities, leaving other ships waiting in the stream until the affair was settled.

Most seriously inconvenienced, of course, were the passengers themselves. As they were held more or less incommunicado during their confinement, little of their predicament or conditions was reported in the press. What we do know is limited almost exclusively to the cabin class passengers. The quarantine facilities were themselves a faithful mirror of the social divisions found aboard ship. Men were housed separately from women, and of course the steerage passengers (nearly all of whom were Asians) were housed in barracks of their own, separate from the cabin class passengers. The cabin class men found the conditions "unfit for any human being."[67] No mention is found of how the Asian steerage passengers suffered their accommodations.

Other ships arrived shortly after the *Nippon Maru*, each coming from plague zones, each having had its share of suspicious deaths on board. The *America Maru* (the *Nippon Maru*'s sister ship) arrived on 16 July, along with the *City of Peking*, and it looked as though a replay of the *Nippon Maru* episode was in the offing. Cohn made plans to be the first aboard the *America Maru* when she entered the Bay, the better to assert his authority, but a dense fog concealed the ship until she reached Meiggs Wharf, where the Federal quarantine launch lay anchored. Cohn's "little *Governor Perkins* steamed out of the Union Street wharf with all her might, only to find herself beaten to the ship. . . . He was ignored alike by the Federal doctors and the ship's officers."[68]

371

For his part, Kinyoun made no effort to pacify his local antagonists. "I have no official acquaintance with that gentleman [Cohn]. He certainly did not interfere with me [aboard the *America Maru*] in the least, and I might say that he was as meek as a lamb. It could not make the slightest difference to me whether he approved of the steps I took. I am not answerable to him. When I get through with the ship and her passengers he can do with them whatever he likes."[69] Kinyoun released the *America Maru* and her cabin class passengers after a mini-quarantine of four days, whereas the Japanese, Chinese, and Korean steerage passengers were sent to Angel Island for disinfection and detention.

Such a relatively speedy release of the ship and its cargo did not allay the anxieties of the city's commercial interests. "G. W. Bramhall of Yokohama, one of the largest exporters in Japan, who landed from the *America Maru*" told the *Chronicle* that uncertainty over the quarantine system was "playing havoc" and was costing the port of San Francisco an immense amount of traffic with the Orient. "The proof is that I myself, with many others, shipped all our exports previously billed for the *America Maru* on the Canadian Pacific's steamer *Athenian* [via Vancouver]. Our action was provoked purely by self interest. I did not know what might happen to my exports when they reached San Francisco, and as it turned out, I did a very wise thing." He then offered some advice to the City by the Bay: "If the people of San Francisco are interested in seeing the commerce of the port built up instead of stifled they should without delay . . . have the unfortunate conflict of authority between the rival quarantine officers settled in the courts once and for all."[70]

Where the *Examiner* had been instrumental in goading the local Board of Health into asserting its prerogatives against the Federal authorities, the Board of Harbor Commissioners cautioned the Board of Health against asserting them any further. Agent Curtis of the TKK hinted rather strongly at legal action against the State and the City to recover some of its losses. The attorney for the Harbor Commissioners, former governor Budd, advised them that owners of a ship could sue them if they enforced a local quarantine after the Federal quarantine authorities had granted pratique. He reminded them that the city was already protected from disease by "the State Board of Health, the city's Board of Health, the Pilot Commissioners and a quarantine fund of $50,000." He had a last, persuasive argument against the Commissioners refusing a request from the San Francisco Board of Health that no ship be allowed to dock without having a certificate of health from the local Board— whether or not it had one from the Federals: the Commissioners might be *individually* liable in any lawsuit.[71]

The *Chronicle* foresaw a continuation of the political dispute between the local health authorities and the Federal government. On 27 July, it predicted that "Quarantine Wars By No Means At An End; A Question of Jurisdiction Which Washington Authorities Will Be Called Upon to Settle Shortly." Reporting on a visit to Angel Island by the *State* Board of Health, the

Chronicle inferred that "an official protest will soon be forwarded to Washington, asking the withdrawal of the Federal quarantine officer from this port on the score of lack of jurisdiction."[72]

In addition to disputes over turf, there was still the question of whether or not there actually had been a case of bubonic plague. Cohn, Lawlor, Barbat et al. were in no doubt: at least one of the two Japanese stowaways had the plague. But Kinyoun's public reports downplayed the *Nippon Maru* controversy. He blithely stated that the two "Japanese stowaways, in attempting to evade the immigration laws and the customs patrol which had been established around the vessel, jumped overboard and drowned, but their bodies were recovered. *These men were perfectly healthy.* [emphasis added]"[73] Later reports by the Public Health Service, however, gave more credence to the possibility that plague might have come to San Francisco aboard the *Nippon Maru.*[74] The *Occidental Medical Times* and the *Pacific Medical Journal* continued to espouse opposing views: the former quite willing to admit the possibility of plague, the latter holding the opposite. As no laboratory inoculations were ever performed, and as Kinyoun found Barbat's slides unsatisfactory for examination under a microscope, the verdict must remain "not proven."

Paralleling the division of opinion within the medical kingdom, the popular press offered its own contradictory post-facto interpretations. Hearst's *Examiner* never wavered in its support of the San Francisco health authorities and their contention that the plague had, indeed, come to San Francisco's doorstep. Both the Republican San Francisco *Chronicle*, and its sister paper, the *Call*, told the public that there had been no plague, not even a possibility of it. The *Chronicle*'s highly biased—but plausible—editorial of 11 July, the day the quarantine on the *Nippon Maru*'s passengers was officially raised, argued that the presence of plague had been concocted solely for the benefit of the Southern Pacific Railroad (owner of the Pacific Mail Steamship Company, the principal competitor of the Nippon Maru's owners) and political bosses hoping to enlarge their patronage powers by expanding the budget of the Board of Health.[75] The editorial concluded:

> (T)he story of the bubonic plague in this city has been widely published ... and exaggerated. Many a tourist who might have come to San Francisco has been turned away by the false rumor started for the purpose of making business for the Pacific Mail and doing politics for [Republican political boss] Dan Burns. . . . Hereafter, the public will be wary. It will take something more than a report from the bacteriologist Barbat to start a scare. . . .[76]

The following year, plague irrefutably made its way across the Pacific. In January, responding to a plague outbreak, health authorities in Honolulu set out to burn several "infected" houses in Chinatown. The fire escaped their control and burned much of Chinatown. In March, deaths in San

Francisco's Chinatown were attributed to the plague. Chinatown and the Chinese would be the locus of death and of blame, and the focus of competing, contradictory interpretations and courses of remedial action. Again there would be arguments over how the plague was transmitted, and even whether or not those dying actually had the plague. Most of the key figures—the state and local political forces, the popular press, and California medical journals—would hold similar positions. Only Kinyoun took a different stand, performing his own laboratory inoculations and diagnosis that confirmed the presence of plague.

Disputes would again erupt between the State and local authorities (spurred on by the city's commercial interests) and the Federal Quarantine Station on Angel Island, this time on a grander scale. Kinyoun's fight with California officials and with the Chinese community would, that time, cost him his career. San Francisco's fight against the plague—and, it would often seem, against its Chinese inhabitants—would cost the lives of 112 people.[77]

Acknowledgments

This article was born a chapter for a book on the immigration industry in early twentieth-century San Francisco. Professor Howard Markel read "Prelude to the Plague" in its early, popular incarnation, and I am indebted to him for suggesting that it be submitted to this journal. Two anonymous referees and Editor Margaret Humphreys made valuable suggestions, for which I am most grateful.

Notes

1 Most recently, Nayan Shah in *Contagious Divides: Epidemics and Race in San Francisco's Chinatown* (Berkeley: University of California Press, 2001).

2 See Shah, pp. 120–57, and Charles McClain, *In Search of Equality: The Chinese Struggle against Discrimination in Nineteenth Century America* (Berkeley: University of California Press, 1994), pp. 234–76.

3 Luigi Lucaccini, "The Public Health Service on Angel Island," *PHS Chronicles*, 1996, *III*, January/February, pp. 92–94.

4 *Annual Report of the Supervising Surgeon-General*, Fiscal Year 1899, pp. 557–58.

5 Ibid., p. 560.

6 Ibid. Report of Surgeon D. A. Carmichael, stationed at Honolulu, p. 550.

7 Ibid.

8 For an explanation of the longer history of the "plague reservoirs" and the spread of the nineteenth century pandemic from southwestern China to urban seaports, see Carol Benedict, *Bubonic Plague in Nineteenth-Century China* (Stanford University Press, 1996), especially pp. 49–71. For an earlier recounting of that pandemic, see L. Fabian Hirst, *The Conquest of Plague: A Study of the Evolution of Epidemiology* (Oxford: Clarendon Press, 1953), pp. 111–20. An even earlier (1905) account of the plague outbreaks in China and (firsthand) India is W. J. Simpson, *A Treatise on Plague Dealing with the Historical, Epidemiological, Clinical, Therapeutic and Preventive Aspects of the Disease* (Cambridge: Cambridge University Press, 1905).

Plague mortality data for India are in *Report of the Indian Sanitary Commissioner*, 1897–1918, *passim*; quoted in Ira Klein, "Plague, Policy and Popular Unrest in British India" in *Mod. Asian Stud.*, 1988, *22*, 4, p. 724.

9 *Annual Report of the Supervising Surgeon-General*, Fiscal Year 1896, p. 547.

10 A possible case of plague in late 1898 so perplexed the Bacteriologist of the San Francisco Board of Health that he rendered a verdict of "not proven." See *Biennial Report of the Board of Health of the City and County of San Francisco for the Fiscal Years 1898–1899 and 1899–1900*, pp.145–47.

11 San Francisco *Examiner*, 7 July 1899, p. 6.

12 San Francisco *Examiner*, 8 July 1899, p.7.

13 See also Simpson, *A Treatise on Plague*. William Simpson was the Health Officer of Calcutta in the 1890s and editor of the *Indian Lancet*. M. P. Sutphen writes (not altogether favorably) on his role in developing the response to the plague outbreak in India in "Not What, but Where: Bubonic Plague and the Reception of Germ Theories in Hong Kong and Calcutta, 1894–1897," *J. Hist. Med. Allied. Sci.*, 1997, *52*,103–13. Writing in 1905, with his extensive experience with the plague, even Simpson was unable to identify with assurance the mechanism that linked rats, humans, and the plague.

14 *Pacific Med. J.*, 1900, *43*, p. 123.

15 Simpson, *A Treatise on Plague*, pp 218–19.

16 *San Francisco Examiner*, 28 June 1899, p. 3. Similar views were expressed in San Francisco's other dailies, none of which were noticeably sympathetic to the Chinese.

17 See Alan Kraut, *Silent Travelers: Germs, Genes, and the "Immigrant Menace"* (New York: Basic Books, 1994) and Howard Markel, *Quarantine! East European Jewish Immigrants and the New York City Epidemics of 1892* (Baltimore: Johns Hopkins University Press, 1997).

18 From *Pacific Med. Surg. J.*, 1876, 19, pp, 36–37, quoted in Joan B. Trauner, "The Chinese as Medical Scapegoats in San Francisco, 1870–1905" in *Calif. Hist., LVII*, Spring 1978, No. 1, 70–87, p. 7. A more recent, and much lengthier, discussion of how white San Franciscans viewed Chinatown as a medical menace can be found in Shah's *Contagious Divides*.

19 McClain, *In Search of Equality* p. 238 ff.

20 San Francisco *Examiner*, 11 July 1899, p. 3.

21 Duncan Carmichael, originally from Canada, had a long and distinguished career with the Marine Hospital Service/U.S. Public Health Service, 1881–1915. He was Superintendent of the Marine Hospital Service in the Hawaiian Islands from 1898 to 1901, when he was transferred to San Francisco as that port's quarantine officer. Source: Mamiya Medical Heritage Center, http://hml.org/mmhc/mdindex/carmicha/html, 7 February 2002.

22 *Public Health Rep., XIV*, No. 27, 7 July 1899, pp. 1066–67.

23 *Public Health Rep., XIV*, No. 33, 18 August 1899, p. 1313.

24 San Francisco *Chronicle*, 28 June 1899, p. 7.

25 See the report by Surgeon Kinyoun, Quarantine Officer at Angel Island, in *Public Health Rep, XIV*, No. 33, 18 August 1899, pp. 1313–15.

26 For a recounting of the off-again, on-again nature of Phelan's political alliance with Hearst, see Swanstrom, *Reform Administration of James D. Phelan, Mayor of San Francisco, 1897–1902* (M.A.Thesis, University of California, Berkeley, 1949), pp. 94–97.

27 Dr. Anderson's career included censure by the state medical society, suspension from the University of California faculty, and the founding of the insurgent College of Physicians and Surgeons of San Francisco. See Henry Harris, *California's Medical Story* (Springfield, Ill.: Charles C. Thomas, 1932), pp. 249–52, and J.

Marion Read, *History of the San Francisco Medical Society*, volume I (San Francisco: San Francisco Medical Society, 1958), pp. 114–15.

28 San Francisco *Call*, 27 June 1899, p. 4.

29 San Francisco *Examiner*, 30 June 1899, p. 1.

30 *Pacific Med. J.*, 1900, *43*, p. 125. This notion of San Francisco as a "healthy" city was not particularly well-founded. Census data from 1900 show San Francisco having a crude mortality rate of 21 deaths per thousand inhabitants; this compares unfavorably with other large cities, such as Seattle (11.8), Chicago (14.6), Cleveland (16.1), New York (19.6), and Philadelphia (18.8). Only large southern cities, such as Atlanta (22.3) and New Orleans (23.1), had higher death rates. Significantly, Oakland, with a climate virtually identical to San Francisco's, had a 20 percent lower mortality rate (15.9). See Bureau of the Census special report, *Mortality Statistics, 1900 to 1904* (Government Printing Office, 1906), pp. lxv–lxvii.

31 *Annual Report of the Board of Health of the City and County of San Francisco for the Fiscal Year Ending June 30, 1898*. Chart No. 1.

32 Article III, Section 3005, of the California Political Code, quoted in the *Sixteenth Biennial Report of the State Board of Health of California, for the Fiscal Years from 30 June 1898 to 30 June 1900*, p. 89.

33 Ibid., p. 90.

34 See Swanstrom, pp. 43 ff.

35 The most recent *Annual Report of the Board of Health of the City and County of San Francisco, for the Fiscal Year Ending June 30, 1898* had listed 248 positions, everything from Health Officer to nurse intern to janitor. Presumably not all of these positions were political appointments.

36 Appointments noted in the *Examiner* on 14 June and 22 June 1899.

37 *Sixteenth Biennial Report of the State Board of Health of California for the Fiscal Years from 30 June 1898 to 30 June 1900*, pp. 9–10.

38 Biographical material on Kinyoun from the web site of the National Library of Medicine, http://www.nlm.nih.gov/hmd/manuscripts/ead/kinyoun.html. Also see Victoria Harden, *Inventing the NIH: Federal Biomedical Research Policy, 1887–1937* (Baltimore: Johns Hopkins University Press, 1986) and Bess Furman, *Profiles of the Public Health Service.* (Washington, D.C.: National Institutes of Health, 1973).

39 Quoted in Kraut, p. 96.

40 Joseph J. Kinyoun, letter dated 29 June 1901, from the Kinyoun papers, MS C 464, History of Medicine Division, National Library of Medicine.

41 See *Annual Report of the Supervising Surgeon-General for 1896*, pp. 957 ff. Rosenau had the last word on the mail.

42 *Annual Report of the Supervising Surgeon-General, Fiscal Year 1897*, p. 503.

43 See Markel, *Quarantine!*, pp. 153–82, for an excellent treatment of the quarantine/ immigration restriction nexus.

44 All quotes are from the *Annual Report of the Supervising Surgeon-General of the Marine Hospital Service of the United States for the Fiscal Year 1897*, pp. 541–59.

45 Figures quoted in the press differ slightly from those of the Immigration Service and those given by Kinyoun in the 18 August 1899 *Public Health Reports*. I have used the latter.

46 San Francisco *Examiner*, 26 June 1899, p. 5.

47 San Francisco *Call*, 28 June 1899, p. 23.

48 San Francisco *Chronicle*, 28 June 1899, p. 7.

49 San Francisco *Chronicle*, 1 July 1899, p. 3.

50 San Francisco *Chronicle*, 28 June 1899, p. 7.

51 San Francisco *Examiner*, 28 June 1899, p. 3.

52 San Francisco *Examiner*, 29 June 1899, p. 8.
53 Ibid.
54 San Francisco *Chronicle*, 1 July 1899, p. 3.
55 Letter from Kinyoun to Health Officer Lawlor, quoted in the *Examiner*, 1 July 1899, p. 1.
56 San Francisco *Chronicle*, 1 July 1899, p. 1.
57 Ibid., p.9.
58 San Francisco *Examiner*, 2 July 1899, p. 1.
59 Reported, of course, in the San Francisco *Examiner*, 2 July 1899, p. 1.
60 Ibid.
61 San Francisco *Chronicle*, 3 July 1899, p. 10.
62 San Francisco *Examiner*, 11 July 1899, p. 3.
63 Ibid.
64 San Francisco *Chronicle*, 30 July 1899, p. 25.
65 Census figures cited in Daniels, *Asian America: Chinese and Japanese in the United States Since 1850* (Seattle: University of Washington Press, 1988), pp. 112 and 115; the quotation p. 114. Also by Roger Daniels: *The Politics of Prejudice: The Anti-Japanese Movement in California and the Struggle for Japanese Exclusion* (Berkeley: University of California Press, 1977), pp. 21–27 and pp. 107–18.
66 San Francisco *Chronicle*, 3 July 1899, p. 10.
67 San Francisco *Examiner*, 11 July 1899, p. 3.
68 San Francisco *Chronicle*, 20 July 1899, p. 7.
69 Ibid.
70 All quotes from the San Francisco *Chronicle*, 21 July 1899, p. 10.
71 San Francisco *Chronicle*, 12 July 1899, p. 10.
72 San Francisco *Chronicle*, 27 July 1899, p. 9.
73 *Public Health Reports*, 14 July 1899, *XIV*, No. 28, p. 1079.
74 See Hirst, *A History of Plague in the United States*, p. 1.
75 Gunter Risse finds some credibility in the latter claim, noting that "the Board of Supervisors in 1899 cut the budget of the Health Department from $80,000 to $31,000." See "The Politics of Fear: Bubonic Plague in San Francisco, California, 1900," in Linda Bryder and Derek A. Dow, eds., *New Countries and Old Medicine* (Auckland, NZ: Auckland University Press, 1995). Undoubtedly, the budget cut had less to do with perceived diminution in public health needs and more to do with Democrats in San Francisco punishing the new majority on the Board of Health, which had been appointed by Republicans in Sacramento.
76 Editorial in the San Francisco *Call*, 11 July 1899, p. 6.
77 Excellent accounts of this are in McClain, *In Search of Equality*, Chapter 10, "Medicine, Race, and the Law: The Bubonic Plague Outbreak of 1900" and Shah, *Contagious Divides*, Chapter 5, "Plague and Managing the Commercial City." Kinyoun was relieved of his duties at Angel Island on 6 April 1901 and transferred to Detroit. Subsequently, he was assigned as a Sanitary Inspector in Yokohama and Hong Kong, then sent to investigate smallpox in British Columbia. He resigned from the Service on 19 April 1902. After serving for a short time as research director for the H. K. Mulford Co. of Glenolden, Pa., he returned to Washington where he took up a private practice and directed the bacteriological laboratory for the District of Columbia. At the time of his death on 15 February 1919, he was serving as Director of the Army Medical Museum. Biographical material on Kinyoun is from the web site of the National Library of Medicine, http://www.nlm.nih.gov/hmd/manuscripts/ead/kinyoun.html.

INDEX